AS I WAS SAYING

NYC
1/02

AS I WAS SAYING

Recollections and Miscellaneous Essays

V   O   L   U   M   E   T   W   O

C   O   R   N   E   L   L   I   A   N   A

Colin Rowe

edited by Alexander Caragonne

The MIT Press   Cambridge, Massachusetts   London, England

This book was set in Garamond 3 by Graphic Composition, Inc., and was printed and bound in the United States of America.

Library of Congress Cataloging-in-Publication Data

Rowe, Colin.
    As I was saying : recollections and miscellaneous essays / Colin
Rowe ; edited by Alexander Caragonne.
        p.   cm.
    Includes bibliographical references and index.
    Contents: v. 1. Texas, pre-Texas, Cambridge. — v. 2. Cornelliana.
    — v. 3. Urbanistics.
    ISBN 0-262-18167-3 (v. 1). — ISBN 0-262-18168-1 (v. 2.). —
    ISBN 0-262-18169-X (v. 3)
    1. Architecture—Philosophy.   2. Architecture—Aesthetics.
I. Caragonne, Alexander.   II. Title.
NA2500.R74   1995
720'.1—dc20   95-15191
                                                          CIP

Contents

AS I WAS SAYING

Introduction

About Cornell University, in spite of the very long time which I spent there, I find that I have very little to say; and this is not because nothing ever happened. Rather it is the reverse. Somewhere or other, Wordsworth said something about "emotion recollected in tranquillity," which may be all very well; but myself is still insufficiently detached from whatever emotions I might have experienced in Ithaca, New York, to envisage them with any precision of contour let alone to consider the possibilities of repose.

Less eruptive than Texas, less exasperating than Cambridge, Cornell of course is a somewhat schizoid institution—not quite a land grant college and not quite something else. Did its founders, Ezra Cornell (1807–1874) and Andrew Dickson White (1832–1918), come from different strata of society? And one has to presume that they did because even their names illustrate their distinction. A Quaker, Ezra Cornell was self-made and achieved a

modest opulence by the supply of telegraph poles—the first telegraph message, I believe, was made between Washington and Balti-
more in 1844, and then there followed a largely forgotten boom
until the laying of the Atlantic cable in 1866. But Andrew White
was something quite different. Born in Homer, New York, representative of Syracuse banking interests, he was educated at Yale, the
Sorbonne, and—predictably enough—in Berlin. He was an attaché
at the American Legation in St. Petersburg in the mid-1850s and
afterward U.S. minister to Berlin from 1879 to 1881, to St. Petersburg from 1892 to 1894, and, yet again, minister (though now
called ambassador) to Berlin from 1897 to 1903.

So what a pair of disparate characters! On the one hand
Ezra Cornell, who would insist on placing telegraph poles with his
own hands and who would go out, through the ice and snow, to re-
pair the wires; and, on the other, Andy White, whom, one imagines, except in Paris, Berlin, St. Petersburg, could scarcely abandon
his library.

But, although a somewhat bruising contradiction remains
inherent at Cornell, to continue in this style will not exactly be
helpful. For Andrew White combined bibliophilia with a passion
for architecture. He amassed a very large architectural library—I
rather think that he envisioned himself in the role which Charles
Eliot Norton had already assumed at Harvard—and it must have
been a prominent part of his policy to make his library highly
accessible. Hence, therefore, the establishment of an architecture
school at such an early date (one of the first three in the U.S.) and
hence, too, the very great profusion of its associated library.

Coming to Cornell in 1962, I found myself preceded by fac-
ulty refugees from Texas—Lee Hodgden, Werner Seligmann, John
Shaw—with quite a few students to follow; and I also found myself
in what I can only call an immensely diverting theater of New York
Jewish wit. And this was supplied, mostly, by Alan Chimacoff and
Tom Schumacher; as for example, this little number to a tune from
Gilbert and Sullivan's *Trial by Jury:*

When I went to the school of planning research,
    I'd an appetite fresh and hearty.
I had visions of making our cities grow,
    both commodiously and arty.
I soon was confronted with statistical analysis,
    Parking studies, and sociology.
And never did I ever get to draw a line,
    in the whole city planning collegee
And never did he ever get to draw a line,
    in the whole city planning collegee.

I walked uptown and down for a year
    counting cars at intersections.
And I made a chart with Zipatone,
    statistical perfections!
I then was ready to draw a plan,
    but they said, "No, forsooth, you are not ready.
You must first calculate, analyze, and comprise,
    more nonsensical, irrelevant data!"
"He must first calculate, analyze, and comprise
    more nonsensical, irrelevant, data!"

In the basement I stayed for another year,
    filling up the calculator.
There were jobless and homeless and dogless and boneless,
    and some with no refrigerator.
They all had a number but never a name,
    not a face for identification.
But they all had a chicken in every pot,
    perfection of standardization.
But they all had a chicken in every pot,
    perfection of standardization.

Then, excepting Tom and Alan and Tom Beeby and Stuart
Cohen, I had only the most attenuated contacts over the drawing

Introduction

board with undergraduates; and, as I guessed then and learned for sure later, it was not considered desirable that my contacts should *be* close. For, to those strange academic dinosaurs of late Beaux-Arts origin who were like yet another edition of Texas, I was too much of an overt intellectual; and, therefore, it was decided that I should be isolated in what, in those days, was *not* known as a theme park but went by the name of *graduate architecture.*

It is for these reasons that it will be convenient for me to split what was written from 1962 onward into two parts: my observations with reference to my theme park—to be talked about later under the general title of *Urbanistics*—and my observations related to other interests, Modern architecture, architectural education, and Italian *maniera*—which are published, or republished, in the pages which follow.

I should however add that there were further publications of these years, such as the two parts of "Transparency: Literal and Phenomenal," written with Robert Slutzky in Texas and published in *Perspecta,* no. 8 (1964) and *Perspecta,* no. 13/14 (1971);[1] and, thanks to Peter Eisenman, "Neo-'Classicism' and Modern Architecture I and II," in *Oppositions,* no. 1 (1974), and also "Character and Composition," which derived from my time at Yale, in *Oppositions,* no. 2 (1974), and which had all of them been languishing in obscurity for years and years. Then there were a number of introductions beginning with *Five Architects* (New York: Wittenborn, 1972) and continuing with Robert Krier, *Urban Space* (New York: Rizzoli, 1979), to lead to *James Stirling,* edited by Peter Arnell and Ted Bickford (New York: Rizzoli, 1984); and, finally, after a collection of essays under the title of *Mathematics of the Ideal Villa and Other Essays* (1976), there was Colin Rowe and Fred Koetter, *Collage City* (1978), both published by the MIT Press.

As far as I am aware, at Cornell the only thing which I did very, very wrong was in 1967. It was in Berlin in late December; it was in Westend; it was in the house of Matthias and Liselotte Ungers; it was late in the evening and most people had left; it was gently snowing outside and I was talking to Peter Blake, both of us thinking about Matthias as a species of Galahad; and it was in this way that Peter Blake instigated my move. "Why don't you walk down the room," he said, "and invite Matthias to Cornell?" So I did; and, since my politics prevailed, Matthias became installed as chairman at Cornell in 1969, that fateful year of revolution following the events of Paris the year before.

But the silliest thing I ever did. For my politics were injurious not only to Matthias and myself but also to Cornell. Coming from the Berlin of Rudi Dutschke, Matthias had caught something of that ardor, that fervor to make a clean slate and, during a six-month absence in Rome which I enjoyed in late '69, a clean slate he had become determined to make at Cornell.[2]

Not at all necessary. Not at all to be desired. But, since he could scarcely get rid of the faculty dinosaurs, it was now the younger faculty whom he was prepared to make expendable. A very sad story; and it was hence that something like a minor holocaust ensued. He had tried to get rid of Jerry Wells while I was away in Rome but he had failed; and then, in '71–'72, it all broke out again, resulting in the firing of Alan Chimacoff, Fred Koetter, Roger Sherwood, and in Klaus Herdeg's disgusted resignation. Finally resulting in a charge of the dinosaurs which brought about Ungers's own withdrawal.

In the articles which follow there will be discovered some wearisome repetitions and perhaps that is inevitable in a collection of essays like this, in which the same themes seem constantly to recur. Thus, though I have tried to eradicate repetition, I have not entirely succeeded.

Notes

1. The second "Transparency" article is reprinted in the first volume of the present collection, *Texas, Pre-Texas, Cambridge*.

2. There is a further song by Alan Chimacoff, derived from Gilbert and Sullivan's *H.M.S. Pinafore*, about the Ungers period as chairperson at Cornell:

Introduction

I am the chairman of this architecture school.
And a very good chairman too.
I'm very, very good, but be it understood
You must never mention the name Corbu.
What never?
Well, hardly ever.
We must never mention the name Corbu.
We must never mention the name Corbu.
Then give three cheers and ring a bell
For the energetic chairman at Cornell.

Program versus Paradigm: Otherwise Casual Notes on the Pragmatic, the Typical, and the Possible

This article came about as the result of an invitation from Jorge Silvetti and Rodolfo Machado, who were then in Pittsburgh, Pennsylvania, to deliver a lecture at Carnegie-Mellon University, probably in 1980. It was then rewritten for publication in The Cornell Journal of Architecture *3 (1982/83). Because it involves a rumination upon Austin, Texas, it might just as well have been included in the first volume of this series, however I have thought it best that it be published here with other writings related to its time.*

I should add that Austin, nowadays, is not as I here describe it, that it has been largely wrecked by a quantity of office towers which have fatally destroyed its skyline and have completely compromised the original priority of the State Capitol.

It is a town that deserved a better fate.

Those who refuse to go beyond the facts rarely get as far as fact. . . . Almost every great discovery has been made by "the anticipation of nature," that is by the invention of hypotheses which, though verifiable, often had little foundation to start with.

—Thomas Henry Huxley

Facts, then, come to be like figures in hieroglyphic writing. . . . There they are, holding up their clean profiles to us so ostentatiously; but that very appearance of clarity is there for presenting us with an enigma, of producing in us not clarity but confusion. The hieroglyphic figure says to us, "You see me clearly? Good—now what you see of me is not my true being. I am here to warn you that I am not my essential reality. My reality, my meaning, lies behind me and is hidden by me, and this means that in order to arrive at the true and inward meaning of this hieroglyph, you must search for something very different from the aspect which its figures offer."

—José Ortega y Gasset

Facts, then, are like sacks. They won't stand up unless you put something in them.

—Luigi Pirandello

What follows concerns the status, the virtues, and the disabilities of two prevalent and rival proposals as to the 'correct' means of architectural and urbanistic problem solving. In other words, what follows is concerned with the examination of two mental orientations of the present day which are often presented as mutually exclusive. One of these is the widespread presumption that an act of analysis will automatically result in an act of synthesis; and the other is no more than the inversion of this point of view—the presumption that a synthetic statement is intrinsically an hypothesis for the discovery of significant empirical detail.

So, evidently, I find both these positions to be, if not false, at least inadequate, and it is for this reason that I have entitled this fairly brief collection of notes "Program versus Paradigm."

A program is defined by the Oxford Dictionary in relation to theater, concert, prospectus, syllabus: and then, with a date of 1837, there is a further definition. A program is "A definite plan or scheme of any intended proceedings: an outline or abstract of something to be done"; and it is in this sense that the word program has penetrated the architectural vocabulary.

Then, as to paradigm, which the Oxford Dictionary, with a date of 1843, defines as a "pattern, exemplar, example." In this case Thomas Kuhn's *The Structure of Scientific Revolutions* may, for present purposes, give a more useful specification. For, according to Kuhn, paradigms are "universally recognized scientific achievements that for a time provide model problems and solutions to a community of practitioners."[1] Thus, on the one hand, there is the presupposition that a document entitled the program is the legitimate and neutral *fons et origo* of all acts of synthesis; and the proponents of this belief are both very excited and very certain about it. To quote:

> The Challenge for Process, the Program: The practice of design has increased in complexity. Interrelationships and constraints previously unrecognized or considered less important demand increased attention. No single discipline, let alone individual can hope to sufficiently address the multi-faceted problems of building. New disciplines spring into existence; creating new bodies of knowledge: the number of specialists increases, owners, users and consumers become more aware of potential solutions and constantly look for comprehensive design services. As a result, the organizations and operations of the professions creating and maintaining the built environment are rapidly changing. Integrated team design, project management, technical and management operations concepts, for instance, become a reality.[2]

Program versus Paradigm

The foregoing was conveniently accessible to me and it may be a statement of the programmatic argument at its most extreme. But, on the other hand, we are increasingly bombarded with a notion that an entity generally specified as the typical or the typological and apparently a reserve of collective memories and Platonic indiscretions is, whether we will or not, always the insuperable starting point for investigation. And this position, as a general drift of ideas, will clearly place high value on the concept of paradigm.

Therefore, we are confronted by two doctrines, and let me repeat that I am convinced by neither. The first (which might be called program-worship) is in decline and is increasingly deplored. The second is emergent and increasingly gains the cultural upper hand. To me, the first seems to be unduly determinist and the second to disclose an unwarrantable pessimism. For surely both of them disallow the possibilities of genuine novelty and, in the end, both of them envisage the solution, the synthetic statement, as no more than an extrapolation of the existing. On the one hand, the procedures are too flat and empirical and, on the other, they are too exalted, too idealist, and too *a priori*. Both positions, I think, leave the world without hope.

For in both cases the possibility of intrinsic novelty (by which I do not mean what Whitehead calls "novelty in the use of assigned patterns") is implicitly denied. In the first case, the future is to be no more than a prolongation of the present (surely intolerable) and, in the second case, both present and future are to be no more than a continuation of the past (surely no better). And, by this, may one not suggest that both of these implied theories condemn us to no more than simple repetition? For the possibilities of breakthrough and revolution neither of them allow; and, saying so much, I mean to suggest that alternative theories which can neither of them envisage the emergence of significant novelty must be in rather a bad way. For, in spite of all academic belief, newness continually does occur within the world; and, without any sense of this permanent effervescence (too often like the corks of cheap champagne bottles popping), without this continuous—and erratic—regrowth, serious existence would be even less than faintly tolerable.

Therefore to agitate and to animate a very few ideas we will begin with a set piece which is going to be partly history and partly parable.

To imagine that the time is 1839, and the place is a new political society: the problem is the location and plan of a capital city; and the result, which will here be used as a counter in an argument, is Austin, Texas. Should one say a miniature Washington as contrasted with Galveston Island's miniature Manhattan? In any case, the problem itself—the inability of the Republic of Texas,[3] in all its initiatory innocence, to accept the apparently obvious choice of Galveston as capital—is extremely American in its nature. One only needs to think of that pairing of major cities with state capitals, of New York/Albany, Chicago/Springfield, Philadelphia/Harrisburg, San Francisco/Sacramento, to recognize the issue. For all of these couplings of cities disclose a conviction (whether right or wrong) that the seat of government and associated bureaucracy should, preferably, be far removed from the freewheeling associations of commerce and from corruptions even worse.

And, therefore, and even at its inception, the mere project of Austin, Texas reveals a cultural prejudice of probably Jeffersonian articulation. Plausibly either New York or Philadelphia just might have become the capital of the United States, and, just possibly, either of these choices might have been to the general good. But the plausible sinks into insignificance when confronted with the preferred, when exposed to the still persisting ideal that both government and law, not to mention education, should be intensively protected from the theaters of temptation and the blandishments of vice. And hence Washington, which presumably repudiated not only the potential evils of Manhattan but also the Quakerish idiosyncrasies of Philadelphia; and hence Austin, almost certainly conceived of as a critique of likely, though scarcely obvious, goings on in Galveston.

Program versus Paradigm

Now this is to guess; but, very probably, such were the almost innate prejudices of the founders of Austin. Galveston was inappropriate because it promised to be wicked. However, very visibly, there existed the alternative of San Antonio, almost—"Remember the Alamo"—a sacred site: but the iconography of battle and slaughter apart, San Antonio was equally unavailable. Its associations were Spanish and Mexican.

Thus, if a properly gringo and Anglo-American demonstration could not there be made, then Austin is to be construed as the result, relatable to American ideas of purity (absurd though these may often seem) and to American ideas of destiny (exaggerated though these may occasionally appear). So, in 1839, the problem of a capital city for the Republic of Texas—at least as regards its location—was solved in what could nowadays seem to be a highly perfunctory manner; and, one imagines, the choice was made without ceremony. A location was chosen sufficiently close to the ocean but sufficiently far removed from the appalling climatic excess, the sweatbox of the Gulf Coast.[4] The location, at the intersection of what promised to be acceptable cattle and cotton country, was, almost certainly, provided with an adequate agricultural base; it was provided with good water; and, if the founders of the city thought about such things, then toward its western extremities the site was also equipped with a brilliant topography where Poussin and, later, Cézanne might have felt at home, a topography which could never be lacking in stimulus.

It seems reasonable to assume at least this much and to imagine the founders of Austin as being influenced by most of these arguments which, for the most part, are surely rule of thumb. But, with so much (or so little) said as regards criteria for location, now to approach the plan.

The founders of this contracted Washington were not exactly highly sophisticated beings (colonists rarely are such). They were unacquainted with the splendors of France and Italy which, in any case, they might have rejected—along with London, Vienna, St. Petersburg—as being too profuse, too aristocratical for the democratically inspired and, if not connected to the Pope (the Whore of Babylon as in Fundamentalist Protestant societies he was then conceived), then very probably connected to something even more dreadful.

However, ethnic and religious asides apart, now to examine the plan of Austin (fig. 1). It is a surveyor's grid into which a number of representational gestures have been quite conventionally interjected. Nothing at all ingenious, nothing in the least bit clever; it is more or less a replica of William Penn's plan for Philadelphia which, in its turn, was an approximate replica of so many sixteenth-century and Utopian propositions. A central square is to be the seat of government and around it are to be grouped the various ministries of an independent political society. Four avenues are to converge upon this central square and in each of the resultant quarters there is to be another public place. This is approximately all. It is a highly innocent diagram; it is almost a child's idea of a town; and, indeed, Austin, Texas does possess some of the characteristics of a toy. More grand and less unassuming than what could be considered its offspring—such adjacent courthouse towns as Lockhart and Lampasas—along with these it still displays many of the charms which Lévi-Strauss attributes to the miniature or many of the characteristics which we might associate with the model. In other words, it makes no pretensions to infinity and no proclamations of artistic sublimity. But, with all this, it is not exactly dismissible. A little infantile, it is, almost, the urbanistic equivalent of a large dollhouse; we might feel that we can play with it: we might even feel that we can wind it up. For, like the perspectives of Palladio's Teatro Olimpico (another miniature), it possesses the capacity to engross and even to obsess the attention. Like good toys and like good miniatures, it operates with the maximum of thematic economy, parades the 'essential' and conveniently suppresses the rest. It is one of the most economical of stages, emphatically a stage framed by a proscenium; and, just as a small and one-time capital city, Parma, awaited its Stendhal, so Austin may be imagined as awaiting the writer who will forever celebrate its myth, awaiting that imaginary novel which, no doubt, is to be entitled *The Balcones Fault*.[5]

Program versus Paradigm

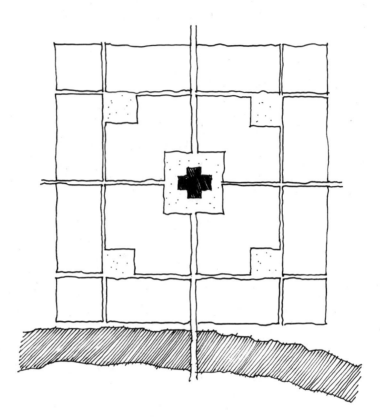

1. Abstraction of Austin, Texas. Alexander Caragonne.

But if it has been intimated that the Austin, Texas diagram
is altogether too laconic to be completely real, there is now some obligation to observe the characteristic style of its failure. It is a diagram recognizing neither aspect, prospect, topography, nor possible
function; and this lack of accommodation, sooner or later, could
only make itself apparent. Increasingly the real could only invade
the ideal; and thus, while activities came to be generated eccentric
to the major motif, certain quarters came to be preferred and others
to experience relative neglect. Only one of the four subsidiary
squares, or parks, was ever undertaken; a casual railroad erratically
entered the picture; and, to the north, an oblique grid (signifying
mostly the university) emerged in indecisive competition with the
primacy of the original statement.

Hence the phenomenon of the city as it was until recently,[6]
a surveyor's grid with some Platonic pretensions: a relatively pris-
tine (if somewhat naive) image which has become warped and dis-
torted by the accumulation of unenvisaged pressures and energies.
It is, nevertheless, an image which continues to be legible, respectable, and, almost, exemplary.

For it is impossible to forget that, inherently, Austin is a
manifesto piece; and an ultimate argument, or admonition, still
there continues to survive, surely to be construed as a very elementary celebration of a basic notion—the idea of government under
law. The central square and the domed capitol are the icons of this
idea. About one hundred and forty years ago, without sophistication, and in the face of awe-inspiring emptiness, the Republic of
Texas wished to illustrate an endorsement of principle, of principle
having nothing to do with the contingencies of time and place, of
principle assumed to be unquestionable. "We hold these truths to
be self-evident. . . . This is a government of laws not men."

Now this is not the occasion to enlarge upon that persistent
theme in frontier Texas, that preoccupation, in spite of violence,
with the ideas of equitability and law (it is in any case rehearsed in
so many almost rustic courthouses which still exhibit great explana-
tory power); but it should still be possible to assert that, in a final

analysis, Austin was propounded as a didactic illustration of just
such themes. For in Austin, with a certain large generality and a
casual unconcern for detail, fantasies related to the *res publica* provide the scaffold and fantasies related to the *res privata* furnish
the infill.

Probably there are few cities in North America—indeed
few cities in the world—which one can address in precisely these
terms, limited terms which may, on occasion, be incomparably gratifying. But if, for these reasons, Austin, Texas may be categorized as
a city of the mind (meaning a city which the mind, without undue
endeavor, can readily comprehend), we are, today, very far indeed removed from the happy certainties and even some of the unhappy
frontier terrors of circa 1839. So, since distance is alleged to provide
perspective, and since Austin is here being used as a clinical specimen, it may now be allowable to envisage the problem—capital
city for a new political society—as, most likely, it might still be
interpreted circa 1982.

Of course, simply by stipulating the time as the present day, there
is a far more complex methodology to be inferred. First, there
would be the minimum of simple deduction and ingenuous do-it-
yourself; and, second, the solving of the capital city problem (location and plan) would be aided by foreign governments and abetted
by research foundations. Indeed the whole interminable parade of
modern knowledge would become focused upon it. The government
of the United States, the Russians, the United Nations, the representatives of the Common Market (with possibly the French and the
British acting independently and separately) would all be eager to
offer aid and expertise. For is not the topic, "A Capital City for a Developing Nation," at present completely irresistible for all those so
very many who are entirely unwilling to leave anything alone? One
would think so; and, therefore, one may conceive of planeloads of
those who know who would be flown in to examine and to advise.
They would be moderately excited, proud of their know-how and,
one can imagine, their appearance. Preceded by a descent of secre-

taries, jeeps, filing cabinets, Quonset huts, air conditioners, computers, calculators, Xerox machines, there would follow a miscellaneous
troupe of geologists, meteorologists, anthropologists, psychologists,
demographers, ethnographers, geographers, statisticians, sociolo-
gists; and, from then on, a positive orgy of expensive but impeccable interdisciplinary collaboration would, hopefully, ensue.

So one perceives the idea; but now to examine the reality.

It should be apparent that the team of experts which is here
predicated would be concerned with an inventory of information
which might then permit an optimum delineation of policy. In
other words, the team would be engaged in the preparation of a program, a comprehensive program, a schedule of requirements not
only for a city but also for a society. For how to locate the site, let
alone trace the model for a city, without the most exhaustive consideration of its empirical context? Or so, one believes, the argument
would run.

And, accordingly, our research team would proceed to issue
questionnaires (although, in a wilderness, one wonders to whom
they would be addressed), to quantify returns, to tabulate specifics,
and to assign priorities. Its operational procedure would be analytical and inductive. It would classify presumable activity and specify
possible performance. As the position papers and the memoranda,
the graphic generalizations, and the printout sheets accumulated, as
the scrutiny of the existing progressively yielded significant guide-
lines for action, then, with all due circumspection, indices of expansion would be traced, rates of growth projected, predominant
'futures' defined, and likely developments extrapolated.

We are all familiar with this approach. Its exponents proceed with
the greatest caution and apparent modesty. Their discriminations
are conducted with a scrupulous regard for local details of every
kind. The site of their city (also its form) is to be rationalizable, not
in terms of any 'arbitrary' or 'intuitive' choice but rather in terms of
an assumed complex of 'necessity': and thus they are prone to award
to indigenous resources—whether human, animal, vegetable, min-

eral, present, or prospective—the most considerate respect. Not at all preoccupied with 'invention', their practical object is to disclose the immanent, to assist a particular condition (presumed to be latent) to 'discover' itself, and, anxious to avoid the least possible imposition, their practice could be said to derive from a never-too-precisely formulated theory—that of maximum non-intervention (*Let us do nothing to impede the course of the future. Let us do nothing to inhibit the creative unrolling of time*).

Now, the theory of maximum non-intervention, which is so evidently conscientious and which seems to be prompted by the illuminations of science and by the dominant mood of an educated liberalism, may proceed to an infinity of ramifications and results. But for the present, it should be enough to notice that though contemporary procedure is incomparably more elaborate than the frontier practice of one hundred and forty years ago, it too is likely to lead to diagrams no less predictable. So the predictable diagrams of today, the outcroppings of a clamoring for 'fact' and of a simultaneous obsession with the 'imperatives' of growth and change, will, as might be expected, vary just a bit from year to year. However, all this being said, quite possibly to date one is still confronted with two versions of the same thing, with two diagrams which both imply high volatility and apparent horror of the *a priori*. There is an old style diagram, probably deriving from the Fifties, exhibiting a loose, curvilinear and biomorphic condition which is vaguely suggestive of Brasília (fig. 2). Then there is a new style graphic piece, rather more jagged in outline and tending to look like a highly complicated specimen of electrical circuitry which invites comparison with, as yet, no known place (fig. 3). All the same and whatever the differences, since the two are very evidently icons, i.e., the contracted representatives of a state of mind, it may now be both entertaining and convenient to compare them with the Austin, Texas diagram of way back.

And the undertaking need not be all that difficult. For if, on the one hand, in Austin we are presented with a highly belated piece of pseudo-Platonism and, on the other, we are the recipients

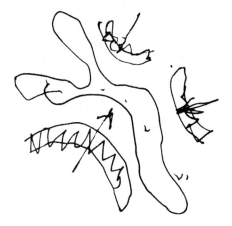

2. Sketch of program without plan. Colin Rowe.

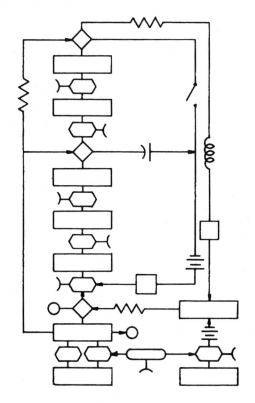

3. Diagram of technical planning process.

Program versus Paradigm

of a fairly easy to recognize analytical maneuver, then apart from certain highly restricted architectural circles, which are never less than cynical, these figures will be widely regarded as:

I.	II.
bad	good
static	dynamic
closed	open
coercive	libertarian
retrospective	anticipatory
sterile	exploratory

However, if one can restrain the far too easy assembly of a repertory of quick value judgments, these opposed evaluations are perhaps somewhat differently to be construed.

Therefore, and by the way of critique, once more to return to the year 1839 and to assume the impossible: to imagine a gang of performers, comparable to our interdisciplinary team, happily descending upon the Republic of Texas. A miscellaneous collection of Benthamites, Owenites, Saint-Simonians, Comtists, disciples of Fourier, with possibly the stray Hegelian philosopher no doubt sponsored by the influence of the Prince of Solm-Braunfels,[7] they too would have remorselessly accumulated data and sponsored predictions and they too would have attempted to formulate a city uncontaminated by cultural *parti pris,* a city of innocence, a mechanism, or alternatively an organic event, which would be no more than responsive to reason and circumstance.

But then, after a lapse of one hundred and forty years, what value would appertain today to those facts and annexed predictions upon which their program and its graphic conclusions might have been based? Would these facts and predictions simply have been invalidated by time, coming to appear as no more than the engaging components of an early Victorian, Biedermeier period piece? Would the never-to-be-anticipated vagaries of history long ago have falsified whatever facts and predictions our interdisciplinary team of 1839 might have thought it judicious or plausible to frame? And, indeed, just what developments or events might our experts and savants of that date have been able, or disposed, to predict?

A railroad up from Galveston they might well have supposed: but the transcontinental railroad network so shortly to arrive might not have appeared so likely. An economy based upon cotton would perhaps have seemed a logical inference; but, since neither the refrigerator nor the internal combustion engine could have been envisaged, the importance which cattle and petroleum were to assume would barely have impinged upon the horizon of possibilities. Then, what to say about an economy giving quite a few indications that it promised to be based on slavery?[8] And, precisely, how would our team have addressed this highly delicate issue? But, if, very reasonably, our interdisciplinary team might well have predicted that the Republic of Texas could never survive, then, just as reasonably, this is a prediction which, almost certainly, it would have refrained from uttering. For in the case of this particular prediction, there were surely the dangers of being run out of town on a rail and, consequently, the virtues of silence and discretion might very likely have prevailed.

This, by proposing the impossible and by inserting present-day procedures into a context within which, under no circumstances, could they have been found, is to caricature certain contemporary modes of analysis (and presumptive synthesis) but not seriously to distort their implications. Back in 1839 (if we can sustain our fantasy) an 'all-accommodating' plan would have been prepared; but, based on an illusory 'fact' structure and a still more illusory 'future' structure, like the executed plan of 1839, this too would have become equally deformed and invaded by events which could in no way have been anticipated.

Now, if these remarks are approximately relatable to common sense, we thus face two issues, one or the other or both of which are germane to any urbanistic problem solving. And if, implicitly, these are divergent theories as to the means by which authentic and useful configurations are to be generated, to illustrate

Program versus Paradigm

these issues I have constructed a parable. Perhaps for reasons little
more than the accidents of autobiography, sentimental addiction,
and a taste for a specific landscape (live oaks, tumbleweed, mes-
quite, *barrancas,* and the beginning of mesa formations), I have exhibited Austin, Texas as a retarded descendant of the ideal cities of
the Renaissance: and then, with a more polemical purpose, next to
it, I have presented a pair of planner's diagrams deriving from a far
more complex pedigree. Which, so far as I am concerned, means
that I have, more or less, arranged the confrontation of two phenomena about neither of which should it become necessary to become
unduly excited.

No doubt, except in terms of a pathos-inducing conflict
between purpose and result, the Austin, Texas diagram is not very
satisfactory and almost the best thing which can be said about it is
that it is saturated with a not unrewarding iconic intention. All the
same, as the representative of a species, as a *plan without a program*
(fig. 4), it may still invite us to consider the alternative predicament, that present day and strange confusion of the analytic with
the synthetic, *the program without a plan.* And do not all of us know
this species so well—the overt denial of typology and then its surreptitious endorsement, the programmatic research and then 'the design leap', the 'irrefutable' collections of data and then the populist
veneers, the planners' investigations and then the cosmetic vi-
gnettes? However, the program without a plan, that curious undertaking conceived to be democratically and iconographically neutral
but which is patently an icon of what is thought to be scientific
method (both physics in terms of 'certainty' and biology in terms of
'growth') is surely a topic which involves many issues—the constitution of 'fact' and the constitution of 'history', 'nature' versus 'culture', predestination versus free will—as abundantly to indicate
that the time has now come for a change of gear.

So the issue is still pragmatics and program versus idea and
paradigm; and, having used Austin, Texas (where, incidentally, idea
and paradigm were almost certainly largely employed as simple empirical convenience) as a piece of litmus paper, which, according to

4. Sketch of plan without program. Colin Rowe.

approach, turns red or blue, remaining observations will be concerned with possible movements through that glaring no man's land ensuing from the architect's unwillingness to think except in terms of built solid and the planner's disdain to be preoccupied with any thing so crude as physical statement. And it is particularly with reference to this unassigned territory, sometimes rather imperfectly entitled 'urban design', where no elegant logic prevails and where the rival contestants conceal their largely inarticulate differences by a joint use of smarmy graphics and other would-be alluring tactics of cheap diplomatic maneuver, that something now must be said about the declining status of the program and the reviving status of the paradigm.

"The problem with the behavioralists is that they always manage to exclude themselves from their theories. If all our acts are conditioned behavior, surely our theories are too." This perhaps helpful little quote is extracted from the *obiter dicta* of W. H. Auden.[9] A useful prop like this aside, it becomes increasingly clear that the whole existential situation of the program, the high valuation placed upon

Program versus Paradigm

an allegedly neutral compilation of data, which Sir John Summerson once proposed as the crucial component, almost the motivating force, of Modern architecture,[10] is a very vulnerable affair: and, particularly is this so when the program professes to include a predictive dimension. For, insofar as the structure of the future is to be related to the structure of future ideas, evidently no predictions can be made about it. "For to predict an idea is to have an idea, and if we have an idea it can no longer be the subject of a prediction."[11] And, if the truth of this assertion should be no less than apparent, then it should be equally evident that, in the wild super-tropical jungle of almost self-proliferating information which we all inhabit, in the end, a prejudiced discrimination of relevance will always occur. Even with the greatest of good will, some aspects of a problem will always be downgraded and others preferred. In other words, the program will always (and, mostly, inadvertently) be biased. It will never be the simple statement of a problem so much as the implication of a solution. It will be like almost any question. It will frame a highly restricted repertory of possible replies. And, if a question can only rarely be neutral, then what to say about that complex of largely dissimulated value judgments which seems invariably relatable to any extreme infatuation with programmatics?

About this topic, quite the best remarks have been made by Alan Colquhoun,[12] who has accused the devotees of data as being, quite naively, the not so innocent victims of an aesthetic doctrine. But, apart from Colquhoun on the program, what else does there remain to suggest? That the program, except for the iconographical program, must be of fairly recent origin? That the program, as a listing of empirical requirements, begins as mostly a French business of the third quarter of the eighteenth century?[13] That preoccupation with the program is possibly the great thread which unites the 'doctrines' of Modern architecture with the practice of the Ecole des Beaux-Arts? That the role of the program was probably immensely reinforced by the characteristic conviction entertained by nineteenth-century positivists, that the enlightened individual, the apex of intelligence, was—at last—capable of making judgments (like those of the ideal and mythical physicist) which would be absolutely objective and impartial? "Je ne suppose rien, je n'impose rien, je ne propose rien. J'expose."[14] One has forgotten the name of the nineteenth-century French character who made this intellectually bizarre remark but its abundant response is surely to be found in a rather more famous piece of mid-Victorian repartee—Disraeli to the Dean of Windsor. The very old, very skeptical, very romantically minded, very Jewish Prime Minister of England had, one imagines, become infinitely exhausted by the dinner table prattling of the desperately open-minded Dean who, most depressing of all, had confessed to a disbelief in dogma; and the tone of Disraeli's reply is completely opposed to that of French Positivism: "Well, Mr. Dean, well—I am sadly disposed to say no dogma no dean, Mr. Dean." And Disraeli was here, surely, implying a critique of the whole Positivist point of view. He was surely invoking the ultimately prejudiced nature of all observation, that we see what we wish to see and we are honest when we admit this limitation.

So, with the respective attitudes of French Positivism and Benjamin Disraeli in mind, then what to say about the constitution of 'fact' that has not already been intimated by the prefatory quotes to this particular essay? Do we add another quotation, this time from Dorothy L. Sayers, one of whose stupid and mildly rustic cops suddenly produces the statement that "Facts are like cows. If you look at them in the face long enough they will probably go away?" Or do we concern ourselves with issues much more stern and serious? With, for instance, such issues as: *are* 'facts' invariably external to the human consciousness, and is an accumulation of 'facts', apparently without any human intervention, infallibly equipped to promote its own controlling hypothesis? Stern and serious, these questions, or absurd? In any case they are rarely confronted by the devotees of programmatics and the enthusiasts for data collection whose practice (otherwise known as waiting for printout) might, as a policy, be summarized as follows: we can't act until we have all the facts, and then we won't need to act, since then the facts will automatically arrange themselves.

Program versus Paradigm

About the cultural ingenuousness of an attitude of mind which, in the end, is scarcely able to envisage the existence of mind, which can in no way conceive of a transcendence of the tyranny of the contingent; which, in the name of 'scientific', 'historical', and 'democratic' exigency, is impotent to imagine even the most modest theater for the exercise of free will, no doubt there is much which requires to be said. All the same, since in this particular essay we are already part of the traffic of an *autostrada* and can in no way permit ourselves the luxury of digression, there is no more that need be said other than to remark that, in the failure of the tradition of Modern architecture and the related tradition of the contemporary planning establishment to address the value-impregnated quality of all observation, there is to be discovered a large part of the reason for our present urban squalor.

For, as the retarded descendants of positivism, these traditions retain the presumptions of their origin, and, not the least, a basic notion that between 'matter' and 'mind', between 'reality' and 'speculation', between 'fact' and 'fantasy', there exists an asbestos and fireproof stage curtain which is never to be breached. 'Matter', 'reality', and 'fact' are apprehensible without serious problem. They are irreducible, irrefutable, and—if we abandon prejudice—painlessly easy to articulate. They are what can be measured and what can be quantified; and, of course, if such are to be considered the criteria of 'reality', if 'reality' is to be such a very small affair, there is no way to be imagined in which factual substance might also appertain to the circumstantial statements of important intelligence—to such intellectual constructions as the Declaration of Independence, Liberté-Egalité-Fraternité, the Communist Manifesto, the Dogma of the Immaculate Conception, to itemize just a few among the ever so many. For, if metaphysics is to be excluded from any conspectus of the real, any propositions such as these must be considered irrelevant, null, and vacuous.

There are, therefore, thoroughly ample reasons as to why the architectural community, and particularly the community of students, over the last few years, has come to divorce its attention from strict programmatics. For, increasingly, and particularly since 1968–69, the pretensions of an old intellectual consortium—academic liberalism, technophilia, and every form of determinism—have become intolerable, have ceased to appear either enlightened, progressive, or reasonable; and, as a consequence, it has been among the great virtues of the protagonists of *architettura razionale*—of Aldo Rossi, the brothers Krier, et al.—to have staged an extremely noisy, revolt, implicitly against a theory of the program which is an assault upon common sense, against the unspeakably odd assumption that at best the architect should be no more than a transparent filter, a lens (interjecting nothing) between the 'scientific' program and the 'popular' result. Because, no doubt about it, it is evidently *architettura razionale* which has effected this revolution and so suddenly called into question the credentials of that consortium which, only recently, seemed to be so solidly established.

Which, certainly, must now be the occasion to transfer attention from what, so far, has mostly been an Anglo-American to a Continental focus, from what one knows only too well—by experience, to what one knows only too slightly—by hearsay, from the innocent empiricists whose activities are to be discovered wherever the English language prevails, to those many others, equally innocent, who can never undertake the slightest intellectual journey unattended by Pascal's *esprit de géométrie* (very rarely by his *esprit de finesse*), who, without Baedeker, always make their cultural trips with Descartes in the one pocket and Marx in the other.[15] For, conceding all its merits and all it has sought to redress, just how to respond to that spectrum of typological (and anti-programmatic) brilliance to which the world has lately been exposed?

How to react to that spectacle of semiotic argument, circular courtyards, neo-Grec peristyles, high staccato, Fellini billowing curtains, semi-Tuscan *altane,* the pseudo-Boullée, the neo-Schinkel, the revived Von Klenze, and all the other current, and 'metaphysical', graphic paraphernalia? That the visuals are too easy and the apologetics too opaque? That, when it comes with all the now standard decoration of quotes from early Structuralist criticism, prob-

Program versus Paradigm

ably from Adorno, and (emphatically) from Quatremère de Quincy, it is almost but not a completely convincing transaction? That, if one is quite willing to suppress the more exacting requirements of the pragmatic intelligence and to avail oneself of the equivalent of stencils, then, surely, one will be enabled to arrive at results of engaging schematic ideality? That, all the same (and even with the pleasant possibility of a sale of the drawings to Leo Castelli), Durand, De Chirico, and Morandi cannot entirely be the solution to all the problems of the city and all the quandaries of the drawing board?

In my preceding exhibition of Austin, Texas I have, I hope, disclosed my own sympathy with the typological concerns of the neo-Rationalists and my own absence of too much belief in those assorted (and often still highly advertised) academic doctrines which presume that a factual accumulation will lead—quite simply—to a scientific conclusion with the corresponding liberation of a disciplined and completely authentic creative impulse. But, all the same, having said so much, though frequently charmed I am still left unpersuaded by neo-Rationalism's formal repertory and particularly unpersuaded by its attendant polemic.

So, as we speculate on the problems of program versus type, on the problem of an academy become recently extinct and the problems of another academy not yet in full working order, might it not, possibly, be argued that we find ourselves confronted with no more than the superficial alternatives of a false empiricism and a false idealism? And, if an empiricism which refuses to concern itself with the fabric of ideas can only be illusory, and if an idealism which rejects involvement with empirical detail will only be inadequate, then must it not further be argued that it is exactly within this theater of the mind that today we find ourselves placed?

But I also think that this argument should not be allowed to impede a recognition of that diverse but devoted band which has done so much to restore the possibility of a renewed debate between architecture and the city. So I refer again to Leon and Robert Krier, to Aldo Rossi, and, most particularly, to Matthias Ungers. But, in saluting these individuals (and others could be included), I also ask why, with the occasional exception of Ungers, the neo-Rationalists in general are to characteristically uptight? *Just why do so many of them, while rejecting the morphology of Le Corbusier, feel obliged, after a good fifty years have gone by, to recapitulate the extravagant pitch of his polemic?* Why, when forms are repudiated, does a certain psychology persist?

And might there be suggested the very obvious affiliation of architecture and urbanism to left-wing politics? And might there further be suggested the very characteristic preference of left-wing politics for an abstracted, a generalized, a simplified, a diagrammatic diagnosis and prognosis of the human condition?

And such questions, if they may be answered in the affirmative, are in no way intended to denigrate left-wing politics. For, from this source and ever since its inception in the late eighteenth century, such enormous ameliorations have ensued that the world would seem a very small and smelly place were it not for this particular contribution. No. Such questions are not, in any way, intended to illuminate the virtues of the political right—possibly, though not always, apt to proclaim an adherence to specificity, to things as found, and to the obdurate complexity of existence. Nor are they intended to draw attention to that ironical condition of the present day in which multinational corporations, oil companies, and the most callous exploiters of real estate regularly clothe themselves in what were once the vestments of an architectural and social Utopia. Rather, these questions (and after all these qualifications, the initial questions are becoming slightly remote) are propounded in order to advertise the interrelationship between a too simple political style and what may be a too simple architectural strategy. For, if everyone is more conservative today than many people were in the 1920s, if imaginable horizons and spaces have shrunk, it may still be argued that, for all the shrinkage, in its ideological essence the *città nuova* of *architettura razionale* is, far too often, not so very remote from the *ville radieuse* and the appalling figments of Ludwig Hilberseimer's imagination. For far too often it displays itself as no more than more of the aprioristic same.

Now we all know a lady from Latin America. Does she mostly come from Mexico, from Caracas, from Havana, or from Buenos Aires? I suspect principally from Buenos Aires. But she spreads herself wide, she is Utopian, and she arrives in a variety of related editions. Invariably she is elegant, energetic, intellectual, ambitious, perhaps a little loud. Almost a *femme type* of a certain background, she is dedicated to the memory of De Saussure and the texts of Adorno, to semiotics and to fashionable Marxism; and, here, I shall call her La Passionaria. But, always a pleasure to meet, La Passionaria is invariably a problem to consider—and myself often spends quite a lot of time considering her. For her tastes and her intellectual passions are at variance. Indeed, La Passionaria's emotional life is unconsciously but scrupulously divided. For, in terms of percepts and things to buy, La Passionaria is never to be imagined too far away from the perpetual parade of Madison Avenue, the Rue St. Honoré, Knightsbridge, and the Via dei Condotti, never too painfully divorced from the prospect of endless shopping in the capitalist bazaars *de luxe*. But in terms of concepts and sociopolitical toys, apparently, for her, Moscow is a basic necessity. And just how would La Passionaria be enabled to shop in Moscow, either for shoes (no Gucci) or for ideas?

So, at every meeting (in her various editions she isn't hard to find), I always love La Passionaria: and I always think how very quaintly similar is her predicament to that of so many of the neo-Rationalists, with their not so sophisticated damnations of the pillars of the capitalist world, the banks of New York, Zurich, London, and their apparent willingness to avail themselves of the products of just these institutions.

Thus my trouble with the neo-Rationalists may be quite simply expressed. In terms of practical politics they may be astute (and hence their rapid rise to prominence); but, in terms of theoretical politics—their *ideal* world—they are prone to be simplistic.

Nevertheless, to repeat, the neo-Rationalists have done very much
to restore a possible balance between the circumstantial and the representational; and, with their graphic campaign, probably one only
argues that, perhaps, the balance has been over-restored with an excessive preference for the Platonic dimension. For how can we who
have surely lived with the influence of Mondrian, who have been exposed to his superlative equilibrium of contingency and ideal state,
just calmly and without more ado, simply wish contingency (and
therefore programmatics) a perfunctory goodbye? For surely,
confronted with any overt classicism, most of us, for better or
worse, are protestant and equipped with an embarrassment of
reservations. And, with all these reservations, can we—so very
easily—revert to a pre-Enlightenment condition of unempirical innocence? And can a romantically proclaimed Marxian devoutness,
the verbal campaign, be seriously imagined as helping to bring such
a condition about? And, for that matter, are not Marxism and classicism (however sophisticated their presentations may be) incompatible states of mind which can only be held together with
rhetorical glue?

In spite of the discriminations of the late Joseph Stalin one
would have thought so. For, surely, one is obliged to think of classicism as an heroic and magnificent attempt to defy the limitations of
chronology, geography, latitude, longitude, and all the rest. And, if
in universalistic terms such as these, one *may* also think about Marxism, then one should also consider the profoundly retrospective and
pessimistic components of classicism, a doctrine which, presuming
the existence both of the Golden Age and the Platonic Idea, locates
the one at the *beginning* of time and conceives the other to be *perma-
nently* inaccessible. A closed and tragic doctrine which can only invite stoical response. Surely, in the end, such is classicism. And, by
comparison with such an attitude, then what an overture to Marx
are both the music and the words of the fourth movement of Beethoven's Ninth Symphony!

The words are not to hand but the music is persistent: and,
compared with classicism (which one may well prefer), how expan-

Program versus Paradigm

sive, how future oriented, how exuberant all this is. And, surely, it
is in such a framework, the 'dynamic' context of nineteenth-century
Romanticism, against the Hegelian background of historical melodrama, against the background of *Weltschmerz,* optimism, and skepticism, against the whole tumult of mid-Victorian London and
Second Empire Paris, that Marx should properly be placed. Indeed,
to imagine his walkings, backwards and forwards (with Engels)
from Haverstock Hill to Regent's Park Road, to know this terrain
and to imagine the two negotiating the Chalk Farm Underground
Station, is already to place Marx in an historical context as a manifestation of a culture and a period almost completely estranged from
any comprehension of the classical idea.

But even if (without some sneaky creeping up from behind)
the physique of classicism and the morale of Marxism might be
imagined as precariously fusible, the question remains: Would the
private sweat, the intellectual effort, and the bureaucratic tyranny really be worthwhile? And, so far as I am concerned, they would not.
One must, of course, concede the need of the architect to avail himself of highly simplified critical schemes (exactly like those which
have here been under review). But, when heuristic convenience becomes interpreted as universal panacea, when useful metaphor becomes translated as naive prescription, when paradigm (without
apology) is simply substituted for program, then surely the fundamental error of Modern architecture is yet again rehearsed (this
time in reverse), and, yet again, we are confronted with the glare
from the eyes of Medusa, which so much theoretical concern seems
determined to impose upon the world.

Which is almost to complete an argument. Worship of program (or
data addiction) and worship of paradigm (or excessive typological
concern) are, both of them, relatively easy to destroy. Neither position is even faintly adequate, and here I wish simply to notice that,
when confronted with two doctrines which are both incomplete, intelligent humanity—when it thinks—will be inspired to consider

the possibilities of their dialectical inter-animation, the method of not only Marx, but also of Aquinas and the Talmud.

So why not try? And as a first step (and not to be pretentious), I suggest that, when confronted with a problem, it might be a good idea to observe the inferential evidence of the detective novel, allegedly the invention of Edgar Allan Poe, so much admired by Baudelaire and the French and by his own compatriots never sufficiently regarded.

And what to say about Edgar Allan Poe except that he was the progenitor of Sherlock Holmes, Arsène Lupin, Hercule Poirot, Nero Wolfe, Peter Wimsey, and all the rest? That, before Karl Popper was born, Poe was Popperian *avant la lettre*. That quite privately and still scarcely noticed, he invented the hypothetico-deductive method, the proposition that in all problem-solving operations, it is the hypothesis, the paradigm, which, of necessity, precedes all empirical investigation? For, with Poe as with Popper, it is the initial conjecture that awaits either refutation or confirmation. In other words, related to a particular situation or crime, the investigator should have a knowledge of the great criminal paradigms because without it he will not be able to place 'facts' in their proper place.

This was Poe's invention, one for which he deserves to be more celebrated than he is. He invented—or recognized—a particular structure of mental interaction. In other words, he postulated a classic strategy of investigation between not-so-amateur amateurs and not-so-professional professionals: and, since his time, his method has persisted as the traditional presumption of the detective novel.

For the great detective has very little use for simple induction. He leaves this to the idiot-friend, whom, so very often, he has conveniently acquired; and while the idiot-friend constantly prescribes action, energy, movement, the great detective is prone to sit at home and to contemplate the typology of crime. Indeed, for him, it is almost a matter of intellectual *chic* to be, physically, highly immobile. So he restricts his *in situ* investigations. He meditates and he postulates. And, meanwhile, the police who mostly despise the

Program versus Paradigm

great detective, scurry around, active as little ants, collecting the most absurd accumulations of typically irrelevant detail and, usually, arriving at the most wildly premature conclusions. For, in the mythology of the detective story, the police must surely be the equivalent of those supposedly many Anglo-Saxon empiricists who it is often supposed can never know *very* much because, with a fatal facility, they so instantly reject speculation and so readily assume the painless accessibility of 'fact'.

But, also, it is of the essence of the great detective, working from hypothesis, to be equally skeptical about hypothesis. For, whatever his private opinion about the police, who, for the most part, are the idiot-friend turned into an institution, the great detective never wavers in his politeness and patience towards them. For though his essential intellectual style seems to be mostly a stereotype of what is conventionally thought to be 'Latin', in spite of a preponderant ability to leap to abstract conclusions, the great detective also knows that naive and disembodied abstractions will never help the solution. He remains responsible and he knows very well that only the police—with all their official resources—can provide him with the ultimate, empirical *matériel* to which, otherwise, he could have no access. And, of course, the great detective further knows—and quite infallibly—just how and in terms of which typology (or paradigm) all this material is, usefully, to be organized.

So Who Cares Who Killed Roger Ackroyd? But if, along with Edmund Wilson, one neither can nor should care extremely much, all the same (and literary snobbism apart) there still persists the suspicion that, both psychologically and heuristically, the detective story is an illustration of the problem-solving process (deprived of funny mystifications) as it is widely understood to be. Meaning that, in spite of the showy histrionics of the final presentation, the detective story is always a relatively modest affair. It is two-pronged and hybrid; and its success derives from a conflation of findings— the often naive discoveries of unsuspecting cops and the alternative suppositions of the all-suspecting detective, the ultimate skeptic, who, in spite of his temperament, never imagines that pretentious speculation will conceal the lesion between things as they seem and the solution as it must be.

Which is so much for the model and the orchestration of the detective story. But, considering the detective story, *is* it apparent that anything so positive and interesting is to be said for the current styles of urbanistic/architectural investigation and projection? And, to me, it is not very apparent that there is. For, so far as I am concerned, there still exists a highly presumptuous and institutionalized empiricism (fictional cops, real planners, and, in spite of its disarray, the predominant apparatus of architectural education). Then, in contradistinction to this, there is a slightly hysterical something else which exhausts itself in unavailing protest against a prevalent ethos.

But, with all this observed—an empiricism which is dreadfully tedious and a Platonism/Marxism which is appallingly abstract, both of them intellectually undistinguished (much more undistinguished than Corbu)—then what to say?

In Berlin, in November '81, I made a lecture related to these topics and I ended with a little exhibition of things which gave me joy. Conveniently, they came from Berlin, 1967; but to me they are universal. They are the graphic speculations of Rainer Jägals who, about to die, felt obliged to draw. He was only twenty-seven and he was dying; but almost following Michelangelo's instructions to Tommaso del Cavaliere—*Disegno, disegno e non perd' il tempo*—he drew and drew and he used whatever time was available.

So, to the results of all this I gravitate; and about this individual I think that one might say, as Henry-Russell Hitchcock used to say, that if Friedrich Gilly was the Giorgione to Schinkel's Titian, then maybe Jägals is the Gilly-Giorgione to something which is to come. He has not been paraded by the exponents of *architettura razionale*. He well could have been. But meanwhile with his drawings— derivatives from Klee, Miró, and the primitive—he indicates what I believe: that a visual idea, properly recorded, will always transcend, if not polemic, at least practice. Because, in the end, I am compelled to suppose that it is drawings such as these—desperate,

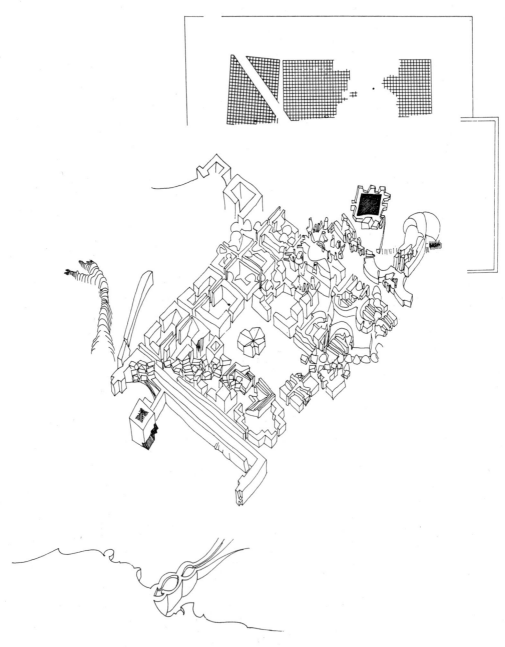

5. *City Dream-Fantasy or Vision,* 1967. Rainer Jägals.

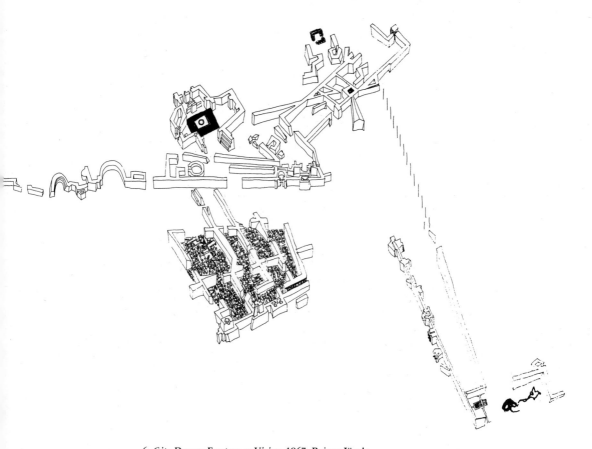

6. *City Dream-Fantasy or Vision*, 1967. Rainer Jägals.

Program versus Paradigm

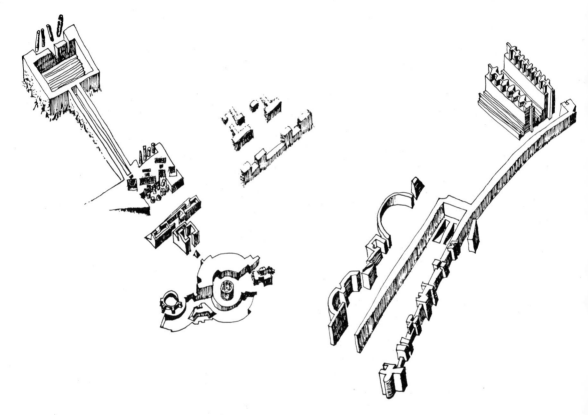

7. Sketch, 1967. Rainer Jägals.

translucent, eclectic, elegant, and ironical—and not the program-matic compilations of the data collectors that are going to affect our vision of the city.

Whether so much might be said for the products of the Cornell Urban Design Studio—over a period of nineteen years—I do not know. I have been too connected with it to be able to judge; and, therefore, I am left simply with a recapitulation of what I might have been trying to say: that a reliance on either program or paradigm is impoverishing; that if we are to talk typology, then a more expanded conception of type becomes necessary; that if the programmers are on the way out, then the neo-Rationalists have received only a very small slice of the typological pizza and, out of it, they are trying to erect the substance of a large urbanistic dinner party.

Notes

1. Thomas Kuhn, *The Structure of Scientific Revolutions* (Chicago: University of Chicago Press, 1962), viii.

2. Mr. Hardtkopff in the *AIA Journal.* The title, month, and year of this publication are unknown.

3. The first permanent Anglo-American settlement in Texas was established in 1821 at San Felipe de Austin on the Brazos River; and as further settlements came into being, in 1830 the Mexican government issued a federal decree prohibiting further immigration from the United States. Hostilities between the Texas colonists and the government of Mexico broke out in 1835; and, preceding the final defeat of the Mexicans at the Battle of San Jacinto, the Texas Declaration of Independence was issued on March 1, 1836. In 1837 the Republic of Texas was recognized by the United States, Great Britain, France, and Belgium. It survived for exactly nine years; and on March 1, 1845 it became a component of the United States.

4. General Sherman's remark (presumably of the 1840s) is still possibly the best observation on the climate of the Gulf Coast—"If I owned both Texas and Hell, I'd rent out Texas and live in Hell."

Program versus Paradigm

5. There already exists a novel about Austin entitled *The Gay Place,* published one imagines before the term *gay* acquired its present connotations. The Balcones Fault is a geological rift which travels to the west of the city.

6. 'Today' is somewhat of a misnomer. Not having set foot in the place for some twenty years, I cannot seriously speak of Austin today. But, all the same, the configuration of the city as it then was (and perhaps the changes have not been so very great) does remain indelibly inscribed upon my mind.

7. The Prince of Solm-Braunfels one assumes was one of those, hopefully, illustrious characters—Lafayette, Rochambeau, Pulaski, Von Steuben are others—who seem to infest the byways of early American history. I know little about him nor do I wish to know very much; and, in any case, his introduction, in 1839, is certainly an anachronism. Probably he was a patron of the Deutscher Adelsverein which, in 1844, founded New Braunfels, some forty miles southwest of Austin and in the heart of what is now Lyndon Baines Johnson country. As to whether Solm-Braunfels ever visited Texas, I have no idea; and as to whether a presumably mediatized prince might have sponsored "a stray Hegelian philosopher," I am equally in the dark. But both seem to be plausible assumptions; and, if they are not, then, in the place of Solm-Braunfels, as a member of our team we might—perhaps just as well—substitute a *protégé* of John Stuart Mill.

8. See Willis W. Pratt, *Galveston Island or a Few Months off the Coast of Texas* (Austin: University of Texas Press, 1954). This book is a publication of the journal of Francis G. Sheridan, grandson of the playwright and apparently a mildly Byronic character who, at the instigation of Lord Palmerston, was sent to Texas in 1839 more or less to smell out the scene. At this time the Republic of Texas seems to have been anxious to secure a British loan; but, if there were certain interests in the City of London which might have been willing to oblige, one is told that the Abolitionist lobby in the House of Commons was unable to tolerate any such transaction. So it may have been the question of slavery (though scarcely a crucial issue in Texas) which helped to bring about the rapid demise of the independent republic.

9. See Charles Osborne, *W. H. Auden: The Life of a Poet* (New York: Harcourt Brace Jovanovich, 1979), 329.

10. See John Summerson, writing in the *RIBA Journal.*

11. See P. B. Medawar, *The Art of the Soluble* (London: Methuen, 1967), 99. From a presidential address to the British Association first published in *Nature,* September 25, 1965.

12. Alan Colquhoun, "Typology and Design Network," first published in *Arena* 83 (June 1967).

13. Reasonable intuition seems to suggest at least so much; and if the promptings of intuition may not be considered adequate, then see Peter Collins, *Changing Ideals in Modern Architecture* (London, 1967), 219.

14. Who *really* was it who made this highly arrogant and extremely silly remark? Myself once knew but, long since, have forgotten. It was revived in my mind by Marty Kleinmann who, also, once knew but who, also, has forgotten.

15. I am indebted for this specification to Richard Etlin, who has probably forgotten that he said so much.

Matrix of Man

A *review of Sibyl Moholy-Nagy,* Matrix of Man: An Illustrated History of the Urban Environment *(New York and London: Praeger, 1968). First published in* The New York Times, *1968.*

"This is a book about faith in the historical City" (p. 11). With her first words Sibyl Moholy-Nagy advertises that what she intends is a polemic; and, for this reason, *Matrix of Man* is not, in any conventional sense, so much a history of the city as an attempt to exemplify the importance of certain urban values which the author conceives to be of permanent significance.

Such a book requires a target; and, after some eight pages of introduction, we are left in no doubt as to what is here to be the principal focus of critical attack. Mrs. Moholy-Nagy finds cities to be "like men . . . embodiments of the past and mirages of unfulfilled dreams" (p. 11). They "are governed by a tacit agreement on multiplicity, contradiction, tenacious tradition, reckless progress, and a limitless tolerance for individual values" (p. 12). "They thrive on economy and waste, on exploitation and charity, on the initiative of the ego and the solidarity of the group. They stagnate and ultimately die under imposed standardization, homogenized equality, and a minimum denominator of man made environment" (p. 11). "The city is the symbolic configuration of a place in history and a place on the surface of the globe" (p. 14); and, if this is 'the historical city', then its enemy is to be found in a combination of ideas associated with such words as crisis and total architecture.

We are all familiar with what ideas are here involved and with the various themes which gather around them. There is, first of all, the insistence that there is very little time left, that change is now so intense as to create a situation quite exceptional in human history. This is the threat of the all-engulfing disaster which can only be averted by the general acceptance of a call to decisive action. The architect or planner, it is proclaimed, must now display an absolute readiness to achieve a new orientation of his discipline. He must be prepared to discard all its previous manifestations as being no longer relevant.

The issue being said to be one of architecture versus catastrophe, it is pronounced that unless the architect faces this issue he will vanish way; and he is therefore exhorted to accept a new calling. What is required on his part is an exalted sense of social responsibility. He must therefore model his activity upon the supposed behavior of the physical scientist. He must honestly concern himself with 'facts'; and then, voiding his mind of all except the measurable, he will at last find himself making authentic contributions both to history and to the good of mankind.

This bundle of highly pervasive and often plausible assumptions is the principal object of Mrs. Moholy-Nagy's attack; for, though 'crisis' may be real, she is still prone to dismiss too much talk about it as, at best, a thin disguise for absence of mind and, at worst, a dubious public relations facade. And, in all this, the author is a child of the Weimar Republic; she was accustomed in those

now remote days, around such institutions as the Bauhaus and elsewhere, to the circulation of just such ideas as these and feels now an
obligation to warn as to where they might lead.

But, apart from certain biographical reasons which could
cause Mrs. Moholy-Nagy to react to particular ideas as, in this
book, she does, there is a further basis for her objections. In another
publication she has expressed her dismay at the belated "rehash of
the functionalist Götterdämmerung of the 1920's"; but, though
there is an element of the personal in this dismay, Mrs. Moholy-
Nagy is a rationalist who is unable to tolerate the bringing together
of ideas from incompatible sources; and thus, if she is dismayed by a
standardized apocalyptic threat followed by an expected promise of
instant millennium—an entirely conventional item in architectural
theory over the last forty years—then she is particularly dismayed
when, alongside these ritual messianic exhortations, there crops up
the neat little mind of a technocratically oriented positivism.

The words 'a technocratically oriented positivism' are jargon if not defined—and there will be here no attempt made to define them; but it is still with a technocratically oriented positivism
that the ultimate argument of this book lies. Mrs. Moholy-Nagy
does not assent to the doctrine of the sacred statistic and the compu-
terized judgement. Her apparent argument is with such personages
as Constantine Doxiadis, Buckminster Fuller, Christopher Alexander, members of the English Archigram Group, and probably others
whom she feels to be a little ludicrous. For, if the historical city is
built up as something various, contradictory, illogical, interesting,
unassessable, and very specific, it is also presented as something
which is being destroyed by the well-intentioned but irrelevant activities of those who suffer from "the technocratic illusion that man
made environment can ever be the image of a permanent scientific
order" (p. 12), of those who "try to solve qualitative problems . . .
with quantitative statistics" (p. 12).

However, there is also a subsidiary critical activity in which
Mrs. Moholy-Nagy involves herself. This is with academic art history. She feels the insufficiency of simple historical categorization

and consequently she distrusts familiar set pieces with names like the Medieval City, the Baroque City, the Hellenistic City, and so on. She seems to feel these to be artificial and platitudinous abstractions; and, therefore, she attempts a discussion, not so much in terms of stylistic evolution, but rather in terms of types of urban configuration which are assumed to be ubiquitous, archetypal, and as basic in Yucatan or Mesopotamia as in Thailand or wherever; and these types she classifies. They are: geomorphic, concentric, orthogonal-connective, orthogonal-modular, and clustered.

The result is stimulating; and, if it acts to inhibit any very adequate presentation of the Renaissance tradition, it does permit a great deal of interesting material to be brought into the picture which a simple history of styles would have been obliged to disregard. *Matrix of Man,* however, has a final chapter called "Options" in which its author is not exactly at her perceptive best. "Options" is an anthology of possible strategies for future development, but if what is here anticipated is some more comprehensive model for the future than any which the idealization of numbers or technology can provide, then it is not too easy to discover traces of such a model in the selection of buildings and projects here exhibited. Which is a pity because at this stage it almost seems that Mrs. Moholy-Nagy, who has been so consistently both brilliant and pointed, is suddenly denying her own arguments. For if crisis mongerers, technocrats, and art historians have all alike by now been put in their place, there are still the simple admirers of good, old-fashioned, Modern architecture who could, until this point, assume that their views were being espoused.

Perhaps this is a small issue. This book is likely to involve its author in a good many battles of which this is one of the minor. It is an important book and an impressive one. Between its covers a good many fireworks are exploded; but because, deriving from a collision between history and polemics, there also remains something inconclusive, some admirers of what she has here done are going to hope that, sooner or later, Mrs. Moholy-Nagy will set down her basic arguments in a manner less involved with historical detail.

Eulogy: Martín Domínguez

This was delivered at a memorial convocation in Sage Chapel, Cornell University, October 1970. Martín Domínguez Esteban (1897–1970) was Professor of Architecture at Cornell from 1960 to 1970.

To have been asked to make a eulogy of Martín Domínguez was, for me, a great honor; but to be speaking about him now is very much more of a great pleasure. And I am compelled to use the word *pleasure* deliberately because how could it be other than, in the deepest sense, pleasing, how could it not be gratifying, to be able to contemplate the memory of a life which was so entirely consistent as his?

When people are dead, we are supposed, for some time, to gloss our tone and to exude the accents of conventional grief; but for Martín Domínguez we should make every attempt not to do this. This was not his style. Martín Domínguez would have expected a situation of this sort to be celebrated without undue effusion, with a considerable deference towards himself, with such protocol as could be improvised, and with some conspicuous sense of irony. Martín Domínguez was an impeccably honest person, indefatigably rational, morally highly fastidious; and a most severe critic of intellectual impressionism, of sanctimony and sham.

He was also irrepressibly vivacious, and it was a part of his feeling for the tragedy of existence that he was never deserted by his deep sense of the ludicrous. Thus, today, though he would have allowed, and would have insisted, that we were doing the right thing, though he would have wished us to do it, he would have missed no details; and, finally, he would have been determined to extract from the event his own and his very sardonic interpretation. This was his character: a controlling awareness of the efficacy of form, with no ability to accept such forms as he found were irresponsive to circumstance.

It was a profoundly Puritan character; but, if we are to do credit to it, we must play with it in far other than orthodox Puritan fashion. We mut try to assume Martín as present here and now, and as, also, our most severe critic. He knew, because he said that on occasions like this people gather together not so much out of grief for the dead, as because they observe in the situation their own fate, and they grieve over their own destiny.

But, such bitter observations apart, the room in which we find ourselves, with its would-be Gothic warmth, with its cozy aura of liberal, late Victorian religiosity, is a place which might have provided him with entertainment. The gluey and the saccharine were not tolerable to him, and certainly to commemorate him we should find ourselves in a building much more austere than this. We should be in the presence of nothing so gaudy, half-hearted, and elaborate. The situation requires stone, little color, and, primarily, black and white. All that would really serve would be a small Escorial—a small one because anything big he would have thought to be pretentious and inflated. But a small building with great severity of outline is what we require. That we are not in a small Escorial should be evident, and I simply call attention to the *mis-en-scène* in the attempt to establish the dimensions of Martín's character. Because *he* would have called attention to it.

But, at this stage, we begin to approach our preconceptions of what we understand as Spanish pride, distinction, dignity. This is a pride without condescension, a distinction without affectation, and a dignity which is not assumed. It is also a condition which never has existed, nor ever can. It is an idea. But, though it is an idea which Martín Domínguez knew to be illusory, it is an idea which his life attempted to embody.

Thus there was the acute and the punctilious sense of honor and obligation, the incapacity to make a divorce between conscience and word, and there was a power of indignation. Which means that, with an elevation of character, with a sincerity and simplicity of manner, with a complete conviction, there was entire absence either of boasting or of bluff.

These are the great outlines of the character, and we may fill them in according to our experience and our knowledge. Thus, with the implacable devotion to principle, there was some stubbornness and asperity; with the liveliness there was always censoriousness; and with the pride—which was also humility—there was the essential knowledge of being someone apart. For stupidity, there was intolerance; for ingenuousness, compassion; for politics, no forgiveness; for himself, no pity. But the outlines of the character threaten to become too large; and though, for Martín Domínguez, we ought to use words which come to us with great difficulty, though we ought to be able, and quite simply, to say: "This was a righteous man"; himself would have found such words not to be acceptable. The formula would have belonged too much to the idea of the hero. He would have rejected it, and indeed one can almost hear him saying: "Oh, you, with your melodrama, why, you almost threaten the Gettysburg Address!" To attempted rhetoric, Martín would have preferred understatement; to lavish appraisal he would have said, "But don't try"; and to the undue building of himself as the impersonation of a Spanish idea he would rather have suggested the subversiveness of paradox.

Eulogy: Martín Domínguez

For he was, above all else, someone whom the expression the INTEGRITY OF WIT entirely fits. The INTEGRITY OF WIT is not an idea which comes easily to the English language, which makes separation between the idea of wit and that of seriousness, which fails to recognize the relationship between wit and spirit, which is unwilling to concede—since etymology is frivolous—the relationship between the notions of taste, wit, spirit, a jest, and the Holy Ghost.

But Martín Domínguez was free of these limitations, and he understood and lived these relationships. Like Unamuno and Ortega, among persons he much admired, he knew that authentic perception is always shocking. He knew that without a constant ability to erect and dismantle scaffolds of reference, without the moral athleticism which this implies, without this form of never-relaxed mental gymnastic, we are quite unable to penetrate those sanitary climates of feeling in which alone truth, goodness, and beauty move and flourish. All this he knew; and, again, I have worked myself up to a pitch of rather too much rhetoric—either for his taste or his purposes. He is dead; but he insists, and all the more strenuously, that certain things should not be carried too far.

And so, the full Baroque eulogium we cannot allow ourselves; and instead, we must be satisfied to witness details: the refusal to wear an overcoat (the climate is not the climate), the Basque beret, the twisting of the mustachio, the determination to pour his own oil and vinegar upon the salad. But these are genre details which he would have considered irrelevant; and so, rather than focus upon such, it will be more illuminating and opportune to deploy attention upon what was to him much more interesting, upon himself as a master of the most apt and rapid judgement.

Like all great conversationalists, no one can recapture his quality; and no one who has heard him will ever be able to communicate his effect. For all this, though without the voice and the physical presence, we may still be allowed to inspect details. We may be allowed, for instance, the Martín which, in a faculty meeting, everyone remembers. There was much vociferation. Being discussed was the closing of Sibley at night. And Martín, who never believed that locks and keys were going to improve either morals or manners, just simply said:

> But you remind me of the man who, in Madrid, came
> home from work one afternoon to find—what did he find?
> His wife in flagrante delicto on the couch.
> > So what did he do?
> > Of course—he sold the couch.

One cannot even attempt to present Martín Domínguez faithfully without the notice of such a remark as this. And I have one more which Peter Cohen has communicated to me. The place is Rochester, and the question is: "Well, Mr. Domínguez, and what do you think about our new Law Courts?" To which the reply is: "What I have always been told—that justice is blind." I realize that I can say little more about Martín Domínguez and nothing about himself as the political refugee. I also realize that, in my appraisal of Martín, I have just possibly presented him too much as a work of art. And, for this, I make no apology. For by cultivation his character had achieved certain classic outlines. There was a firmness and economy of moral contour. There was no silliness, no vulgarity, nothing bizarre. We can judge him by the highest standards, without embarrassment or equivocation. There is nothing to extenuate. Martín Domínguez was strong, intelligent, magnanimous, without rancor; and, just as he deserved, so I believe he owned the respect of all who knew him.

Eulogy: Martín Domínguez

Architectural Education: USA

A statement first delivered at a conference at the Museum of Modern Art, New York City, in 1974 and then published in Lotus International, *no. 27 (1980).*

Bernard Berenson somewhere describes himself as being "a Christianity graduate." He is, he says, highly indebted to the Christian tradition and, to a large degree, formed by it; but he continues that he would no more wish to be immersed in that tradition than he would wish still to be a student at Harvard and hence, just as he is a college graduate, so he is a Christianity graduate. His argument is a useful one—at least for me, because I wish myself to claim to be a Modern architecture graduate, which I suppose means that, while I acknowledge a debt and a derivation, while I am constantly moved by the magnificence of the original idea of Modern architecture and while I can scarcely think except in terms of its repertory of forms,

I cannot really believe in it any longer, or, when I almost can, it is a case of the *credo quia absurdum,* the (not so Dada) I believe in it because it is absurd.

I have adopted a pseudo-theological tone which I do not consider to be altogether inappropriate to the subject matter of this conference; but then—and after having adopted this tone—it was forced upon my mind that the published image of this conference is an apple. The apple is first of all complete; then bitten into; and, finally, almost totally consumed. And is this a case of frivolous graphics? Or do we have here, with the fruit of the Tree of Knowledge, a reference to the Fall of Man and to the introduction of Original Sin? Or again, could it just possibly be that the whole and unimpaired apple represents ourselves at the beginning of this conference, ourselves intact and in a state of grace, and that its wreck prefigures ourselves at the end, corrupted, sophisticated, and having received intimations as to the nature of good and evil?

The apple may, no doubt, be given other explanations; but I shall proceed as though these were the significant ones, as though the apple were, simultaneously, a temptation and the index of some immensely involuted and labyrinthine trap.

Which does not mean that I believe architectural education to be so involuted, labyrinthine, and fraught with problems as is often supposed. Indeed rather the reverse. I presume architectural education to be a very simple matter; and the task of the educator I am convinced can be quite simply specific as follows:

1.   to encourage the student to believe in architecture and Modern architecture;
2.   to encourage the student to be skeptical about architecture and Modern architecture; and
3.   then to cause the student to manipulate, with passion and intelligence, the subjects or objects of his conviction and doubt.

But, having said this, I could be accused of quite massive dissimulation.

I have declared myself to be an unbeliever but have also prescribed for myself a missionary role; I have implied that I wish to instigate faith but also to subvert it; and, worst of all, I have confessed to an interest in 'manipulation'—presumably of both ideas and forms. But these apparent inconsistencies can, I believe, be made to go away; and, meanwhile, their introduction only serves to preempt an argument because, supposing the sequence faith-doubt-manipulation, then just how this sequence is initiated and developed will ultimately derive from what one conceives architecture and Modern architecture to be or to be about to become.

So we have first of all the public and the received idea of Modern architecture as an important response to the impact of technology, as a more or less rational approach to building which is to be discriminated from all previous architecture by the designer's lack of formal preoccupation and his greater refinement of scientific knowledge. Modern architecture, it is averred, is or will (or should) become no more than a logical derivative from data which are, in themselves, the factual components of the contemporary world; and it is from this wholly commonsense relationship to reality that it acquires the authority which it enjoys or, alternatively, will come to enjoy.

Such has been the typical bias of much writing or talking about architecture during the last thirty to fifty years. A breach has been made with irrationality and with morbid sentimentalism; the architect is no longer interested in forms to the exclusion of everything else; he is no longer a purveyor of private luxuries for the rich and the privileged; instead he is an enlightened builder "for a population with nothing like the leisure for luxuries" which patrons of earlier ages enjoyed; and he is the painstaking student of function who, if he is to build a soap factory, will discover all about the process of soap manufacture and who, if he is to build a nursery school, will promptly acquire the most intensive knowledge of kindergarten practice.

Architectural Education: USA

This is the line of explanation which haunts the later pages of Nikolaus Pevsner's admirable and usually subtle *Outline of European Architecture;* but, without difficulty, one could excerpt something very like it from a large variety of other sources. For, wherever it was a question of 'putting Modern architecture over', wherever it used to be a question of persuading the naive and the unsuspecting, these were the standard arguments which were rehearsed; and, for all their debilitating blandness, it cannot be denied that they are scarcely a complete misrepresentation of what Modern architects, at one time, believed that they were up to. Finally and fearlessly, the architect is at last able to confront things as they are. He is free from prejudice, exempt from bias, innocent of dogmatic presumption; and now he has almost won through to the objective neutrality of the physical scientist. He has repudiated fantasy and he can now concern himself with 'building' rather with 'form', with the 'public' rather than the 'private', with 'needs' rather than 'wants', with the 'dynamic' rather than the 'static', with 'innovation' rather than with 'custom'. If this was not the message of the Bauhaus and the prevailing tone of the polemic of the 1920s, then something very like it certainly was and still continues to be highly obtrusive. We have at last discovered, so the message ran and half a century later the would-be revolutionary message still continues to run, a new approach to building. It is a style which is not a style because it is being created by the accumulation of objective reactions to external events and which, therefore, is pure and clean, authentic, valid, self-perpetuating.

This mystical vision of a new architecture, impeccable and incorruptible, was so necessarily seductive that, even when, as now, it has shrunk and become pathetically attenuated, it should not be surprising that this is a vision which is still extensively, perhaps unconsciously, invoked; and it should certainly not be surprising that these presumptions as to Modern architecture's mode of being, now strangely influenced by ideals of management, should still continue to exercise a controlling influence upon educational frameworks which are conceived to be progressive and enlightened. Thus, since

a seminal myth alleges that the Modern architect is properly concerned with facts and has abjured speculation, architectural education becomes increasingly what is believed to be 'fact'-oriented.
That is: while for bohemian and liberal reasons, architectural education conveniently approves the so-called 'counter-culture' (which is
a not so implicit protest against both management and technology),
architectural education becomes increasingly a compilation of
courses devoted to the presentation of information designed to assist
management and derived from technology, sociology, psychology,
economics, cybernetics, etc., with the inference that no adequate,
let alone valid, design decision is possible until all this information
is digested, and with the even more tempting subliminal proviso
that, once this information is digested, no design decision will be
necessary anyway. Since, should it not be apparent that, given the
'facts', these will automatically arrange themselves, will, presumably, promote their own hypotheses irrespective of any human
intervention.

That such a point of view should, in the end, extinguish or
paralyze initiative should surely be obvious; but that, when its epis-
temological foundations are so very slight, when so painfully vulnerable, it yet remains predominant should not be considered strange.
For any criticism of this point of view has now become an assault
upon an entrenched establishment, upon an establishment with a
presumptive empiricist, naturalist, behaviorist, and technophile
bias, an establishment which represents a major investment of emotional and political capital and which, therefore, can never react
with more than a minimum show of rationality.

For, notoriously, and it should not be necessary to stress the
matter, behind the so reasonable public (and public relations) facade
of Modern architecture, there boils a largely uninvestigated metaphysical and psychological volcano. Metaphysically, one imagines
that its lava is of a largely Hegelian origin; and psychologically,
one supposes that its detritus is, for the most part, of a Platonic-
Hebreo-Christian provenance. Which is to say that, behind or beneath the alleged neutral surface and underpinning, the so often

Architectural Education: USA

expressed ideals of scientific objectivity and/or direct social commitment, by anyone who chooses evenly randomly to examine, there is
to be discovered—to mix metaphors—a whole jungle of largely un-
observed and entirely unverifiable assumptions; and these, like Spanish moss, are all the beautiful parasites which the tree of ingenuous
rationalism so abundantly encourages. And thus, there is the notion
of ineluctable social change which must in some way be accommo-
dated; then there is the notion of the spirit of the age, of the *Zeitgeist,* envisaged as establishing moral imperatives which can in no
way be rejected; and finally and allied to all this, there are those
never to be subdued fantasies of the architect as a composite of Mo-
ses, St. George, Galahad, Siegfried, as the messianic hero, as he who
leads the people to the promised land, as the killer of the dragons
and as the one who keeps the faith.

Now, however much we may, sometimes, be led to disavow
these, they are all of them presumptions and personifications which
we know and which, when we acknowledge them, are all of them destructive of the received idea of a simply rational, or rationalizable,
Modern architecture and of the increasingly established propensities
of architectural education. Or so they ought to be. But to uncover
an attitude is not to dispose of that attitude; and the idea of a 'total'
architecture which, in spite of its implied brutality, still seems to be
so widely desired, the idea of an architecture 'scientifically' based
upon 'facts' is, again and again, so much complemented and interpenetrated by a profusion of eschatological enthusiasms, chiliastic
illusions, Utopian fantasies, and millennialistic dreams as to be virtually irresistible to criticism. Indeed, it is an amalgam which, like
Marxism, ultimately enshrines a faith in science and an irrational,
contrary conviction in the immanence of the New Jerusalem; and
which, like any primitive religion, effectively guarantees its devotees a very large immunity from the intrusions and promptings of
common sense.

It goes without saying that Modern architecture was always—or perhaps I should say was always in its heroic period—an
implicit denial of the consequences of that aboriginal eating of the

apple, of the consequences of the alleged Fall and of its later explanations. That is, it was—for better or worse—always an implicit denial of the doctrine of Original Sin. It knew very, very little of "the
good that I would that I do not, the evil that I would not that I do."
Instead it was born, let us say, under a strange astrological combination: on the one hand Oswald Spengler, on the other, H. G. Wells;
on the one hand the predictions of an imminent cataclysm, on the
other the prophecies of an effulgent future. And so, Modern architecture, recoiling from the threat of catastrophe, assumed a faith in per-
fectibility and in the possibilities of a, perhaps final, cultural
integration.

I do not wish further adversely to criticize an antiquated
and now somewhat sclerotic religion of architecture—particularly
since myself is highly susceptible to most of the doctrines and much
of the poetry of this religion. Instead, simply all that I wish to suggest is that its repertory of contradictory assumptions, conscious
and unconscious, could usefully be subjected to a modicum of theological finesse. I agree with Janet Daley that those two tendencies of
Modern architecture, the architect as errand boy of the sociologist
and the architect as cosmological systems man—are coming to com-
plement one another in a pernicious and "a potentially terrifying
conceptual framework," in a framework which also threatens to be
authoritarian; but I also imagine that, given sufficient comprehension, irony, compassion, wit, good sense, somehow these terrifying
and pernicious effects which I assume lie latent in all primitive religions can be made, if not to go away, at least to recede and to come
to occupy an overt and a discussable place.

Back in 1765, in what I suppose must have been his second
publication, the Abbé Laugier begins his *Observations* with the entirely fetching notice that "Everything is not yet said about Architecture. There rests," he says, "an enormous field, open to the
researchers of artists, the observations of amateurs, and the discoveries of men of genius"; and it is because, more than two hundred
years later, the same remarks are true and the field remains equally
immense and open that one is emboldened to continue.

Architectural Education: USA

So, one is emboldened to continue and to allow the big
question to emerge: With reference to any specific work of architecture, what statements can be proved to be false or true? And this is
the question which is almost never propounded—and, presumably,
because its results are so entirely unreassuring. That is: though one
may verify certain statements about a building, about its materials,
cost, maintenance, etc., most of these statements are—in the end—
not going to be widely regarded as being very interesting. But, if
equally verifiable and much more interesting indeed there may be
proposed statements relating to the laws of statics, there certainly
also will proliferate a super-abundance of strenuously maintained
positions related to use and appearance.

And this predicament, as to the ultimate impossibility of
proof or disproof, one is obliged to propose as supremely important,
since a truly scientific approach to architecture and the problems of
teaching it should surely begin, not with an aprioristic method derived from the physical sciences (or from anywhere else) but rather
with the nature of the institution of architecture itself, with its limitations, its mode of being, its most intimate and intrinsic qualities.

That there is almost total reluctance to look at these and to
envisage any scientific base for their discussion, I have already intimated. But, pursuing such an approach, we might choose to recognize that, though a work of architecture in its practical aspects is
very largely an affair of assembling bricks, mortar, steel, concrete,
glass, timber, tubes, and entrails according to the principles of certain known statical laws, that the supposition which is generally
received that architecture itself is a coordination of these very miscellaneous materials for the purposes of use and pleasure already
does intrude most of the ultimate problems of metaphysics. For, if
the laws of statics can be safely assumed to be established beyond
dispute, the laws of use and pleasure, of convenience and delight,
have certainly not as yet been subjected to any Newtonian revolution; and, while it is not inconceivable that in the future they may
be, until that time, any ideas as to the useful and the beautiful will
rest as untestifiable hypotheses. And this we might propose as archi-

tecture's central glaring problem—a problem which neither the brisk conclusions of common sense, the refined intuitions of enlightened sensibility, nor the application of scientific veneer will ever quite suppress.

Like the exponent of theology, political theory, philosophy, or any other discipline which seeks to order random experience, which cannot possibly await an ideal future solution of its problems, which is obligated to disentangle significant and workable structures from a continuous flux of evidence, the architect is obliged to work upon an essentially 'uncertain' substratum; and, in the end, his formulation of concepts of use, beauty, improvement, etc. will rest upon ideological, or at last idealistic, foundations. That is: behind any architectural system or approach, or even behind any single work, there will always be implicated a variety of assumptions as to the nature of reality, the significance of novelty, the natural man, the good society, and all the other criteria which typically are intruded in order to arbitrate problems of value.

This ultimate basis for almost everything that he does, though he is prone to recognize its presence throughout the whole history of architecture, the architect is almost always determined to disavow as regards himself. And this is to be expected. He feels guilty about it and he hopes to shift the guilt to others whom he wishes to believe have none of the doubts about their own disciplines which he entertains about his own. But the continuous identity crisis of the architect is certainly no help to architectural education; and it is because architecture, in the end, is concerned with the simultaneous recognition and solving of highly complex and value-informed problems that what could be called the neo-Positivist tone of so much architectural education can only be seen as obscuring rather than illuminating the central issues.

I may, so far, have been largely negative; and, even, I may have given the impression that I am hostile to computers, statistics, technology, sociology, cultural anthropology, and all the rest. I should therefore attempt to correct this impression. So far as I am concerned, all these things and pursuits have their place and their

Architectural Education: USA

contribution; but, also, their place and their contribution will never be valuable to the degree that they serve as surrogates for the architect's social guilt and permit, indeed facilitate, his abdication of responsibility.

To switch the scene and to be pragmatic; I am skeptical of institutionalized systems and much more skeptical of institutionalized objectives; I am skeptical of too much research—because how can the student conduct research until he is informed about what is already known; I am also convinced that once a thing is teachable, can be specified and codified, it is, almost certainly, not very much worth learning; and, for these reasons, I find myself believing very much in the virtues of confusion and the impromptu. Which means that I believe, and sometimes maybe to extravagance, in the centrality of the design studio and of its issue, the presumptive physical product. And I quote, "The design studio is probably the most rich and advanced system of teaching complex problem solving that exists in the university," and "even as courses stand now, they have so much to offer students which cannot be obtained in any other university department that I am amazed that nobody has the faith to give them the hard sell." This is a quotation from the *RIBA Journal* for January 1970 but is the opinion of a sociologist rather than an architect and is therefore, just possibly, all that more significant.

But, how we conduct the design studio will depend on how we believe about the apple and original sin, how we feel about program versus archetype, how we evaluate the role of empirical information versus that of myth, whether we consider the purpose of information to be that of a determinant or simply that of a test; and, in general, the degree to which we are willing or not willing to recognize any work of architecture to be a conglomerate of both empirical facts and value judgements. Further, the strategies of a design studio will depend on attitudes taken up, on the one hand, towards research and, on the other, towards that still almost incredible constellation of novelties which emerged in the opening years of this century, towards what we think about the student discovering for himself and what we think about the student becoming immersed in a tradition of which he cannot but be a part.

Now which of these approaches is conservative and which is radical, I am at a loss to know; and, probably, neither designation is very opportune. But, if among my personal convictions there remains the belief in the supreme importance of certain discoveries of approximately sixty years ago, then for present purposes, I wish to rescind this belief. Instead I wish to present an argument for which I am indebted to Fred Koetter. It is about a linear descending sequence versus the rotations of a wheel; and it concerns the manner in which the architect should accept the intimations of parallel disciplines which he should rightly consider important. The one style of acceptance—the linear descending sequence—is hierarchical. There is the sociologist and then the techno-man and then the computers, and then, at the end of the line, the architect.

But the other style of acceptance, the wheel, is much more egalitarian, and, in this, everybody shares the responsibility and the guilt, because when we are talking about the wheel, we are recognizing that everybody wants to and will invent a model but that everybody's models are partial, incomplete, and subject to check by somebody else's.

So in this wheel style, the architect, even though he may not want it, is 'raised' to the level of the sociologist and obliged to assume responsibility, while the sociologist, which I should imagine would make him happy, is 'reduced'. But the idea involves neither raising nor reduction. Rather it involves the validity of all kinds of contradictory models and perceptions. Nobody is at the center. Everybody is at the perimeter; and all models are subject to qualification by all others.

However it is just possible that, given the architect's social guilt and his anxiety to enjoy a sulphuric acid douche twice a day, a proposal of this kind, so obvious and so easy, so tolerant and so rational, could never be effective; and, if this is the case, and even if it is not, then I would like to end as I began with a falling back upon a quotation and this time a quotation from that impeccable liberal, Alfred North Whitehead. In his lecture, "The Aims of Education," way back in 1912, Whitehead condemns what he calls the tyranny

Architectural Education: USA

of inert ideas, of "ideas that are merely received into the mind without being utilised, or tested, or thrown into fresh combinations"; but, with these overcome, finally he says,

> there should grow the most austere of all mental qualities, I mean the sense for style. It is an aesthetic sense based on admiration for the direct attainment of a foreseen end, simply and without waste. Style in art, style in literature, style in science, style in logic, style in practical execution have fundamentally the same aesthetic qualities, namely attainment and restraint. Here we are brought back to the position from which we started, the utility of education. Style, in its finest sense, is the last acquirement of the educated mind; it is also the most useful. It pervades the whole being. The administrator with a sense for style hates waste; the engineer with a sense for style economises his material; the artisan with a sense for style prefers good work. Style is the ultimate morality of mind. With style the end is attained without side issues, without raising undesirable inflammations. With style you attain your end and nothing but your end. With style the effect of your activity is calculable and foresight is the last gift of gods to men. With style your power is increased, for your mind is not distracted with irrelevancies, and you are more likely to attain your object. Now style is the exclusive privilege of the expert. Whoever heard of the style of an amateur painter, of the style of an amateur poet? Style is always the product of specialist study, the peculiar contribution of specialism to culture.

Style, "the most austere of all mental qualities," "the ultimate morality of mind," "the peculiar contribution of specialism to culture." Evidently Whitehead did not understand style in the art historical sense, but I still feel obliged to quote him because of the pregnancy of definitions such as these and because, in the end, and after everything may have been said, he has cited, for us, what must be the object.

On Conceptual Architecture

An almost completely ad hoc little talk given at the Art Net conference on Conceptual architecture, London, January 17–18, 1975. First published in Art Net *(1975).*

My first reaction was, but all architecture is conceptual; and that must be the very crude reaction that a lot of people must have. And, then, my second reaction was: well, no—it can't be quite like that—it must have something to do with Marcel Duchamp— but surely.

And then I discovered that I was supposed to make a more protracted form of utterance, and that information was received a little too late because I would have liked to assemble a number of slides which turned out not to be possible.

Anyway, I gather that, among the relevant themes, are *process* rather than *product,* and, of course, *the dematerialization of the object:* which I find immensely difficult. You see, in so far as I am able to receive information, this dematerialization seems to have been going on for so very long now, that one might imagine that the object could very well have disappeared quite a long time ago. But, on the other hand, it seems to be extraordinarily persistent. Then, and also involved in this business, there is undoubtedly something called *the presence of absence;* and, naturally, one may justify the presence of absence by all kinds of arguments relating to Zen Buddhism, the mystical traditions of Christianity, and, probably, Elena Petrovna Blavatsky.

I was talking to Cedric Price upstairs a few minutes ago about this business of *the presence of absence,* as to whether this conceptual thing (though mystical—and I have no objection to that) is something you can specify and send the specification by telegram. Also, if it is about buildings to be dematerialized and without corporeal presence, whether it is something which can, possibly, exist. But I also know that it *can.* You don't touch it, you can't smell it, you can't measure it; and again, in this matter, we are, obviously, talking about some kind of mystical essence.

So, talking to Cedric, I was intrigued about the possibility of conceptual cooking. And one imagines a situation in which you invite people to a conceptual dinner party and everybody is equipped with a cookbook which they proceed to contemplate, the nature of the specification being the equivalent of the meal itself. And, again, I can see *that* as having value. I would infinitely prefer, for instance, to sit with a good cookbook than go into the establishment next door and eat those deplorable English sausages and consume that abominable beer. A frivolous aside? But of course.

What I decided that one could do, was to throw out a number of things for discussion, since this is supposed to be a conversation. The things are awfully (sort of) old-hat and 'churchy'. I think they are in some ways relevant—though their relevance may be a little bit dubious—and the connections to relevancy are a little bit tenuous—shall we say?

Anyway, my first quote was (and it should please the semanticists and the semiotic people), "In the beginning was the Word,

and the Word was with God, and the Word was God." (That should
captivate Chomsky freaks, I think.) And that is followed up by
the subsequent statement, "The Word was made flesh and dwelt
amongst us." O.K. I take it that this can be translated as, "In the beginning was the Idea and the Concept, and the Concept was made
palpable," was equipped with length and breadth and height and
texture and if you like, smell and substance, that whatever it is
you're dealing with was made incarnate in some way or another.
And I don't really see much to argue about here. I'm perfectly willing to concede that in the beginning may have been the Word.
Why not?

But the business of "the Word was made Flesh" raises question marks. I think.

You might ask: Can the Word be made flesh? Or was that
not a Christian fantasy? Should the Word be made flesh? Is this
embodiment of the Word in flesh to make it intelligible? Or is it
simply to adulterate the Word?

I'm going to answer (for myself) all those questions in the
affirmative. The Word can, I suppose, be made flesh—up to a
point—and this embodiment does help to make the Word intelligible. However, to make the Word flesh is also to adulterate the
Word.

So that deals with one text; and my next text is equally
'churchy', this time from St. Paul's Epistle to the Romans, and it is,
"The law came in that the offense might abound."

This is one of those more captivating things in the Bible
and obviously a much, much more difficult statement to handle.
Does it mean that the normative has a kind of use as a surface or
background for the display of the deviant? I think it means that
amongst other things. Does it mean that the typical is useful as
validating the exceptions? I think it also means that. I think it
also means that the Ground—if we're talking Gestalt stuff—the
Ground stimulates the intimate apprehension of the Figure. I think
also, if we're using Lévi-Strauss language, this is what Lévi-Strauss
would call "the precarious balance between Structure and Event,"

On Conceptual Architecture

which is also the balance between Scaffold and Happening and Grid and Episode.

Then there is that little piece of Serlio which says "by an error I mean to do contrary to the precepts of Vitruvius." It also indicates somehow the two-way commerce which should (and always does) exist between those corollary things which one might distinguish in present-day jargon as the Establishment and the Revolutionary Principle—of course, as interdependent activities.

O.K. That's the second of my texts: "The law came in that the offense might abound," and I think it's very important for the subject being discussed—it could be discussed for hours: you can imagine Talmudic types and Medieval scholastics going on with this for days, if not for years.

O.K. My next is that famous occasion in the 1860s when the Dean of Windsor said to Disraeli that he did not believe in dogma. And then of course, there is Disraeli's reply, "Well really, Mr. Dean, I'm afraid no dogma no Dean, Mr. Dean." Now that, I suppose, is a criticism (on Disraeli's part) of certain aspects of Liberalism. A criticism—from a Jewish point of view—of English empiricism: and of very much else too. It's a criticism of French Positivism. It's a criticism also of English utilitarianism; it's a criticism of many of the pretensions of the social sciences. It's a criticism before the event, of Modern architecture and the doctrine of Walter Gropius not to mention the characteristic mentality of the planner. I can see in it a criticism of all those things. It implies that there is no such thing as neutral observation: that all observation is culture-biased (as we know); that we can never hope for an objective view of things; that the best we can hope for is for arguments between different styles of subjectivity.

Having given that quotation, I wish now to take up the issue of tradition. Several people used the word tradition yesterday, and sometimes you hear of these-and-these traditions of Modern architecture.

If you look in the *Shorter Oxford Dictionary,* one of the first meanings given to the word *tradition,* apart from a "handing over" and all that business, is "a giving-up, surrender, or a betrayal." And it follows with the statement that "a tradition is also particularly a betrayal of sacred books in times of persecution."

In other words, you can 'commit' a tradition—which entertains me as a possibility. I do not claim to know about economics and that kind of thing, but related to the word tradition are notions of trade. And treachery, and bargaining, and the betrayal of principle, and the making of treaties. And low-class diplomatic skills; and, also, translation: you get it obviously most clearly in French when a *traité* is a treaty and a *traitre* is a traitor: and the implication surely is that somebody who makes a treaty is a traitor. He is betraying principles in the interests of survival. But, in this sense, one has to see, I think, Judas as the absolute *homme idéal* of the traditionalists. He performed a necessary act of betrayal in order that the Christian religion could be institutionalized. This is a profitable desertion to the Establishment—profitable for the Revolutionary Principle. What Judas does, surely, is to save humanity from the deserts of the spirit to which unmitigated Christianity condemns it, and to make it safe, to steer it yet again towards the warm, soft harbors of the flesh.

O.K. So these are different arguments, which surely one might take.

The business about "In the beginning was the Word and the Word was made Flesh and dwelt amongst us," and then this funny business about "the law came in that the offense might abound." And this thing about 'tradition' as treachery and betrayal. But, perhaps every day, in that context, art *has* to betray principle. And perhaps every day one has to *revive* principle—something you have to kill in order to make it truly alive.

Then it occurred to me this morning that I could even at this stage interject another quotation. This is from Doctor Johnson, from his magazine *The Rambler* for January 25, 1752, and it goes as follows:

On Conceptual Architecture

Wit, you know, is the unexpected copulation of ideas. The discovery of some occult relation between images in appearance remote from each other. And an effusion of wit therefore pre-supposes an accumulation of Knowledge; a memory stored with notions which the imagination may cull-out to compose new assemblages. [That might actually be assemblage—I don't know.] Whatever may be the native vigour of the mind, she can never form many combinations from new ideas, as many changes can never be rung on a few bells. Accident may indeed sometimes produce a lucky parallel or a striking contrast, but these gifts of chance are not frequent, and he that has nothing of his own and yet condemns himself to needless expenses, must live upon loans or theft.

There are here subsequent themes which are, I think, relevant to the present position, which include the idea of 'wit', the idea of 'collage', of 'ready-made', of all that kind of business, which are implicated in the statement.

Then I thought I would briefly reminisce, which is always a deplorable thing to do. I suddenly remembered, while somebody was talking yesterday, an occasion in Texas. Long ago in the High Eisenhowerian period, the University had what was called 'Religious Emphasis Week'. It really didn't matter what religion you emphasized—after all we are a pluralist, liberal society, and we merely want people to *emote* and to *feel* religious. We're not really interested in the substance of their beliefs, or the structure of their beliefs. Anyway, there was this Religious Emphasis Week. It related to that period, you know, when you got those dreadful slogans like "A world at Prayer is a world at Peace." Which is preposterous. And that even more deplorable statement "The family that prays together stays together." Which, in the High Manson period a couple of years back, was turned into "the family that slays together stays together."

O.K. So there we are in mish-mash land. And sooner or later we're all going to enter mish-mash land if present tendencies of pluralism continue. But I was walking down the street in Texas, with John Hejduk, of all people, and he suddenly said, "Ch-r-rist, isn't it really wonderful that there really is a Pope in Rome." And I'm not an enthusiast for the Pope. But there are certain circumstances, certain predicaments that you find yourself in, when he becomes a useful entity to presume. You can delete 'the Pope'—quite the easiest thing in the world (that was what Protestantism was all about to begin with)—and you can substitute, if you like, the Supreme Court of the United States. Or you can delete 'the Pope' and propose that we all skip around with Superstudio, preferably naked, in the Cartesian coordinates of freedom. That is another thing that you can do. But what we are talking about, again, is surely a version of "the law came in that the offense might abound." We're talking about the ordered guarantee that has to exist if spontaneity may also exist. We're talking again about the infinite two-way commerce between Establishment attitudes and Revolutionary Principles. And you can't get along without *both*.

I was also reminded this morning, and I will not give the name of the person to whom this relates, but it was back in Cambridge (England). But somebody rang up—a person who stammers rather a lot, and said, "C-C-C-Colin, d-do you think that we might possibly have d-d-dinner?" I said "Well yes, why not, what about tonight?" "Well, I'm afraid that I'll be in t-town, and be dining at the Reform Club." So we went through this list of possible dates and the first time we could have dinner was in three weeks' time. And then, the end of the conversation was, "You see, What I r-r-really wanted to talk about was s-s-s-spontaneity." That is a little cruel but I haven't mentioned any name. However, sometimes I feel that one is in the presence of a protracted *talking* about spontaneity which means that a true spontaneity will surely never come about.

Then there is that piece of Shelley: "Rarely, rarely comest thou, Spirit of delight"; and obviously you want it to come fre-

On Conceptual Architecture

quently, you want things to come spontaneously, but that is much more easily said than done.

If I had been going to make a proper talk, I would like to have had as a primary image that picture from Albert Speer's book of memoirs, during the first Nuremburg Rally, in which the arena was built up out of floodlights, which were centrally inclined, which Sir Neville Henderson spoke of as a "cathedral of ice." And Speer was particularly moved by this structure of floodlights, by what one imagines was the rather Wagnerian movement of clouds backwards and forwards between them. And, again one might see this as Structure and Event; the clouds being 'Event'. But I suppose that this arena for the Nuremburg Rally was a very perfect illustration of a dematerialized architecture. You turn the switch and it's there. You turn the switch and it goes away. It is also an architecture that obviously could be specified by telegram. I think it is really an eloquent sort of image.

I'm sure that, again, Marcel Duchamp does drag his way in and one would like to bring somebody like Duchamp into a parallel (say) with Fernand Léger. I infinitely more enjoy Duchamp, who seems to me to be lucid, illuminating, entertaining, and all that, fragile, poetic, lyrical. Whereas, surely by comparison, one would find Léger turgid, opaque, heavy, and after a little, wearisome. On the other hand I suspect that Léger is maintaining the Establishment—to some extent against which the Duchamp type of personality might possibly be able to perform.

Again I suppose one ought to produce the Maison Domino as the instance of a contest. And also to notice that *it* was never built. In other words, the Maison Domino is a kind of conceptual necessity, an heuristic device. But then, in reality, this thing has to be modified because of the exigencies of perception, and it becomes modified in the most extraordinary variety of ways.

Now I presume that there must be a two-way commerce between Concept and Process. Which means between intellectual and physical stimulus. And I am a little baffled—but I am waiting to be instructed—by how one is to react to something that quite simply is not there. (Except in one's more Zen moments.) Its specifications are there, but nothing more. Again, it is the presence of absence. And in order for the absence to be felt as presence—in a lot of other places there's got to be a lot of presence. Otherwise, you know, "No hole is visible unless there is a solid for you to make the hole in."

(In answer to a question from the audience)

There is something in Modern architecture called 'object-fixation', probably at no other time than in the twentieth century have people been so concerned with making significant objects, and at the same time as making them they have had great guilt about making these objects and wish them to go away. A complete ambivalence in reaction to 'the object'. It's notorious in a little quote from Corbu, in which he said, "Great blocks of dwellings run through the town—what does it matter, if they're behind the trees? Nature has entered the lease." This is simultaneously an affirmation of the object and then inhibition about the object; and I think that it has a lot to do with Conceptual architecture.

Waiting for Utopia

A review of Robert Venturi, Complexity and Contradiction in Architecture *(New York: Museum of Modern Art, 1966), and Reyner Banham,* The New Brutalism: Ethic or Aesthetic *(New York: Reinhold, 1966), published in* The New York Times, *1967.*

Not so many years ago, when Modern architecture was allegedly no more than an objective approach to building, implicitly it was much more. Implicitly it was a prophetic illustration of the shape of things to come, the revelation of a world in which difficulties would vanish and conflicts would be resolved. The Modern building was both a polemic and a model, a call for action and an assertion of those ends to which action should lead; and therefore it is not surprising that the architect should have often conceived of his buildings, not only as the *images* of a regenerated society, but also as the *agents* which were destined to bring that society about.

The future of yesterday, one might suggest, is the present which we now occupy; and, evidently, it is not quite the anticipated future. Modern architecture now exists in abundance; but the hoped for Utopia has scarcely ensued. Nor is it clear that mankind is so very much further ahead on the road to its redemption; and hence, there has followed a certain deflation of optimism.

Such is one interpretation of today's situation. It is the predicament which anyone wishing to understand recent architecture must accept as some sort of base line; and, further to this, it is an issue which links together and somewhat explains the two books which are the subject of this review: the one American, the other English.

In *Complexity and Contradiction in Architecture,* the first of a new Museum of Modern Art series, Robert Venturi presents a critical essay which is also, as he stipulates, a personal apologia. Venturi, like some other architects—and many literary critics—is preoccupied with the uses of paradox, redundancy, and ambiguity. He uses these devices in his buildings, wishes others to use them, and proposes these as the valid and animating elements of a mature architectural approach. Deploring the unaccommodating simplicity which he associates with the International Style and its continued influence, Venturi discovers most of his inadequately reproduced illustrative material in the architecture of the sixteenth to the eighteenth centuries. In other words, via a catalogue of Mannerist motifs, Venturi explains in detail those visual phenomena which excite and inspire him. Then he concludes his book with a catalogue of his own work in which he exhibits the evidence of this inspiration.

From only six hours away across the Atlantic, but appearing to emanate from another time and world, comes Reyner Banham's latest book, *The New Brutalism,* an account of that architectural movement which was centered in London and which, stimulated by the later works of Le Corbusier and Mies van der Rohe, was partly reaction against the specious prettiness of so many English buildings c. 1950. Banham once thought the New Brutalism to be a hopeful architectural manifestation. Its commitment to technology he believed to be unquestionable. The seriousness of its leading proponents he knew at first hand; and he believes their production to have been distinguished. But, ultimately, this book is a record of disappointment and its subtitle, *Ethic or Aesthetic,* is an index of its message. "For all of its brave talk of 'an ethic not an aesthetic' Brutalism never quite broke out of the aesthetic frame of reference. . . . The ethic of Brutalism was a campaign of 'mens sana in corpore sano' but no one should have doubted that the mind and body would prove, ultimately, to be the mind and body which had always belonged to architecture." And so the great renovation did not really occur. The Brutalist episode was hygienic and salutary but architecture did not become something-other-than-itself; and therefore it is with pessimistic awareness of insufficiency, with the renewed knowledge that, after all, architects wish to produce works of architecture rather than pure technological constructs, that Banham concludes.

It is a virtue of *The New Brutalism* to have brought together, between covers, a number of stylistically related buildings—some of them of considerable quality. It is a curiosity of the book that its author would probably consider such a stylistic determination to be superficial and against the cause of true architecture. It is the merit of *Complexity and Contradiction* that its author has publicly exposed personal predispositions—though not entirely unique to himself—which, in terms of the orthodox credo of Modern architecture, would certainly be dismissable as deviationist. Vincent Scully, in introducing Venturi's book, has claimed for it a significance possibly equal to Le Corbusier's *Towards a New Architecture;* and he explains that, to the degree that Le Corbusier provided the manifesto of the International Style, so Venturi here may have issued the manifesto of some imminent—and perhaps equivalent—development. If Scully is right, and if this is the case, then one can only imagine that there is about to be built up an enormous reservoir packed with future irritants for the author of *The New Brutalism.* For Banham's book, which is not so much a manifesto of Brutalism as it is an obituary notice, is likewise construable as an epitaph ahead of time for any such attitudes as those which Venturi propounds. For, if a modest analysis of Brutalist production and of

Venturi's own could plausibly demonstrate some stylistic affinity, then a modest analysis of Banham could plausibly suggest that, while he now feels himself to have been deceived by the Brutalists, at least—knowing the ropes in this area—he will scarcely dispose himself to be deceived again.

Banham, in this context, provides a useful measure for Venturi's achievement. His principal publication, *Theory and Design in the First Machine Age,* is one of the most important contributions to the literature of Modern architecture; but, while a study of avant-garde ideas and practice in the 1920s, it is again—like the book under review—the record of a disappointment. Practice did not completely reflect theory. Masterpieces were produced; but these masterpieces only served further to indicate the gaping chasms which intervened between theory and practice. One can understand the dismay. Theory and practice, the ideal and the real surely should converge, and it is Banham's great contribution to have insisted throughout his whole critical activity on just this. Banham has believed, and continues to believe, that Modern architecture should be, and can be, exactly what it was claimed to be: i.e., an objective approach to building deriving from an unprejudiced scrutiny of facts. Venturi would probably consider this to be conservative and irrelevant. Yet, to Banham, and to quote Scully, to "those technological homogenizers who crowd our future" it will be Venturi who is the reactionary.

It is Banham's strength to be in possession of a crucial and simple idea. It is Venturi's strength to be the possessor of an enlightened sensibility. Had Venturi's sensibility resulted in more than a collection of stimulating visual insights, entrenched establishments would be more seriously threatened than they will be. Could Banham's attitude be confirmed by concrete illustrations of its possibility, the aspirations of the 1920s would be realized.

Connoisseurs of the ironical might extract considerable satisfaction from the simultaneous appearance of these two overtly unlike but intrinsically related offerings: the two attitudes they disclose represent the polar extremes between which architecture now oscillates.

Robert Venturi and the Yale Mathematics Building Competition

Published in Oppositions *(Fall 1976).*

    I first met the Venturis in Rome in 1969, and I found them quite as charming as I found their architecture to be more than acceptable. But why should this not have been the case? I had written an article, "Mannerism and Modern Architecture"—I think not very good—in 1949–1950, in which I had used almost the same language which Venturi himself used in Complexity and Contradiction in Architecture *(New York: Museum of Modern Art, 1966) (see C. Ray Smith,* Supermannerism *{New York: Dutton, 1977}). So it must have been appropriate that we met in the* cortile *of Palazzo Farnese on a late Sunday morning while we were, all of us, waiting to go upstairs to the Carracci Gallery. And it was further appropriate that, afterward, we all went to lunch at a restaurant very adjacent.*

    Therefore I was not surprised—since we had achieved almost a marriage of the minds—when I received an invitation to write a review of the Venturi and Rauch winning design for the Yale Mathematics Building Competition. This was for a book to be published about the competition; and, of course, I complied.

I wrote, as I thought, dispassionately (fundamentally the program was too rough to make sense, and the accommodation too large to be amenable to the site); but, even writing so—and attempting to make an empirical critique equivalent to my earlier piece on Churchill College[1]—I found myself involved in all the viciousness of academic politics as conducted by absurd fanatics. The criticism, I had thought, was sympathetic; but it was not so received by a faction at Yale,[2] and, as a result, the book was never published.

But to say more about this would be to exhibit paranoia. It distressed me; it distressed Charles Moore; and it so much distressed Peter Eisenman that, in February 1971, he felt obliged to write to the Yale University Press about it.

A dreary dredging up of fatuous scandal of course this is; but, meanwhile, I just want this review to stand as evidence of my regard for Robert and Denise, and also my distaste for the cultural imperialism at one time emanating from certain East Coast American universities.

Robert Venturi continues to be the victim of what seems to be a campaign to enlarge him beyond what he really is—a thoughtful, attractive, and, so far, insufficiently considered figure. This seems a pity. For Venturi has integrity, talent, and an interesting point of view. He has written a book which discloses him to be something of a mandarin; he has designed a number of buildings which suggest something equally elitist; and, because he admires paradox, he also professes a feeling for the commonplace.

Thus, for the Yale Mathematics Building, he has made a project of which he says that "the image is ordinary" and "the substance is ordinary," and though there should be nothing wrong or remarkable about that, still, if a genuine commonplace is indeed to arise in Hillhouse Avenue, then what should there really be to talk about? And why should criticism be solicited? Because, surely, if

the Mathematics Building is to be what it is said to be, then it will
be no more than the equivalent of any old Main Street job, and
though, as such, it might afford casual gratification (native genius
in anonymous architecture?), presumably it could, quite well, be
left unprovided with critical notice.

The answer is, of course, that the Mathematics Building is
not what it is said to be. For, in the context of Venturi's project, is
it not evident that the word "ordinary" belongs not so much to the
public realm as to a quasi-private language? That it implies values
which are not so much commonplace as they are arcane? That being
"ordinary" is the low-key advertisement of a point of view which
implies not so much a passive condition as a polemical one? That,
while to be "ordinary" is to seem to be ordinary, it is, also, to be difficult, to be cryptic, to be cute?

This said, it would be agreeable if we could approach Venturi's project without more verbal ado; but, unfortunately, we cannot. For the direct approach seems to be blocked—by words which
intervene to disallow any immediate, analytical contact.

These are, primarily, words concerning Venturi's reputation. "He has so far enjoyed little popular success and incurred surprising professional resentment"; however, he is, "one of the few
American architects whose work seems to approach tragic stature in
the tradition of Furness, Sullivan, Wright, and Kahn"; moreover, he
is "an Italian architect of the great tradition"; and, if Le Corbusier's
Carpenter Center has been "in all ways more understood, apparently, by Venturi than by any other architect in America," then also,
though his *Complexity and Contradiction in Architecture* is as "graceless
and inarticulate as only the new can be," it too is "probably the
most important writing on the making of architecture since Le Corbusier's *Vers une Architecture* of 1923." [3]

These are among specimens of the critical hyperbolics with
which Venturi's name is now enmeshed. Apparently a niche has already been prepared in the architectural hall of fame; and, since the
image has arrived, it now only awaits installation. Venturi has, after
all, not only the most elaborate recent pedigree—Sullivan, Wright,

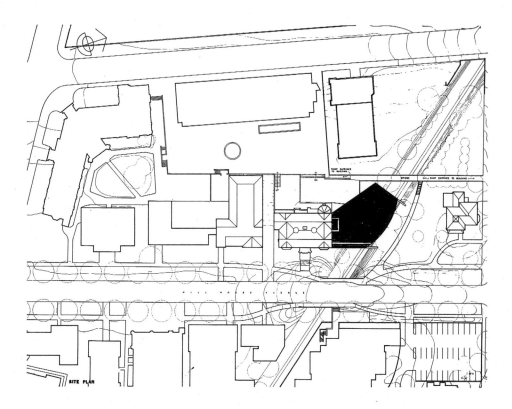

8. Yale Mathematics Building, New Haven, site plan. Robert Venturi.

Le Corbusier, et al.—but we know that we only have to search a bit and we shall find both Aalto and Lutyens acting as sponsors; while we are well aware that, if we prolong our investigations, a whole host of more remote but equally important figures—Vanbrugh, Vittone, Soane, and almost any architect of the last four centuries who has displayed moderate sophistication—may safely be conscripted to decorate the lower branches of the genealogical tree.

This is to exaggerate an only too prevalent critical tone which, by claiming too much, can only incite disbelief. Simply, we feel that the credentials are being forced; and, even when the stereotypes of aggressive art history become qualified by 'gentle' information as to Venturi's ironical insights, his modest feeling for compromise and 'accommodation', his 'inclusiveness', and that unerring common sense such as few others possess, still our skepticism is not allayed. We continue to wish to expel at least some of the clouds of critical incense which fog the air.

For, in spite of the insobriety of his admirers which inhibits approach to his buildings and virtually defeats all possibility of a logical handling of his ideas, Venturi must be recognized as somebody with something to say; and, as Alan Colquhoun has pointed out, if his *Complexity and Contradiction in Architecture* is something less than consistent, there are many aspects of his general theoretical position which ought to command a very easy assent.[4]

Thus Venturi finds it hard to accept the dated naïveté of that body of ideas which still circulates as Modern architecture's apologetic; and, though he does not say as much, one suspects that he would be just as prone to condemn the Bauhaus ideal of a total architecture as being something dangerously Wagnerian. That is, while he is appalled by simplistic explanations and aspirations, rather than any "survival through design" (with all the real brutality *that* implies), he would prefer to insist upon the usefulness of a dichotomy between high and low culture, between fine and crude art, and upon the complete normality of a two-way commerce between the polite and the vulgar.

Robert Venturi and the Yale Mathematics Building Competition

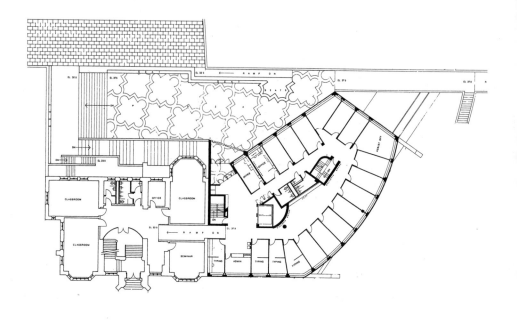

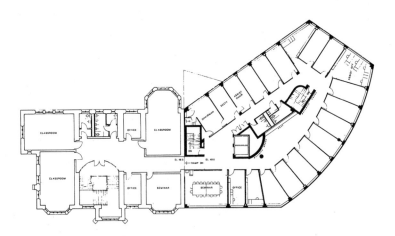

9. Yale Mathematics Building, first- and second-floor plans.

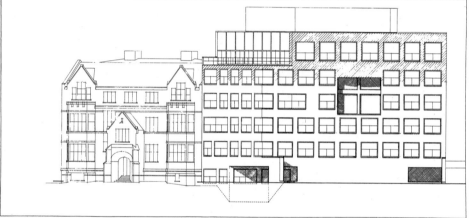

10. Yale Mathematics Building, east and northeast elevations.

Robert Venturi and the Yale Mathematics Building Competition

Having no faith in the efficacy of any single, universal, world-transforming principle, Whitehead's observation that there is no reason to suppose order more fundamental than chaos would seem to approximate his point of view; and this feeling for the empirical multiplicity of any given situation rather than for any cosmic vision of a millennium also carries over into what seems to be anxiety to emancipate architecture from the grip of historicism— meaning not from *the styles* but from the very Germanic supposition that history, irrespective of persons, is an irresistible force, that obedience to it is a moral imperative, that to deny the *Zeitgeist* is to invite catastrophe, and that the architect's most elevated role is to act as no more than the agent of necessity, as midwife for the delivery of historically significant form.

In *Complexity and Contradiction in Architecture,* Venturi only hints at a criticism of these ideas, but such criticism may still be recognized as distinctly implicit in his eclectic choice of illustrations. Mostly of Mannerist, Baroque, and Edwardian provenance, these are presented without apology; and there should be no more than this unabashed advertisement of his taste required to indicate his conviction that we are not entirely the victims of ineluctable historical process, that we are equipped with, at least, some freedom of choice. All this is what his illustrations seem to say. They are exemplary, and he infers that there is no embargo upon their employment as models.

But it is, at this stage, that Venturi seems to become a little evasive. He has—and perhaps not quite consciously—been concerned with demythologizing Modern architecture; and, in the process, he has arrived at drastic, if not unique, conclusions. Neither the apocalypse-Utopia nor the *Zeitgeist* myth is he able to accept; while it may be surmised that for the dependent myths, both the scientific and the ethico/technological ones, he also feels very considerable reservations. This leaves us with the problem that, though one cannot object to Venturi's skepticism, one might agree with him all the more readily if he were to have provided any indication of an awareness of the seminal role played by myth in the development of any architectural approach, strategy, or style. For, if it is myth—in collaboration or conflict with social and technological conditions—which is the ultimate architectural determinant, Venturi scarcely subjects this issue to examination; and, certainly, he never stipulates that the forms he admires came about through the activity of just such fantasies as he seems prone to reject.

Such scrutiny, it could be claimed, lies outside the scope of *Complexity and Contradiction in Architecture;* but, by its absence, evaluation of Venturi becomes more difficult and we are finally left wondering what, in this area, he does think or believe. Does he, for instance, conceive of a world in which myth has gone away and in which reason is, at last, ideally free? Or does he, desperately, hope that Main Street and Las Vegas can provide an adequate base for a continuing mythic structure? Or does he, with even more justified desperation, assume that, in a world where all myths can be uncovered, wit—with its allusiveness and integrity—can operate as the skeptical equivalent of belief?

His buildings would suggest that something like the last question frames his ultimate position; contrariwise, his Las Vegas study implies that the second question does profoundly interest him while one can only suppose that the first question he would find to be a merely rhetorical device.

And so Venturi shuttles between an esoteric ideal—the game of the learned reference and the calculated footnote—and a would-be esoteric and populist one. Hence his preoccupation with ambiguity, whether of meaning or form, Honky-tonk and Caserta, Frank Furness and Hawksmoor, Parisian *hôtels particuliers* and the Capella Sforza, small town America and McKim, Mead and White; anything which can be ironically considered or is itself ironical has been absorbed if not always digested, and Venturi has then felt amazingly free to play with these discrete items as though they were the ingredients of a collage. We paste on allusion to the Villa Aldobrandini; we make clear, *to the happy few,* our infatuation with the William Low House at Bristol, Rhode Island; we make commentary upon Stupinigi, Pavlovsk, Howard Johnson's, or Route 66; and then we syncopate the mix.

Robert Venturi and the Yale Mathematics Building Competition

Given the arguments of reasoned disbelief, this procedure via collage and innuendo is, in principle, not to be faulted; but, if it is a procedure which can produce the most enviable results and also a genuinely twentieth-century discovery, the idea of the ironical juxtaposition of things taken out of context has, in general, been profoundly antipathetic to the conscience of the so-called Modern movement; and, even though Le Corbusier was himself a great master of the architectural collage, the general bias of the contemporary architect's morality has contrived to inhibit the use of any technique so obvious and so rewarding.

But, if Le Corbusier, with what William Jordy has called "his witty and collisive intelligence,"[5] could bring into headlong confrontation the most diversely significant images and metaphors, this is something of which he rarely talked and which, though it was fundamental to him, he made no attempt to rationalize. Instead, what Le Corbusier talked about were "the great primary forms," the *ville radieuse,* and other equally grand abstractions; and what he attempted to rationalize were such normative facts as the column-grid. In other words, *publicly,* he upheld a structure which he could then, *privately,* proceed to contradict. For contradiction does imply something valuable and known in that which is contradicted; and, just as Le Corbusier's complexities are located in simplicity, so his contradictions assert a situation conceived to be public.[6]

Now, with Venturi, this does not appear to be the case, and, because it may seem a little ludicrous, overtly, to set up a situation in order, covertly, to shoot it down (Le Corbusier's pretended Platonic structures which are then riddled with whole salvoes of pretended empirical detail), Venturi's position may be more logical than that of Le Corbusier. Though perhaps logic, like morals, presumes always a question of geographical (and temporal) location.

For, in spite of a logic which one may wish to attribute to Venturi, he seems never to specify (except verbally?) the simple scene within which he wishes to be complex, nor any received order which he wishes to contradict, and thus, while one may understand,

and share, his anxiety to criticize certain myths, one can scarcely understand, or share, the supposition that such criticism leads where it appears to lead. Thus, apart from a taste for ambiguity in itself, which may be sponsored and guaranteed by the best authorities, and may be understood, just what is it that Venturi is trying to contradict? The received myths of Modern architecture? The doctrine of Walter Gropius? But then *who* is not trying to contradict just *these?* It is not easy to do so, and thus, and even after Venturi has dilated, things are still left insubstantial and not promising. For the delights of Las Vegas are principally delightful because they violate the sanctions of 'good taste', and pseudo-Mannerist exercises are the pleasure that they are because their erudition can be communicated to the connoisseur. But neither taste nor connoisseurship are possessed of any very public substance; and it may be for this reason that what have here been called Venturi's collages have appeared, in their frameworks, to be too researched and, in their ingredients, to be too fragile to admit of any very deep satisfaction. They have seemed clever and decorative, evocative and nostalgic, the entertaining *scherzi* of someone definitely informed rather than anything profound. Not, really, quite *collages,* not quite Dada, insufficiently mod, or Pop, or Op, sometimes engaging but always insufficiently witty, they are a little pedantic; and, though one may enjoy them up to a point, they are apt to leave us with the knowledge that, so far, Synthetic Cubism has provided a far more solid collection of images for collage (*objets à réactions poétiques*) than anything that art history and the various cults of Americana have been able to supply.[7]

Possibly this is a dismal conclusion, but it should not be allowed to obscure a further observation as to what seems to be Venturi's position. One alludes to an apparent Americanism, to a seeming desire to make, not so much architecture, as to make American architecture. Whether this is good or bad, who is to say? But it may, probably, be assumed that Le Corbusier never set out to be French; that, though his images are indisputably local, he conceived of both them and his procedures as being universal in their meaning and application; and it may be, as a result, that his local images thus be-

Robert Venturi and the Yale Mathematics Building Competition

came imbued with the most poignant generality. They were related, not to the world as it is, but to the world as he supposed it should be. For, whatever his passion for empirical detail might have been, Le Corbusier still proposed the issue of Utopia versus empirical life; while, by contrast, Venturi may be seen as appealing to 'life' itself, to ordinary life, the life of the art historian, the Mafioso hick, or the owners of the ranchburger around the corner, all being assumed to be equally significant.

And, if the notion of the 'ordinary' ('people' as found without overt Utopian idealization) begins thus to acquire some specific meaning, we might now also notice how the world of Venturi's images is without homogeneity, how it seems to be rifted, how there here seems to be signified a world of ancient culture—aristocratic and primarily European—which is juxtaposed alongside a world of immanent culture, an incipient modern world which is, primarily, American.

This cleavage, I think, should be evident to anyone who is not hopelessly prejudiced either in favor of Venturi or against him; and it would seem to be important. For it allows Venturi the best of all worlds; he can be, simultaneously, the Jamesian American in Europe, indisputably more refined (and less Marxian) than any European could ever be, and a Whitmanesque type in the United States. He may be privately esoteric and can publicly extol the democratic virtues. He can enjoy all the comforts of connoisseurship and may still have at his disposition the myth of America's incompleteness and potentiality, that myth of America's youth which Oscar Wilde called its oldest tradition.

With this notice of a probably harmless nationalism, which may not be entirely irrelevant to a consideration of the Mathematics Building, we may now approach New Haven and Hillhouse Avenue; and, in doing so, we may wonder how it is that, in the last twenty years, the quality of the Yale campus has become so dissipated, and why it is that, after this time, Yale's more spuriously eclectic buildings should now seem to be so much more authentic and convincing than those which have deliberately set out to be so.

The two questions are interconnected and the first is more easy to answer than the second.

"Not Gothic but Modern for Our Colleges" was the somewhat retarded title of an essay published by Walter Gropius in 1949, which could still win a prize in 1951,[8] and, if by that time the practical results of a new approach were already to be seen in the Harvard Graduate Center, it was probably the Massachusetts Institute of Technology that immediately pushed furthest the idea of a university campus as a kind of picture gallery for the exhibition of works by Modern architects believed to be distinguished. And the policy proved irresistible. For was it not patently progressive? *Is not Modern architecture the outward and visible sign of progress? And do we even have to look at it to know this? And, after all, have we not been told?* So that, as one unconnected gesture followed another and as academic communities, from coast to coast, proceeded to erode their environment, they could always do so with the pleasingly liberal conviction that they were definitely not left behind, that they were *au courant* and completely abreast of the march of history.

It must all have been immensely reassuring and some of the more unhappy illustrations of this policy are to be found standing around the Yale campus as the icons of a new world that never came about. It is not desirable and should not be necessary to itemize these horrors. For, officially, Yale is still "proud of its modern monuments"; and, in any case, anyone has his own list. Instead, it is enough to say that the Yale campus is scarcely the "open air museum of modern architecture" that is proclaimed, but rather that it is a theater of the architectural pseudo-event—not so much a museum as a version of Madame Tussaud's, a waxworks exhibition displaying important simulacra of the good, it being assumed that, for practical purposes, these must be quite just as good.

One fake performance after the other, and all in the ostensible name of honesty, have constituted a horribly protracted joke; but, while Yale, like other institutions, seems to have been unaware of this and journalism has consistently acclaimed it, apparently somebody has, finally, intimated that it has all been more than

Robert Venturi and the Yale Mathematics Building Competition

enough and, therefore, it is now again the value, not of individual buildings, but of the campus as an entity that is beginning to be asserted.

To speak of the "strong existing" and "the superbly integrated fabric unifying the central part of the campus" is, at New Haven, no exaggeration; and the Yale courtyards and quadrangles of the years around 1930 will increasingly come to be regarded as one of the greater urbanistic achievements of that period. Stylistically, indeed, they are far from avant-garde; but are they, for that reason, any less historically significant? Few great urbanistic achievements ever are avant-garde, and the acknowledged achievements of the years around 1930 (mostly in the area of European housing) may now seem to be less useful, so far as we are concerned, than the example of the Yale campus. But, if the Yale campus, in its classic phase, is now to be pushed forward as paradigmatic, there is still something dubious we might feel about this operation. In the first case, because it may seem a little inbred; and, in the second, because, just as one policy was pressed too far in the spirit of innocent optimism, one may feel that another is now about to be too cynically and pessimistically pursued.

None of this denies the concern that has prompted the Yale Mathematics Building competition. Indeed, one can imagine only too well the maneuvers necessary to put over this idea of deference for the existing. One can almost smell the lobbyings, the arguments, the rebuffs, the sophistries, the drinks poured; and, in the end, one can sense a bureaucratic resignation: *Well, and why not make of the Mathematics Building a test case, something which will certainly be new but which will still recognize "the superbly integrated" and the "strong existing" fabric? And why, for that matter, should the Mathematics Building not be the subject of a competition?*

These, then, might seem to be the anterior circumstances of the competition: a good idea which was insufficiently presented, inadequately received, and then deployed neither in a proper place nor at a reasonable scale; and, in the results, one can sense the conditions of the compromise: deference for the existing, perhaps more than should be required, and excess of accommodation which makes the possibility of such deference largely illusory.

From what has been published, so far as can be judged, it seems certain that, out of the five finalists, Venturi's project was the most deserving. Yet what can be said about it? That it displays a certain bald authority? That because it does not set out to seduce, it succeeds in doing so? That it promises to be the best building at Yale since about 1952? That it is certainly far better than Venturi claims it to be?

To answer all these questions in the affirmative is, probably, to be only fair; but it is also to abandon the strict sequence of logical discussion. We have, so far, inspected Venturi and inspected Yale—the two contexts to which the building must ultimately relate. A product of Venturi's mind and temperament, it is also a response to a specific situation in New Haven; and, in so far as it is possible to make this separation, it will be convenient to review the proposed building from these two standpoints.

So it is an 'ordinary' building. So 'ordinary' indeed that it is almost supposed to be not there. But the problem of the bulk of the building (and this must surely be a fault of the program) made it a little difficult for it to wither away like the state after the Marxist millennium. However much wished or willed, and whatever the ideal of the unobtrusive, it could just not be made to go away. It was indefeasible and, therefore, the argument that something so huge could become neutral simply had to be propounded. But a dependency (the extension to the Mathematics Building) cannot very well become all that much larger than that upon which it depends (Leet-Oliver); and one may observe Venturi struggling with this problem. He has altered the color of the brick in the upper floors, he has combined extensive references to Alvar Aalto with, maybe, more distant memories of the Palazzo Massimo, he more than hints at an old style New York City ziggurat; but, with all this, the problem of bulk he has not been able to reduce—simply because it was not to be reduced.

But with so much (or so little) observed, it is comparatively easy to travel to the back of the building and to notice that, although problems of bulk are painful on the Hillhouse Avenue exposures, they become little short of agonizing when we survey the confrontation of old and new at the rear; and, if much may be written off to irony, if it may be claimed that this abruptness of juxtaposition, however amateur it may appear, was willed, then, where there lurks around that willful framing plan, when there has been all that care about Gothic paving patterns, when we observe a pseudo-Gothic entrance screen arbitrarily arranged at a self-consciously clumsy angle, it might be best to withdraw attention from these obvious and easily discernible failures and to ascribe their apparent irresolution to the program. It might be best to concentrate attention not upon the details of Venturi's building, but upon the whole.

As regards the whole, we are, again, faced with the problem of its being 'ordinary', a condition which Venturi's personality and the details of the competition both, alike, act to deny; and, here, the ideal of the 'ordinary' has led to a manifestation that is supposed to be the equivalent of Main Street but which is not that equivalent because it assumes towards Main Street a sentimental attitude. It has led to a building that, in its refusal to communicate, in its determination not to reveal, in its assumption of the primitive and the banal, in its supposed innocence and its very great formalism, in the profession it makes of being addressed to the 'average' man, is, externally, supremely affirmative of the pathos, the unassuming beauty, and the hopelessness of a matter-of-fact pragmatism. It has led to a building that both celebrates and calls into question a Rotarian ethos; and that, in its supposed rejection of quality, becomes almost ostentatious.

It has also led to a building that assumes the Puritan disguise—external reticence as camouflage for private luxury—and that, because of its enigmatic and deceptive exterior, can afford, inside, to elaborate the scenographic richness of an entirely other tradition. The public face is deadpan; the private world is chic. We rest upon our privileges and we dissimulate their existence, which is all a little like Park Avenue—externally, facts (Connecticut know-how?) and, internally, subjective performance (Ralph Waldo Emerson for purposes of decor and public relations?).

And certainly Venturi, inside, insists upon everything other than factuality. But, if his circulations are to be enjoyed, if they are more spatially playful—in a European sense—than anything which has lately been witnessed in the United States, if they assert a primary dependence upon Le Corbusier and a subsidiary reliance upon Aalto, there could be a quality of interior decoration about them which might not be entirely pleasing. A *coup de théâtre* they certainly are, but might it not be wondered whether this effect has not been secured at the expense of an undue lesion between inside and outside; and, though this lesion could be thought of as something deliberately intended to disturb, though Le Corbusier practiced similar lesions, it could possibly be argued that Venturi's exterior and interior are, maybe, just a little too disrelated.

But, theatricality apart, in spite (or because) of his refusal to assume a grand image, with Venturi, we are still dealing with an aboriginally American building. We look at it. It is not to be rationalized with ease or without introspection. It is—if we like—quite mundane; and it is also—if we like—quite respectable. It has many virtues; but, this being said, the obligation now remains to relate Venturi's proposal to the Yale campus.

So we have what is alleged to be an important attempt to make art out of vernacular material, and we have something which is further alleged to be the rigorous solution of exacting functional problems. But we also have something which claims to be a significant contribution to the expressed idea of Yale as a spatially integrated campus, a campus in which, once again, buildings and their context will become components of equal value. And it is here that it is very hard not to repress a doubt.

Of course, once again, we may be in the presence of a defect of the program. The program proposed deference to an existing building, but seems barely to have envisaged deference towards a po-

Robert Venturi and the Yale Mathematics Building Competition

tential space. And thus, the oblique archway of Strathcona Hall, leading into an area that might have become something but that now threatens to be never anything, could plausibly have been expected to receive some equally public gesture from the Mathematics Building. This need not have been excessive—perhaps something in the form of a comparable opening leading through to Hillhouse Avenue. But nothing of this sort has been envisaged or provided; and, as a result, having been admitted to a court via the rhetoric of the Strathcona archway, we are compelled to make our egress through a variety of back alleys. And, most notably, we are compelled to move between the rear of the Sheffield Laboratory and the end of the Mathematics Building, to proceed alongside the kitchen entrances of the Dana House to arrive ultimately in Trumbull Street—an architectural promenade which, while it may be rough and tough, should scarcely be regarded as any instance of spatial integration and which, certainly, is no experience that any one of even far less than average sensibility would, willingly, wish to undergo.

This is to observe an urbanistic failure and to notice what should be regarded as the most glaring defect of Venturi's proposal. For the courtyard now becomes a back space, not the useful link between Woolsey Hall and Hillhouse Avenue, which ought to have been its destiny, but, instead, something condemned to existence as a stagnant cul-de-sac. Thus, while the Mathematics Building may very well defer to the Cotswold pastiche of Leet-Oliver and the public facade of Hillhouse Avenue, it cannot seriously be considered as deferring to the spatial themes of Yale.

And it is here again that we return to the problems of the building's bulk with which we have already observed Venturi struggling. That is, simply by its sheer size, the building cannot ever be a mere addition to Leet-Oliver; but, instead, because of its size, it must inevitably function as one of the more important ingredients of the whole block lying between Prospect Street and Hillhouse Avenue. Also, because of its size, however neutral it may aspire to be, the building cannot ever behave as not more than a passive infill; essentially, its obvious life must be that of assertiveness rather than diffidence.

Perhaps the about-face from the object-like establishment architecture of the sixties, now decried as monumental, has been all too abrupt. Or, possibly, the rapidly prevailing idea of building as not so much object but texture has been interpreted all too completely; but, in any case, it could be suggested that Venturi has produced a building which, while it has been conceived as texture, operates as object, and that, however much he may wish to intellectualize his contribution away, he has made something more prominently assertive than most other buildings which have deliberately set out to be so.

It is thus we may have the feeling, after protracted contemplation of Venturi's project, that we are in the presence of a distended balloon, that something is about to burst; and, though this may not be an unpleasing sensation, because it is so engrossing it may be doubted whether it is appropriate. Maybe the project demands too much of our participation. We wish to puncture the balloon (to introduce an opening?), to relieve the tension, and to allow texture, once more, to become texture and object, object. What we wish is to relax a too artificial posture which, perhaps, the program has imposed and which prevents the building from collaborating as it should in the real community of Yale's older buildings.

If only the building could become more itself and less of a stylish cultural act, if, instead of setting out to be 'ordinary', it had attempted to be *easy* . . . but these are values which, again, perhaps the program acted to inhibit. The program was fashionable and could scarcely do other than elicit, to some degree, irrationally self-conscious behavior. It presumed a modesty that, if pressed too far, could only be indiscreet, a discretion that could only become immodest, and, in this bashfulness of good taste, it left, apparently unexamined, the problem which we have already touched upon— How can a dependency become so much bigger than that upon which it depends?

Robert Venturi and the Yale Mathematics Building Competition

A willingness to consider which was minor and which was major, which should be subsidiary and which not, what is tail and what is dog, would have helped this competition enormously, and, in a genuinely Main Street situation, this issue would probably have been sensibly discriminated in terms of the real volumetrics. Leet-Oliver would have been downgraded as the primary element, its extension would have been upgraded and, by these means, a good deal of strain and artificiality would have been avoided and the buildings might then have been assured of a far more congenial co-existence.

By these means, too, the real spatial themes of Yale, so well understood and elaborated by John Russell Pope, might have been awarded infinitely greater respect. For, in its classic phase, the Yale campus is a place of courts, implying walls, and of entrances to courts, implying archways; and, if there is about it a distinct flavor of hysteria, it is one of hysteria checked by very great reserve. It is an extreme situation; but one which succeeds admirably in appearing not to be so. Instead, it excellently succeeds in insinuating the ideas of ease and geniality. There is texture. There are objects. But we are not made aware of either violent contrast or extreme cerebrality. Instead, whatever happens is able to occur as no more than the inflection of a single wall. There are entrance gateways and there are pavilions, things assertive in themselves, but only as things emerging from a wall to contradict, and thereby, to emphasize, reassert, and participate in its functions.

It is all a triumph of common sense, knowledge, passion, reasonable dissimulation, and money; and we must therefore ask why it is that, given common sense, knowledge, passion, and a willingness to dissimulate (Venturi), and given money (Yale), something comparable but a little different could not have been achieved.

And what is the reason why not? Or do we have to scrutinize our undue intellectuality and sense of social guilt which, both alike, prevent us from being 'ordinary' or even very easy? Presumably we do, and therefore, because we are irrepressibly concerned with rediscovering innocence, with the Garden of Eden, with the noble savage and his primitive hut, we might recognize that our reductionist fantasies impede our logical capacity. For in New Haven, an acceptable archetype is almost completely given; and, therefore, one may well ask for what reason the attitudes of knowing dissent, why the sophistication, and why—when modesty is declared—the inability to accept the existing message?

For the attempt to bring Main Street to Yale (however charming) is, iconographically, just as exotic as, in the last twenty years, has been formally exotic the importation of freestanding, so-called Modern building. Neither one is, or was, necessary. One *may* admire Main Street for one body of reasons, and one *could* admire the City Beautiful (of which the Campus Beautiful is an offshoot) for another. But, if we are to be truly 'inclusivist', we are not compelled to make any choice, and we should know that both are available to us. We can feel for the brashness, the infelicity, the integrity, the alleged innocence of Main Street, but we can also feel for the decorum and the, almost, genuine social concern of the City Beautiful; and, in this consideration, we may also recognize that Main Street is not more real because it is more ugly.

But ugliness, of course, seems to us always to be more real and beauty to be always so much more false; and, therefore, although what we inherently require is something astringent and well argued, we are constantly misguided; which is to continue for too long, for perhaps it should be enough to say:

(1)   that the proposed building is not, like so many recent Yale buildings, an embarrassing public relations performance;

(2)   that, though it will certainly not be what it is supposed to be, it will surely be satisfactory; and

(3)   that, though it will not, in any way, contribute to the greater themes which inform the Yale campus, its existence might still lead to the gradual re-establishment of these themes.

Robert Venturi and the Yale Mathematics Building Competition

And, apart from all this, it might be suggested that the cult of ambiguity could become an excuse for irresolution, that the cult of the 'ordinary' might become an alibi for non-performance. Am I being fastidious or am I being careless? One sees already where the question leads. Blatant failures can become explained as ironies and total lack of distinction may become exonerated by asserting the ideal of the average. We are here in the presence of something which professes to be active but, in reality, is more passive than it knows; and, if Venturi is in no danger of becoming the dupe of his own apologetics, there is the eminent, and imminent, threat of others becoming so.

Finally, it could be added that, because the Mathematics Building has quashed establishment architecture as we have known it—which is a very great credit to Venturi—there are few recent buildings (or projected buildings) that a serious critic could discuss with less equivocation than has here been displayed.

To be worthy of criticism a building must possess qualities.

Notes

1. See "The Blenheim of the Welfare State" in the first volume of this collection, *Texas, Pre-Texas, Cambridge.*

2. See "Scully Blasts Math Building Critics as 'Despicable Scum,'" *Yale Daily News,* September 29, 1971.

3. Presented as a specimen of pro-Venturi literature, the preceding quotations are from Vincent Scully's introduction to Robert Venturi, *Complexity and Contradiction in Architecture* (New York: The Museum of Modern Art, 1966).

4. See Alan Colquhoun, "Typology and Design Method," in *Meaning in Architecture,* ed. Charles Jencks and George Baird (New York: George Braziller, 1970), 267–277.

5. William Jordy, "Symbolic Essence of Modern European Architecture of the Twenties and Its Continuing Influence," *Journal of the Society of Architectural Historians* 22 (October 1963): 182.

6. Is the assumption of a situation conceived to be public and standard necessarily and always a 'good' undertaking? Perhaps not always; but, nevertheless, the normative and the typical do possess their roles and it may be doubted whether themes deriving from nineteenth-century suburbia can ever be promoted as usefully comprehensive generalizations. The role of these themes is essentially private and perhaps one should never ask for the public parade of private virtues.

7. Surely for the most part true, but the name of Kurt Schwitters and, preeminently, that of Marcel Duchamp should equally belong in this area.

8. Walter Gropius, "Not Gothic but Modern for Our Colleges," *New York Times Magazine,* 23 October 1949. Later republished as "Archeology or Architecture for Contemporary Buildings," in Walter Gropius, *Scope of Total Architecture* (New York: Harper and Row, 1955). In 1951 it was awarded the Howard Myers Memorial Prize.

Giulio Romano's Palazzo Maccarani and the Sixteenth Century Grid/Frame/Lattice/Web

This was first presented as a lecture given in the big salone *of the Palazzo Massimo, March 14, 1987, on the occasion of the opening of the Rome studies program of the Cornell College of Architecture, Art and Planning; and, since we were where we were and quite a few specimens of Roman* maniera *were within a short distance of us, it was my supposition that the private agenda of my talk might not be considered irrelevant.*

However, since students from the Hertziana who were present found it a little strange that anyone should seek to make comparisons between sixteenth- and twentieth-century production (after all this is not *what art history is all about), for a publication by the* Cornell Journal of Architecture, *no. 4 (1989), I took the opportunity of modifying my opening remarks by deleting reference to the buildings of Chicago's Loop; and it was in such revised form that this piece came to attract the attention of Javier Cenicacelaya, at the time the editor of* Arquitectonica, *who asked for permission for a further publication.*

Now, through no fault of my friend Javier but rather as a result of some palace revolution within its editorial body, the publication in Arquitectonica, *March 10, 1993, is, by my standards, utterly senseless, tasteless, and deplorable. Though the text, supplied by the* Cornell Journal, *is accurate, the visuals—also supplied by the same source—were, incomprehensibly, disregarded and, quite fatuously, substitutions were then made. The resulting layout is, consequently, incorrigibly abandoned and erratic, with diagonal views substituting for frontal and frontal for diagonal, with related images become disrelated, with blatant omissions and gratuitous additions, in short with everything that can only obfuscate intelligent reading.*

But why go on? The original lecture was delivered to cause students, brought up on a different architectural diet, to look at details in Rome and elsewhere which they might, otherwise, fail to see; and, then, the version of the lecture as published in the Cornell Journal, *I think, is to be interpreted as a conjecture awaiting refutation. Or, if that is not possible, as a hypothesis waiting for qualification and amplification.*

Evidently it is something of an adult, and pedantic, recapitulation of a former juvenile enthusiasm as represented in my article "Mannerism and Modern Architecture" (The Architectural Review, *May 1950); and, as such, I can scarcely expect it to be received with the wildest enthusiasm or the most penetrating understanding. Nevertheless, I know that there are some, all of them architects and most of them American, who will find it an amusing diversion for an evening's reading; and, if not equipped with all the* seriosità *of Germanic art history, possibly as something equipped with sufficient insights to allow for useful annexation.*

An increasingly basic component of building for something like the last hundred years has been the steel or concrete frame, grid, or skeleton; and, for the most part, the results have been less than satisfactory.

A basic element of sixteenth century masonry construction was the frequent employment of a frame, grid, or lattice as a structural metaphor; and the results, generally, continue to be interesting.

It is a matter of curiosity that twentieth century architects have been largely blind to the richness and suggestiveness of *maniera* precedent which, quite often, seems to be closely allied—peripheric composition, etc.—to what they have been attempting.

This may have been because of the neo-Classical exposition of modern architecture offered by so many (we have taken up where the eighteenth century left off) and, particularly, offered by Emil Kaufmann in his *Von Ledoux bis Le Corbusier*. Then, Kaufmann's *Three Revolutionary Architects* went a long way to establish that various 'revolutionary' architectural happenings in the Paris of the 1780s were absolutely precursive of twentieth century innovations conducted under the auspices of Cubism, Constructivism, and De Stijl.

But what matter?

It is still glaringly obvious that, however much one aspect of Le Corbusier may derive from the late eighteenth century *hôtel particulier,* his intrinsic resources remain *maniera.* Pity it is that, with his Neuchâtel origins and his Ruskinian education, he should have had no access to Vignola—except as a monster of the Ecole des Beaux-Arts; but, no matter, for was he not, always and simultaneously, *Modern, pre-Modern and Post-Modern?*

With good reasons and because of elective affinity, almost at the beginning he equated himself with Michelangelo; and what follows is, more or less, a highly removed substantiation of his claim. The slave writhes in the marble block to which Michelangelo has consigned him; and, in the same block, there is also tormented Giulio's Palazzo Maccarani—not to mention the Dominican monastery of La Tourette.

Giulio Romano's Palazzo Maccarani is dated by Frederick Hartt 1521–23; and of course, there is always a problem as to what such dates mean.[1] However, Giulio left Rome for Mantua in October

1524 and it seems plausible to assume that much of the building was complete by that date. An engraving of the house was published in the mid-sixteenth century by Lafréry (fig. 11), and again in the mid-seventeenth century by Falda (fig. 12), both recording somewhat different ideas as to what it looks like (Lafréry accentuates the verticals, Falda the horizontals); but, since Palazzo Maccarani is a north facing house with the upper parts of its facade developed in low relief, none of its photographic presentations have done too much justice to the complexity of its ideation (fig. 13).

Then it should further be noticed that, though in a prominent location, after about 1700 Palazzo Maccarani increasingly failed to engage attention. Simply, during the eighteenth and nineteenth centuries, it came to escape the eye; it became part of the Roman background; and it is only fairly recently that it has re-emerged as a building of importance. German picture books of the 1920s[2] give it little attention; and I suppose that my own rather exaggerated consciousness of this house derives from the appearance of Frederick Hartt's monograph on Giulio of 1958. Of the Italian historiography of the building, regrettably, I know very little; but I believe that it must be safe to assert that present awareness derives mostly from Hartt.

Evidently, Palazzo Maccarani depends for its principal facade motifs upon that group of Roman palaces inspired by the last phase of Bramante's career—most notably the Casa Caprini (fig. 14), demolished by Bernini for the construction of Piazza San Pietro.[3]

Ideally, these houses are majestic and serious, five windows wide, with a basement and mezzanine of shops—tough and rusticated—which support a *piano nobile* almost excessive in its declamation. Down below, in the *piano rustico,* there is one theme of society which is celebrated; but, up above in the *piano nobile,* with its aloof distinction of walls and columns, there is an alternative (and intellectual) social distinction which is advertised.

Such is the paradigm; but, in Raphael's Palazzo Vidoni-Caffarelli of circa 1515 (fig. 15), Bramante's basic distinctions already come to appear blurred; and now *piano rustico* and *piano nobile*

11. Palazzo Maccarani, Rome. Giulio Romano. Engraving by Lafréry.

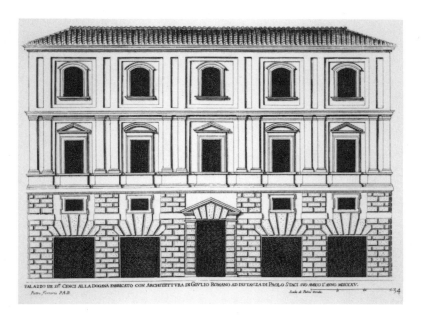

12. Palazzo Maccarani, engraving by Falda.

The Sixteenth Century Grid/Frame/Lattice/Web

13. Palazzo Maccarani.

14. Palazzo Caprini, Rome. Donato Bramante. Engraving by Lafréry.

15. Palazzo Vidoni-Caffarelli, Rome, facade.

The Sixteenth Century Grid/Frame/Lattice/Web

have come to share a common delicacy. Down below the *bugnati* become streamlined; they cease to be savage; they begin to declare an entirely new message; and, correspondingly, interventions upstairs—horizontals beginning to contradict verticals—may be the preliminary announcement of themes which, perhaps, Bramante could scarcely have imagined. However, Maccarani expands upon the topic of Caprini and Vidoni by yet another reference. Reaching back beyond Bramante, it annexes aspects of the facade of Palazzo della Cancellaria of circa 1490 (fig. 16). Not too many; but, in the low relief style of its upper floors, perhaps enough to indicate an affiliation.

Probably too, while considering the morphological pedigree of Palazzo Maccarani, the Palazzo Bresciano should further be cited (fig. 17). This not only for the trabeation of its downstairs openings, which Maccarani more emphatically exhibits; but also for its addition of an attic storey to the Bramante-Raphael formula. Nevertheless, whatever fastidious local complication may also have been introduced, however provocatively elegant the rustication, the three stages of the building—basement, *piano nobile,* attic—remain sharply articulated; and there can be no doubts as to their respective functions in the hierarchy of the facade. The name of Baldassare Peruzzi has been traditionally invoked in connection with Palazzo Bresciano and some of its more enigmatic details might support this attribution;[4] but, if Casa Caprini may evoke the world of Julius II and Palazzo Vidoni that of Leo X, if their respective strengths and refinements may correspond to the regimes of these two Papal personalities, then what more remains to say about Palazzo Bresciano (also attributed to Raphael)?[5] With Palazzo Vidoni it belongs, of course, to the world of Leo; but, at the same time, do not its so many footnotes on Bramante-Raphael begin to rehearse that dissolution of their confident assumptions, which is made almost complete in the great subversive act of Palazzo Maccarani?

With Bresciano and Maccarani brought into conjunction, it will now be expedient to approach Palazzo Alberini (otherwise Cicciaporci-Segni), where passages of detail comparable to Macca-

16. Palazzo della Cancellaria, Rome, facade.

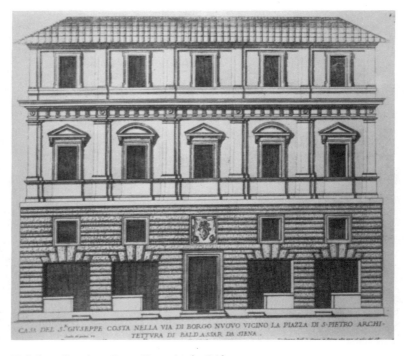

CASA DEL Sr GIVSEPPE COSTA NELLA VIA DI BORGO NVOVO VICINO LA PIAZZA DI S.PIETRO ARCHI-
TETTVRA DI BALDASSAR DA SIENA.

17. Palazzo Bresciano, Rome. Engraving by Falda.

rani receive a preliminary display. Palazzo Alberini is best to be explained via the agency of Lafréry's engraving (fig. 18); but, then,
just *who* was the architect? Lafréry presumed the impossible—he
thought that it was Bramante; and then there were the attributions
to Giulio, rejected by both Wolfgang Lotz and Frederick Hartt.[6]
The date, 1515, was impossible—for Giulio; but then there comes
along Paolo Portoghesi who seems to opt for a later date; and there
might be some obligation to think about this.[7] For, if not Giulio,
then what brilliant, destructive, and vanished reputation was here
concerned? Is the latest attribution—to Raphael—to be accepted?

Certainly the two upper floors of Palazzo Alberini are an approximate prevision of what was going to occur at Maccarani. Cor-
nices and entablatures become condensed; the axes of pilasters are

18. Palazzo Alberini (Cicciaporci-Segni), Rome. Engraving by Lafréry.

enigmatically projected in the form of panels; and the wall of the
upper floors is organized in a system of three closely implicated relief layers. Palazzo Alberini is a far more important premonition of
what Giulio was to do at Maccarani than the much more careful,
and brilliant, Bresciano.

Meanwhile, there is one further building which may serve
to illuminate the strategies which are presented at Palazzo Maccarani. According to Hartt, Giulio's exquisite Villa Lante on the Gianicolo dates from before 1523 (fig. 19);[8] and very noticeable on the
loggia facade is the tracing of an exceptionally delicate grid serving
as the merest suggestion of a link between the loggia and the upstairs windows; but, then, there are the downstairs windows which
receive the intimations of the gridded scene up above and then project downwards something of its traces.

The Sixteenth Century Grid/Frame/Lattice/Web

19. Villa Lante, Gianicolo, Rome, facade. Giulio Romano.

But, now to approach the much more lurid Palazzo Maccarani; and it is infinitely more assertive. There are three stories, apart from the basement their respective heights not very distinguishable; the *piano rustico* is divided, ruthlessly divided, by an immense Doric doorway; the *piano nobile* is set up in terms of coupled pilasters with separate podia for windows. The Casa Caprini rustication is of massive *bugnati;* in Palazzo Vidoni rapid horizontal motion was introduced; but, in Palazzo Maccarani, rustication is discontinuous, comprised of vertical strips with gigantic interlocking lintels; and, on the lintels, are balanced the horizontal oblongs of the mezzanine windows. Then the upward thrust of the vertical strips is sustained by the pilasters and is further emphasized by the deliberately willed 'deficiency' of their entablature and cornice; and, above all this, what at first reading may appear to be pilasters finally disclose themselves to be no more than frames in a system of panelling which operates just as much in the horizontal as it does in the vertical dimension.

After more than four hundred and fifty years language exhausts itself in the contemplation of Palazzo Maccarani and the attempt to record such phenomena as these becomes almost dismissable as hopeless. According to Ernst Gombrich (but, in what follows, I do not know how much is him and how much is me), at Palazzo Maccarani there is no distinction between the carrier and the carried.[9] Members emerge from the building block only to be drawn back into it again. The portal is swallowed; rustication overwhelms the finer architectural membering; pilasters become not only the articulations but also the prisoners of the building mass. Elegance and savagery are both at work. There is the rational, intellectual order of the column grid and there is the explosive, primeval order of the rustications. The primitive building which is here present is constrained in a sophisticated corset. It palpitates; it is volcanic; it is about to erupt; but, in the end, it concedes to a cerebral order of things. Bramante had kept these two worlds apart. In Casa Caprini the savage, rustic world had formed the basis for the *civilized* achievement of the *piano nobile.* Raphael had hoped to harmonize these worlds. In Palazzo Vidoni he had imposed the same linear elegance upon them both. But, with Giulio, they have now become two worlds which have burst into blatant collision. A momentous step has been taken. Whatever the High Renaissance synthesis might have been, irretrievably, it is now at an end.

So much is almost to conclude a first phase of argument; and, in what will later be said about the sixteenth century grid-frame-lattice-web, it should become apparent that this is something very different from the fifteenth century grid of Brunelleschi. Brunelleschi's normative and mathematical perspective grid establishes a network of lines which prescribes a position for all of the figurative elements which might be introduced. Lines are drawn upon the floor of the architectural or pictorial space and columns or human forms became rooted in this network. They became interpolations of the grid and there can be no doubt about their location.[10]

No: the sixteenth century grid is decisively different and may best be approached by the introduction of pictorial evidence. Thus, Bramante's Casa Caprini and Raphael's *School of Athens* may be considered related events; and, if the *School of Athens* (fig. 20) celebrates the High Renaissance achievement of a deep space in which human figures and architectural detail move equipped with their own internal animation (now quite independent of the Brunelleschian grid), then Casa Caprini may be construed as a representation of this deep space condensed within the limits of a facade. It is an affair of arches below, columns in the round above, and, then, the energetic projection of the entablature. If it is not hopelessly absurd to talk about *the space of a facade,* then Casa Caprini is a facade presenting a deep space; but, when one comes to examine Palazzo Maccarani, upstairs almost all significant depths and all rotundities have vanished in favor of a system of layers in low relief.

Now this condition of a flattened facade in Rome may, only too obviously, be compared with the contemporary contraction of pictorial space in Florence; and Rosso's Volterra *Deposition* (fig. 21) might make the point. The *School of Athens* is dated 1510–11, the Volterra *Deposition* 1521.[11] In other words, they are separated by the

20. Raphael, *School of Athens,* Stanza della Segnatura, Palazzo Vaticano, Rome.

The Sixteenth Century Grid/Frame/Lattice/Web

21. Rosso, *Deposition,* Volterra.

119

same length of time as that which elapsed between the buildings of
Bramante and Giulio. So Giulio grids his building and Rosso grids
his picture; and, in both cases, there has occurred a loss of depth
and middle distance, a compression of action into a shallow relief
layer in which angularity of architectural episode and figures prevails. At Volterra the organization is rectilinear. There is a crucifix
and there are ladders; but the attendant figures are also conditioned
by the same implied grid from which the only exception is the
slumping body of the dead Christ.

It might, of course, be said that it is altogether too easy to
make a grid out of a cross and a couple of ladders; and who could
not agree? But at exactly the same time there is the Pontorno *Pietà*
in the Capella Capponi at Santa Felicità in Florence (fig. 22); and,
here, one may observe the same collapse of deep space, the same
compression of figures towards picture plane, a comparable pursuit
of angular gesture. Pure accident this coincidence of architectural
and pictorial phenomena? Perhaps not.[12]

This much is to establish the polemic of Palazzo Maccarani.
Just as Villa Lante is, maybe, the first of those airy, openwork structures which distinguish the cinquecento (Hartt), so, maybe, Palazzo
Maccarani is the first, dramatic, presentation of those gridded,
framed, or panelled wall surfaces which were even more characteristic of *maniera* achievement, particularly in Central Italy.[13]

But now for a brief, and relaxed, gallop among the more accessible
illustrations of what here is called the sixteenth century grid.

At Velletri we are in the provinces; and, in the Municipio
of approximately 1575 (fig. 23), we may see the grid presented with
a devastating simplicity. There are almost no mouldings. There is almost nothing—a basic presentation of the frontal surface, backed
up by the complete absence of any detail around the sides. There is
a kind of mad and elementary excitement about the blind arcade,
also, in the conflict between the two entrances and the two *cordonate*.
Minimalist, it displays, above all, an excessive presence. This is the
grid or frame as received by a sophisticated disciple of Vignola.[14]

The Sixteenth Century Grid/Frame/Lattice/Web

22. Jacopo Pontorno, *Pietà,* Santa Felicità, Florence.

23. Palazzo Comunale, Velletri.

The Sixteenth Century Grid/Frame/Lattice/Web

But now to approach Vignola himself. At the Loggia dei
Banchi in Bologna, 1565–68 (fig. 24), one may observe the pilasters
down below which are equipped with profusely developed capitals
—though with only the most tenuous and abbreviated of entablatures—and, then, one might begin to construe the behavior of the
upper wall, where what one is disposed to think must be pilasters
receive no trace of anything like a capital and, instead, merge into
something like an entablature to become—backed up by another
relief layer—the framing of a series of panels.

Derived from the repertory of Palazzo Maccarani of course
all this is: but this ambiguous *parti* is then further strapped together by an obtrusive horizontal motion, that of the mezzanine and
its supporting apparatus. But, also, the typical bay of this facade becomes augmented by significant local manipulations. Minor, but
highly assertive, motifs interlace the composition; and, of these, the
most notable must be the inversion of the *serliane.* In both the mezzanine and upstairs the window in the middle is not arched. Instead, being trabeated, it can scarcely prevail over the flanking and
arched openings which are its necessary companions; and a result of
this peripheric emphasis is to spread a peculiar condition of animation throughout the entire vertical surface. The strapping predicates
a flatness; and, from out of this condition, the only details which
emerge protuberant are the capitals of the pilasters down below
and, more unexpectedly, the pediments of the central windows
up top.

However, in terms of elaboration of grid, the Loggia dei
Banchi (though later in date) is little more than a preface to what is
exhibited at Caprarola, 1559, where, in spite of the apparent identity of all facades, their complexity is most readily to be examined
from a position in the gardens (fig. 25).

Except for the highly specialized drama of the entrance
front, ostensibly the facades of Caprarola are a highly standardized
affair of one order piled up on another; but, needless to say, any
more than casual scrutiny discloses this to be scarcely the case. For,
below, there are pilasters which do not project very far; and, then,

24. Loggia dei Banchi, Bologna, elevation. Jacopo da Vignola.

The Sixteenth Century Grid/Frame/Lattice/Web

25. Villa Farnese, Caprarola, garden facade. Jacopo da Vignola.

travelling behind these, there is a business of further members, with which the pilasters are inextricably connected. So, down below, there is already revealed the presence of contrary systems of organization; the ordonnance of the pilasters and their entablature is basically contradicted by the behavior of a presumably minor arcade. This is a flat cardboard cut-out affair and, within it, the great projection of the window heads which it encloses establishes a horizontal reading across the facade almost as assertive as the entablature itself.

Then, if interpretations of the lower level favor a movement of the eye from side to side, in the upper level it is a vertical reading which is imposed upon the spectator. The windows become as though they were items on so many skewers; and, while down below the wall surface is frontally presented, up top there are almost the implications of a *dal di sotto in su* perspective; and, given sufficiently patient analysis, no doubt much the same could be said about the courtyard facade of Villa Giulia (fig. 26). It is a testimony to comparable strategies.

The Collegio Romano of about 1582 (fig. 27), generally attributed to Ammanati, in a rough way also belongs to the phenomena which are the present subject of scrutiny; and two further Ammanati buildings may also be added to the evidence. In Lucca the Palazzetto della Provincia of 1577–83 (fig. 28) implies the presence of a grid or frame by means of the checkerboard syncopation of its facade; and in Rome the courtyard of the Palazzo di Firenze (fig. 29) displays a structure intimately related to that which is to be discovered in Vignola. Pilasters are backed up by strips, downstairs and upstairs; and, as with Vignola, the wall appears to have been subjected to some kind of intense anatomical dissection.

Similar inferences are to be found in Peruzzi's loggia facade for the courtyard of Palazzo Massimo of 1532 onwards (fig. 30) where an underlying gridded structure is highly explicit. The strange, undecorated, intermediate area (which responds to the barrel vault behind) appears visually problematic until one assumes the existence of a skeleton up and down which the accessories of architecture can slide; and this skeleton becomes all the more evident

The Sixteenth Century Grid/Frame/Lattice/Web

26. Villa Giulia, Rome. Jacopo da Vignola.

27. Collegio Romano, Rome, facade. Bartolomeo Ammanati(?).

The Sixteenth Century Grid/Frame/Lattice/Web

28. Palazzetto della Provincia, Lucca, facade. Bartolomeo Ammanati.

29. Palazzo di Firenze, Rome, courtyard. Bartolomeo Ammanati.

The Sixteenth Century Grid/Frame/Lattice/Web

30. Palazzo Massimo, Rome, courtyard. Baldassare Peruzzi.

when it is recognized how clearly this area between the two loggias is allied with the attic or mezzanine up top. For, now, the Doric and the Ionic orders become almost like so many items of clothing— pants or sleeves; or, more provocatively, the building becomes something like a skin which simultaneously both conceals and discloses the musculature and the bone structure lying behind it.

Vesalius, the great anatomist of the period and physician to the Emperor Charles V, published his *De Humani Corporis Fabrica* in 1543; and his plates on the process of dissection (figs. 31, 32), stripping the human figure down from skin, through muscles to bone, might be a commentary upon so many sixteenth century buildings. Specifically, it might be a commentary upon Vignola, Ammanati, and what is going on at the Palazzetto Spada where the usual apparatus of multiple relief layers makes an early appearance (fig. 33).[15]

Nor is an elaborate display of columns necessary to stipulate the activity of this grid-frame-lattice. For instance, it occurs in Pirro Ligorio's Villa Pia of circa 1560 (fig. 34); and, equally, this taste for rectilinearity is exhibited by the garden facade of Villa Medici (fig. 35).

Neither is this taste simply central Italian. Like so much else in the Veneto, of course, it arrived up there somewhat late; but Palladio's Palazzo Porta Festa of about 1549 (fig. 36) provided much more than a mere footnote to Bramante's Casa Caprini. Vitally important for the international distribution of Bramante's paradigm, with Palladio there are none of the central Italian provocations. There is no question of low relief; but, this being noticed, the grid still results in an influential presence. The columns of the *piano nobile* produce a series of interruptions of their entablature and cornice; and these interruptions are then transmitted into the attic.

Then Palladio's Palazzo Barbarano (fig. 37) and Scamozzi's Palazzo Bonin-Thiene (fig. 38) might make commentary upon later Venetian manipulations. Allowing for the asymmetrical disposition of Palazzo Barbarano as built, both show, with their super-imposed orders, an approximately identical distribution; but, in Palladio, local accents are less obsessive. For instance, the Ionic order down-

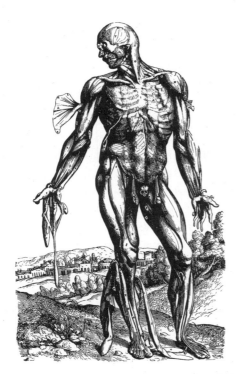

31. Andreas Vesalius, *De Humani Corporis Fabrica,* pl. 27.

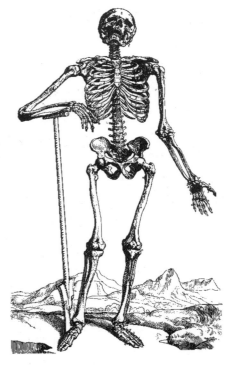

32. Andreas Vesalius, *De Humani Corporis Fabrica,* pl. 21.

33. Palazzetto Spada, Rome, facade. Baldassare Peruzzi.

The Sixteenth Century Grid/Frame/Lattice/Web

34. Casino of Pius IV, Rome, facade. Pirro Ligorio.

35. Villa Medici, Rome, garden facade. Annabale di Lippi.

The Sixteenth Century Grid/Frame/Lattice/Web

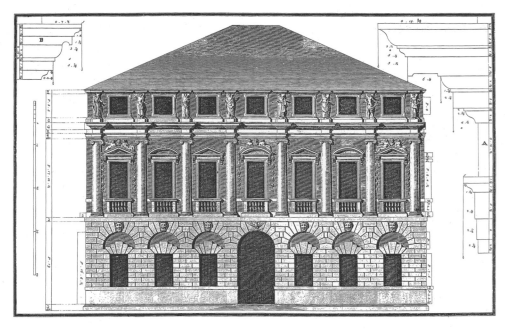

36. Palazzo Porta Festa, Vicenza. Andrea Palladio. Engraving by Bertotti Scamozzi.

37. Palazzo Barbarano, Vicenza. Andrea Palladio. Drawing by Bertotti Scamozzi.

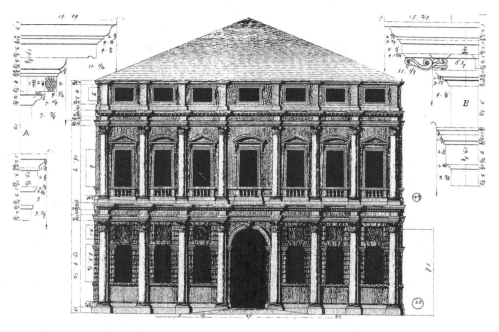

38. Palazzo Bonin-Thiene, Vicenza. Vincenzo Scamozzi. Drawing by Bertotti Scamozzi.

stairs rises to an uninterrupted entablature whereas, in Palazzo
Bonin, the axes of the Corinthian columns are vertically projected
so as to destroy any simple commitment to horizontal continuity.
By these and other means Scamozzi records a pronounced conflict of
the horizontal and the vertical; he is above all else the intellectualistic writer of footnotes and the results of his editorial process are to
secure a building of great and refreshing astringency. Operating on
a fundamentally Palladian vocabulary his somewhat alembicated
mental condition is more approximate to that of Vignola.

    But, apart from these facades, internally, similar spatial dis-
tributions are also to be observed, and, thus, from 1520 onwards,
Giulio Romano was involved with the decoration of the loggia at
Raphael's Villa Madama (fig. 39) and, about 1527, he was responsible for the loggia of the Palazzo del Tè (fig. 40). But, in these
two works so close together in time, just may we not observe the
significant difference between the curvilinear and rotund taste of
the High Renaissance—apses, pendentives, cross vaults, domes—
and the more aggressive and rectilinearized products which so
quickly followed?

After this highly casual survey the evidence for the origins of rectilinear strategies in the sixteenth century all seems to lead back to
Michelangelo.

    The basic motif for the typical bay of Vasari's Uffizi, of
1560 onwards (fig. 41), is derived from the loggia of Palazzo Massimo (the river facade is presumably a heavier orchestration of Giulio's Villa Lante); but the space of the Uffizi as a courtyard or street
(fig. 42)—conceptually it is a sort of wire cage to which every part
of the building responds—can only seem to be the inevitable result
of Michelangelo's Laurenziana of 1525 onwards (fig. 43); and, here,
the implications of a three-dimensional grid or cage are particularly
assertive.

    But something very similar is also to be observed in Michel-
angelo's interpretation of Antonio da Sangallo's courtyard at Palazzo
Farnese (fig. 44). In this courtyard, Sangallo's proposals were fully re-

39. Villa Madama, Rome, loggia. Raphael.

The Sixteenth Century Grid/Frame/Lattice/Web

40. Palazzo del Tè, Mantua, loggia. Giulio Romano.

41. Uffizi, Florence, typical bay. Giorgio Vasari.

The Sixteenth Century Grid/Frame/Lattice/Web

42. Uffizi.

43. Laurentian Library, Florence, interior of the reading room. Michelangelo.

The Sixteenth Century Grid/Frame/Lattice/Web

44. Palazzo Farnese, courtyard. Michelangelo and Antonio da Sangallo.

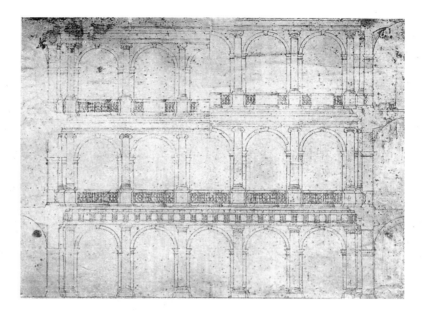

45. Palazzo Farnese, Rome. Antonio da Sangallo. Drawing by Sangallo.

The Sixteenth Century Grid/Frame/Lattice/Web

alized only on the ground floor; and then, from 1546 onwards, Michelangelo proceeded to 'correct' what he had found (fig. 45). What he introduced is a plane travelling through the two upper storeys, introducing flatness in the second stage with flatness and trabeation in the third; and it is the third floor which provides this space (perhaps via exaggerated height) with its overwhelming intimations of rectilinearity. Sangallo evidently intended the courtyard to be something like the Colosseum turned inside out; but, by Michelangelo's interventions, it becomes something radically different.

The entrance facade of Palazzo Farnese (fig. 46) also exhibits comparable manipulations. Here it is possible that Sangallo intended the central window of the *piano nobile* to become a triumphal arch—perhaps on the model of a drawing for a palace in that long-since-vanished Farnese town of Castro (fig. 47).[16] But, primarily through added height and the activity of the central window, Michelangelo, again, produces a relentless trabeation (fig. 48).

Then, since it may be amusing to contemplate Michelangelo's long struggle with members of the Sangallo family, in this connection there must be cited the flanking palaces of the Campidoglio (fig. 49) where it is often said that the giant order made its first appearance. But this is to ignore the elder Antonio da Sangallo's Palazzo Tarugi at Montepulciano (fig. 50). Not necessary to say that Michelangelo should have known this, it is sufficient to notice the relationship and the differences.

At Montepulciano, columns are semi-round and protuberant. On the Campidoglio they become pilasters, aggressively flat. On the Campidoglio (as at Palazzo Farnese) arches are wished away and the whole rectilinearized composition is expanded by the abruptness of the cornice and then, beyond this, by the balustrade and by the figures which it supports. But, on the flank, the typical bay becomes compressed and flatness becomes corrugation (the extra bay added by Carlo Rainaldi). In other words the typical bay can expand or contract—Frederick Hartt talks about this in connection with Giulio; and so we have expansion-contraction, the grid or lattice behaves like an accordion or concertina.

46. Palazzo Farnese, entrance facade. Antonio da Sangallo.

47. Palazzo Ducale, Castro, entrance facade. Antonio da Sangallo.

48. Palazzo Farnese, detail of central window of *piano nobile*. Antonio da Sangallo.

49. Palazzo dei Conservatori, Rome. Michelangelo.

50. Palazzo Tarugi, Montepulciano, entrance facade. Antonio da Sangallo the elder.

The Sixteenth Century Grid/Frame/Lattice/Web

However, in his commentaries upon others, Michelangelo may, of course, be taken further; and the contrast of the Medici Chapel of 1519 onwards (fig. 51) with Brunelleschi's Old Sacristy of San Lorenzo (fig. 52) is the painfully evident move. In the Medici Chapel, between the orders of the lower wall and the pendentives of the dome, there is now interpolated an upper stage so that the space becomes vertically attenuated and the activity of arcuation becomes diminished. Brunelleschi's *pietra serena* entablature is now split apart, interrupted by a white plaster equivalent to the rest of the wall. Then, the shape of the windows leading the eye upwards introduces a false perspective (more *dal di sotto in su*). And, further, there are the wall tombs which, by contrary perspectival implications, are absolutely locked into place.

In the Florence Baptistery the early fifteenth century tomb of the anti-Pope John XXIII of Donatello and Michelozzo, 1425–27 (fig. 53), is almost like a big piece of furniture. Given energy, one may feel that one might shift it around and that it won't too much matter where it is located. But Michelangelo's tombs are implacably related to the vertical surface. They are emanations of it and in no way to be detached from it.

Still continuing to move backwards in time now leads to the facade of San Lorenzo of 1515 or thereabouts and to Michelangelo's model for it in Casa Buonarroti (fig. 54). Intended to supersede Giuliano da Sangallo's proposals, there is a rarely published drawing, Uffizi 279a 45 (fig. 55), attributed by Giovannoni to Giuliano, which may indicate Michelangelo's point of departure.[17] It shows a rectangular composition—superimposed orders three bays wide with a central pediment; and, possibly, this drawing might have constituted the basis for Michelangelo's operations. But, whether or not this could be the case, it is rewarding to look at how he translated such material for his purposes.

Primarily he adds height by the introduction of an attic or mezzanine between the two orders. A premonition of maneuvers which are going to occur at Palazzo Massimo, Caprarola, and elsewhere, the appearance of this attic or mezzanine both *extends* and *dis-*

51. Medici Chapel, San Lorenzo, Florence. Michelangelo.

52. Old Sacristy, San Lorenzo, Florence. Filippo Brunelleschi.

53. Baptistery, Tomb of Pope John XXIII, Florence. Donatello and Michelozzo.

The Sixteenth Century Grid/Frame/Lattice/Web

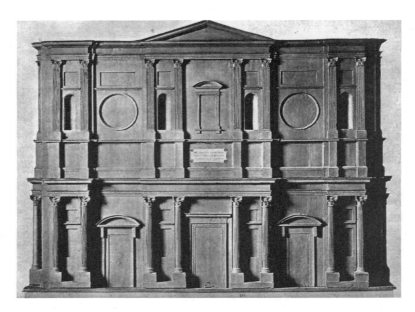

54. San Lorenzo, model of proposed facade. Michelangelo.

55. Uffizi 279a, Palazzo dei Penetenzieri, Rome. Giuliano da Sangallo.

tends the field of activity. Not only does it contribute height (as at Capella Medici); but it also seems to contribute breadth and—incidentally—flatness. And, thus, with further memberings—like the tight lacing together of the side bays up top—it acts to enforce the reading of Michelangelo's project as a grid. But, meanwhile, this flattened and gridded surface is then equipped with further intimations. The flanking doors down below, with their curved pediments, collaborate with the central aedicule up above, with its own curved pediment, to introduce an entirely crucial triangulation—again involving a reading of perspective recession.

So, somewhat rashly, it will now be argued that this San Lorenzo proposal, generally spoken of as Michelangelo's first major architectural performance, a scaffold for the display of sculptural apparatus, is very much a result of the ceiling of the Sistine Chapel, 1508–12 (fig. 56), in its turn a scaffold for the display of pictorial apparatus.

Before Michelangelo the Sistine ceiling presented a night sky studded with stars (fig. 57), and perhaps the most incredible aspect of the change which he effected (as in the Medici Chapel) is the immense amplification of scale. De Tolnay lists the strategies available in the early sixteenth century for a painted ceiling over a volume of this kind.[18] These were:

1. The illusionistic solution as in Mantegna's Camera degli Sposi in the Palazzo Ducale at Mantua (fig. 58). Later employed by Correggio in the Duomo at Parma and brought to a culmination in the late seventeenth century in the vault of Sant'Ignazio, this became the favorite solution. Apparently the space is opened to the heavens; and, up above, there float around a variety of angels, saints, *putti, allegories*, etc.

2. The painted simulation of coffering—Raphael and Sodoma's strategy for the ceiling of the Stanza della Segnatura of 1511 (fig. 59); and

56. Sistine Chapel, Vatican. Michelangelo.

57. Sistine Chapel, reconstructed view of 1508 (after Steinmann).

The Sixteenth Century Grid/Frame/Lattice/Web

3. Pinturicchio's tactics for the ceiling of the Piccolomini Library in Siena, later adopted by Peruzzi at the Farnesina for the ceiling of the Sala di Galatea (fig. 60); and in this version—possibly the most logical—there is floated a big central panel about which the accessories congregate.

But, according to De Tolnay, Michelangelo would have nothing to do with any of these. Instead, on the vaulted ceiling he imposed a rectilinear and attenuated *galleria*.

De Tolnay suggests that in doing this, in opposing the curves of the vault with a rectilinear structure, Michelangelo both affirms and contradicts the shape of his surface.[19] Figurative motifs emerge as vital energies conceived to be immanent in the ceiling itself. The ceiling is a monolith carved in relief with at least three planes. There is the gravitational role of the prophets and sybils pulling down the architectural skeleton and explaining the shape of the vault; and, then, there is the levitational role which pilasters, *putti,* and caryatids all implicate. But, at the same time, there is the band of the *ignudi,* possibly the binding force which holds the whole organization together; and, about the ceiling in general, De Tolnay uses the same language as does Hartt with regard to Giulio Romano's frescoes of the Sala di Costantino.[20] He speaks of a trellis, and, of course, this reading of the Sistine may be further assisted by the disparate vanishing points of each and every panel.[21]

Meanwhile, it may be interesting to look at the background against which the nude figures are placed (fig. 61). First of all there is a frontal plane which is flat and rather wide. It might be equated with a pilaster. But, then behind this there is a further surface and, behind this, yet another before the observer escapes from the domain of simulated 'architecture' to arrive at the surface of 'pictorial' subject matter.

Now, there seems to be a conspiracy of silence to regard the Sistine ceiling not as the work of architecture which, most indubitably, it is; but, being 'painted', apparently 'architecture' it can *never* be.

58. Camera degli Sposi, Palazzo Ducale, Mantua.
Andrea Mantegna.

59. Stanza della Segnatura, Palazzo Vaticano, Rome.
Raphael and Sodoma.

60. Sala di Galatea, Villa Farnesina. Baldassare Peruzzi.

The Sixteenth Century Grid/Frame/Lattice/Web

61. Michelangelo, Sistine Chapel ceiling, Vatican: nude youth above the Libyan Sibyl.

However, we might attempt to overturn this 'conspiracy' by looking at a detail of the apses of St. Peter's (fig. 62). Almost exactly it
replicates the *modenatura* of the Sistine. There are pilasters and,
then, layers upon further layers. In other words, the *modenatura* of
the ceiling almost completely previsions what was later to occur. If,
in the chapel, Michelangelo rectilinearizes and opposes the vault, at
St. Peter's he uses something like the idea of the gridded palaces of
the Campidoglio for the purposes of an attack upon a centralized
church. And it is this collision between the apsidal surfaces and the
cutting behavior of the grid, each acting to warp and distort the
other, it is this interaction of constraint and expansion which was so
penetratingly understood by Le Corbusier, that later major exponent of the dialectic between the flat and the round.

But, in contrast to the Sistine ceiling, it should now be
obligatory to notice Raphael's Stanza della Segnatura and, one has
to say, its lamentable corner (fig. 63). Two deep-space frescoes are arranged at right angles together, with nothing to intervene and to
separate; and about this deplorable scene, it is comparatively easy to
imagine the confusion of Raphael and his *garzone* when the Sistine
ceiling was disclosed in 1512. Quite simply, brilliant though they
might have been, they had not *done it right;* and, to observe the reaction, one need only pay attention to Giulio's Sala di Costantino of
about 1520 (fig. 64).[22] For, here, a solution to 'correct' the corners is
adopted. The corners of the room become occupied by simulated
deep niches in which various Popes, allegories, and virtues sit
around (fig. 65). Abundantly they disclose their Michelangelesque
origins; and, around this framework, the frescoes—the Vision of
Constantine, his Battle, his Baptism—are located.

But, walking through the Sala di Costantino, some forty
years ago people shuddered. It was an expression of crudeness and
vulgarity. Bernard Berenson says as much; but, nowadays, one may
wonder. For, whatever its defects might be, in terms of its sophisticated spatial development, the Sala di Costantino should, surely, be
linked to the Medici Chapel. Of approximate date, which came
first? Giulio under the insistent influence of Michelangelo? Or Mi-

62. St. Peter's, Rome: detail of the apse.

63. Stanza della Segnatura, Palazzo Vaticano, Rome. Raphael.

The Sixteenth Century Grid/Frame/Lattice/Web

64. Sala di Costantino, Palazzo Vaticano, Rome. Giulio Romano and assistants.

65. Sala di Costantino, Palazzo Vaticano, Rome, Pope Urban I fresco. Giulio Romano.

The Sixteenth Century Grid/Frame/Lattice/Web

chelangelo himself? The dates (there is confusion about these) are almost the same; but both are specimens of the first delivery of a famous sixteenth century spatial *parti* and, as such, it is astonishing that they have not been so related.

Did Giulio do it first or did Michelangelo?

By historians of architecture this question, like the issue of Michelangelo's remorseless trabeation, has scarcely been addressed. On the whole, historians of architecture have preferred to involve themselves with the empirical details of particular *commissions* rather than with the empirical detail of particular *temperaments* and, on the whole, we may be thankful that so they have done. Research—in the archives—diminishes the possibilities of dangerous speculation. However, like speculation itself, research can never be neutral. Whatever attempts may be made to clean it up it will remain theory-impregnated. There will be rewarding discoveries which may be made; but, in spite of these, the 'researcher in the archives' will still find (with Germanic thoroughness) exactly what he wishes to find.

So, there can *never* be absolute certainty but, all the same, having talked about Michelangelo—the flat versus the round, the rectilinear versus the protuberant—it may still be permissible to resurrect a drawing from Le Corbusier's *Vers une Architecture* (fig. 66); and the overdoor in the Vatican from which it derives. By Paris Nogari, 1536–1601 (fig. 67), it presents everything which, ineptly, I have been trying to say. There is Michelangelo's St. Peter's (as it never could be) in a vast plenum of gridded space. All over again, but dare one say it, it is the vaulted ceiling of the Sistine Chapel and the grid imposed upon it.

Notes

1. Frederick Hartt, *Giulio Romano* (New Haven: Yale University Press, 1958), 45.

2. Such as Corrado Ricci, *L'Architettura del Cinquecento in Italia* (Paris: Librairie Hachette, 1923); and Julius Baum, *Baukunst und dekorative Plastik der Hoch und Spätrenaissance in Italien* (Stuttgart: Julius Hoffmann, 1920).

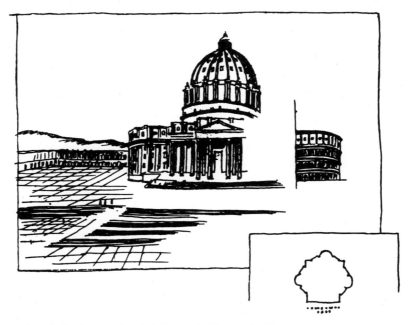

66. Le Corbusier, drawing of St. Peter's, in *Vers une Architecture*.

67. Vatican overdoor. Paris Nogari.

3. See Nikolaus Pevsner, *Outline of European Architecture* (London: John Murray, 1948).

4. See Pietro Ferrerio and Giovanni Battista Falda, *Palazzi di Roma* (Farnborough: Gregg Press, 1967).

5. C. L. Frommel, "Palazzo Jacopo in Brescia," in *Raffaelo Architetto* (Milan: Electa, 1984).

6. Hartt, *Giulio Romano,* 65.

7. Paolo Portoghesi, *Rome of the Renaissance* (London: Phaidon Press, 1972), 358.

8. Hartt, *Giulio Romano,* 62.

9. Ibid., 65.

10. A very obvious case in point would be Piero della Francesca's *Flagellation.*

11. Sydney Freedberg, *Painting of the High Renaissance in Rome and Florence* (Cambridge, Mass.: Harvard University Press, 1961), 554.

12. However, scarcely a sufficient coincidence to encourage the postulation of some all-devouring and convulsive *Zeitgeist.*

13. Hartt, *Giulio Romano,* 90.

14. The reconstruction after the bombardment of Velletri in World War II has radically altered these readings.

15. Portoghesi, *Rome of the Renaissance,* 225.

16. Gustavo Giovannoni, *Antonio da Sangallo, il giovane* (Rome: Tipografica Regionale, 1959), 49.

17. H. Millon and C. H. Smith, *Michelangelo Architetto* (Milan: Olivetti, 1986), 6.

18. Charles De Tolnay, *Michelangelo* (Princeton: Princeton University Press, 1975), 31.

19. De Tolnay, *Michelangelo,* 24.

20. Hartt, *Giulio Romano,* 47.

21. De Tolnay, *Michelangelo,* 31.

22. Hartt dates the completion of the Sala di Costantino to no later than October 1524, as Giulio was to be in Mantua later that same month (Hartt, *Giulio Romano,* 45). De Tolnay cites the beginning of the construction of the Medici Tombs as the spring of 1524 (De Tolnay, *Michelangelo,* 38).

The Provocative Facade: Frontality and *Contrapposto*

Way back, part of my stock-in-trade was a little pet of a lecture which was useful for almost all occasions, and I remember having delivered it in Chicago, in Houston, in Lexington, Kentucky, at Princeton, Columbia, Harvard, Yale, Syracuse, and, before I lost all patience with this repetition, I don't know how many other places besides. During this protracted exposure details could vary, and one of its virtues was that it could receive a variety of titles—like "The Flat versus the Round," "Wall and Superwall," and even "The Wall: An Extinct Species?"

It was based upon two stimuli: the side wall of the church at La Tourette and a long contemplation of the paintings of Piet Mondrian.

In December 1960 I was privileged to stay in Le Corbusier's Dominican convent because of my association with certain Dominicans in Cambridge, England, most notably because of my association with

Father Illtyd Evans, whose presence and wit were always a very great pleasure and whose imitations of the Archbishop of Canterbury and even the Cardinal Archbishop of Westminster were something quite wild. So Father Illtyd led to Père Couturier, and Père Couturier led to my three nights' stay at La Tourette.

This was an infinitely rewarding experience and particularly so in the refectory, where none of the monks were allowed to speak but where, read to in a Gregorian voice, they were obliged to listen to an incantation not about religion but rather about aspects of French archaeology. And I can still hear the voice: "un sarcophage Gallo-Romain découvert à Belfort, comme a dit Viollet-le-Duc, ainsi comme a dit Prosper Mérimée."

But, apart from this diversionary and Dominican stuff, my three days at La Tourette were spent in thinking about its relations to Maison Domino, Maison Citrohan, to Garches and to Poissy; and the side wall of Maison Citrohan, promoted to prominence, has obsessed me ever since.

Then the paintings of Mondrian—the white ground, the blue, red, and yellow figures, and the grid of black lines—my present interpretation of them must derive from my association with Robert Slutzky at Texas, which himself must have derived from Josef Albers at Yale; and this reading is apt to insist that the paintings of Mondrian's maturity represent a fluctuation between ideas of surface and depth and, perhaps also, between ideas of flatness and concavity. Thus, in terms of this reading, the white ground becomes a signifier of deep and probably concave space, and it is within this space that there are to be found the 'accidents' of the picture, those rectangles of blue/red/yellow, which are the reason for its being; while, via the activity of the black quasi-grid, all of this apparatus of the background is grabbed. It is brought forward and it is discharged into the surface of an enigmatic picture plane.

But now, to introduce a bifora *window from a twelfth- or thirteenth-century house in Venice (fig. 68) and to observe what it is causing to happen. Apart from the central column and its accessories, everything here is flat, though not without certain significant intimations.*

68. *Palazzetto,* Salizzada S. Lio, Venice, twelfth or thirteenth century, *bifora* of the *primo piano.*

The Provocative Facade: Frontality and *Contrapposto*

Deriving from the recessed wall below the window, this flatness may further be construable as the product of two layers of wall traveling in close proximity. However, the central column is cylindrical and, therefore, it may be felt that it causes a cylindrical space to gyrate around itself, a space which, though subject to different vicissitudes, is to be found half within the depths of the building and half outside it. Then the sense of this cylindrical volume of space is further augmented by the Byzantine profile of the two arches which, though they partake of the semicircular, are not in themselves semicircular. And it is at this stage that analysis becomes almost defeated, that such words as are available to record what is visible are, virtually, rendered useless to describe what should be said.

Were these two arches obedient to a post-Byzantine system of logic, they would either be pointed or semicircular and they would spring fairly directly from the capital of the central column; but, being what they are, they comprise aspects of both the vertical and the semicircular—neither of them highly articulated. And also, being what they are, these two arches further encourage a determination on the part of the eye to perceive a vertical projection of the axis of the circular column into the rectilinearized situation just above the capital and, thereby, to engender a highly stimulating miscegenation of all received ideas of the round versus the flat.

Nor is this all. Because, if one follows the career of this column downward, while it retains its same form, it is now to be found subject to restraints and, at bottom, simply to be standing upon a highly exiguous shelf. In other words, the circular volume of space has, down here, become the victim of the transverse shearing action of a vertical stratification of planes.

An anomalous but crucial destiny for the column? But it is surely from this surreptitious compounding of its spatial functions that there is to be discovered the very particular predicament of both this window and its setting. This condition, which I became accustomed to think about as a matter of making surface pregnant with depth, some architects have always understood and some others will never comprehend. It was understood by Alberti, by Michelangelo, and by Borromini. It was not understood by Bernini. It was understood by Hawksmoor—though not by Vanbrugh; and, I think that it was always understood by Jim Stirling.

So the very old story of the protuberant versus the planar, which is the ultimate story of "Grid/Fame/Lattice/Web" and will continue to be the story of "The Provocative Facade." And this because the combination of gridding, flatness, and rotundity always continued to be basic for Le Corbusier.

As first published, "The Provocative Facade: Frontality and Contrapposto" *was a contribution to the catalogue of the exhibition "Le Corbusier, Architect of the Century" (London, 1987) and was later republished in* Arquitectura, *no. 264–265 (Madrid, 1987).*

In *Vers une Architecture* Le Corbusier publishes a drawing of what in the early 1920s was a little-known fresco, an overdoor in the Vatican of c. 1587 (fig. 69). This is Nogari's presentation of Michelangelo's St. Peter's set in an ideal piazza and it displays an accumulation of rotundities standing on a rectilinear pavement in a rigidly rectilinear space (fig. 70).

Then, to the bottom right of this drawing, he appends another one which, presumably, we are supposed to recognize as Michelangelo's plan; and this, quite possibly, is highly revealing in terms of the details which Le Corbusier chooses not to disclose. Thus, there is absolutely no specification of interior voids and solids. There is simply perimeter; and, related to this 'failure' to record *poché,* there is yet another 'failure' which may be even more interesting. If Le Corbusier's rendition of Michelangelo's plan is compared with the engraving from which he derived it (fig. 71), it is apparent that he has further excised a whole spatial episode—the eastern apse of the centralized church which leads to (or from) the entrance portico.

Now this may be the result of pure carelessness—the graphic equivalent of a Freudian lapse; but, with an architect so self-conscious as Le Corbusier, it would be less than perceptive not to interpret this drawing as some sort of significant editorial revi-

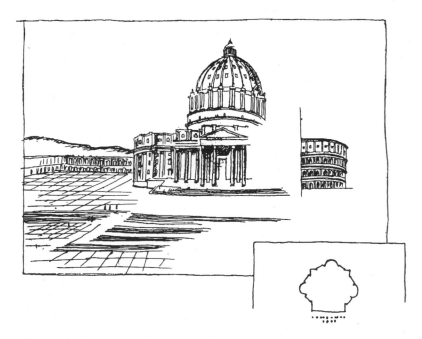

69. Le Corbusier, drawing of St. Peter's (after Nogari), in *Vers une Architecture.*

sion. And this for the reason that, in *Vers une Architecture,* the writer's preoccupation with Michelangelo is so very well advertised. "Michelangelo is the man of the last thousand years as Phidias was the man of the thousand years before."[1] (With the millenary years so well articulated the next slot can only be left open for we know whom.)

> And so we have the rotundas, the setbacks, the intersecting walls, the drum of the dome, the hypostyle porch, a gigantic geometry of harmonious relationships. Then we have renewed rhythms in the stylobates, pilasters and entablatures of entirely new sections. . . . The whole scheme was a complete unity; it grouped together elements of the noblest and richest kind. . . . The mouldings are of an intensely passionate character, harsh and pathetic.[2]

70. St. Peter's, Rome. Overdoor fresco by Nogari.

The Provocative Facade: Frontality and *Contrapposto*

71. St. Peter's, Rome. Plan, after Michelangelo.

Apart from his predilection for big hands, big feet, big biceps, etc. (after all, the Modular Man is an explicit descendant of David), this great eulogium should be enough to suggest the intensity of Le Corbusier's involvement with Michelangelo and, correspondingly, it may be allowed to elicit the argument that his amputation or suppression of a whole phase of the centralized St. Peter's could scarcely have been accidental. Le Corbusier abbreviates and almost mutilates the entrance arrangements which he professes to depict; and, witnessing this and thinking about those mouldings "of an intensely passionate character, harsh and pathetic," almost inevitably one is obliged to think about the Villa Schwob (fig. 72).

The first of Le Corbusier's highly provocative facades—flat frontispiece and miscellaneous turbulence/protuberance behind—it

72. Villa Schwob, La Chaux-de-Fonds, 1916–1917, facade. Le Corbusier.

The Provocative Facade: Frontality and *Contrapposto*

is relatively easy to propose antecedents for the vertical surface of the Villa Schwob. Auguste Perret's garage in the Rue Ponthieu (Paris, 1905), as a probable (fig. 73); Frank Lloyd Wright's Hardy House at Racine, Wisconsin of the same approximate date (fig. 74) as a casual maybe (the two entrances just might indicate such affiliation); but, all the same, there still remains the glaring *maniera* content, and with reference to this—the blank panel—one remains compelled to cite the highly obvious precedents of the so-called Casa di Palladio in Vicenza (fig. 75) and of Federico Zuccheri's studio in Florence (fig. 76).

However, the gesture of the blank panel (which contributes astringency to the visual field) is not the crucial issue; and much more important is the contention that Villa Schwob should be recognized as a somewhat juvenile, distinctly bizarre, and highly domesticated version of Michelangelo's St. Peter's.

Of course, such a proposition is too implausible to acquire immediate acceptance. This in spite of those mouldings "harsh and pathetic"; this in spite of the excavation of the wall as a series of relief layers; this in spite of the cycloramic effect of the manifesto panel which can only insinuate apsidal suggestions of depth; this in spite of Villa Schwob's plan (fig. 77) and Le Corbusier's 'editorial' version of Michelangelo's; and, therefore, while registering this general argument, it will be more opportune to go on to another.

The facade of Villa Schwob is a billboard or a surface for enigmatic advertisement; and, in terms of the whole building's anatomy, this excessive statement of plane and frontality is then disengaged or dissected from what lies behind by a vertical slot or cut (fig. 78). In front all is flat; behind happenings are of a distinctly different order; and something along these lines continues to be a Corbusian dispensation.

For instance, if one considers the vertical slot or *dégagement* at Villa Schwob (distinctly clumsy), not only will one find it rendered more elegant/laconic at Garches (fig. 79), but one will also find it persisting in far later buildings like La Tourette (fig. 80) and Millowners, Ahmedabad (fig. 81), not to mention others. And,

73. Garage, Rue Ponthieu, Paris, 1905. Auguste Perret.

The Provocative Facade: Frontality and *Contrapposto*

74. Thomas F. Hardy House, Racine. Frank Lloyd Wright.

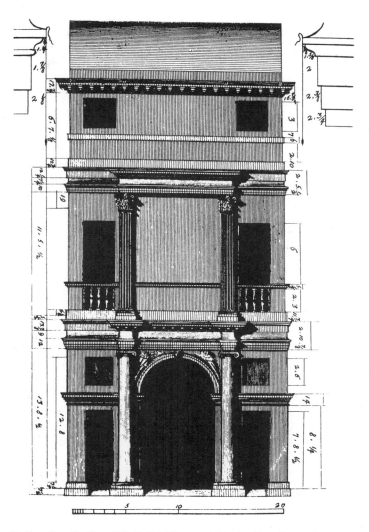

75. Casa Cogollo (Casa di Palladio), Vicenza, 1572. Attributed to Andrea Palladio.

The Provocative Facade: Frontality and *Contrapposto*

76. Casino dei Zuccheri, 1578. Federico Zuccheri.

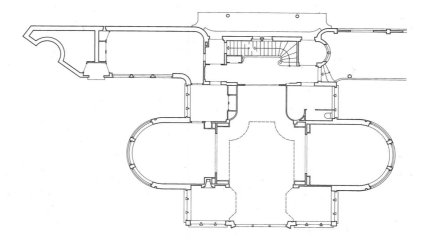

77. Villa Schwob, plan.

78. Villa Schwob, view.

The Provocative Facade: Frontality and *Contrapposto*

79. Villa Stein de Monzie, Garches, 1926–1928. Le Corbusier.

80. Monastery of Sainte-Marie de La Tourette, Eveux-sur-l'Arbresle, 1953–1959. Le Corbusier.

The Provocative Facade: Frontality and *Contrapposto*

81. Millowners' Association Building, Ahmedabad, 1954, west facade. Le Corbusier.

therefore, there is certainly one safe argument which may be advanced about Villa Schwob: the juxtaposition of front and rear which it displays establishes at least one basic datum for the interpretation of a quantity of Le Corbusier's more important achievements—though, needless to say, accepted exegesis has not been prone to develop any such strategy.

Not published in the *Oeuvre Complète,* the initiatory role of Schwob has been decisively obscured by the far more assertive novelty of Maison Domino (fig. 82), which is so transparently the icon of a new beginning. Like the primitive hut of the Abbé Laugier, Maison Domino appears to declare the primacy of columns and the largely superfluous nature of any opaque enclosure; and, going beyond Laugier, it then appears to announce the 'inevitable' nature of a space conditioned by a 'Modern' structure. Horizontal planes predominate; the building becomes something like a club sandwich or a Neapolitan wafer; and, when these enticing suggestions become allied with ensuing deductions about plan and 'free plan', then it might seem that the whole box of tricks has been presented.

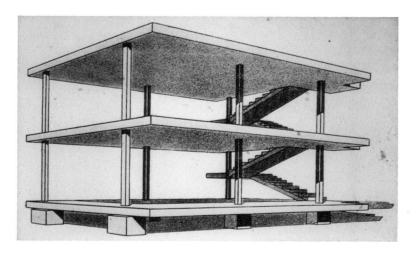

82. Maison Domino, 1925. Le Corbusier.

The Provocative Facade: Frontality and *Contrapposto*

But, alas for so facile a route from Maison Domino to Villa Savoye. For there are horrible roadblocks to be negotiated. There is, first of all, Maison Citrohan (fig. 83), a general statement which, contrary to Domino, proposes a space with restricted horizontal extension, an open-ended tunnel space; and then, as something supremely difficult to cope with, in terms of the critical clichés of 'Modern architecture', there is the magisterial entrance surface at Garches (fig. 84).

> Now the plan is the generator, the plan is the determination of everything; it is an austere abstraction, an algebrization, and cold of aspect. It is a plan of battle. The battle follows and that is the great moment. The battle is composed of the impact of masses in space and the morale of the army is the cluster of predetermined ideas and the driving purpose.[3]

So much is Corbu rehearsing French academic doctrine (Guadet and Choisy); but when he continues that: "A building is like a soap bubble. This bubble is perfectly harmonious if the breath has been evenly distributed from the inside. The exterior is the result of an interior,"[4] then it is at this stage that one wishes to produce his self-contradiction. Contrary to Corbu's insistence upon the plan and contrary to his academic "soap bubble" one wishes to produce his equally fundamental idea of *wall as declamation.*

> Our elements are vertical walls . . . the walls are in full brilliant light, or in half shade or in full shade. . . . Have respect for walls. . . . Light is intense when it falls between walls which reflect it. The ancients built walls which stretch out and meet to amplify the wall . . . light and its reflection by the walls and the floor, which is really a horizontal wall.[5]

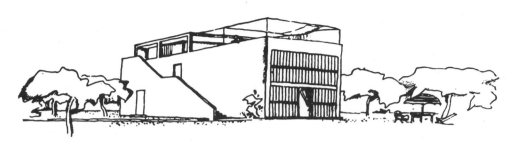

83. Maison Citrohan, 1922. Le Corbusier.

84. Villa Stein de Monzie, entrance facade.

The Provocative Facade: Frontality and *Contrapposto*

"The floor which is really a horizontal wall." Throwaway remark though this might be, it is, just possibly, Le Corbusier's most rewarding observation. For, if walls become floors, then sections become plans; and, as the building becomes a dice to be thrown on the table, then all the rest results. We throw around the dice: and, as facade becomes side elevation, as Domino becomes Citrohan, a continuous twisting of meaning and presentation is obliged to occur.

It is thus that the vertical surface of Garches, neither a logical sequel of Maison Domino nor a flat contradiction of its structural precepts, becomes a visual document equivalent in status to the alleged, and more abstract, priority of its horizontal planes and the spatial delimitations of its interior. The facade of Garches is only the most arcane record of its plan; and, while Maison Domino *may* have been a *conceptual* necessity for Le Corbusier, it *must* be apparent that an expressive frontispiece—an allegory of what lies inside (?)—was an entirely equal *perceptual* imperative.

However, "The floor which is really a horizontal wall" insists upon further interpretation. *Obiter dicta* though it might be, this remark is entirely inconceivable coming from Frank Lloyd Wright, Mies van der Rohe, Gropius. All these had too much respect for the laws of gravity which Le Corbusier here seems casually to despise (he evidently preferred the laws of dialectic); but, if the idea of a building as an entity gyrating around horizontal (and vertical) axes is, in any way, to be considered seriously—as less than a joke—then we will be compelled to invent a term which has not yet been heard of. And the only available term seems to be *architectural contrapposto.*

The pictorial and sculptural phenomenon known as *contrapposto* may be said to derive from a preference for frontality and a subsidiary pleasure in the delights of the oblique view. Dependent on the supremacy of a vision which is related to one point perspective, as a second category it then admits all those movements of turning and revolution which a two point perspective is enabled to observe—though, perhaps, not appropriately to value. In other words, the existence of *contrapposto* presumes a pictorial or a sculptural condition of permanent argument. The figure is simultaneously static and is also set in motion. There is the primary surface of attack, the frontal picture plane, and, then, there is the convoluted and serpentine territory which lies behind.

As a piece of sculpture a Michelangelo slave (fig. 85), with all its torsion, tension, muscular excess, may illustrate the issue; and, as a work of architecture, the rear of St. Peter's may illuminate it still further (fig. 86). For, at the rear of St. Peter's the observer may be in some doubt as to which planes are to be considered frontal and which diagonal. But, then, to remember that it was precisely those ambiguous planes, which, in *Vers une Architecture,* threw the writer into such frenzies of critical delirium.

This said and in spite of his ambitions, Le Corbusier's ultimate product is never quite so titanic. As his buildings twist (twisting at Garches is mostly a function of the garden front), Le Corbusier may manipulate their vertical axes so that they will not only present the evident *façades* but will also exhibit (with something like the same prominence) those not very interesting exposures which, supposedly, are *elevations.* And hence, published big in the *Oeuvre Complète,* there is that empty side wall from Pessac (fig. 87). This image, cropped so that it resembles some major statement about flatness from Juan Gris or Fernand Léger, is the side elevation of a Maison Citrohan; but in terms of display, it is presented as a rhetorical piece equal in pitch to the 'representative' frontispiece at Garches.

Hence too the church at La Tourette—really the observer's primary notice of the building—is a later exhibition of Maison Citrohan at its most banal. It is nothingness; but also, in its absence of revelation, it is surely to be interpreted as the ultimate recapitulation of the 'exciting' emptiness of Villa Schwob. Indeed the quartet, Schwob, Pessac, Garches, La Tourette, when seen as interactive with Domino and Citrohan, clamor to be envisaged as a basic *matériel* for explanation of how ideas of frontality (Schwob and Garches) became compounded with the promotion of side to the eminence of front

The Provocative Facade: Frontality and *Contrapposto*

85. Michelangelo, *Captive,* 1519.

86. St. Peter's, Rome, rear view.

The Provocative Facade: Frontality and *Contrapposto*

87. Cité Frugès, Pessac, 1925–1928. Le Corbusier.

(Pessac) and how there eventually resulted an elaborate system of rotation partially shielded by a front which is deprived of all the pretensions of a front (La Tourette).

But, if La Tourette is a descendent of Schwob and Citrohan, it must also be seen as affiliated to Poissy, where there is something like a corkscrew motion—the pedestrian ascent of the ramps. A sketch and an airplane view may illustrate the similarities (figs. 88, 89); and, in both cases, it is to be noticed how muted, and almost sad, is the initial presentation. The other three sides of both buildings are developed in depth; they display conspicuous attention to *chiaroscuro;* but, at both Poissy and La Tourette, if the first message which the buildings advertise is not actively hostile at least it is an affront. There is nothing seductive; there is nothing ingratiating; and, in this paralysis of the power to please, evidently there lurks the presence of that blank panel at La Chaux-de-Fonds.

88. Monastery of Sainte-Marie de La Tourette, aerial view.

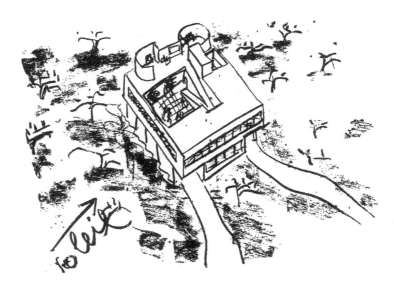

89. Villa Savoye, Poissy, 1928–1930. Le Corbusier.

Apart from a generous lyricism, as at Poissy, it seems impossible to deny an important sado-masochist content in Le Corbusier's architecture, as at La Tourette. Domino, one might suggest, is expansively kind; but Citrohan, one might believe, is potentially coercive. And it is with this observation (which is not a value judgement) that one must finally approach the problem of "the floor which is really a horizontal wall."

Traditionally *contrapposto* has implied a priority of picture plane with accessory revolution around a *vertical* axis. The simple idea of an image gyrating around a *horizontal skewer* (like shish kebab at a barbecue cookout) was scarcely to be considered. Nevertheless, in the 1920s, the notion of revolving an image around a horizontal axis became an important topic. No doubt it was considered a breach of the acceptable; but, in any case, a Picasso of 1925, *Musical Instruments on a Table,* may illustrate the condition (fig. 90).

Spatially a flat surface, while guitars or whatever they may be provide intimations of roundness and depth, Picasso presents a horizontal plane, the table (a floor?), and then the table's supports, the residue of a vertical plane (a wall or, at least, a number of columns?) which are all compressed into a more or less elliptical figure in a field which will scarcely permit recession.

Now, in Paris rather more than sixty years ago, it is entirely possible that such performances as this particular Picasso were everyday events; and it is mildly possible (though not likely) that from them Le Corbusier derived his, otherwise, strange idea about the inter-changeability of walls and floors. But, in any case, at La Tourette, this inter-changeability occurs within the *parti* of Poissy; and within this *parti* there are then insinuated assertions of both Citrohan and Domino.

Thus the church is Citrohan and the rest is Domino. Conceptually one or the other is turned sidewise (Le Corbusier was never exactly profligate with his inventions; his architectural game was deployed within highly restricted parameters); and it is just possible that, from this compacting of the horizontal and the vertical—a simultaneous attack from three sides—the peculiar density (almost Romanesque) of his late style was engendered.

90. Pablo Picasso, *Musical Instruments on a Table*, 1925.

The Provocative Facade: Frontality and *Contrapposto*

So, if all this seems to be laboring a minor point, there is a quotation from himself which might help to correct accusations of pedantry: "In a complete and successful work of art there is a wealth of meaning only accessible to those who have the ability to see it, in other words to those who deserve it."[6]

Mildly *élitiste*, these sentiments may be; but, if nowadays Le Corbusier is becoming distinctly *persona non grata*, to fail to register his achievement is quite as completely stupid as was the eighteenth century failure to 'see' either Michelangelo or Borromini— within which succession, in terms of the animated wall, Le Corbusier assuredly belongs. All the same, just what was his relation to Italian *maniera?* Schwob indicates a relation; at Garches the excessively high visual center of gravity may suggest a Michelangelo dependence (top floor of Palazzo Farnese?); but, when one contemplates Pirro Ligorio's Villa Pia (fig. 91), then what to say? Shave Villa Pia, crop Garches (fig. 92), and there is stylistic convergence? There certainly is; but as accents flee to the perimeter, it may still be amusing to introduce a little Buontalenti chapel from Figline, Valdarno (fig. 93). Minute, its physiognomic declaration—face, aperture, eyes—a little like a Bronzino portrait, infallibly it belongs to the same world as Schwob and all the rest.

Notes

1. Le Corbusier, *Vers une Architecture,* rev. ed. (Paris: Vincent Fréal, 1958), 133.

2. Ibid., 137.

3. Ibid., 145.

4. Ibid., 146.

5. Ibid., 149–150.

6. *Le Corbusier, Architect of the Century,* exhibition catalogue (London: Arts Council of Great Britain, 1987).

91. Casino of Pius IV (Villa Pia). Pirro Ligorio.

The Provocative Facade: Frontality and *Contrapposto*

92. Villa Stein de Monzie, cropped view.

93. Oratorio, Figline, Valdarno. Attributed to Bernardo Buontalenti.

The Provocative Facade: Frontality and *Contrapposto*

Classicism, Neo-Classicism, Neo-Neo-Classicism

This essay was written in 1984 while I was Thomas Jefferson Professor at the University of Virginia where, obviously, I must have been highly affected by the genius loci *of Charlottesville; and it was proposed to me by Vittorio Magnago Lampugnani as part of the catalogue of an exhibition, "Die Abenteueren der Ideen," which he was organizing in Berlin.*

At the same time similar proposals on different topics were also made to Alan Colquhoun and Kenneth Frampton, who both responded by sending their own contributions.

Judge the surprise of the three of us, therefore, when, on receiving our copies of the catalogue, we discovered that, though the texts had been printed, they had been printed in each case with a quite different choice of illustrations! A strange freak of editorial policy? Or so it seemed; and, thus, one could not be surprised when a review of the exhibition in House and Garden *applauded the show but described its "message" as "muddy."*

However, this piece seems to have acquired an Italian publication about which I must confess that I know nothing; and, apparently, it was in this form that it came to the attention of the editors of Arquitectura y Vivienda *in Madrid, who, to the best of their considerable ability, reassembled it in* A y V, no. 21 (1990).

What follows is the text of 1984 and an imperfect attempt to reconstitute the original illustrations as they were found in the library at the University of Virginia.

There is a statement of Nietzsche's to the effect that only that which is without history is capable of definition; and, if this is true, then we may safely assume that Classicism (with such a very long history) is a highly indefinable topic. Nevertheless there is a pronouncement of Sir Joshua Reynolds which effectively defines the classical ideal. Said Reynolds "The whole beauty and the grandeur of the art consists of being able to get above all singular forms, local customs, particularities, and details of every kind."

Now to us, who depend so much upon the idea of contingency, a notice of this order can only be just a little shocking: but for a very long time statements of this order were representations of the conventional wisdom, only to be invalidated by the findings of English Romanticism and German *Sturm und Drang,* in other words by the discoveries of an era which, stylistically, was dominated by an approach which, more than sixty years ago, Sigfried Gidieon defined as *Romantic Classicism.*

Classicism, Romantic Classicism, Neo-Classicism, the designation may vary; but, as a first act of understanding, it will be convenient to approach the subject through the agency of three monumental gateways which may be regarded as among the grandest descriptions of the style. These are from Berlin, Langhans' Brandenburg Tor of 1789 (fig. 94); from Paris, Chalgrin's Arc de Triomphe de l'Etoile of 1806 (fig. 95); and from Munich, Von Klenze's

94. Brandenburg Gate, Berlin, 1789. Carl Gotthard Langhans.

Classicism, Neo-Classicism, Neo-Neo-Classicism

95. Arc de Triomphe de l'Etoile, Paris, 1806. Jean-François Chalgrin.

Propylaen of 1848 (fig. 96); and collectively, they may illustrate the range and the aspirations of the period. Predictably the German specimens are Greek in inspiration, and the French specimen is Roman. Langhans introduces the theme, but it is terminated by Von Klenze in an archaizing statement of extraordinary subtlety.

But, prefatory to all this, we must now observe the signs of incipient change which became visible in the 1750s. Bach died in 1750, Handel in 1759. Winckelmann arrived in Rome in 1754; James Stuart and Nicholas Revett went to Athens in 1750. In the same year Cochin and Soufflot were at Paestum measuring the temples. In the same year, also, Piranesi produced his *Carceri,* what Sir John Summerson has called those "fantastic compositions of meaningless architecture festooned in ropes and chains and cluttered with monstrous tackle of uncertain purpose." The Abbé Laugier published his *Essai sur l'Architecture* in 1753, Edmund Burke his *Sublime and the Beautiful* in 1756. Robert Wood's *Ruins of Palmyra* and *Ruins of Baalbek* date from 1753 and 1757. In 1757 Robert Adam was measuring the Palace of Diocletian at Spalato. In 1751 there appeared Le Roy's *Les Ruines des plus beaux monuments de la Grèce.* The first volume of Stuart and Revett's *The Antiquities of Athens* came out in 1762. Sir William Hamilton became British Ambassador to the Court of Naples in 1764. And, somewhat distant from all this aesthetic and archaeological excitement, in 1756, at the perfectly rational instigation of the King of Prussia there began what should properly be called The First World War—the first war to involve not only the European theater but also those distant places in India and North America.

So, in the 1750s the evidences of important change were almost excessive; and, as the world became contracted, the historical imagination became inflamed. The decade, as one now can see, was one of the great historical watersheds. About eighteenth-century architecture the English used to say "early curly, later straighter," referring to the very obvious differences between late Baroque-Rococo and the Neo-Classical ideal; but, if in England this style was disguised by a general mask of reticence and uniformity, then, as we

96. Propylaos, Munich, 1848. Leo von Klenze.

approach the Germanic lands and Paris, the transformation of intellectual mood becomes rather more extravagant.

Balthasar Neumann's Vierzehnheiligen was begun in 1743 (fig. 97) and Soufflot's Sainte-Geneviève (fig. 98) (otherwise the Panthéon) was initiated in 1757. Thus, in terms of ideation, they are separated by a gap of only fourteen years; and yet what a cultural chasm separates these two monuments! On the one hand the magnificent Neumann, who, like Bach and Handel, is in full possession of a superb late Baroque repertory; and, on the other, the pedantic, revolutionary Soufflot. On the one hand an historical cul-de-sac; and, on the other, the wave of the future. On the one hand a sophisticated provincial exuberance; and, on the other, a cosmopolitan and a highly nervous, graphic tightness.

Absolutely no doubt that Neumann is preferable to Soufflot. However, to look for origins of this mood of the 1750s we must retreat further backward in time. For, almost certainly, the origins of Neo-Classicism (as of Rationalism) will be found to be Venetic and French. In other words: Palladio. And so, two Palladio images are produced.

One is from the *Quattro Libri*. It is a plan of the Villa of the Ancients (fig. 99). It interested the Rationalists, particularly among the French; but it scarcely interested Neo-Classical sensibility. And the other is the garden facade of the Villa Pisani at Montagnana (fig. 100), a specimen of that somewhat elegiac Palladio which, for almost three hundred years, received incessant world attention.

However, attention must now be shifted, first to seventeenth-century Paris and Rome where, inevitably, a line of affiliation will descend through Poussin. And therefore, let us briefly notice Poussin's *Rape of the Sabines* (fig. 101), with its primitive Tuscan temple as a backdrop and its miscellaneous assembly of *maniera* palaces and rustic stoa to the right. And then let us consider his *Ordination* (1647) (fig. 102), with that surprising pyramidal temple in the near background. For both of these pictures (not to mention many more by Poussin) belong to the repertory of highly prophetic architectural rehearsals. The *Rape* is a grand set piece, in a way that

Classicism, Neo-Classicism, Neo-Neo-Classicism

97. Vierzehnheiligen, near Bamberg, 1743. Balthazar Neumann.

98. Sainte-Geneviève (Panthéon), Paris, 1757. Jacques Germain Soufflot.

Classicism, Neo-Classicism, Neo-Neo-Classicism

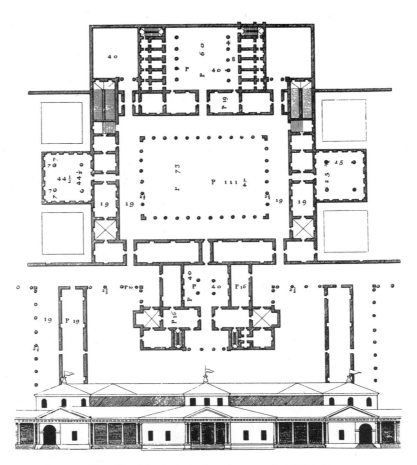

99. Andrea Palladio, *Villa of the Ancients,* from *Quattro Libri dell'Architettura.*

100. Villa Pisani, Montagnana, 1553. Andrea Palladio.

Classicism, Neo-Classicism, Neo-Neo-Classicism

101. Nicolas Poussin, *Rape of the Sabines,* c. 1637. Louvre, Paris.

102. Nicolas Poussin, *Ordination,* 1647. Duke of Sutherland Collection.

Classicism, Neo-Classicism, Neo-Neo-Classicism

Romantic Classicism would find it extremely easy to assimilate; while, as for the *Ordination,* that Egyptoid and Roman temple belongs to a category of buildings which, outside painting, one could scarcely expect to find until a hundred and thirty years later; and, then, with a slight shift of perspective (from frontal to moderate diagonal), a general view of Poussin could lead us, very easily, up to Schinkel's *Antike Stadt an einem Berg* (fig. 103).

Then, Poussin aside, there are other French seventeenth-century events to notice, and to cite only two: Perrault's east front of the Louvre represents the defeat of Bernini and of the Roman Baroque (just what Colbert and his advisers wanted?). It represents a style of secular establishment, *toutes proportions gardées.* It is Gallican rather than Papalist; and, belonging to this same category of things, one should now notice Jules Hardouin-Mansart's chapel at Versailles (fig. 104). Because this too may be interpreted as a very determined French protest against Baroque extravagance.

All the same, as Louis XIV declined, so did this early period of French Classicism. The *Régence* wished nothing so public or severe; and, though something like the style of Louis XIV was to be resumed shortly after the mid-eighteenth century in Gabriel's two buildings for the Place de la Concorde (fig. 105) and his Ecole Militaire (fig. 106), in the interim the most important activity (in terms of Neo-Classical evolution) was to take place in England. Indeed it is often said that the origins of Neo-Classicism are to be found in England: and, of course, for these arguments there is much support.

Richard Boyle (1694–1751), third Earl of Burlington and fourth Earl of Cork, was the promoter in England of a revival of interest in Palladio. Anglo-Irish, rich, travelled, an important patron and connoisseur, he was an early representative of the Enlightenment—his uncle was Robert Boyle of Boyle's Law and his tutor was Lord Shaftesbury, friend of John Locke and the author of *Characteristics.* Also, in his own right, he was an important architect and innovator.

His Chiswick House (fig. 107), begun in 1725, is not the slavish imitation of Palladio which, at one time, it was presumed to

103. Karl Friedrich Schinkel, *Antike Stadt an einem Berg,* 1842.

Classicism, Neo-Classicism, Neo-Neo-Classicism

104. Palace Chapel, Versailles, 1698. Jules Hardouin-Mansart.

105. Place de la Concorde, Paris, 1753–1770. Ange-Jacques Gabriel.

Classicism, Neo-Classicism, Neo-Neo-Classicism

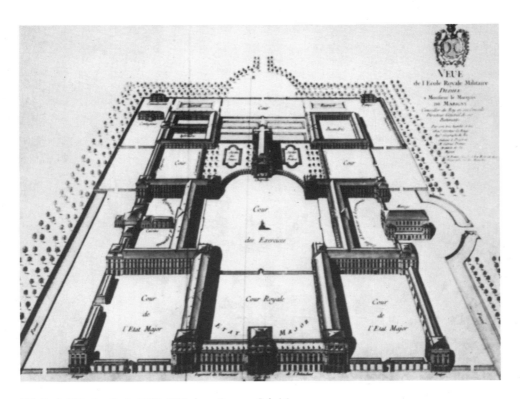

106. Ecole Militaire, Paris, 1752–1772. Ange-Jacques Gabriel.

107. Chiswick House, Middlesex, 1725. Lord Burlington.

Classicism, Neo-Classicism, Neo-Neo-Classicism

be. Maybe it is a little too cerebral for Palladio: maybe it is a little too *staccato:* maybe in its dome it makes too many allusions. Certainly it is a little too theatrical and, in its internal distributions, too Rococo. But, as one looks at this villa on the side of the Thames (supposed to be the Brenta) and, particularly, as one places it in its landscape setting, the argument that here were the first premonitions of Neo-Classicism becomes more than plausible.

Nevertheless, Burlington and the English demonstrations he sponsored, for present purposes, must be considered minor to the more concentrated impact of that international society of scholars, artists, and *dilettanti* that began to assemble itself in Rome after 1750: and some of the names that illuminated that benign and hospitable Rome of Benedict XIV and Clement XIII have already been called out.

So these were cultured and eclectic reigns which indulged visitors and foreigners who stayed. Now a very minor political power, Rome had almost ceased to be the capital of a religious empire and become the capital of the arts. It had become, as Robert Adam called it, "a Holy See of Pleasurable Antiquity," and, of all the foreign presence the Académie de France enjoyed first place. It was then established in the Palazzo Mancini, Via del Corso, and almost opposite to it was installed the shop of that Venetian and scarcely private personality, Giambattista Piranesi.

In other words, those *pensionnaires* of the Academy were placed in a highly privileged and explosive position. Mostly they must have been architecture students in their mid-twenties—and one knows the type: mostly, perhaps they did not like Rococo; mostly, perhaps, they hoped to contribute to a *restauration* of the style of the *grand siècle,* but meanwhile, there was that magnetic shop across the street and, in this extraordinary shop, its equally magnetic proprietor.

At the same time, apart from immediate exposure to excessive, energetic, passionate Piranesi, these same boys might also have been reading the *Essai* of the Abbé Laugier: and must this not, immediately, have been a very major problem? On the one hand there

was Piranesi's profusion and *terribilità,* and, on the other, there was
the exaggerated simplicity of Laugier's Primitive Hut, that very par-
simonious presentation alleged to be the origin of all architecture.
And need one say more? For the French students at Palazzo Mancini, from this dialectic of proximity, there must have ensued a
highly elevated sense of mission.

The refrigerated mood of Laugier and the tropical excitements of Piranesi, the very cold and the very hot, may be considered
as illustrating the two most extreme positions that Neo-Classicism
embodies: but a glance at Stuart and Revett's *Antiquities of Athens*
will disclose this inherent conflict in a more muted form. In their
volume of 1762 the *Choragic Monument of Lysicrates* (fig. 108) is presented in incredibly precise, linear terms. It is presented as archaeological 'science'; but, in the volume of 1794, the message is
completely contrary. The *Incandata at Salonica* (fig. 109) is a strictly
'pictorial' piece. Everything is 'as found'. An elderly Turk is ac-
cepting a cup of coffee and a younger one is making a rhetorical gesture, while, all the time, the principal object of attention is mostly
screened by recent and obviously 'interesting' accretions. But we
may now drop the Choragic Monument down into an English garden, Shugborough (fig. 110), and the three images together may
then be proposed as another advertisement of the Neo-Classical
predicament.

In a brief article it is impossible to give adequate credit to
anybody or anything. All the same it is easily possible to regard
George Dance's Newgate Prison, London (1769) (fig. 111) as a distant tribute to Piranesi and Peter Speeth's Frauenzuchthaus in Würzburg (1809) (fig. 112) as belonging to the same category. However,
far more perfectly than either of these, in terms of crime and punishment (a favorite Neo-Classical theme), a French drawing of 1778
may serve to suggest how the Piranesian position became both exaggerated and tamed by the didactics of Laugier (fig. 113).

It was Henry-Russell Hitchcock who once said (to me):
"But, in Robert Adam, is there not a very curious mixture of the
ritzy and the subterranean and is it not all like putting Marie Antoi-

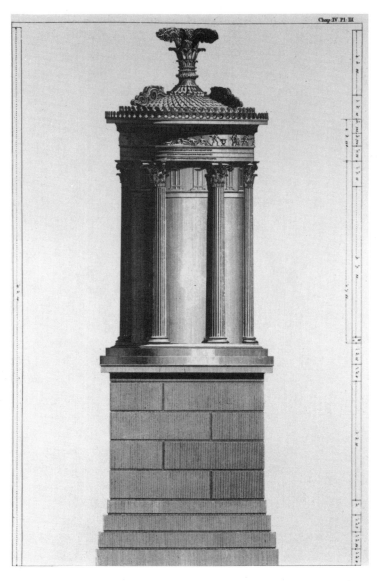

108. James Stuart and Nicholas Revett, *Choragic Monument of Lysicrates*, 1762. From *Antiquities of Athens.*

109. James Stuart and Nicholas Revett, *Incandata at Salonica,* 1794.

Classicism, Neo-Classicism, Neo-Neo-Classicism

110. Shugborough, eighteenth century.

111. Newgate Prison, London, 1768–1780. George Dance the Younger.

Classicism, Neo-Classicism, Neo-Neo-Classicism

112. Frauenzuchthaus, Würzburg, 1809. Peter Speeth.

113. L. J. Desprez, *Intérieur de prison avec scène de torture,* 1788.

Classicism, Neo-Classicism, Neo-Neo-Classicism

114. Interior, 26 Grosvenor Square, London, 1773–1774. Robert Adam.

115. La Chambre du Perroquet, Santa Trinità dei Monti, Rome, 1776. Jacques-Louis Clérisseau.

Classicism, Neo-Classicism, Neo-Neo-Classicism

nette in the catacombs?" And Robert Adam's parlor at no. 26 Grosvenor Square (1773–1774) (fig. 114) is some indication of the justice of this remark. It is Piranesi abbreviated, domesticated, and made luxurious for English purposes: and, as such, it deserves to be placed alongside that extraordinary room in the conventual buildings of Santa Trinità dei Monti, La Chambre du Perroquet (fig. 115), which was executed a few years earlier by Adam's teacher and Piranesi's disciple, Charles Louis Clérisseau (1721–1820).

Then a further English specimen may serve as reiteration. Patently inspired both by Piranesi's publications and the doctrine of Laugier. This is George Dance's All Hallows, London Wall: and the reverberations of this interior are persistent all the way through the career of Sir John Soane. His Privy Council Chamber (fig. 116) will illustrate the point.

However: a further sequence of Soane may still be permissible: his own Breakfast Room (fig. 117) showing the remarkable clutter (again miniature Piranesi?) which his collections finally came to present.

So English Neo-Classicism is apt to be a rather private affair. The English architect is prone to be a bit like Hamlet, Prince of Denmark, always thinking about thinking and, therefore, it is only when we turn to Paris that the full glare of publicity begins to appear.

Gondoin's lecture hall of the Ecole de Chirurgie (1769–1775) (fig. 118) is an evidence of this much more assertive French voice. From all those years in Rome the French had acquired a didactic solemnity later to become gigantomania: but, unlike the English, they were prone to be far more doctrinaire about the positions of their two architectural heroes. For were not many of them inflamed by the vision of a new and rational world that would be both sober and sublime; and, must not many of them have also received further fantasies about the Masonic order? For certainly that remarkable eye, an image of astonishing psychological profundity, which Ledoux used in the presentation of his auditorium at Besançon (fig. 119) must be related not only to Gondoin's oculus but also to an-

116. Privy Council Chamber, London, 1824–1827. John Soane.

Classicism, Neo-Classicism, Neo-Neo-Classicism

117. Soane Museum, Lincoln Fields, London, 1808–1824, section through the cupola and breakfast room. John Soane.

1·18. Ecole de Chirurgie, Paris, 1769–1775. Jacques Gondoin

Classicism, Neo-Classicism, Neo-Neo-Classicism

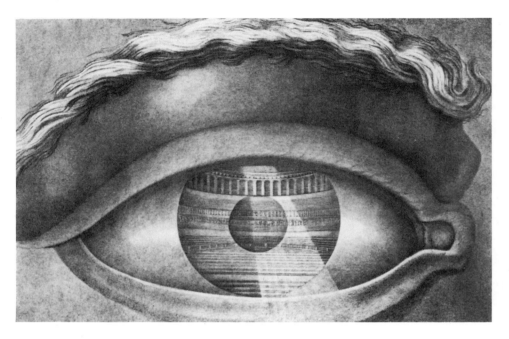

119. Claude-Nicolas Ledoux, *Auditorium of Theater of Besançon Seen as Reflected in the Pupil of an Eye,* 1775–1784.

120. Reverse side of a dollar bill.

other primary Neo-Classical and Masonic symbol: the Dollar Bill
(fig. 120).

Boullée, in his theater project for the Place du Carrousel of
the early 1780s (fig. 121), may be considered an adequate illustration of the excited state of mind of that decade in Paris: but it is necessary to recognize that very little of this sort was ever built and
that most of French production was still inspired by a conservatism;
by a desire to mediate between the Rococo and the *grand siècle,* an
attitude represented by Blondel and Gabriel. For, while in London
Palladio had become an influence in the 1720s and there was the
minimum of Rococo tradition to supersede, this was hardly the case
in Paris: and an observation of Ledoux's Hôtel Guimard (1772) (fig.
122) might underscore this point. For, whatever the revolutionary
reputation of the architect, the internal distribution remains approximately Rococo.

In any case, the great creative impulse of French Neo-
Classicism had mostly exhausted itself before the Revolution of
1789 which, apart from abbreviation of detail and a great many
very extravagant quasi-architectural festivals, seems to have exer-
cised little influence upon the continuity of French production. But,
all the same, as we move through the Directory to the Empire,
there is still a significant change of style to be observed. The Directory and Napoleonic projects are not less grandiose; but, just probably, they are a little more down to earth. Quite quickly they come
to present fewer museums and libraries, no more cenotaphs for
Newton; instead, there is a growing number of perfectly acceptable
warehouses and barracks. And did this owe something not only to
the policies of Napoleon but also to the teachings of Durand at
the Ecole Polytechnique, published in his *Précis des Leçons* of
1802–1805?

However this question may be answered, it must be admitted that, at what should have been the climax of Neo-Classical development, there is not all that much in Paris to show. For instance,
in St. Petersburg Thomas de Thomon's Stock Exchange of 1804–
1810 (fig. 123) is of incomparably better quality than Brongniart's

Classicism, Neo-Classicism, Neo-Neo-Classicism

121. Project for a Theater at the Place du Carrousel, Paris, 1781. Etienne-Louis
Boullée.

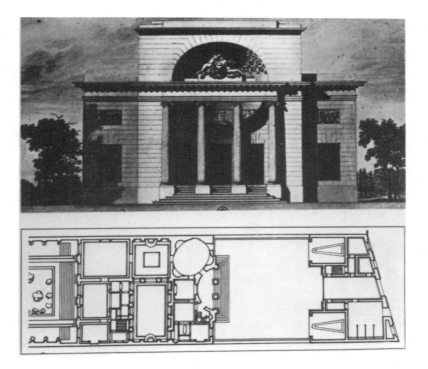

122. Hôtel Guimard, Paris, 1772. Claude-Nicolas Ledoux.

Classicism, Neo-Classicism, Neo-Neo-Classicism

123. Stock Exchange, St. Petersburg, 1804–1816. Thomas de Thomon.

124. Stock Exchange, Paris, 1808–1815. Alexandre Théodore Brongniart.

Paris Bourse (fig. 124) of, more or less, the same date. But, since for some twenty-three years the French were mostly involved in aggressive war, this decline in major production is to be expected. On the whole Bonaparte was too *soldatesque* to be civilized; and, therefore, in terms of the center of political power, the great triumphs of Neo-Classicism are not where they ought to be. For were not these triumphs almost exclusively German? And is not Neo-Classicism in the Germanic lands a movement which originated some thirty years later than it did in France and England?

Nevertheless, it is obviously possible to assemble the allure of the *style Empire* from an enormous quantity of fragments. From Paul Mebes we can extract pieces from Trier and Breslau: from Hector Lefuel a whole collection of shop fronts which formerly existed in Paris; from the pages of Percier and Fontaine a sequence of highly spectacular bedrooms: from the Palazzo Pitti the bathroom of Elisa Baciocchi (fig. 125); from far away Pavlovsk the Lantern Study of the Tsar Paul (fig. 126); and, from London, circa 1800, the long vanished interiors of Thomas Hope's house on Duchess Street (fig. 127). And, out of all this, Duchess Street deserves a more extended commentary.

Like the house of Sir John Soane, for which it probably provided the model, Duchess Street was simultaneously residence and museum; and then there is something about these interiors that seems to anticipate the general *Stimmung* of Schinkel some twenty years later. In Duchess Street, we almost could be at Tegel.

But consideration of Thomas Hope's town house can only lead us to his country place, in Surrey, where there is a deliberate pursuit of disarray and disjunction. Deepdene of 1818–1823 (fig. 128) is intended to be Hadrianic. An intentionally picturesque accumulation, it clearly derives from such a much smaller house as John Nash's Cronkhill of 1796 (fig. 129): and, almost certainly, it prepares the way for that greatest accumulation of the Neo-Classical Picturesque, the villa and the associated buildings at Charlottenhof, all intimately associated with the landscape.

125. Bathroom of Elisa Baciocchi, Palazzo Pitti, Florence, c. 1800.

CORNELLIANA

126. *Lantern Study of Tsar Paul at Pavlosk,* St. Petersburg, 1782–1786, interior.

Classicism, Neo-Classicism, Neo-Neo-Classicism

127. Hope Mansion, Duchess Street, London, c. 1800. Thomas Hope.

128. Deepdene, Surrey, 1818–1823. Thomas Hope.

Classicism, Neo-Classicism, Neo-Neo-Classicism

129. Cronkhill, Shropshire, c. 1802. John Nash.

130. Altes Museum, Berlin, 1824–1828. Karl Friedrich Schinkel.

Classicism, Neo-Classicism, Neo-Neo-Classicism

So it is a great historical irony that Neo-Classicism should have climaxed not in Paris/London but in the Berlin of Friedrich Wilhelm III; not in the portico of the Madeleine but in the peristyle of the Altes Museum (fig. 130); not so much in the gardens of an English country house as at Charlottenhof. But thinking about all this could also lead us to think about Schinkel's Bauakademie (fig. 131). For while the Altes Museum advertises the idealist content of Romantic Classicism, the Bauakademie is much more a highly intentional statement of fact and circumstance. The source material of one is simple, the provenance of the other much more complex. One is stone, the other a more humble brick and terracotta. In terms of an iconography of gesture, presumably the Altes Museum represents an idea of culture and the Bauakademie an idea of technology. In other words, in the purity of one and the hybridness of the other there is produced an hierarchical discrimination of purpose that is expressed in terms of stylistic difference. The primacy of *Kultur* demands a full-dress demonstration, but the subsidiary theater of *Baukunst* requires a far minor (though equally rigorous) display. And this distinction of genres was surely inevitable since, properly understood, the whole history of Neo-Classicism relates to a loose alliance of attitudes and sympathies.

It involves a mythical and ideal Greece and a mythical and ideal Rome: but it is apparent that, on the way to Paestum or Delphi, the traveller was apt to be side-tracked. In Regensburg he may have seen a great *Dom;* in Florence a *palazzo* that seized his attention; around Lucca or Viterbo he may have seen an engaging *casa colonica,* to Sicily he may have gone to look at Agrigento and remained to be seduced by Islamic fragments; and, out of all this very mixed experience does it not become apparent that, in search of Greece and Rome, our tourist of 1750–1830 might have become desperately worried by all the alternative information that, inadvertently, he had come to acquire? Obviously, Greece and Rome were pre-eminent: but then, just how to explain the rest? Indeed a rational explanation could not be made except by assuming some

131. Bauakademie, Berlin, 1831–1836. Karl Friedrich Schinkel.

Classicism, Neo-Classicism, Neo-Neo-Classicism

inherent essence of architecture which, irrespective of stylistic phenomena, had been active at all times and places.

A description of something like the experience of Schinkel and before him Soane this may be; but it was also the experience of many others. In their time, Laugier and Durand had implied as much; and in practice, the doctrine of an informing essence of architecture seems to have led to two major results which should not be considered diametrically opposed. It tended to sponsor an assembly of disparate stylistic reference within the same building; and, simultaneously, it served to promote (yet again) a rationalist concern with austere structural origin. Thus it tended to inspire an inventiveness so far as concerns local particulars and a minimalist reduction of episodic detail so far as concerns the total ensemble.

This is perhaps only incipient in the Bauakademie; but now to produce two buildings exclusively related to the second position. One is undoubtedly affiliated to Schinkel and the other to the typical facades of the *Rundbogenstil.* They are both from, then, modest and provincial Zurich and they are both works of the relatively unknown Gustav Albert Wegmann. The Kantonschule, with its elementary gridded surfaces, is of 1839–1842 (fig. 132) and is a little like a basic diagram for the later Kunstgewerbe Museum of Martin Gropius, and the Grossmünsterschulhaus is of 1850–1855 (fig. 133); but both of these buildings should be accepted as defining a late Neo-Classical state of mind which was already present in Schinkel and which later became very overt in Paris.

Therefore, now to approach the Paris of Louis Philippe, and the personality of Henri Labrouste and his greatest work, the Bibliothèque Sainte-Geneviève (fig. 134). It has always been admired: in the nineteenth century for its facade and later, by the protagonists of Modern architecture, for its interior. For the outside there have been cited Michelozzo's Banco Mediceo in Milan and Alberti's side elevations of the Tempio Malatestiano at Rimini as prototypes; and, for the inside, it has often been suggested that there is a dependence on one of those French medieval churches with double naves.

132. Kantonschule, Zurich, 1839–1842. Gustav Albert Wegmann.

No doubt, all true. For this building emphatically represents both a servitude to archaeology and an independence from it. It is *Rundbogenstil* become hyper-exacting. It is extravagantly flat. All at once, it is intensely private, enormously public, incredibly simple, Egyptian, Greek, Roman, *quattrocento, Louis Seize,* dogmatically technicist, and entirely convincing. It could be called a product of Positivist Neo-Classicism because, undoubtedly, it derives from an intellectual descent: Ecole Polytechnique, Henri de Saint-Simon, Auguste Comte, César Daly, and *La Revue Générale de l'Architecture et des Travaux Publics.*

An unfortunate intellectual descent? Perhaps. But all the same, it remains the incomparable French nineteenth-century monument, more or less the terminal monument of Neo-Classicism, and a building that has been widely proclaimed (by Sigfried Giedion and others) to have been completely seminal as relates to the pedigree of twentieth-century architecture.

Classicism, Neo-Classicism, Neo-Neo-Classicism

133. Grossmünsterschule, Zurich, 1850–1855. Gustav Albert Wegmann.

But Classicism, or Neo-Classicism, is an elderly *prima donna.* There is always the farewell performance (with retreat into the sunset); but apparently she is never allowed to bow herself off the stage. She might seem exhausted. However, the powers of recuperation continue to be insuperable; and, therefore, it will now be a good idea to direct attention to the United States and to the 1880s.

No need to say that Greek Revival architecture in America was of a brilliance, abundance, and diversity still unsuspected in Europe. Instead, it will be more opportune to propose that the United States comprise a natural arena for Classicism. And, with the oldest constitution in the world, a constitution deriving from the Enlightenment, it is hard to imagine how this could be otherwise. Atavistically, Americans will always return to the formulations of 1776; and, after the First Centennial, this tendency became more highly pronounced.

However, on the whole, the idea of this revived Classicism was cosmopolitan rather than nationalist. For major buildings, it was Francophile or apt to involve the Roman Renaissance. For domestic buildings the precedents were likely to be Anglo-American eighteenth century but, sometimes, could also be French. According to McKim, Mead and White, their Boston Public Library of 1888 (fig. 135) onwards was not inspired by the Bibliothèque Sainte-Geneviève but rather by Alberti at Rimini. However, its descent seems to be very obvious; and then there is that Frank Lloyd Wright project of 1893 for the Milwaukee Library and Museum (fig. 136) which is clearly related to Perrault's east front of the Louvre (fig. 137). Then there is Wright's George Blossom House in Chicago (fig. 138) which, in academic 'correctness', possibly exceeds any other work of its date: and, as a *finale* for this American excursus there could be introduced John Russell Pope's superb Temple of the Scottish Rite in Washington, D.C. (fig. 139).

So it was formerly the custom (influence of Walter Gropius and Sigfried Giedion) to dismiss the American work of these years as a dangerous irrelevance. The 'real' America was supposed to disclose itself elsewhere. However, confronted with the obvious quality

134. Bibliothèque Sainte-Geneviève, Paris, 1838–1850. Henri Labrouste.

135. Boston Public Library, Boston, 1888–1892. McKim, Mead and White.

136. Milwaukee Library and Museum project, 1893. Frank Lloyd Wright.

Classicism, Neo-Classicism, Neo-Neo-Classicism

137. Louvre, Paris, 1667–1674, east facade. Claude Perrault and others.

138. George Blossom House, Chicago, 1892. Frank Lloyd Wright.

139. Scottish Rite Temple, Washington, D.C., 1911–1915. John Russell Pope.

of American late Neo-Classical production (it was the best in the world), this very selective position is impossible to maintain: and it becomes very apparent that the United States provided a most important bridge serving to link the world of Labrouste and the Paris of Louis Philippe with that of early European Modernism. Frank Lloyd Wright's brief flirtation with academic Classicism in 1892–1893 has never received the notice it deserves. All the same, it must be regarded as a precedent for similar involvements in the early years of the twentieth century which, on the whole, the apologists of Modernism preferred to ignore. So these are embarrassingly many; and, therefore, to call out just a few: the rarely published entrance facade of Adolf Loos's Villa Karma outside Montreux (1904) (fig. 140); the buildings by Behrens for the Nordwestdeutsche

Classicism, Neo-Classicism, Neo-Neo-Classicism

140. Villa Karma, near Montreux, Switzerland, 1903–1906. Adolf Loos.

141. Nordwestdeutsche Kunstausstellung, Oldenburg, 1905. Peter Behrens.

142. Feinhals House, Cologne, 1908. Josef Maria Olbrich.

Kunstausstellung at Oldenburg (1905) (fig. 141); the Feinhals
house at Köln-Marienburg (1908) (fig. 142) by Olbrich; again by
Behrens, the Schroeder house at Hagen (dated 1909) (and supposed
to have involved, in the office, both Mies van der Rohe and Le Corbusier); the palace of the German Embassy at St. Petersburg (1912)
which, apparently, left an indelible impression on the mind of Mies;
and, last but far from least, by the remarkable Paul Mebes, author
of *Um 1800:* that brilliant building in Berlin-Schöneberg for the
Nordstern-Versicherungsgesellschaft (fig. 143), which dates from
the ominous year 1914. Now evidence of all this classicising activ-

Classicism, Neo-Classicism, Neo-Neo-Classicism

ity—without even introducing the now fashionable Heinrich Tessenow or, from Stuttgart, the mostly forgotten Paul Schmitt-henner—may be obtained by a quite casual turning over of the pages of Gustav Adolf Platz, *Die Baukunst der neuesten Zeit* (Berlin, 1927); and it could be further augmented by producing illustrations of later works from Scandinavia—Asplund, Lewerentz, Aalto. But this is being excessive; and, therefore, from Scandinavia only to produce Asplund's Lister County Court, Sølvesborg (1921) (fig. 144). Meanwhile, all this evidence can only lead to a series of questions:

1. Were these architects merely *retardataires?* It seems difficult to make this claim.
2. In some mysterious way, were all these architects totalitarians well before the emergence of the thing itself? Though Classicism is often supposed to be coercive, this is even less likely to be believed.
3. Was there some trans-Atlantic influence at work? In general there may have been but scarcely so as regards detail.
4. Did the Classical or Neo-Classical stage operate as a useful platform, able to receive and accommodate the bombardments of Cubism, Constructivism, and De Stijl? And it is this question that I am prone to answer in the affirmative.

By which I mean to suggest that a Classical/Neo-Classical substructure was, probably, an imperative field to support the figural attack of Modernism. Without that basis the attack was simply not to be conducted. It needed the Abbé Laugier's Primitive Hut (alias the Maison Domino of Le Corbusier) in order to succeed: and, about that 'success' of Modernism, what is there now left to say?

Certainly the attack exhausted itself very quickly; and, very quickly, the anticipated brave new world disclosed itself to be extremely sordid. Hence the accepted story and the pretensions have become a little too ridiculous: and hence, the revived interest in Classicism that is so prominent in the present day.

143. Nordstern-Versicherungsgesellschaft, Berlin, 1914. Paul Mebes.

Classicism, Neo-Classicism, Neo-Neo-Classicism

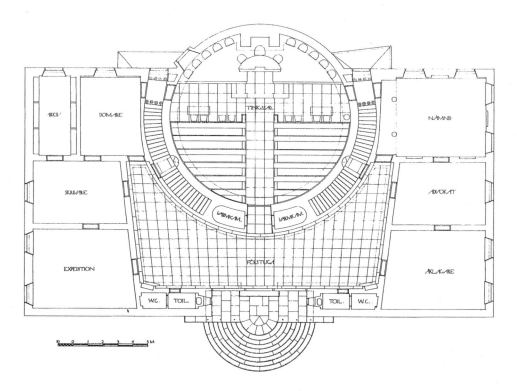

144. Lister County Court, Sølvesborg, 1921. Gunnar Asplund.

Who, but Stirling?

A review of the Sackler Museum at Harvard. Published in Architectural Record, *no. 174 (March 1986).*

"The Arthur M. Sackler Museum—as beautiful on the inside as some observers find it ugly on the out—opens to the public." In an announcement of coming issues *Harvard Magazine* (July–August 1985) reiterated what has now become something of an entrenched evaluation which, at best, proceeds like this. A building by James Stirling is more or less predictable. A breach of the normative, a calculated distribution of local perversities; it is expected to be difficult but good, cerebral but a solution. However, the Sackler is not quite the pyrotechnical display which was to be expected. Instead it is a firework that has failed to explode; and, though the galleries are not without interest, the exterior is certainly no invitation to applause.

The disappointed observer may then proceed to excuse. There was the site, too small; the program, too complex; the budget, too skimpy; and then, of course, there was the client, and it is surely notorious how difficult a client Harvard is apt to be.

On the whole such is the received critical litany which culminates in something approaching a crescendo of dismay as it addresses the Quincy and Cambridge Street exposures of the building. The entrance facade is an overblown attempt at Postmodernism, and then, so the story goes, the two further exposures are distressingly inept and, even more dreadful, they are inexcusably reminiscent of public housing at its lamentable worst.

Against this consensus of judgment, it is often hard to intervene; but, given a building so frequently deplored (in terms not so much vehement as gently bored), it finally becomes a positively refreshing undertaking to point out its virtues. And, therefore, to deal first of all with the "so beautiful" inside.

I shall later argue that the entrance is in the inevitable and the only correct position and I shall now notice that from this inescapable entrance the dispositions of foyer, lecture room, galleries, offices, and service areas—all grouped around the great chasm of the central staircase—follow as a compact, logical, and elegant corollary. All this is ingenious. With its great height the foyer acts as a sort of grandiose, very splendid, internalized portico. The lecture room occupies an accessible but otherwise dead area of the basement floor, and the galleries are the modest neutral containers—four walls, and specific points of entrance, with occasional use of *enfilade*—which one might expect to find in a traditional nineteenth-century museum.

But, after all this, then what of the staircase? Is it to be regarded as a cause or as a result? As a monumental declamation or an opportune convenience? And, if it certainly has an end, an end which recapitulates the main entrance to the building itself, then what is to be said about its beginning?

The implacably protracted staircase, open from the bottom of the building to the top, is a theme which one is tempted to asso-

145. Sackler Museum, Harvard University, Cambridge: view of the entrance. James Stirling.

Who, but Stirling?

ciate with variations of Le Corbusier's Maison Citrohan; and the published axonometric of the Sackler does seem to disclose something of this affiliation, with the staircase as an item approximately clipped on to the volume of the galleries.

However, there is a further species of continuously visible mono-directional stair. It is the type of the Scala Regia, which, after its seventeenth-century appearance at the Vatican, equipped with neo-Classical emendations, was then to enjoy a distinguished early nineteenth-century career. Solemn, simple, processional, this is the type of stair which one finds in the Tuileries during the regime of Napoleon, in Leo von Klenze's Hermitage at St. Petersburg, in von Gartner's Munich Staatsbibliothek, and, probably, in a great many further occurrences, large and small.

Not the type of staircase of Aalto's Baker Dormitory at MIT, which is very much a picturesque annex to the building which it serves, the Scala Regia category is inherently a centralizing and symmetrizing maneuver; and typically it presents a vaulted hall in which one is propelled from an enclosing basement to a columned *piano nobile* where the promise of more expanded movement is then fairly conspicuously advertised.

So might the Sackler staircase also relate to this category? And it is not too far-fetched to suggest that it does. For, just as the neo-Classical Scala Regia, with its basement supporting columns above, presents an internal recall of the outside goings-on, so the stripes of Stirling's stair hall are just as much a recall of the stripy business displayed on Quincy Street.

All the same it is with this notice that we may begin to approach a problem. The neo-Classical Scala Regia is unambiguous. You climb it to reach the *piano nobile* and then you go no further. But, with five office floors of equal value on the one side and three gallery floors on the other, then to what are fantasies of *piano nobile* related? Or, as the entrance facade with its big window up top seems to be announcing, is the *piano nobile* simply the top of the stairs?

Perhaps not a very painful issue this one; but, in any case, it is questions related to the walls of the staircase which now transpose themselves with regard to its section and its plan. In section there is the roof light which is part of the idea of the staircase; but a quarter of the ascent lies outside this coverage, and the passage of the staircase from one lighting condition to another remains without articulation. Possibly a conscious choice of subtly graded lighting? But, in plan, the beginning of the stairs is not so easily to be rationalized; and it is now time to say that, in local episodes towards the bottom of the stairs, one may discover the imperfect resolution of a highly impressive gesture.

Anybody who wishes may interpret the stairs as a steeply inclined and highly animated street; but I myself will continue to suspect that these evocations of the marketplace are the less than appropriate disguises for a lapse in the clarity of identification. Both in plan and in section, the commencement of the stair is without overture, apparently unconsidered, and unhappily *ad hoc*. In fact it is just at the bottom of this staircase, where the building reveals the defects of its virtues, that one feels the interior has been invaded by a particularly impenetrable fog. The staircase is visible; but, all the same, one feels optically deprived.

Apart from noticing that jumbo semi-cylindrical, wooden columns (presented without benefit of any paint) are, probably, not the best frames for openings in a series of exhibition galleries, this is to conclude any negative remarks which will here be made. The bottom of the stairs may be less than adequate but, with this said, it is now a great pleasure to contemplate the building's exterior which, on the whole, has been provocative of so much private grief.

It is, I think, best to be appreciated from some way outside Richardson's Sever Hall, from where its entrance contributes a frontal and enclosing presence, Cyclopean and Mycenaean, which one can only think that Richardson would have enjoyed. Then other points of view are from much closer, perhaps from the immediate sidewalk of Quincy Street where the building's personality is somewhat more abrasive and tactile, something which impends rather than something merely visual.

Who, but Stirling?

But Quincy Street is a thoroughfare of architectural parade and, among Sackler's immediate neighbors, one should observe not only the Fogg Museum and Gund Hall but just across the way what must be surely the most delightful fire station in the world—brick with limestone trim, neo-Georgian, looking a bit as though Robert Adam had condescended to take hints from a late seventeenth-century Dutch town hall. It is evidently in terms of these neighbors (and maybe particularly the last) that decisions about entrance were taken.

To have entered facing the fire station would have been difficult because of the disposition of its pediment; and, in addition, it would have loaded the street with a further gratuitous point of punctuation. To have entered from the Gund Hall side would have been to divorce the new building both from the Fogg and the center of Harvard. And hence the entry from Broadway facing the side of the Fogg was not so much a choice as an obligation. Hence, too, a further justification of the *parti* in terms of its externals rather than its functions: a representational facade, which proclaims public purpose, and a couple of no less visible vertical surfaces which infer a somewhat different destiny. And all of this has added immensely both to the acceleration and the scenery of Quincy Street, where stimulus for the eye now provides excitement for the feet. For, inherently, the Sackler Museum is a major revision of the street. A delightful street but never a distinguished one, a major architectural exhibition without apparent objective, the arrival of the Sackler has provided the articulant which was always needed; and not only has the street gained in terms of more understandable transversals but it has further been augmented in terms of a more developed perspective.

Previously to set out from the Fogg to reach Gund Hall was a psychologically hazardous enterprise. There was Broadway; there was Cambridge Street; and, in between these two intersections, there was the little, early Modern Burr Hall. And, needless to say, in negotiating this territory, Burr Hall gave *no* help whatsoever. On the left there was the fire station, with the firemen always ready

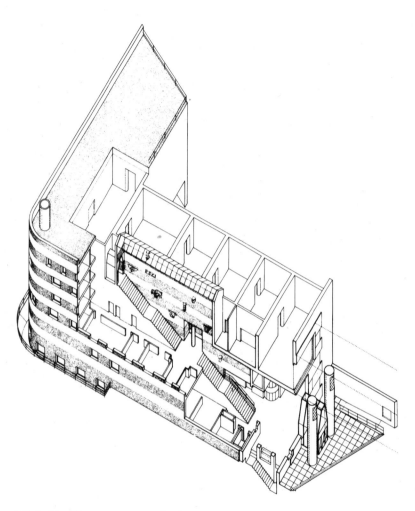

146. Sackler Museum, axonometric view.

Who, but Stirling?

147. Sackler Museum, view of the grand stair.

to look out (from what appeared to be a ballroom) and always ready to pay attention to whatever feminine specimen of interest came into view. But, in spite of the fire station, which acted to block the line of vision, the pedestrian navigation of that single block was invariably a minor torture; Burr Hall was altogether too indented to direct the eye forwards. But now, thanks to the Sackler, the continuity of the street has become surprisingly affirmed. Though Broadway and Cambridge still cut across the line of Quincy, the effect of Stirling's aggressive orthogonal counter statement is greatly to minimize their impact.

Such is the result of graphite gray and butterscotch horizontal stripes; and, since it is—almost certainly—the use of these which is considered inordinate and a little cheap, it would be as well if they were to engage a more concentrated attention. Stirling would have liked his brickwork to display the hard metallic resonance of Sever; but, in terms of production and budget, this was an unobtainable quality. However, though in terms of local precedent his stripes are patently related more to the mid-nineteenth-century polychromy of adjacent Memorial Hall than to Sever, they must also be placed in a completely different line of descent. The two striped elevations, and particularly the rounded corner in which they converge, have the obvious look of a German department store of the 1920s; and, if the graphite gray stripes were windows, anybody might swear that they were looking at such a building by Erich Mendelsohn in Stuttgart, Chemnitz, or wherever. But, since Sackler is much more opaque, it is not at some German Expressionist masterpiece that one happens, at this corner, to be looking. Rather it is at some end product, exported to Holland and there restyled, and then commercialized to become internationally available in the 1930s.

But, however discovered—whether picked up in the streets of Berlin, Amsterdam, London, or New York—these striped elevations represent an exceptionally opportune appropriation; and who, but Stirling would have thought of taking over the school of Mendelsohn at what would seem to be its most debased and unreward-

Who, but Stirling?

148. Proposed bridge between the Sackler and Fogg museums.

ing? Far more versatile than the contemporaneous stripes of his Wissenschaftszentrum in Berlin, the zebra game has been astonishingly productive and, as the most obvious instance, how brilliantly this Expressionist corner has allied itself with the red and the white of Memorial Hall diagonally opposite!

Then this corner, its curve acquiring resilience from the repetition of its stripes, may also serve as a further source of information. Contemplation of the Sackler's plan suggests that the building is predicated upon an argument about spiral motion versus a statement about flatness. The ascending stairs and the top floor gallery comprise one spiral. The wrap-around of office and service accommodation comprise another. The second spiral, the more fragmentary and the more expansive (thanks to the curved corner), supports an inference that the whole organism is located within a curvilinear field of disturbance which is inhibited from completing itself by rectilinear restrictions—most notably by the frontalizing statement of the entrance facade. In other words, one may discern within the plan a commerce between two spatial ideas, rotundity versus flatness, which also carry the connotation of the massive versus the planar; and these may be seen as each informing and transforming the other. Thus the pre-eminent statement of flatness, the entrance facade, becomes invested with implications of depth and penetration which derive from the configuration of what ultimately lies behind it; and thus facade and elevations are interactive. That is: the two elevations united by a curve profess something of the quality of paper, while the building's frontispiece possesses a quality of almost insuperable density. That is: roles and attributes are inverted and, as side and rear are the intended complements of front, so the flat stripes of the one dispensation come, as it were, to be discharged as the heroic rustication of the other.

Though too briefly stated, I believe that this may be a not too fanciful explanation of the very great vitality with which Stirling has endowed this relatively small museum and teaching facility. Not only a versatile solution to an almost incompatible array of problems, not in any trivial sense a shocking building, it is a major and tragic statement of physiognomic intensity; and, as if all this were not enough, its urbanistic performance is exemplary. All in all it is far, far from the indifferent work which ignorance is led to presume. Not quite the Neue Staatsgalerie at Stuttgart; but, for all that, one of the best Stirling realizations to date.

And about the bridge?

Well, surely, the bridge is both conceptual necessity and functional desideratum. But, since things are so much more than satisfactory as they are, since the general scenery is so good, might it not be the better part of wisdom to desist?

Who, but Stirling?

Ideas, Talent, Poetics: A Problem of Manifesto

Written 1987, published in Lotus International, *no. 62 (1989), what follows is for the most part the text written for the annual Walter Gropius Lecture at Harvard in December 1987; and, at the insistence of Franco Purini, repeated with variations at the University of Rome, La Sapienza, May 4, 1988. At Harvard, as I thought, the lecture had been given with great success—to an audience, I was told, of approximately six hundred people, many of them sitting on the floor. But, all the same (in spite of acclamation), I believe that I had committed a tactical error: in the Walter Gropius Lecture I had been less than enthusiastic about Walter Gropius. I had addressed an audience in Cambridge, Massachusetts, as though I were addressing an audience in New Haven, Connecticut, while the cultural/architectural climate and politics could not be more dissimilar.*

So, inadvertently, I must have caused anguish, distress, and irritation to some persons; and it is to them that I would attribute the failure of the Graduate School of Design (contrary to what I understand to be its practice) to publish this text and these illustrations.

So what was the outcome of the performance in Rome?

Primarily a request from the editors of Lotus International *to be able to publish this little piece.*

So I tried to explain. This piece was not at all Lotus *(far too much concrete evidence and far too many pics, it just did not respond to the traditions of Italian rhetoric). But all this to no avail. My friend Pierluigi Nicolin was, in the usual Italian way, charming and persuasive; and, needless to say, I succumbed to his pleadings. But all the same the results turned out bad. Did they have with them a tape by Purini? Or was it a case of* traduttore-traditore? *I suspect a translation from English into Italian and a translation back again. But what matter? For if, for its own editorial purposes,* Lotus *had reduced this text by about three thousand words, it has proved comparatively easy to reassemble it.*

It was Mies van der Rohe, in his Chicago days, who made the famous proposition that you can't have a revolution every Monday morning; and, of course, this is a statement extremely endearing to cultural conservatives.

All the same, whatever may be the charms and the heroics of revolution, whatever the generosity of sentiment which may provoke the upsurgence of oppressed peoples and oppressed ideas, whatever the sudden acuity of vision which may derive from revolutionary excitement, it must be obvious that the idea of a 'permanent revolution' (revolution every week or every day) is an intellectual chimera.

For revolution to be truly revolution it can never be institutionalized. There can be no easy repetition. To be able to shatter the conventions of privilege, the condition of ruling elites and ruling ideas, can *never* be the prerogative of *every* generation of humanity. For revolutionary change to become effective there must *always* be

intervals of stasis and digestion. In spite of Marinetti, movement—without intervals of stasis—ceases to be recognizable as movement. Common sense and the evidence of history may suggest at least this much; but the temperament of what used to be called "the Modern movement in architecture" has remained curiously impervious to any argument
so obvious.

What used to be called "the Modern movement" has, typically, conceived of itself as a continuous opposition; and it does so even now—now when there is nothing left to be opposed to but itself. Derived as it is from positivist notions as to the nature of scientific method and Hegelian propositions as to the behavior of the *Zeitgeist,* for all the incompatibility of its components, one may understand how this attitude survives. It survives because of the intellectual laziness (and, ironically, the conservatism) of those who subscribe to its *parti pris.* With its accessory (and equally antique) fantasy as to the obligatory *avant-garde* role of the architect, this body of ideas is the psychological equivalent of a lavish insurance policy. By citing this body of ideas all failures may be extenuated. They will become either the simple products of 'science' or the inevitable results of 'the spirit of the age'.

For these reasons one should only be skeptical of those many 'revolutionary' manifestoes which seem to be concerned, not so much with the fate of culture and society, as with the self-dramatization of their authors. And, while one may—sometimes—acclaim the validity of 'revolution', one must also insist upon the simple existence of its categorical opposite: the survival or the activity of 'tradition'.

Now 'tradition' is not apt to be a very profoundly intellectual value. Unlike 'revolution', it has little to do with ideas as such. Its recourse is to precedent and prescription. But nowadays, when so much criticism, so much teaching, so much production is painfully, and pretentiously, intellectualized (let us, at all costs, be arcane), maybe there might remain at least something to be said on behalf of 'tradition'.

Ideas, Talent, Poetics

From long ago it was the contention of T. S. Eliot that 'tradition', subjected to the evaluations of an alert sensibility, has always provided something like the essential manure of talent. But, meanwhile, to put the question: Are we in search of an architecture of 'revolution' and 'ideas'? Or are we in search of an architecture of 'tradition' and 'talent'? Since these propositions are interdependent, myself would hope both; but, all the same, I can only believe this to be a counsel of perfection. For, as far as I can perceive, we are at present in the grip of equally cheap 'revolutionary' and 'conservative' cultures; and, considering the cheapness of both, they may each be considered to be unduly aggressive.

However, not to continue in this way; and, simply, to assert one's bias.

In the stress of 'revolution', when 'intellect' becomes extravagantly prominent, simply the voice and the constituency of 'talent' is likely to be swept away. Just as 'craftsmanship' is hardly likely to be a topic of 'revolutionary' chatter, so 'talent' (a kind of stepbrother to 'craftsmanship') is prone to be regarded as slick, insincere, *ancien régime,* and meretricious.

Hence, it is for these reasons that I wish to address what follows to the predicament of 'talent' in a milieu where, currently, prevails a crude overestimation of 'ideas'.

It is a fashionable milieu. It is, almost desperately, chic. It is familiar with the most prestigious, contemporary, critical references—from Frankfurt, Venice, and Paris. And within it I find a great many of my friends.

However, to me, its most gross limitation seems to be that pernicious assumption of a manifesto culture at the present day: *the notion that 'ideas', without any mediation of 'talent' and 'craftsmanship', will automatically result in 'poetics'.*

Some years ago my friend Jacquelin Robertson told me that, shortly, he and his wife were going to Sestriere to ski, and I suppose that I must have said to him something like this, "Dear Jack, if you are going to Sestriere then, absolutely, you must go to Torino. It's

one of the most distinguished cities in the world; and people just
don't go and look at it as they should." So Jacquelin went to Torino,
looked, and when he came back to New York he said to me, "A fab-
ulous city; but you know what the trouble there is? There were two
architects: the first had incredibly good ideas but not equally conspicuous talent; and, while the second had extraordinary talent, he
was almost destitute of any ideas of very great quality."

Now, as regards architecture, this distinction between talent and ideas, I had never heard of before (nor have I heard of it
since); but, apparently, Jacquelin's judgement of Turin concurred
with my own; and, therefore, almost automatically, I said to him:
"I assume you mean Guarini and Juvarra."

Well, of course, this is exactly what he *did* mean; and, therefore, from Jacquelin Robertson derives the pretext for most of the remarks which follow, observations in which I wish to contrast the
attributes of talent and the attributes of ideation.

No doubt about it that Juvarra's Superga is a dazzling, brilliant building (fig. 149). It stands up there on its hill; it insists on
approach; but, when you get there (so far as I am concerned), there
is always a disappointment. The theatrics don't quite add up; and,
as a result one is immensely happy to return downtown to San Lorenzo (fig. 150), which seems so much more to reward a protracted
contemplation. A cruciform church which is, simultaneously, an oc-
tagon; an impacted condition of convexities and concavities, of rectilinear, curvilinear, and diagonal directions, the plan, alone, exhibits
the complexities of Guarini's thought; while fish-eye views of the
dome of Superga and San Lorenzo only serve to reiterate these observations (figs. 151, 152). In its display of light and gold, the dome of
the Superga is scintillating; but it still fails to absorb attention.
While the dome of San Lorenzo presents, I think, an image which
ultimately, indelibly, penetrates the mind.

The one is a shell with ribs upon it. The other is a ribbed
cage which acts as a summation of all the activity beneath it.

So this is one version, as seen by Jacquelin Robertson and
myself, of the issue of talent versus ideas.

Ideas, Talent, Poetics

149. Basilica of Superga, Turin. Filippo Juvarra.

150. San Lorenzo, Turin. Guarino Guarini.

Ideas, Talent, Poetics

151. Superga, fish-eye view of the dome.

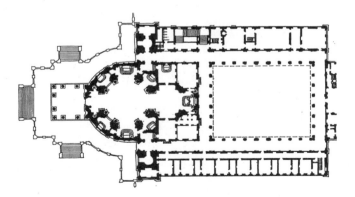

152. San Lorenzo, fish-eye view of the dome.

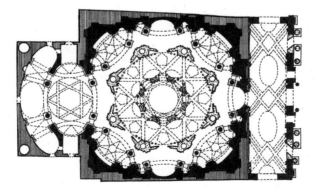

Ideas, Talent, Poetics

But meanwhile I remember saying to Jack: "But what about Vittone? Though a provincial—more or less—did he not superbly mediate between the closed and intricate dialectics of Guarini and the more expanded, extravert imagination of Juvarra?" However, at that time the phone rang, we went out to dinner, and the conversation was never resumed.

All the same one might follow its lead; and for some time we might play an architectural/intellectual parlor game, a game which will be very dependent upon intuition, a game which—since it is without rules—can never be preceeded by aprioristic definition of either talent or ideas. It is a game which requires a certain amount of knowledge (though not too much); and immediate access to a library (though not too large). It's a game in which the players may, occasionally, become hyper-excited, though—usually—judgement is surprisingly unanimous. And it is a game which, also, may permit reference to a further essay in not so casual discrimination: Sir Isaiah Berlin's *The Hedgehog and the Fox,* 1957.

Isaiah Berlin's topic is Russian literature of the nineteenth century; and, about what might be thought to be his own too simplistic procedure, he elaborates reservations:

> Of course, like all over-simple classifications of this type, the obvious dichotomy becomes, if pressed, artificial, scholastic, and ultimately absurd. But, if it is not an aid to serious criticism, neither should it be rejected as being merely superficial or frivolous; like all distinctions which embody any degree of truth, it offers a point of view from which to look and compare; a starting point for genuine investigation.[1]

This particular starting point (the fox knows many things, the hedgehog knows one big thing) allowed Isaiah Berlin to reach the conclusion that, although Pushkin, Gogol, and Turgenev were foxes, and Dostoevsky was certainly a hedgehog, then Tolstoy was a fox who chose to disguise himself as a hedgehog—a complication which might suggest that the ultimate discrimination between talent and ideas will not be easy.

However, as all the world knows, the really great artistic personality—Mozart, Michelangelo, Shakespeare—will always possess both ideas and talent in almost perfect equilibrium; but, meanwhile, there exist the possibilities of masquerade and disguise. However, if these may be an amusing dimension to the crude opposition of talent and ideas, it will be much better to pursue the game and to allow it to take us where it leads us; and Henri Labrouste and Charles Garnier might now substitute for Guarini and Juvarra.

Almost without the need for words the Bibliothèque Sainte-Geneviève and the Opéra make the point (figs. 153, 154). Crudely expressed, Garnier is a case of the dominance of talent and Labrouste a case of the dominance of ideas. Not that Garnier was without ideas; the plan and section of the Opéra disclose these, the rear composition much more so. Not that Labrouste was deficient in talent. His impeccable contours indicate otherwise. Notwithstanding, one must argue for a preponderance of ideation in Labrouste, a preponderance of talent in Garnier. At the Opéra all is sensuousness: at the library all is cerebration. In Isaiah Berlin's terms Garnier is a fox—he combines Sansovino, Michelangelo, and Perrault's east front of the Louvre; and Labrouste is a hedgehog—for the motif of his facade he is content simply with Alberti's side elevations of San Francesco at Rimini with, maybe, just a trace of Michelozzi's Banco Mediceo in Milan. Profusion and austerity; but, for the purpose of the game, Labrouste and Garnier are the perfect opposites.

Then, from London, shortly after 1700, there might now be introduced James Gibbs and Nicholas Hawksmoor; and, of course, Gibbs is very much the type of Juvarra. Educated in the studio of Carlo Fontana (as was Juvarra), Gibbs is another case of the ability to say everything but of nothing much to say. Genial, garrulous, his great talent invented one of the major paradigms of history. St. Martin-in-the-Fields (fig. 155) is the WASP (white, Anglo-Saxon Protestant) alternative to the Gesù; and, when, a year or so ago, I was last in Dallas, Texas, I saw at least five of these

153. Opéra, Paris. Charles Garnier.

154. Bibliothèque Sainte-Geneviève, Paris, facade. Henri Labrouste.

Ideas, Talent, Poetics

churches still being built. For Protestants in the United States, Gibbs exerts an irresistible fascination. Everything which might be required, Gibbs expounds. But then there is Hawksmoor, with his infinitely profound Christ Church, Spitalfields (fig. 156)—a difficult, reserved, poignant, serious, and tragic building—and Hawksmoor's far more ideated church has been entirely without influence or issue. (Like the Bibliothèque Sainte-Geneviève it is not in a highly visited part of town.)

However, with talent and ideas conceived as simple opposites, particularly in the case of Hawksmoor, I know that I am operating in terms of an extremely crude argument. Amusing though it may be for this purpose of an intellectual parlor game, the confrontation of talent and ideas will scarcely serve the purposes of a general architectural critique; and, therefore, to a simple dialectic I feel obliged to add the further dimension of poetry, not independent of either, but also serving as an irradiation of both. It is, perhaps, a special invasion, visitation, annunciation of grace—in the theological sense; and so, might one suggest that the poetics of Gibbs are approximate to Alexander Pope (and very nice, too) but that the poetics of Hawksmoor are an equivalent to the musical meditations of Georg Friedrich Handel in his *Messiah*.

But now to enter the early nineteenth century world of John Nash and John Soane, and the examples are Cumberland Terrace, Regent's Park, and the Privy Council Chamber, Whitehall (figs. 157, 158). So what do these represent?

Nash, I think, a highly flamboyant talent and mostly the talent of a histrionic land speculator. And Soane? Was he talent disguised as ideas—as a friend of mine suggests? Or was he ideas, equipped with conspicuous talent, as myself believes?

And then there is the question of Soane's poetics which, in a neo-Classical way, are apt to be slightly lugubrious, slightly subterranean. Completely devastated by all his vaulting, his disengagements, his slits and slots as I am, as I contemplate Soane, I often receive the idea that I am already dead, that, though still observing life, I am looking at it, Egyptian style, from a very luxuriously equipped mausoleum. The poetics are sombre and provocative.

And now, as the parlor game leaves England behind, what about Bernini and Borromini—Sant'Andrea al Quirinale and San Carlino (figs. 159, 160)—less than three hundred yards apart, almost contemporary in time?

Is it that Bernini shows a preponderance of talent, and Borromini a profundity of ideas? Very difficult this; but nevertheless, I suppose something like this answer to be approximately the case. Bernini superb in his scenic displays, like Piazza San Pietro and Scala Regia; but Bernini less than superb (in fact, slightly banal) in his churches at Castelgandolfo and Ariccia, though *not* at the Quirinale.

To me the Borromini-Bernini confrontation in Rome is a little like a rehearsal for Guarini and Juvarra in Turin—a confrontation less intense but still of the same order. Like the Superga, the whole structure of Bernini's dome is uncomplicated and almost neo-Classical; but, as with Guarini, Borromini's dome is something else. Apart from the perspective intimations of its coffering, it is both a contradiction and a summation of the plan which lies below it. Bernini's dome is a logical product of the plan; but Borromini's dome enters into a stimulating argument with the plan from which it derives. Bernini advertises a rationalized structure in a more or less neutral space; but Borromini cannot be satisfied with so literal a solution. Borromini presents a plan in which the walls are pressured by (and, in turn, pressure) the animation and the activities of the dome. Two, famously, different strategies, and do these exhibit, with Borromini, the energy of an architecture of ideas and with Bernini, in this case, no more than the diffusion of a supremely educated talent? Perhaps they may. However, another Roman confrontation might establish a different estimation of talent and ideas.

On opposite sides of Via di Banco Santo Spirito are the Palazzo Alberini (Cicciaporci-Segni) and the Palazzo Niccolini; and neither of them photograph well. Originally attributed to Bramante (Lafréry), then to Raphael, then to Giulio Romano, the architect of

155. St. Martin-in-the-Fields, London. James Gibbs.

156. Christ Church, Spitalfields, London. Nicholas Hawksmoor.

Ideas, Talent, Poetics

157. Cumberland Terrace, Regent's Park, London. John Nash.

158. Privy Council Chamber, Whitehall, London. John Soane.

Ideas, Talent, Poetics

159. Sant'Andrea al Quirinale, Rome, section. Gian Lorenzo Bernini.

160. San Carlo alle Quattro Fontane, Rome, section. Francesco Borromini.

Ideas, Talent, Poetics

the Palazzo Alberini now occupies the limbo of doubt. However, something of a consensus still permits Palazzo Niccolini (sometimes called Palazzo Gaddi) to be attributed to Jacopo Sansovino. And what to say about these two? The architect of the Palazzo Alberini was, evidently, an intellectual and he must have been close to Giulio. Palazzo Alberini is a primitive, but sophisticated, exhibition of themes which, very soon, were to lead to Palazzo Maccarani. But, then, there is the problem of Jacopo Sansovino. Extravagant accomplishment, luscious capacity for detail, fundamental absence of *mind,* one might say all this about Jacopo Sansovino; and certainly, by the standards of his contemporaries—Perruzi, Serlio, Giulio, Sanmichele—Sansovino really did have little to say.

Nevertheless, in Venice, in the Marciana, there exists one of the very important buildings of the cinquecento; and it is a business of talent all the way. Sansovino was *not* an 'intellectual' architect; and, in his *Outline History of European Architecture,* Nikolaus Pevsner doesn't even list him in the appendix. Too difficult, perhaps, too destructive of certain historical generalizations certainly. But, as we stand in Via di Banco Santo Spirito, and look from side to side, with Palazzo Alberini and Palazzo Niccolini, what are we to say? Palazzo Alberini is 'interesting'; but the far more reserved Palazzo Niccolini just happens to be extremely 'good'? Something like this, I think, one is compelled to say; and now, to produce a further opposition.

Villa Farnese at Caprarola and Villa Foscari/Malcontenta (figs. 161, 162) will further assist the argument. For there can be no doubt about Vignola and Palladio. Vignola is a supreme illustration of talent. He has brilliant ideas but is independent of their control. He is astringent, cerebral, intellectualistic. All he does is intelligent; all he does assists local complication, tight structure, and wit. He is the servant of specificity while, by contrast, Palladio is the agent of generality, the proponent of an elementary basic theme. To use, once more, Isaiah Berlin's distinction: if Vignola is a fox then, evidently, Palladio is a hedgehog.

161. Villa Farnese, Caprarola. Jacopo da Vignola.

Ideas, Talent, Poetics

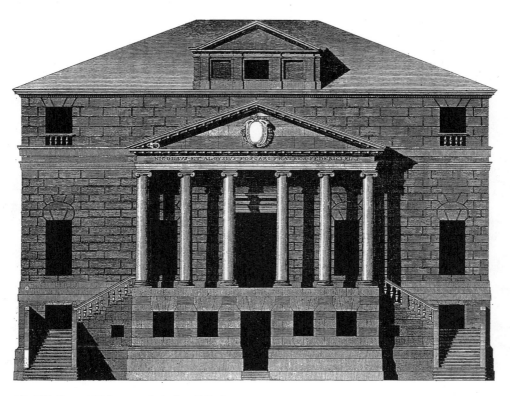

162. Villa Foscari (Malcontenta). Andrea Palladio.

Naturally, taken separately, a wholly different interpretation may be placed on both Caprarola and Villa Malcontenta; but, taken in conjunction, this is surely a plausible inference. Palladio is a case of the 'discovery' of idea; Vignola is a case of the 'invention' of concept; and the opposition between 'discovery' and 'invention' is somewhat crucial for the further consideration of talent and ideas. It seems to imply that ideas are latent, pre-existing, immanent, eternal, and impersonal; while, by comparison, talent is apt to become 'mere' talent, a matter of gratuitous display. This is a prevalent but highly unjust evaluation; but, hence, the persuasiveness of Palladio. To the cosmologically minded his poetry evokes 'the music of the spheres' and it is a quite different admiration which we award to Vignola. If Palladio is an architectural Plato, Vignola is an Aristotle; if Palladio's specialty is poetics, Vignola's specialty is dialectics.

Two late nineteenth century houses of approximately the same date, by two contemporaries, will help to bring us down to a more mundane level of speculation.

Norman Shaw's 180 Queens Gate, London, was built in 1890 (fig. 163); Richardson's Warder House, 16th Street, Washington, D.C. (fig. 164) was finished in 1887; and, in many ways, they are very alike.

In an English context, Shaw's performance will appear to be highly abstracted; but, as one continues to look at it, attention to local detail might come to appear excessive, perhaps something of an aberration. While at the same time, the abstracted look of the Richardson house may come to appear more entirely consistent.

Reference, at the Warder house, is to the density and idealized flatness of vertical surface and to the consequent sharp cutting of window reveals. Reference is, also, to the highly provocative manner in which flatness turns itself into roundness—the low wall as it curves to support the entry to the carriage house and stables and the staircase turret which lies behind, two episodes which ambiguously collaborate to modify any simplistic insistence upon planarity.

Ideas, Talent, Poetics

163. 180 Queen's Gate, London, 1885. Norman Shaw.

CORNELLIANA

164. Warder House, 16th Street, Washington, D.C., 1886. H. H. Richardson.

Ideas, Talent, Poetics

Norman Shaw is, possibly, a specimen of careless talent (a little of the order of John Nash?); but Richardson is surely a case of splendid talent operating upon important ideas.

And what to say about Olbrich's Secession Building of 1897 (fig. 165) and Wright's Unity Temple of 1906 (fig. 166)? They came up during the course of this game and, frankly, I hadn't expected them. Olbrich evidently talent? I think this must be correct. And Wright? A combination of talent and ideas though of not quite so felicitous a combination as that displayed by Richardson? In my reading this must be the case. Viennese *patisserie* versus Chicago bluntness?

So the parlor game (like playing solitaire with slides), if undoubtedly frivolous, may, just possibly, have revealed something; and, obviously, it is capable of extension into other areas than architecture. For instance, in talking about music, Stravinsky also used the opposition of talent and ideas. Berlioz had talent and composed quickly; Beethoven had ideas and composed with great labor; Moussorgsky, Rimsky-Korsakov, Rachmaninoff, Tchaikovsky had talent; and the presumable implication is that Stravinsky had *both* talent and ideas.

But, briefly to continue the game with one or two pictorial images. Canaletto's *St. Paul's* is dated 1750 and the title page from Piranesi's *Antichità Romane* was published in 1756 (figs. 167, 168); but I can only suppose that the opposition between talent and ideas still holds. However, all the same, with Piranesi, it may be noticeable that ideas are being pressed into another service. They are tending to become strident, to become propaganda, to operate as overt manifesto; and this could provoke the notice that the Abbé Laugier's first essay had been published just three years earlier. No influence upon Piranesi, but surely a sign of that new neo-Classical temper of opinion that was about to subvert Piranesi's Roman monopoly?

Now, this must surely be enough for the parlor game; but its breathless trivialities apart, it may have served to advertise the

165. Secession Building, Vienna, 1897. Josef Maria Olbrich.

166. Unity Temple, Oak Park, 1906. Frank Lloyd Wright.

Ideas, Talent, Poetics

167. Giovanni Antonio Canaletto, *St. Paul's,* 1750.

168. Giambattista Piranesi, title page of *Antichità Romane,* 1756.

Ideas, Talent, Poetics

very obvious; *that neither the presence of talent nor the presence of ideas is a necessary guarantee of quality.*

For the overt presence of abstruse ideation, which is so deadly an aspect of the present day, need not result in that arcane and intellectual production which seems so often to be anticipated.

Indeed, the present, and laborious, parade of 'ideas' can only serve further to compromise the already painfully compromised condition of 'important' building.

Moreover, if the 'ideas' projected are, very frequently, little more than the fantasies of cultural primitives, then one should be compelled to recognize that, quite often, 'talent' is a vivacious employment of knowledge and education.

As an opening to further discussion, now to produce a comparison between Erich Mendelsohn and Walter Gropius, between the Bauhaus and the Schocken Store at Chemnitz (more recently called Karl Marx Stadt) (figs. 169, 170); and, of the two buildings I can only think that Mendelsohn's exhibits the most irrefutable evidence of talent and accomplishment.

Mendelsohn has never had a very good press (perhaps because of the Einstein Tower?) and it is to be doubted whether he was ever the recipient of superbly significant 'ideas'. But then, can the Bauhaus building seriously be envisaged as a very clear case of the priority of 'ideas'? And in all conscience I cannot see it as being so. Surely whatever ideas it may display were ruthlessly appropriated from Constructivism and De Stijl. While, as for the presence of 'talent', when compared with the suave and mindless Mendelsohn, with Gropius at the Bauhaus the slightest trace of 'talent' is extremely difficult to discover.

However, very much highly respectable judgement has continued to salute the Bauhaus—both as an institution and as a building. "Apollo in a Democracy" was one, English, specification of Walter Gropius; and his crucial attributes were the continuous critical theme of such eminent observers as Sigfried Giedion and Nikolaus Pevsner. But, apart from a pedagogical program which, now

169. Bauhaus, Dessau. Walter Gropius.

Ideas, Talent, Poetics

170. Schocken Department Store, Chemnitz. Erich Mendelsohn.

more than sixty years later, might be considered highly dubious, just what was it which so much excited those observers?

And the answer can only be very simple. They believed themselves to be in the presence of both an instrument and an emblem of cultural therapy. Persons like Giedion and Pevsner (who would have repudiated any opposition between 'ideas' and 'talent') were almost certainly convinced of a myth, derived from Oswald Spengler, as to the decline of 'the West'. 'The West', which did not seem to include Russia, was obliged (by Hegelian laws?) to decline. Like at no time in previous history, 'the West' was self-alienated, self-divided, diseased; it suffered from 'a schism between feeling and thinking' and, as a result, society was atomized. But meanwhile, first at Weimar and then at Dessau, a cultural reintegration had been made possible. The message had been delivered; and, as a consequence, it was up to the world to take heed.

In a completely cursory way, one may, thus, summarize the mystique of the Bauhaus. Both a proclamation and a building, it was to be interpreted as an incitement to a new 'spirit' and a new way of 'life'. Here was to be seen the twentieth century *Zeitgeist* in full working order.

But was Gropius so completely dependent for his ideas upon De Stijl? His detractors usually suggest so. However, comparing the Bauhaus with the van Doesburg and the van Eesteren axonometrics of 1922, I don't think that these allegations can be regarded as completely proved. Van Doesburg operated with his own private version of what he assumed Mondrian to be about; and he was so agile in his polemics that he caused this view to prevail; but it was surely Rietveld rather than Gropius who made the direct annexation of van Doesburg's strategies. The Schroeder House (fig. 171) is a highly provocative and beguiling little building. But can a manifesto be so literally converted into built form as here seems to be assumed? My ongoing argument will be that this can scarcely be the case; but, meanwhile, to introduce a parenthesis.

Giuseppe Terragni's Casa Giuliano-Frigerio (fig. 172) may rewardingly be brought into conjunction with the Schroeder House; and here, perhaps, one observes more a case of 'talent' than a preponderance of 'ideas'. But *what* a talent! In his slitting and slotting, his cuts and dissections, in the ideal flatness of his vertical surface, in his general virtuosity, at Casa Giuliano-Frigerio, Terragni surely comes closer to Mondrian than either van Doesburg or Rietveld. And is this a case of a Latin sensibility far more capable of responding to Mondrian than any of his compatriots?

The question of course is rhetorical, because press on we must; and, now, to pay the briefest attention to Luigi Moretti's Casa del Girasole of 1950 (fig. 173).

A highly polemical building? Without the interesting complexities of Terragni? Is this a case of 'ideas'? Or is it a case of 'talent' masquerading as 'ideas'?

So, end of parenthesis and to resume the argument.

Ideas, Talent, Poetics

171. Schroeder House, Utrecht. Gerrit Rietveld.

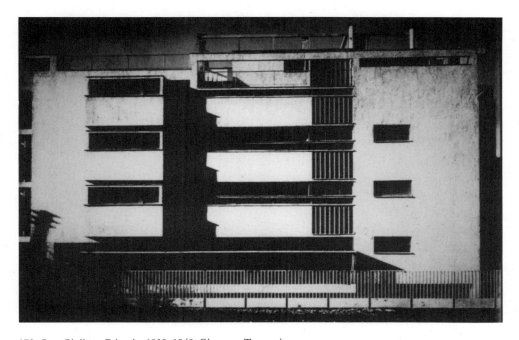

172. Casa Giuliano-Frigerio, 1939–1940. Giuseppe Terragni.

Ideas, Talent, Poetics

173. Casa del Girasole, Parioli, 1950. Luigi Moretti.

The Abbé Laugier's primitive hut of 1753 is the most celebrated and influential of eighteenth century manifestoes; but, while
the genius of architecture points through a tetrastyle of trees towards some imagined future condition, this was not, immediately,
envisaged as any one-to-one transcription of Laugier's image. At
Sainte-Geneviève Soufflot built a highly pedantic church, but this
was by no means the caricature of a bookplate.

No, it was left to the twentieth century to make this attempt; but it must still be noticed that such an attempt was never
made by Le Corbusier. I suggest that apart from its manifesto content, Maison Domino is the most prominent architectural idea
which Le Corbusier put into general circulation. I do not suggest
that an *architectural* idea can be devoid of political overtones, but I
do suggest that it may be distinguished from a political statement,
such as Corbu's Ville Contemporaine of 1922 (fig. 174)—a direct
descendant, one would think, of Maison Domino—but a statement
more about society than about building. And political statements
may become even more seductive when they are disguised as lyrical
poetry (fig. 175). But an important point about Maison Domino is
that Le Corbusier *never* built it; no doubt he found it to be a *conceptual* necessity but perhaps a little too meager for any purposes of protracted contemplation.

And so, as illustrated by *the five points of a new architecture,*
Maison Domino becomes infiltrated by alternative material, most
notably by the diagram related to the free plan. Then, if the Villa
Savoye may be considered a dependent of the Maison Domino, the
original statement becomes further enriched by local differentiation, so that it acquires a beginning, a middle, and an end. Then, in
Villa Savoye's plan, the Maison Domino's ideal distribution of columns is emphatically violated—for purposes of entrance and for the
parking of cars in the garage. Then the ramps constitute another vio-
lation, this time of section. Then there is the, wholly to be unexpected, decoration of the roof. And then, the introduction of wholly
extraneous poetic episodes as in the entrance hall.

Ideas, Talent, Poetics

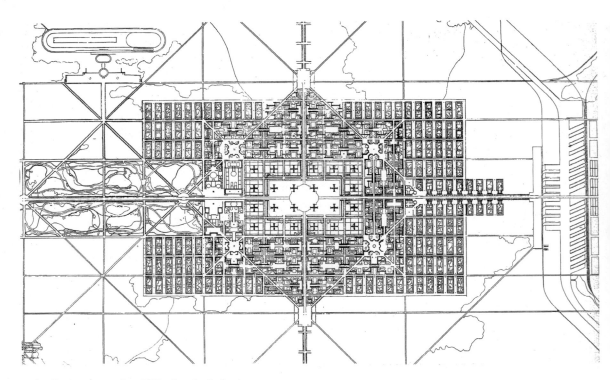

174. Ville Contemporaine, 1922, plan. Le Corbusier.

175. Ville Contemporaine, view.

Ideas, Talent, Poetics

Now, apparently because Le Corbusier proposed to build a rather bad hospital in Venice, the rather sordid quarter of Cannaregio (in which it was to be located) became invested with all the qualities of a sacred site; and a little flurry of manifesto pieces ensued. For the most part, these are quite beyond rational criticism but there are two which still deserve our attention.

John Hejduk's beautiful drawing for *Twelve Towers of the Cannaregio* (fig. 176) is something like a story from Italo Calvino or Jorge Luis Borges. There are to be twelve old men who are to finish their lives in these twelve towers (most recently, in the Triennale of 1987, twelve comparable hospital towers have been proposed for Milan); and one may understand the slightly morbid charm of Hejduk's distinctly 'Gothick' entertainment.

But with his own particular fantasy, Peter Eisenman is very much more esoteric. Eisenman's Cannaregio project was published in *Domus,* November 1980 (fig. 177); and to begin with, the words of Alessandro Mendini deserve to be recorded. Mendini does a paraphrase of Eisenman; and, as his editorial continues, he produces the following bizarre language which he attributes to Eisenman:

> It is not my job to build more or less expressive architecture; I don't try to construct buildings more or less suited to man; I am not interested in belonging to any trend of architectural history as "normal" architects are, who work for "normal" men, all hot-blooded people. I am that unique scientist/architect who, in icy solitude, will attain to the most atemporal and profound essence of the ontological knowledge of the architecture of all time.[2]

But, as though this were not bad enough, the text continues, about Cannaregio, and, for wholly inexplicable reasons (it is now Eisenman's) it suddenly focuses upon Giordano Bruno:

> Giordano Bruno was an alchemist. He practiced the art of memory. He was brought to Venice in 1600 at the request

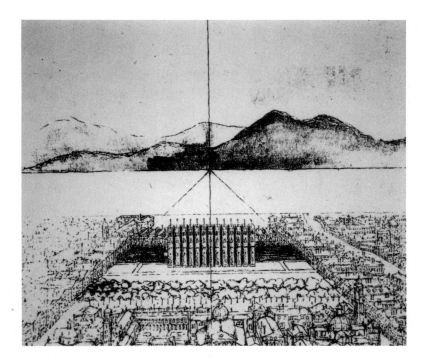

176. John Hejduk, *Twelve Towers of the Cannaregio.*

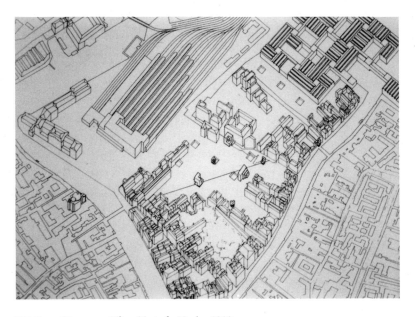

177. Peter Eisenman, *Three Texts for Venice,* 1980.

of a rich nobleman and it was there that he was incarcerated and eventually burned at the stake for practicing his art. The model of Cannaregio is painted gold. It is the gold of Venice and it symbolizes the mysticism of the alchemist. The objects are a pink-red. This is a Venetian red and it symbolizes the martyrdom of Bruno. The colors remind us of the irrationality of a Venice in 1600 turned against the art of memory. Now, in 1980 seemingly rational projects for Venice have embraced memory. All three memories—future, present, past—have their shadows, the loss of memory. Perhaps we must now learn how to forget.[3]

How poetical all this! But *why* didn't somebody tell him—why did not Mendini tell Eisenman the simple facts as related to Giordano Bruno, 1548–1600? Coming, rather unwisely for his opinions, from Zurich to Venice at the invitation of Giovanni Mocenigo, almost immediately he was sent by the Inquisition to Rome, where after seven years, February 17, 1600, he was burned at the stake in Campo dei Fiori—as a Lutheran heretic and not for the practice of alchemy. But the monument to Bruno—there it stands. Very visible, and not very agreeable, it presides over Campo dei Fiori; and anyone who chooses to read the inscription will know that it was made public on June 9, 1889 to the happiness of the liberals and to the scandal of the Vatican.

A pedantic aside no doubt; but important all the same. For, Eisenman apart, it may serve to illustrate the extremely tenuous connections between 'architecture' and some of the manifesto/demonstrations which are made on its behalf. A parade of false naïveté and an uncalled for advertisement of cerebrality, neither of these projects approach Cannaregio as an intrinsic part of Venice; and, if both of them make the pretense of intellectual anguish, then, possibly, they may both be interpreted as attempts to rape poetry without going through the labor of encouraging talent to make love to reason.

After these specimens, which incline to the high, polemical style of *architettura razionale,* it may calm the nerves once more to take a look at Mies van der Rohe's Berlin Exhibition House of 1929 (fig. 178). A grid of columns, very elegantly interpenetrated by an apparatus of sliding planes, an outcome of Maison Domino and related diagrams, this is what Robert Venturi almost certainly would call 'a gentle manifesto', and one must be grateful for its absence of stridency. It exhibits one of Mies's *two* basic ideas; and now to look at the second, the Fifty-Foot Cube House of 1950–51 (fig. 179). As Mies's own primitive hut, this was, presumably, something of a belated response to Maison Domino. A much more aggressive manifesto than the Berlin Exhibition House, it was proposed with an unswerving and total devotion to its inherent idea. Nevertheless, the Fifty-Foot Cube House may permit a few observations on the problems of literal, strict manifesto building as it is today:

(1)   a site is invariably presumed which is platonically flat and completely unequipped with 'accident';

(2)   complications of program are assumed to be without significance;

(3)   the building is typically projected as a solid which, except for landscape, will permit no discourse with anything outside itself;

(4)   urbanistically, the manifesto building can only be adversary to spatial considerations.

All the same, Louis Kahn's manifesto building of 1955, the Jewish Community Center's Bath House at Trenton, is worth thinking about (fig. 180). A platonically ideal site, and an almost platonically ideal plan (almost it might be a church of the late quattrocento), it is the first, *but absolutely the first,* contradiction of Corbu's Maison Domino, and, from the moment that it was available to look at, did it not exhibit a density, a thickness, a crudeness, a lack of elegance, which deserves more exploitation than it has received?

And Leon Krier evidently found it a gift. With its pyramidal roof forms and over-scaled piers (fig. 181), in the "Roma Interrotta" exhibition of 1978, he introduced the Trenton Bath House as a major critique of the Campidoglio (fig. 182).

Ideas, Talent, Poetics

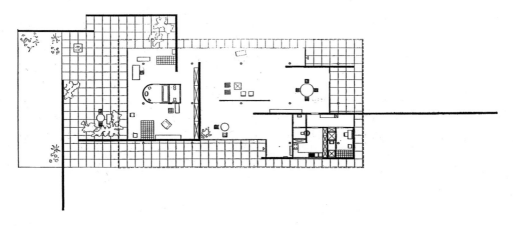

178. Berlin Exhibition House, 1929. Mies van der Rohe.

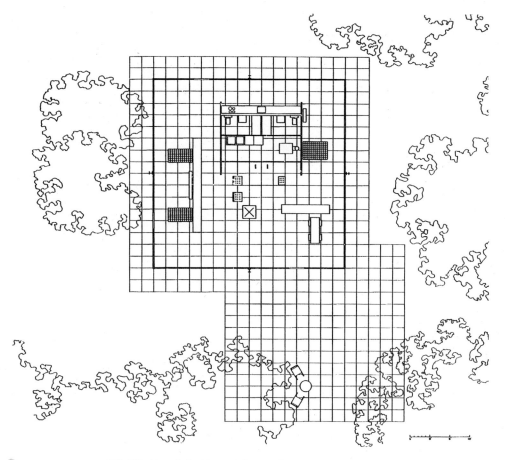

179. Fifty-Foot Cube House. Mies van der Rohe.

Ideas, Talent, Poetics

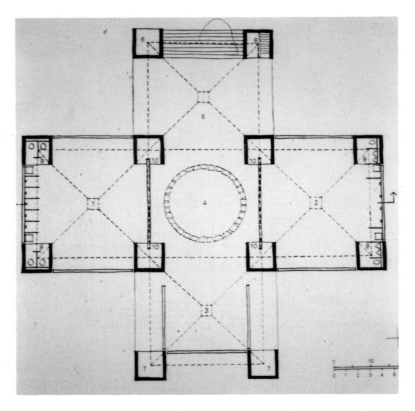

180. Jewish Community Center, Trenton, Bath House, 1965, plan. Louis Kahn.

181. Trenton Bath House, view.

182. Leon Krier, contribution to *Roma Interrotta*, 1978.

But Kahn was always more circumspect; and the motif of the Trenton Bath House he employed with very much more reservation. The project for the Devore and Adler Houses of 1954 (figs. 183, 184), which may be considered a variant of Trenton, is surely an intrinsic novelty (even though different opinion may consider it a staccato revision of Wright's Martin House at Buffalo), and it represents important strategies which still remain to be pursued.

There now follow two Italian pieces; and I don't think that the Franco Albini interior will generate the response which I had hoped it might (fig. 185). However I think that it does explain the Aldo Rossi image. This in terms of a disgust for the versatility of Albini and the like. No doubt about it, Albini was an important (and intellectualizing) talent; and this interior of his own apartment is of 1937. *Domus* for that year tells us that he is *freschissimo sposato* but much more important than this biographical detail is his stylistic preciosity. The mounting of the pictures, the animation of the radio, the tensile structure of the bookshelves, perhaps none of these items have, as yet, become *retardataire,* anachronistic curiosities. But all the same, from the look of this room one may understand the Rossi reaction. It is poetry in the service of *dumb* ideas.

And one may trace this reaction in the Teatro del Mondo for the Venice Biennale (fig. 186). Both in the drawings and in the photo showing it being floated out into the lagoon, more a poetic icon than a theater, this was; and, of course, without the example of Louis Kahn (again *dumb* ideas in the service of poetry), the existence of this floating pavilion would have been inconceivable.

But to repeat: the manifesto piece avoids local contingencies and it only enters the city as the adversary of context. Witness Mies's Glass Tower project of 1922. The manifesto piece avoids complicated sites and complicated programs, which can only infringe upon its theoretical ideality; and, in contradistinction to this condition of mind, it may be instructive and amusing to present the Hôtel de Roquelaure of L'Assurance, 1722 onwards (fig. 187), and the Cité de Refuge (Salvation Army) building of 1929 (fig. 188)—

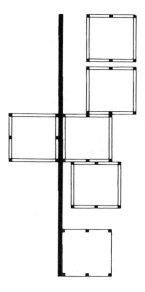

183. Weber DeVore House, 1954, plan. Louis Kahn.

184. Adler House, 1954, elevation. Louis Kahn.

Ideas, Talent, Poetics

185. Interior, 1937, Franco Albini; elementary school
at Fagnano Olona, 1972, Aldo Rossi.

186. Teatro del Mondo, Venice, 1979. Aldo Rossi.

Ideas, Talent, Poetics

both as instances of an old time French virtuosity in solving the issues of an apparently intractable site.

Both of them are highly ingenious and self-conscious distributions, both are evidently addressed to what Stendhal might have called "the happy few," to those appreciative of paradox; and both of them present a normative core—with L'Assurance a version of the accepted format of the *hôtel particulier,* with its sequence of court, *corps de logis,* garden; and, with Le Corbusier, what was already by 1929 a version of that long, skinny slab to which twentieth century architecture has been so addicted. And then, to take up those difficult fringe territories which cannot be absorbed by any normative procedure, both architects make a highly idiosyncratic display of not so local formal manipulations: L'Assurance with the axes, the avenues and the *bosquets* of his gardens, and Le Corbusier with the parade of his entrance arrangements which, in themselves, almost resemble the episodes of a garden.

Might it be correct to suggest that at the Cité de Refuge, through the agency of Winnaretta Singer de Polignac (of the South Bend, Indiana, sewing machine outfit), Le Corbusier created an *hôtel particulier* for the homeless, the dispossessed? Perhaps it might be; but, probably, it is more important to assert that, if L'Assurance offers some sort of brilliant dialectic between different conceptions of Rococo decorum, Le Corbusier makes the obvious point: that, given the activity of a vivacious intellect, even an architecture of 'ideas' may be subjected to the most problematic of local circumstances. For, at the Cité de Refuge as so frequently with Corbu, the abstract message of a manifesto culture is brought into the most stimulating conflict with the empirical confines of specifics.

On the other hand, Richard Meier's Douglas House of 1971–73 at Harbor Springs, Michigan (figs. 189, 190, 191) scarcely displays any comparable argument between abstract message and specific location. Not that the Douglas House is other than a highly potent image. Not that its architect has ever been the victim of crude ideas. He must be judged far too intelligent for that. No, his is a

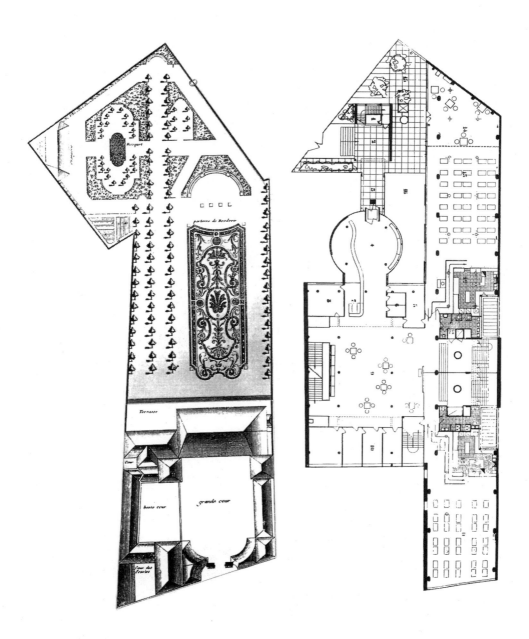

187. Hôtel de Rocquelaure, Paris, 1745. L'Assurance.

188. Cité de Refuge (Salvation Army Building), Paris, 1926. Le Corbusier and Pierre Jeanneret.

case of intelligent and super-abundant talent; but, talent apart, the Douglas House might still be interpreted as a reflection of the current manifesto culture.

Notice, for instance, the restricted plinth on which it stands. In a highly particular topography, seemingly it has been introduced from out of a Platonic void. That it may be envisaged as a ship without secure anchorage, without any relation to docks or piers, need not be deplored; but that the occupants of this ship, or icon, appear to be hermetically sealed within it, with the minimum of any inviting access to adjacent territory, might—just possibly—be considered a minor tribulation.

Now a comparison of the Douglas House with the Villa Aldobrandini at Frascati (fig. 192) might further assist the evaluation of the manifesto piece based upon over-simple ideas. Of course, Villa Aldobrandini (1598–1603) is enormous and the Douglas House is quite small. But, nevertheless, if we forget the presence of the lake and, instead, substitute the distant view of Rome, there is some identity of position; and here it should be noticed how Villa Aldobrandini extends itself in a lateral deployment. But, an inspection of the plan will also assist this notice and may also permit a further observation: that while, for Meier, his external trim tends to salute Corbu, it may be a curiosity that his internal distributions show a propensity to remain Gropius. And this is particularly evident when one examines the minimal bedrooms stacked up at the back of the house with the living room as a sort of promenade deck in visual communication only with the lake.

In other words, the Douglas House makes no positive use of the space between its rear wall and the upward slope of the hill behind it (fig. 191). Simply this is a throwaway. Or, maybe, it was dismissed as too confined a volume to possess the potentialities of interest. But in sixteenth or seventeenth century Italy it was not necessary to be a genius to recognize the value of such a location. On the one side of the house backed up against the hill, there would be the place of intimacy, the *nymphaeum*; and, on the other side, there would be the extended prospect over lake, *campagna,* or whatever;

189. Douglas House, Harbor Springs, Michigan, 1971–1973, view. Richard Meier.

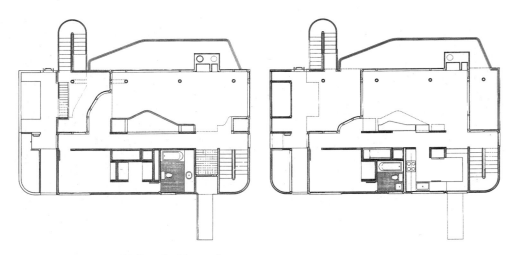

190. Douglas House, plan.

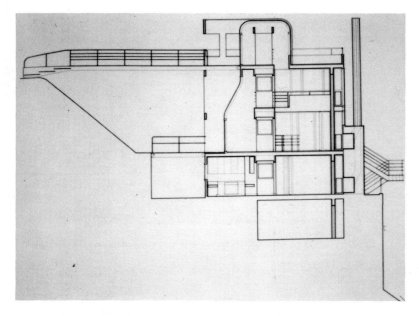

191. Douglas House, section.

192. Villa Aldobrandini, Frascati, 1602.

Ideas, Talent, Poetics

and since, ideally, the living room connects the two, by the briefest of movements one would be always permitted the refreshment of contrasted spatial and landscape conditions—to the rear the reclusive *nymphaeum,* then the passage through the *salone,* and then the great explosion of the big view. Very obvious all this; but it still deserves to be recorded. For an elaborate house on a sloping site, this was long understood to be a logical disposition; and, short of Villa Aldobrandini at Frascati, Villa Carlotta, up the lake from Como, may serve to illustrate this sectional parti (fig. 193).

But then, there is Frank Lloyd Wright's Hardy House of 1906, overlooking Lake Michigan at Racine, Wisconsin (fig. 194). One of the very best of small Wright houses, it almost relates to the same category of problems which are presented in the Frascati and Harbor Springs sites. Without the *nymphaeum* of course it is; but, all the same, it exploits its position with supreme self-confidence. Without *any* pretensions to manifesto, without *overt* intellectual presumption, it grows from the specificities of the site with easy lateral and frontal extensions.

Nor need it be said that manifesto culture (let's make a big 'intellectual' noise quick) has been highly detrimental to elegant and even commonsense planning? Back in 1912 an architect of intelligence, E. R. Carpenter, was responsible for an apartment house in New York City, 635 Park Avenue; and the almost impeccable distribution of a typical floor of this building (fig. 195), with its preliminary entrance, its circular foyer, its two to three living rooms, the seclusion of its bedrooms, is almost a summary of the later phases of the American *belle époque.* An illustration of capitalist *Existenzmaximum?* But one may also safely suggest that the architect of this building indulged himself in no intellectual extravagance, that he was content with his general competence and his, no doubt, minor talent.

However, after this accomplishment of 1912, now to approach a Kahn and Jacobs house, also in Park Avenue, of about sixty years later (fig. 196); and this is to contemplate a *dégringolade.*

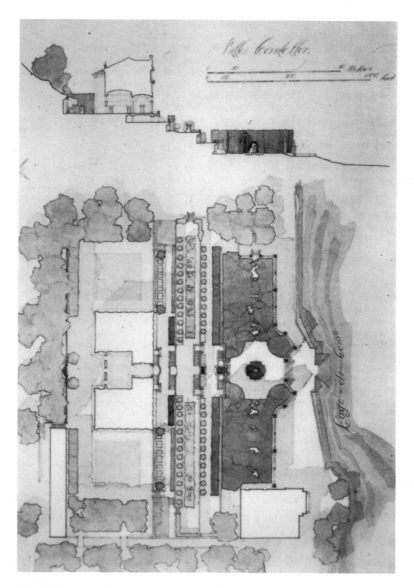

193. Villa Carlotta, Como, section.

Ideas, Talent, Poetics

194. **Hardy House, Racine, 1906. Frank Lloyd Wright.**

The Beaux-Arts policy of placing members of the structural frame within the *poché* has been abandoned but it is not very apparent that anything else has been understood. A message of emancipation has been heard from Weimar-Dessau-Harvard; but the Le Corbusier strategy of separating the columns from partitions has scarcely received attention and, as a consequence, the Kahn and Jacobs house presents incredible crudities. About the same size as 635 Park Avenue, with its incredible confusion, it might begin to explain why the 'rich' are apt to prefer interior decorators to architects. For, looking at these highly inept rooms, it is surely apparent that there can be no possible occupancy without extensive camouflage and cover-up.

All the same let us now recognize that, by 1976, rather than camouflage and cover-up, what might be called extensive manipulation was coming to be 'required' even in the carefully arranged apartments of E. R. Carpenter at 635 Park Avenue. Presumably these did not disclose a 'Modern' message; and, therefore, one of them came to become selected to be either devastated or radically transformed (fig. 197). A manifesto on the part of the owners no doubt this was. For is it not a case of the *ricca borghesia* of New York City making protestations of apostolic poverty? But then, why did they select for this entirely gratuitous performance an apartment so exemplary and an outfit with the integrity of Gwathmey Siegel? But why eliminate the sophisticated entrance arrangements and the circular foyer? Or is this yet another case of manifesto infecting a situation in which it is of only the slightest relevance?

But now to move to Berlin, to the intersection of Kochstrasse and Friedrichstrasse, to the approaches of Checkpoint Charlie. There is an architect and critic who calls herself Claire Obscure (I think that she comes from Münster) who occasionally writes for Maurice Culot's magazine in Brussels. So Claire Obscure describes the present condition of this unfortunate intersection as comprised by: a Catalonian fortress (Bohigas), an *esquisse* (Rossi), *un quadrillage ésotérique* (Eisenman), and a collection of Hanseatic warehouses from Ticino (Reichlin and Reinhardt). A case of pluralism perhaps?

Ideas, Talent, Poetics

195. 635 Park Avenue, New York, 1912, plan. E. L. Carpenter.

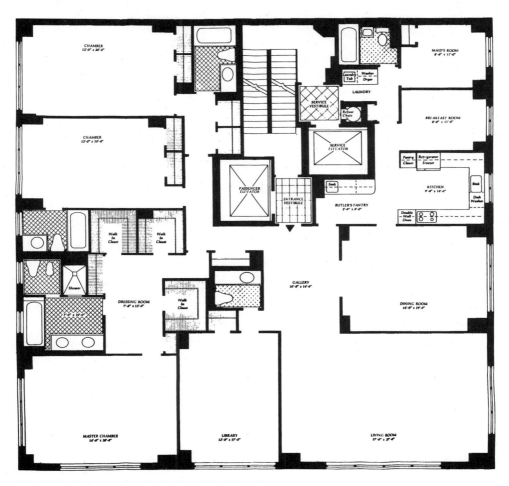

196. 733 Park Avenue, New York, plan. Kahn & Jacobs.

Ideas, Talent, Poetics

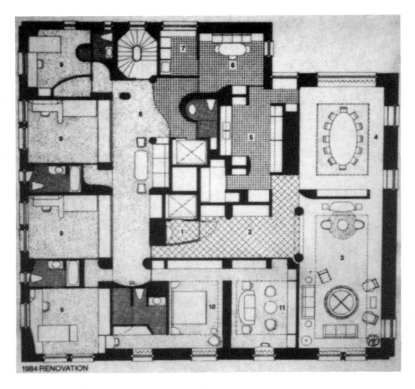

1984 RENOVATION

197. 635 Park Avenue, plan as redesigned by Gwathmey Siegel.

However now to approach quite the most demonstrative of the four components, the *quadrillage ésotérique* of Peter Eisenman and Jacquelin Robertson—although I don't think that Robertson had too much to do with this (figs. 198, 199). Apparently it is predicated, basically, upon a fantasy of two conflicting grids, the eighteenth century grid of the Friedrichstadt and the grid derived from the longitudes of Mercator's projection which, one is told, differ from the Friedrichstadt grid by some 3.3 degrees.

But what an involuted argument! And what are we to derive from this highly abstruse information? Does it mean that the authors of the central Berlin grid were not quite sure about the true location of the geographical North Pole and are, therefore, tactfully to be corrected? Or does it mean that the authors of this grid just didn't care about the North Pole (an unbearable lapse on their part?) and were only anxious to align their new streets parallel and at right angles to the axis of the Unter den Linden and the Tiergarten? Or, is this not very plausible fetish of the North Pole simply an excuse to justify an opportunism which has been deliberately willed?

Patently it is the latter; and, patently like so many others the architect here is operating to 'make it strange', to render the simple complicated and the banal extraordinary; and if this preoccupation with the geographical North Pole must now be allowed to take us where it leads us, to a second opportunism, this time of a psycho-archaeological variety, I suspect my friend Peter of being a devotee of Canina's plan of Rome which was also admired by Sigmund Freud. Or such is the inference of Freud's *Civilization and Its Discontents,* where, though I don't think that Canina is mentioned, the influence of his plan is evident: and where Freud allows himself to imagine that Rome represents an accumulation of psychic debris and that all buildings which have existed on a site may also be conceived of as simultaneously present. An interesting Freudian intuition and fairly inevitable that it should be grabbed, by Peter, as "the excavated city."

Ideas, Talent, Poetics

198. Corner of Kochstrasse and Friedrichstrasse, Berlin, 1988, view. Eisenman Robertson.

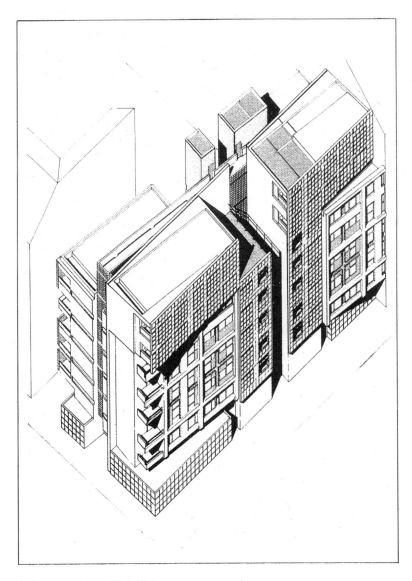

199. Kochstrasse and Friedrichstrasse, axonometric.

Ideas, Talent, Poetics

Permissible in Rome? Just possibly. Permissible in Berlin?
Just possibly not. Permissible in New York? Almost certainly
never. But, if conflicting grids and a city waiting to be excavated
constitute the basic public apologia for an apartment house on the
northeast corner of the intersection of Kochstrasse and Friedrichstrasse, one knows that there is much more likely to follow: an
appeal to the authority of current critical trends and prevailing culture heroes as they have successively prescribed procedures. And
how well one knows what is now becoming quite an anthology: semiotics, structuralism, deconstruction, George Steiner (from his period at Princeton), Noam Chomsky, and, as the pace accelerates and
becomes more exclusively French, de Saussure, Lévi-Strauss, and
Jacques Derrida.

But is all this exegetic excess largely gratuitous? For, after
all, given the impossible banality of the site, the building does just
happen not to be at all bad. So why could not all of this have been
said without calling up the extremes of metaphysical angst? It
would have been so easy. The site is dull and, hence, the conflicting
grids. For was it not reasonable to suppose that a bit of torsion, as at
La Tourette, might very likely liven things up? And, as for the rest,
well, surely, that was a free ride? Like so many others, myself included, Peter Eisenman has been devoted to Italian architecture of
the years 1930–60 and, therefore, here in Friedrichstadt he has
made a compilation of items from those years. Thus, if you look and
if you know, here you will find references to Giuseppe Terragni's
Novocomun of 1929, to his Casa del Fascio of 1935–36 (fig. 200),
to his Casa Giuliano-Frigerio of 1939–40, maybe references to
Cesare Cattaneo's apartment house at Cernobbio, and quotations
from Luigi Moretti, most notably his Casa del Girasole in Parioli
and his Casa Astrea of 1949 (fig. 201) in Monteverde Nuovo. In
other words, what there is here is a pretty tough-minded pastiche of
an Italy which many people just happen greatly to admire.

And is there anything so very wrong about that? And I refer to the predicament of a tough-minded pastiche in a culture
which professes to abominate pastiche and which has surrounded

200. Casa del Fascio, Como, 1939–1940. Giuseppe Terragni.

Ideas, Talent, Poetics

201. La Casa Astrea, Rome, 1949. Luigi Moretti.

the whole idea of imitation by so many, quaintly absurd, prohibitions and tabus—most significantly the tabu upon any exercise of personal preference. And, therefore, the 'I admire' or 'I am utterly consumed by' Terragni, Cattaneo, Moretti (which I think may shortly become 'I admire' or 'I am utterly consumed by' Bruno Taut, Hans Poelzig, Hans Scharoun) can never be an acceptable theme of discourse for purposes engendered under the auspices of Modern architecture. No it cannot; but all the same, the 'I like' was available to Robert Venturi, who opens his *Complexity and Contradiction in Architecture* with the sentence, "I like complexity and contradiction in architecture."[4]

A big difference in intellectual style? No imaginary archaeology, no 'deep' psychotherapy, no pseudo-Hegelian ra-ra, the *Zeitgeist* thing is quite abruptly abandoned; and it was very daring (or was it very naive?) on Venturi's part—for after all, he presented himself as the apostle of the complex—to be able to make such a break in a communication of just seven words.

Just seven words! But, of course, Venturi is scarcely an ideas man. Rather he is a conspicuous talent perhaps only slightly bruised by ideological polemic; and speaking as I am about the persistence of talent in a theater where the crudeness of ideas has become hegemonic, by way of a terminal cadenza I will only take notice of a building in New York City where, though talent predominates, the allegiance to at least one idea is completely emphatic. The University Club (figs. 202, 203) is a Florentine palazzo; and, without any sense of shame, it makes this point. But it exceeds its precedents. Palazzo Medici-Ricardi and Palazzo Strozzi, by its distribution of mezzanines (signifying bedroom floors), a distribution more Roman than Florentine, and by the *maniera* motif of its entrance, which looks as if it ought to be discoverable in Florence but is not there to be found.

So was it about this building that Le Corbusier wrote: "In New York then I first learned to appreciate the Italian Renaissance. It is so well done that you could believe it to be genuine"? I think that it may have been; but I also remember an occasion when Fifth

202. University Club, New York, 1900, view. McKim, Mead and White.

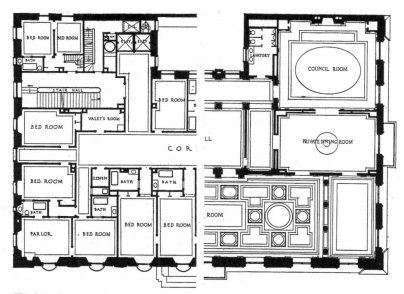

Third Mezzanine Bedroom Floor Plan   Third Floor Plan

203. University Club, plan.

Ideas, Talent, Poetics

Avenue was still a two-way thoroughfare equipped with two-storey buses, when, sitting on the top floor of one of these, I was privileged to overhear the conversation of two Polish fencing instructors who, for the most part, talked French. But, as we approached 54th Street, and almost as a concession to my linguistic inability, both suddenly proclaimed: "Best building on the Avenue! Best building on the Avenue!"

In any case in the debate between talent and ideas which has been the topic of my discourse, I have felt compelled to salute the University Club not only as a great early twentieth century paradigm but as a considerable illustration of the virtues of talent, of an intelligent and severely instructed talent. The University Club can tolerate no cheap nonsense. But, nevertheless, I still feel obliged to add a piece from Karl Marx, from his *Dix-Huit Brumaire of Louis Napoleon*: "All great ideas come around twice, first as tragedy and second as parody."

Postscript, 1994

It was with these words that I concluded my lecture at Harvard in December 1987; and, though I had to stop somewhere, on the whole I hated myself for doing so with this Karl Marx quotation. It is too unambiguous and, altogether, too 'modern'. A first performance is to be applauded. It belongs to the world of tragedy; but, apparently, anything resembling a repeat performance is to be deplored. Thus Napoleon III should never have modeled his coup d'état *on any pattern deriving from the behavior of his uncle; and it is in terms of this 'romantic' myth of originality—only the absolutely new can be absolutely authentic—that, of course, we have all of us been educated. It is, yet again, the impossible story of continuous revolution. And, if this story scarcely agitated the moral scruples of McKim, Mead and White at the University Club, certainly it very much agitated the conscience, the much more delicate moral fiber, of Peter Eisenman at that fatal intersection in Friedrichstadt. "No, I am not a parody as envisaged by Karl Marx," one seems to hear him saying, "and, to prove that I am not, here are my papers of legitimization signed by Jacques Derrida, and they are French, French, French!"*

But, alas, I don't see how even this helps very much. For, in Marx's terms, surely even Deconstruction itself is not anything much more than a parody. Because, in the early years of this century, were not the practitioners of Analytical Cubism, fundamentally, Deconstructionists avant la lettre; and, following from them, is there not a strand of literary criticism, initiated by T. S. Eliot, which, for rather longer than one cares to remember, has proclaimed the virtues and the values of the ambiguous and the difficult—a critical strand culminating in William Empson's Seven Types of Ambiguity, *perhaps itself a parody of Ruskin's* Seven Lamps of Architecture?*

However, I am drifting away from my attempted project—to promote a possible *reciprocity between talent and ideas; and, therefore, I must abandon my sidetrack. I am not hostile to the apartment house in Friedrichstadt. In that area I am only hostile to the condition which brought about such a ludicrous assignment of sites; but, as regards Peter, who, over a very long time, has been my always difficult but often generous friend, I can only say that, though I am always charmed by his histrionics, I am frequently appalled by his exuberance of discourse and the indiscretions to which it leads.*

But enough for that. Peter's intellectualism and his pursuit of cerebrality have, by now, produced a tribe of imitators who are, already, panting up behind him; but it is not about these would-be emulators, these epigoni *of Peter that I wish to speak and, mercifully, I am relieved of doing so by discovering a quite casual statement by John Summerson: "By 1937 the Edwardians were finished. The Modern was ready to take over which, in 1945, it did. It conquered the world and then fell into a dead faint, without, however, actually dying."*[5]

Correct of course. The Modern fell into a dead faint about 1951; and, if it didn't die, it has persisted comatose since that date. Not dead, not exactly alive, a little bit like the body of Lenin outside the Kremlin, it has persisted for almost fifty years, as a cult object with all the good guys trying to help. But how did they help (myself included) except by an extended German Totentanz *or an Irish wake; and should this not have been obvious for an intolerable length of time? In Texas in 1954, Bernhard Hoesli and myself had already presumed the existence of the coma and we had structured a system of education related to, what we thought, was almost certain to lead to Modern architecture's revival. But no matter. The Modern* might have *be-*

come something. However, instead, the cheap allurements of science fiction were enabled to take over.

But again, since much can be tolerated, no very serious sweat; and, instead, to produce another quotation: "Theory mongers, searching for congratulatory applause from the culture voyeurs, fight their quixotic struggles far from the site of the real battle."[6]

But who could not agree and who could not suppose that the site of the real battle is the city?

Notes

1. Isaiah Berlin, *The Hedgehog and the Fox* (New York: New American Library, 1957), 8–9.

2. Alessandro Mendini, "Dear Peter Eisenman," *Domus* 611 (1980): 1.

3. Peter Eisenman, "Three Texts for Venice," *Domus* 611 (1980): 9.

4. Robert Venturi, *Complexity and Contradiction in Architecture* (New York: Museum of Modern Art, 1966), 22.

5. Sir John Summerson, "Classical Architecture," in *New Classicism,* ed. Andreas Papadakis and Harriet Watson (London: Academy Editions, 1990), 16.

6. Mark Jarzombek, "Good Life Modernism and Beyond: The American House in the 1950's and 1960's: A Commentary," *Cornell Journal of Architecture* 4 (1990): 93.

Interview: 1989

My memory for details is, generally, so good that I am entirely baffled on the occasions when it completely deserts me. Thus, as regards this interview and as regards whoever it was who asked the questions and where the questions were asked, I have no certain recollection.

I think that this interview must have taken place in Rome, possibly in 1989 and, probably, in my apartment in the Via del Teatro Valle. But I can't say for sure and I am not even sure that the interrogation was conducted by Richard Ingersoll—though this seems to me to have been likely.

Also, though this interview may have been published well before its appearance in ANY *magazine in 1994, its first publication has escaped my notice.*

But, all the same, I am still enabled to notice how much I am apt to repeat myself—always the same dreary themes. However, the themes do seem to have the ability to erupt from a variety of different contexts.

Q. How do you define architecture?

A. For the most part I don't try; but I assume that any architecture is determined by a myth which is extensively believed. This might be the notion that antiquity was better than the present day, that the future will be better than today, or that the engineer is better than the architect. In any case, I suppose that architecture is always the exhibition of myth and I cannot see how it can ever transcend this condition. In the nineteenth century Gilbert Scott said something like this. If you see a building with windows of a size to admit an appropriate amount of light, it may or may not be a work of architecture; but, if the windows are definitely too big or definitely too small, then you can be almost certain that you are in the presence of an architectural endeavor. And I find this remark very relevant because, surely, architecture always involves an element of theatrical distortion or exaggeration. Myself, I am apt to think of architecture as the fashion trade of the building industry; and I don't mean this as either good or bad. It is simply a condition; because architecture, in so many ways—like clothes and like words and like music—is inherently pre-logical. That is: a work of architecture is rather like a theological exercise. In its later developments it may involve all sorts of sophisticated dialectic; but, at the bottom, its foundations rest upon the precariousness of fantasy and faith. So I am surprised that this condition (which is not discreditable) is not more widely recognized. For, practically, the only propositions concerning a work of architecture which can be proved to be false or true relate to the laws of statics. They relate to the Vitruvian category of *firmitas;* and the other two categories of the Vitruvian triad, *commoditas* and *venustas,* have, as yet, certainly not been subjected to any Newtonian revolution, or revelation. And shouldn't we be grateful that this is so? Because, if it were not so, if the laws of use and pleasure were capable of empirical verification, then surely all diversity and change would disappear, all would be known, all would be predictable. Therefore, the pre-logical condition of architecture (which is its 'mode of being', or its 'existential predicament') should be a cause for satisfaction rather than regret. Architecture requires conjecture; and, for this reason, those many characters who spend their lives in the attempt to render it independent of speculation should be regarded with intense suspicion. The Abbé Laugier began his *Observations* (1765) with the statement that: "Tout n'est pas dit sur l'Architecture"; and, probably, this should be regarded as one of the greatest understatements of all time. That architecture is not an 'exact' science is not a scandal.

Q. And how do you define 'Modern architecture'?

A. I had hoped that this question was not going to arise. For 'Modern architecture' is a very slippery and eel-like concept. I was given a quote from Nietzsche the other day. It is to the effect that only that which has no history is capable of definition; and, therefore how to define 'Modern architecture'—which was, intrinsically, an attempt to render obsolete the contingencies of time? I would suggest that 'Modern architecture' was an approach to building which was penetrated by the sentiment of modernity; and, then, I would suggest that this sentiment also represented a highly odd collection of ideas. It involved (did it not?) fantasies about progress, science, and emancipation. It also involved (certainly?) further fantasies about organism, evolution, and the structure of time. So some of these fantasies were French and some were German. Some relate to the famous seventeenth century *querelle* and some relate to *Sturm und Drang.* So, perhaps, the French sentiments involve ideas of precision, and the German, ideas of continuity and the social fabric. But this must be to overgeneralize. From Denise Scott-Brown I have annexed the term *physics envy* (apart from being amusingly Freudian, it describes a state of mind eminently French, prone to categories and, possibly, descended from Descartes, via Turgot, Saint-Simon, and Auguste Comte); and then, from David Watkin, the term *Zeitgeist worship,* which displays a mostly German origin. So the idea that architecture should be an 'exact science' (like an imaginary version of physics) and the further idea that it should be an emanation of 'the spirit of the age' are, evidently, at variance. The two demands are not compatible. In no way can the 'exact' be made so abruptly an ally of the 'cloudy'; and, if Karl Marx was able to do this, then so much the worse (so much the more ridiculous) for Karl Marx and, also, for 'Modern architecture'. But the sentiment of modernity is something so virulent and so much extremely still with us that it is apt to defy analysis. It is a crazy sentiment of course; but isn't it all the more potent for that reason?

Q. And 'Post-Modernism'?

A. I have already tried to suggest that 'Modernism' was a dangerous intellectual disease; and that Modern architecture was destined to break apart because it combined the incompatible. In terms of 'modernity' the architect was destined to be both the slave of 'science' and the obedient pencil of 'history' ("I'm not responsible for the building; I didn't build it; the building was 'required' by 'science' and 'history' and I had nothing, *nothing* to do with it."). But, if 'Modernism' was an important pseudo-doctrine, then how about your question about 'Post-Modernism'? In the first case I am reminded about a remark attributed to Frank Lloyd Wright. It is probably apocryphal; but the story goes that Wright had been asked what he thought about the architecture of Philip Johnson. So there is then F.L.W.'s alleged reply: "The architecture of Philip Johnson? Why, I never think about it. Why should I?"; and it is in terms approximately like these that I approach so-called Post-Modernism. The so-called Post-Modernists, I think, are still the victims of 'Modernism'; they have shifted the visuals but scarcely the sentiments. For what else is the idea of the avant-garde, what else is the idea of water-skiing over the tides of history, if it is not a very close side product of 'Modernism'? No, the Post-Modernists sustain a leading idea of the 'Modern movement'. Unfortunately they belong to the tradition. They are part of its *dégringolade*; and the most logical position is that of Leon Krier, who (in theory at least) remains classically aloof.

In any case there is a little interchange in Igor Stravinsky and Robert Craft's *Memories and Commentaries* which might here be cogent. Supposedly Stravinsky and Craft have been talking of various matters—academicism, information theory, creativity—when Craft presents his question: "And modern?" To which the following is Stravinsky's reply:

> The only sense in which I think that 'modern' can now be used must derive from, or so I imagine, a meaning similar to the *devotio moderna* of Thomas a Kempis. It is 'romantic', of course and it suffers . . . for it cannot accept the world as it is. 'Modern' in this sense does not so much mean or emphasise the appearance of a new style, though, of course, a new style is part of it. Nor is it brought about merely by its innovations, though innovations are part of it too.

Now a statement of this kind which, to my mind, perfectly illustrates the never completely articulated convictions of the Modern architect some fifty years ago may stand, almost like a species of lighthouse somewhere on the edge of the current rather muddy debate about Post-Modernism, the death of 'Modern architecture', etc. For surely, in the full Stravinskian sense ("it suffers for it cannot accept the world as it is") Modern architecture has been dead for rather more years than most persons connected with it have been alive. But still another quote from Stravinsky may be apropos. Does he attribute it to Stockhausen? I don't remember; but it goes something like this: "My music isn't modern. It is simply badly played."

Q. And what about architectural education?

A. A calamity. But don't you think so? Increasingly a case of the inept leading the inexperienced. Surely, after the Russian Revolution, the two world wars, the Holocaust, and Modern architecture itself, among the greater catastrophes of the twentieth century.

Interview: 1989

I don't want to talk about architectural education; but, since you insist that I should, what further do I say? Do I refer to the horrible legacy of Walter Gropius? I think that this should no longer be necessary. Or do I think about the gruesome planning of so many recent buildings in which one can only feel like Theseus about to enter a labyrinth and slay a minotaur? But you know those dreadful buildings where, invariably, you are lost. They are unspeakably ridiculous (most immediately I think about the Staatsbibliothek in Berlin) and their circulation defies common sense. You enter them at your peril and to move in them you need a guide. Where are the cloakrooms? Where the elevators? Nothing is clear. You are in a contrivance of planned obscurity; and, in this absurd predicament, you inevitably begin to think about the abundant simplicities of the Ecole des Beaux-Arts where everything was quietly advertised and apparent. From Durand to Guadet you knew where you were. Color coding wasn't necessary. You were never lost. There was a portico or a *porte-cochère.* There was a sequence of lobbies. If they wanted to relieve themselves both men and women, without any embarrassing instruction, knew just where to go. But no longer. "The elegance of the plan, the virtues of the solution, eminently French qualities, these are unknown anywhere else. Such a lack of spirituality saddens me." This was Le Corbusier in the 1930s and an implicit criticism of Bauhaus influence; but he could never have imagined how very bad things were later to become.

Q. I think that you are a defeated Francophile; and, therefore, I wonder what you think about France today.

A. It leaves me lost and miserable. I much prefer Italy, the Germanic lands, and the United States. I was educated to the idea of the *grande nation,* the *ville lumière,* and the Ecole de Paris. So I will always respect a period of French intelligence. When the French are intelligent they are devastating and brilliant. They are beyond belief. I think of François Mansart and I have to think about the Duc d'Aumale at Chantilly; but I respected French sensibility the other day in Switzerland. We had come from Bavaria and, you know, we were at Arenenberg (that rustic version of Malmaison), and, coming from all that German stuff we were immensely happy to arrive in a mini-château, absolutely Charles X, which was the summer retreat of Hortense de Beauharnais. Site incredible, literally a hermitage, views incredible, with the Bodensee looking like a Leonardo landscape intended for Germanic consumption and the house itself no more than a pavilion. So Arenenberg is a miracle and via Queen Hortense, I was led to think seriously about what Leon Krier is apt to call the great French restitution. This is the idea, at last to honor the memory of Napoleon III (surely the greatest benefactor of the city of Paris) by an international competition for a monument (no French invited to compete, no French invited to the jury, and the judgement at Baden-Baden). But don't you think a terrific idea? I do. For it is at once a celebration of the great France (which all the world loves) and the contemporary France (which half the world can only abominate).

Interview: 1989

Moneo's Spain

In 1989 I received a letter from Avisa *asking me to write an article about Rafael Moneo; and I replied that I could not, that I knew Rafael in terms of his tenure at Harvard but was quite unable to interpret him in terms of his Spanish persona. So I am apt to be prolix and protracted and, in my letter of excuse, saying that I couldn't write anything, I must, so much, have gone on and on that* Avisa *simply excerpted part of this letter and made it into this little piece.*

Had I been talking seriously about Rafael I would certainly have directed attention to that lecture which he gave at Harvard about his own work when, about a particular building, he was understood to have said "This building was conceived in terms of sickness and death" and everybody looked around at each other and said things to the effect: "Well, with Spain, what do you expect?" But this was before it was later understood that Rafael had been trying to say: "This building was conceived in terms of thickness and depth."

Published in Avisa, *1989.*

I am assuming that Catalonia is not part of Spain; therefore quite truthfully I am able to say that I have never been to Spain. On the other hand, I have been to Barcelona, in January 1985, where I stayed at a hotel opposite to what I would call the *duomo.*

So I was slightly shocked by Barcelona, which in spite of Gaudí and all the rest is a mildly inadequate, destitute city. I had expected perhaps a poor man's version of *Genova La Superba,* but found nothing like it. From this recognition, I took consolation in the knowledge that the Spanish crown had persistently suppressed Barcelona in favor of Genoa, port of entry to Spanish Lombardy, whose bankers had so frequently relieved the financial pressures of the Spanish crown.

But we all know this (or don't we?), and we know that the pressures on Barcelona became relaxed under Charles III of Bourbon, allegedly an enlightened prince. All the same, it was too late to do much good.

In the foregoing, which are the observations of a naive Anglo-American foreigner casually walking the streets, I also had opportunity to think about the folly of Philip II in retreating to Madrid and establishing the capital there. For surely Spain belonged to the sea, on the one side to Barcelona and on the other to Lisbon.

Thinking about all this, I was also obliged to think about innate Spanish distinction (the Escorial and all that); and as I thought about it I returned to my hotel, which abundantly compensated for the walk.

Everything there was well conducted—red morocco all the way—nothing of the usual Statler Hilton horrors, all of it seeming to exhibit a presence, a quasi-antique *tenu* which could surely date no later than circa 1925; so judge my surprise when I learned that this hotel was about forty years newer than I had assumed it to be. And hence more food for thought, not only on Spanish distinction but also on Spanish retardation.

It was thus, sitting in one of the red morocco chairs and holding a drink, that for the first time in my life I found myself contemplating with a mild favor the intolerable and repressive regime of the late General Franco. For after all, was it not as a result of the appalling policies of El Caudillo himself, determined as he was to hold back the course of 'history', that I was able to sit, very briefly, in this modest, sparsely Spanish, and highly elegant room?

I didn't like the idea then, in January 1985, and I don't like it now; nevertheless it still lives in my mind (perhaps festers in my mind) and I feel compelled to enlarge upon it.

Simply, I wish to propose as a topic of thought that brief moment of enlightenment likely to follow the overturning of a bad and impossible order of things and, then, the establishment of an almost equally vicious consumerist society. This, when it occurs, is apt to be the shortest possible breathing space in time. Thus was Italy after the collapse of Mussolini and before the 'economic miracle' and the final triumph of Fiat, when the best of the old world and the best promises of the new were to be enjoyed alike, when craftsmanship was still available and wages were still not excessive.

For was this not a temporal episode illuminated by the performances of Franco Albini, Ignazio Gardella, Vittoriano Viganò, and so many others to whom I feel personally indebted? And do we see any comparable galaxy of vivacity and talent in the Italy, affluent but intellectually depressed, of the present day?

Frightening all these ideas? Of course. And are not most comparisons and most analogies dangerous and foolhardy? But of course. All the same, I remain possessed by the fantasy that the brilliance of the Spanish scene at the moment may be a case of *entre deux économies*. I think of the absolute *luxe* of architectural publication, yourselves in Madrid and Javier Cenicacelaya in Bilbao; and I am grateful to think about it, for you present a standard that is inaccessible in either New York or London; and—I must say it—all of you guys, apart from your obvious intelligence, present this exalted standard via the medium of an underpaid proletariat.

No, don't get me wrong. I am far from being a Marxist agitator, very far. I just want to express my fears. Our friend Rafael Moneo is absolutely related to that interstitial condition between Fascism and 'free enterprise'; and he depends upon this all too transient scene for the wonderful finish of his buildings. But how long before consumerism takes hold of Spain? And how long will be the resistance? Will it be long and hard? I doubt it. And this is why I think about Rafael whose buildings I admire and whose society I enjoy. Rafael is abundantly O.K. But, in a consumerist society, how long, just how long, can this condition of excellence survive?

P.S. All this said, it should be instructive to observe that Ferdinand and Isabella (she who would never remove her chemise until Granada was captured) sponsored not only Columbus but also Bramante. So perhaps there is still the greatest of hopes for Spain, and also for Rafael?

Colin Rowe

Letter: On Precedent and Invention

Written in 1986 for The Harvard Architectural Review, *no. 5,*
"Precedent and Invention."

The Editors,
The Harvard Architecture Review,
Graduate School of Design,
48 Quincy Street,
Cambridge, MA 02138

Dear Editors:

Let me first stipulate that I don't really perceive how your topic, *the use of precedent and the role of invention in architecture today,* can very well lead to profitable dispute.

I can never begin to understand how it is possible to attack or to question the use of precedent. Indeed, I am not able to comprehend how anyone can begin to *act* (let alone to *think*) without resorting to precedent. For, at the most banal level if a kiss may be instinctual, a handshake remains the product of convention, of habit, or of tradition; and in my reading, all of these gestures and whatever they may signify are related—loosely no doubt—to the notions of paradigm, of model, and hence, of precedent.

So much is my initiatory bias which I will now expand upon via the ancient strategy of a series of rhetorical questions:

1. Just how is it possible to conceive of any society, any civilization, or any culture without the provision of precedent?

2. Are not language and mathematical signs the evidence of convenient fables and hence the advertisement of prevailing precedent?

3. Further, in the romantic predicament of interminable novelty, surely one must be at a loss to discover how any discourse (other than a grunt) is to be conducted?

4. Is not precedent, and are not its connotations, the primary cement of society? Is not their recognition the ultimate guarantee of legitimate government, legal freedom, decent prosperity, and polite intercourse?

As painfully obvious and horribly banal as these implicit propositions are, I assume that they belong to the platitudes that anyone operating in a *reasonably* structured society (neither savage nor subjected to overheated revolutionary excitement) will be compelled to observe. I do not assume—*I cannot*—that these platitudes are available to the average architecture student. For he or she has been educated in a much more expansive milieu, with boundaries and limitations fragile to say the least.

In the days when it was understood that all art is a matter of imitation, whether of external reality or of some more metaphysical abstraction, the role of precedent was scarcely to be disputed;

and, needless to say, Aristotle produces the argument very succinctly. "The instinct of imitation is implanted in man from childhood, one difference between him and other animals being that he is the most imitative of living creatures and through imitation learns his earliest lessons; and no less universal is the pleasure felt in things imitated."

So, after this, now to produce another quote related to the doctrine of mimesis. It is from Wordsworth's "Intimations of Immortality" and it is here condensed.

> Behold the child among his new born blisses,
> A four year's darling of a pigmy size!
> See at his feet, some little plan or chart,
> Some fragment of his dream of human life,
> Shap'd by himself with newly learned art;
> But it will not be long
> Ere this be thrown aside
> And with new joy and pride
> This little Actor cons another part,
> As if his whole vocation
> Were endless imitation.

But if Wordsworth expands upon Aristotle and begins to relate mimesis to infant worship (the child is father to the man), one must turn to Walter Gropius to receive the full, the kindergarten drift of this diversion. Inadvertently, Wordsworth describes the architecture student as one knows this creature to be: but the impulsive Walter goes on to specify a *beau idéal* for the species: "Creativeness in the growing child must be awakened through actual working with all kinds of materials in conjunction with training in free design. . . . But this is important; no copying, no elimination of the urge to play, i.e., no artistic tutelage!"

Such is to provide pointers to a condensed history of the doctrine of mimesis and its decline; and such is also to bring into prominence your business about the use of precedent. For with the

Letter: On Precedent and Invention

best will in the world, it is not extremely easy to understand the Gropius distinction between "copying" and "urge to play": "Yer gotta play but yer not gotta copy and that's what you guys have gotta do." But could there be any dictate more perverse and inhibiting?

For is it not evident that any form of play is inherently "copying," related to fantasies of war or domesticity? And, without these models of either battle or building, surely it is extremely hard to imagine how any game from chess to architecture could very well survive. No, all play is essentially the celebration of precedent.

And now, what about the second part of your topic: *the role of invention in architecture today?*

Well, one thinks about the lawyer with a whole library bound in blue morocco behind him. This is the inventory of cases bearing upon the specific case that he is required to judge. So simply to pronounce a legal innovation, to discriminate the new, our jurist is obliged to consult the old and the existing; and it is only by reference to these that a genuine innovation can be proclaimed. For are not precedent and invention opposite sides of the same coin? *I think a better topic might have been: How does the new invade the old and how does the old invade the new?*

Sincerely,
Colin Rowe

Index of Names

Index

Contents

For Margaret and Dorothy Morgan:
Queen Street Girls

Chapter 1

Crème de la Crème

' "I am putting old heads on your young shoulders," Miss Brodie had told them at that time, "and all my pupils are the crème de la crème." '

For anyone wishing to write about the girls' schools of Edinburgh, Muriel Spark's description of these pupils is irresistible as a title. Following her death in 2006 at the age of 88, much of the praise for a remarkable literary career was focused on *The Prime of Miss Jean Brodie* as the book which brought her international recognition. There is a stage version, and the novel's central character was made vivid on film by the actress Maggie Smith. Her exaggerated Morningside accent caught the public imagination and made genteel Edinburgh a part of the theme.

Dame Muriel emphasised in *Curriculum Vitae*, the autobiography of her early years, the value of 'documentary evidence' and lamented the loss of her childhood notebooks. In my case it was an abundance of such material, turned to in retirement, which got things started. A complete series of school magazines for the period when my brother and I attended an Edinburgh boys' school was preserved, along with term reports from age five to seventeen. There were also childhood notebooks. All was passed on, and then taken from one attic to another. When the idea came of writing a book about Edinburgh fee-paying schools, so much material was at hand that the project divided itself in two – ladies first: girls' schooldays with the boys following on.

Are schooldays the happiest days of your life? Not according to literary folk, whose memories of school are often negative: Frank McCourt expressed it in *Angela's Ashes* as 'Your happy childhood's hardly worth the while.' But Muriel Spark rejected the idea that an unhappy start in life was necessary for the creative artist: 'I spent twelve years at Gillespie's, the most formative years of my life, and in many ways the most fortunate for a future writer.' From *Nelson's Infant Primer* by stages to the top of primary school under 'Miss Brodie', and right up to the examination stage at a very selective Edinburgh school, Muriel Camberg (as she then was) had good teachers and positive experiences. The relationship between

James Gillespie's School and Jean Brodie's 'crème de la crème' provides a number of starting points for this chapter.

I taught primary and secondary school children before moving to a teacher-training college in Aberdeen, where there was a general presumption in favour of state-funded schools. Secondary ones were then becoming comprehensive, shedding all sense of privilege. Selection for secondary school was out of favour, but most of our students had been educated in small-town high schools in country areas. Socially, they were 'comprehensive already'. Part of my job was to encourage discussion on educational questions of the day, but it was difficult to persuade students who came from rural areas as far north as Shetland that the question of fee-paying schools was interesting. On learning that eight per cent of English children went to 'public' schools like Eton, as well as private ones you never heard of, students would simply shrug and say that Scotland was different.

It certainly felt different in that northern college of education. In fact the overall fee-paying proportion in Scotland was only slightly less than in England, but most of it happened to be concentrated in Edinburgh. There have always been private schools in Aberdeen, Glasgow and Dundee but Edinburgh was unique – in Scotland, Britain, the world. There, twenty-four per cent of all children attended schools which charged fees. Some were independent and expensive. Others were 'grant-aided' and affordable. When compulsory attendance began, late in Queen Victoria's reign, local education authorities charged fees for all their schools. They were quite low, and parents paid without question. Some Edinburgh local authority schools were still fee-paying in the middle years of the twentieth century and James Gillespie's School was one of them.

Over the years withdrawal of government money has had its effect on Edinburgh, and the number of primary school children being privately educated in Scotland's capital has halved. However a remarkably constant figure of very nearly twenty-four per cent persists for secondary pupils, even though fees for day girls and boys have passed £2,500 per term. Boarding fees are almost twice as high, but there are still plenty of pupils coming to Edinburgh from elsewhere. That partly explains the high attendance figure. Today almost one in four teenage pupils in Edinburgh attends a fee-paying school. Their parents' taxes help to fund schools which are available for nothing, but those parents prefer to spend more for *A School of One's Choice* – title of the last book to be written about fee-paying in Scotland. It was published in 1969. Those of an egalitarian bent may wish to ignore Edinburgh's fee-paying schools, to pretend that their contribution to Scotland's educational system is insignificant or peripheral, but that is far from the case. At the very least they merit the kind of general survey which this book seeks to provide.

Many books have been written about individual schools – often for centennial purposes – with some Edinburgh schools described several times in print. As the idea of attempting an overview developed, I began to collect school histories. Second-hand bookshops were the main source, but sometimes a visit to the school was productive. As a second source of information, front office staff were glad to hand out prospectuses and magazines in glossy colour – much changed from the grey chronicles of my youth. The Edinburgh Room of the Central Public Library yielded up its treasures in the form of old school magazines, and there was also an unpublished nineteenth-century survey there by Alexander Law – a sequel to his *Edinburgh Schools in the Eighteenth Century* which linked them with the Scottish Enlightenment.

Autobiographies were another source, and the creator of Miss Jean Brodie provided more than most in *Curriculum Vitae*. Dame Muriel Spark told the 2004 Edinburgh Book Festival that although she had lived away from the city for most of a long life, it shaped her. Although the early novels were set in London and the later ones in New York, Tuscany and so on, Spark remained a Scottish writer – grateful for the Edinburgh years. Of course her writing is imaginative, and the Marcia Blaine School for Girls cannot be regarded as modelled on life. In a letter of encouragement, Dame Muriel checked my tendency to speculate: 'On the question of *The Prime of Miss Jean Brodie* this is a work of fiction and the character and scenes should not be confused with those of my school James Gillespie's.' Nevertheless (a word she thought of as typically Scottish) there is much to be learned from Muriel Spark's schooldays:

'Now I come to Miss Christina Kay, that character in search of an author, whose classroom's walls were adorned with reproductions of early and Renaissance paintings, Leonardo da Vinci, Giotto, Fra Lippo Lippi, Botticelli. She borrowed these from the senior art department, run by handsome Arthur Couling. We had the Dutch masters and Corot. Also displayed was a newspaper cutting of Mussolini's Fascisti marching along the streets of Rome.

'I fell into Miss Kay's hands at the age of eleven. It might well be said that she fell into my hands… In a sense Miss Kay was nothing like Miss Brodie. In another sense she was far above and beyond her Brodie counterpart. If she could have met "Miss Brodie" Miss Kay would have put the fictional character firmly in her place. And yet no pupil of Miss Kay's has failed to recognise her, with joy and great nostalgia, in the shape of Miss Jean Brodie in her prime. She entered my imagination immediately. I started to write about her even then.'

Works of fiction used to begin with a statement that no real-life character was portrayed, but childhood co-author Frances Niven (they wrote stories together, and Frances beat Muriel to the class English prize at least once) testified that '75% is Miss Kay.' Most people's memories of primary school are dim compared to the stronger impressions of later years, but not with Miss Kay/Brodie around. She is there in the 1930 Junior Class photograph looking serious in the midst of thirty-eight smiling girls. This is odd. The stage play, the film and the book itself combine to give an impression of the kind of small class which parents are

1. *Miss Kay's class 1930, Muriel Camberg third row second from right.*

willing to pay for. A 'Brodie set', held together in the teenage years despite separation into classes and houses, almost requires it. Yet thirty-eight was a large class even by the standards of that day.

Then there is the question of Mary Macgregor who was 'famous for being stupid'. The class photo is remarkable for the alertness of expression on faces, and it is hard to imagine a stupid girl finding herself in it. It was Miss Kay who first described her girls as the 'crème de la crème', and they truly were. There was an informal selection process for Gillespie's at five, though unrecalled by the bright Muriel who had already been reading for a year or so: 'It was an early start, although in Edinburgh at that time it was not unusual for children to read and write fluently before they were five…' It was a bright class as well as a large one. The Gillespie's roll reached 1,400 about the time when Muriel left, with a substantial proportion of those pupils enrolled in the seven years of the primary department. There were two classes in each primary school year and streaming was only to be expected. (Muriel and Frances were in 2A at fourteen, with 2B and 2C beneath.) Miss Kay's class was the top set at the top of the primary department with never a Mary Macgregor in sight.

But Muriel Spark's experience of schoolgirls ranged wider than Gillespie's. Having decided against going on to higher education, the prize-winning young poet went to work at the Hill School in Merchiston, close to her Bruntsfield family home. This was an unpaid teaching post which the future writer took for the sake of in-house lessons in shorthand and typing. The Hill School's principal asset was advertised in terms of 'Young ladies prepared for Commercial Examinations.' Miss Camberg taught English, arithmetic and nature study to small classes limited by the size of a suburban house. She found it easy to keep them occupied: 'School work here was not assumed in the serious light I was used to… The girls were only filling in their school-days until it was time for them to go to a finishing school somewhere on the Continent.'

Here, perhaps, was a composite source for the real Mary Macgregor – transposed by imagination into a setting where she would indeed have been 'famous for being stupid'. But the author delivered a Sparkian rebuke to me: 'Mary Macgregor, the character in my novel, is a pure figment of my imagination. In general one can make fiction out of fact but not fact out of fiction.' However that may be, the Hill School was typical of many small institutions serving families which, more than anything, sought to marry their daughters well. An early proprietor of what became St Denis School moved on from headmistressing to bringing out debutantes in London.

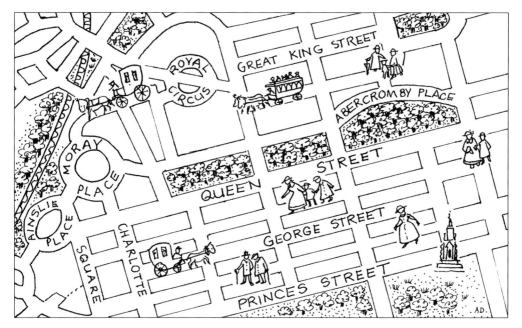

2. *The New Town.*

By the Thirties it had become acceptable for young women to work for a while after leaving school. Secretarial qualifications were almost as useful for marrying well as was the veneer of sophistication provided by *The Finishing School* – Muriel Spark's last novel. The times were changing, and the Hill School specialised in secretaries.

Small schools, large schools… One answer to the question of why Edinburgh has so many fee-paying pupils can be summed up in a phrase: the Merchant Company. The Company of Merchants of Edinburgh was formed shortly before Mary Erskine made a bequest, in 1694, of 10,000 merks for the maintenance of 'burges children of the female sex'. After opening in the Cowgate, the Merchant Maiden Hospital was provided with better accommodation on the edge of the Meadows (by the second last act of the Scottish Parliament, as it happens). Soon after that George Watson's Hospital began providing a similar service nearby for boys in need who were associated with the city's mercantile community. These Merchant Company charitable boarding schools were transformed in 1870 (by another Act of Parliament, this time at Westminster) into four large day schools for boys or girls. The former Merchant Maiden Hospital kept the name Mary Erskine's, after the founder. However the school became familiarly known as Queen Street, the thoroughfare below Princes Street and George Street from which its north-facing windows looked down to the Firth of Forth. Pupils came mainly from homes in the streets, squares, crescents and circles which had been designed by the Adam brothers as the New Town. As will appear, their school went under various names including the Edinburgh Ladies' College (or ELC) but to avoid confusion Queen Street is used here while the school was on that site for almost a century. Thereafter it became the Mary Erskine School at Ravelston.

The other Merchant Company girls' school, George Watson's Ladies' College (GWLC), was also known by its location, George Square, serving Edinburgh's South Side. Queen Street opened to 1,200 girls, George Square to fewer than half that number, but by the turn of the century both had about a thousand pupils aged five and upwards. By contrast, St George's in the West End (an extension from the New Town) was based on the English model of Miss Buss, Miss Beale and the Girls' Public Day School Trust. Only two hundred girls were admitted, and from the age of seven. At St George's two extremes were equally rejected: it was neither very small like the Hill School nor very large like those of the Merchant Company.

James Gillespie's School started as part of the Merchant Company scheme of things, feeding boys and girls into the larger schools. It was sold to the Edinburgh School Board in 1908 but continued to resemble the schools of its old proprietors: 'The Company's schools were deservedly popular with Edinburgh parents. Their academic reputation was high, their facilities for sport and extra-curricular activities far ahead of what the local authority could provide. Smart uniforms, a high standard of discipline and above all low fees made them popular with Edinburgh parents.' Thus Lydia Skinner, author of a fine tercentennial history of the Mary Erskine School.

Muriel Camberg's high marks (she had an equal aptitude for science) were rewarded by a bursary after she left Miss Kay. Her education was now paid for, and Muriel even studied Greek for nothing in an early morning extra class. Parents of slightly less clever girls at Gillespie's paid about half the Merchant Company rate. In 1938 the school was overcrowded and had a waiting list of four hundred. When higher fees were proposed the chairman replied: 'Every time we raise the fees the number of pupils desiring to attend has risen.' The classes at Gillespie's were larger than those of the other girls' schools, but with these very able pupils that hardly mattered. And without Miss Kay's high numbers there would have been no novel, perhaps no novelist: 'I had always enjoyed watching teachers. We had a large class of about forty girls. A full classroom that size, with a sole performer on stage before an audience sitting in rows looking and listening, is pure theatre.'

The physical setting of Gillespie's was described in the school magazine by a fourteen-year-old pupil of the mid-twentieth century – a kind of spiritual successor to Muriel Camberg. She noted a historical development – the opening of Boroughmuir School nearby: 'On 7th April, 1914, the old "Boroughmuir" became the new "James Gillespie's". At last "we" had a comfortable and well-situated school on Bruntsfield Links, on the historic Burgh Muir. This building was a "dream" school compared with the old building in Gillespie Crescent. It is probably the highest school in the city. From the windows on the middle floor and upwards there is a magnificent view to the north and north-east of the city. The building itself has many long corridors, and big airy classrooms with large windows.'

Edinburgh does indeed have marvellous vistas, including Arthur's Seat and the Castle across Bruntsfield Links. Muriel Spark's best known novel also evokes the cramped Old Town and the slums of the Grassmarket, where her encounter with Thirties poverty was likened to visiting a foreign country. Normal life was different: 'I loved crossing the Links to school in the early morning, especially when snow had fallen in the night or was still falling. I walked in the virgin snow, making the first footprints of the day. The path was still lamplit, and when I looked back in the early light there was my long line of footprints leading from Bruntsfield Place – mine only.'

Nostalgia brings out the 'mine only' in all of us. Having lived away from Edinburgh for many years, I found myself rediscovering the city of childhood through its school buildings. Some were impressive to look at, but the process went beyond architecture. Location was all-important in the days when most children walked to school. The first end-paper map shows an early cluster of schools in the New Town and the West End – which was the next area to be favoured by the business and professional classes – and south as far as George Square. The second end-paper map shows how, in the 1890s, new streets, houses and schools extended south to the suburbs of Newington and Morningside. The creation of a tramway system followed which made schools less dependant on districts. A suburban railway also helped parents to avoid the local school: that sense

THE EDINBURGH LADIES' COLLEGE

Is distant from (*a*) Princes Street Station about 5 minutes' walk; (*b*) Waverley Station, about 12 minutes; (*c*) Haymarket Station, about 15 minutes.

TRAIN TIME-TABLE.

CAR TIME-TABLE.

Times of departure of morning Cars which leave in time for School:—

	A.M.	A.M.		A.M.	A.M.
Bernard Street, Leith	8.18	8.28	Morningside Drive	8.23	8.20
Colinton Road	8.15	8.25	Murrayfield	8.30	8.35
Comely Bank (Cable)	8.28	8.32	Newhaven	8.10	8.20
Gorgie	8.30	8.35	Portobello and Joppa	7.50	8.5
Golden Acre (Cable)	8.15	8.20	Nether Liberton	8.10	8.14
Jock's Lodge	8.15	8.30	Seafield, Leith	8.5	8.20
Morningside (Church Hill)	8.30	8.34			

NOTE.—The Tramway Company issue Tickets at 1d. each to scholars if purchased in bundles of sixty. These Tickets are available at any time of day, any day of the week, all the year round.

3. *Horse car for Morningside.*

4. *To school on time.*

of escaping from 'rough' children lies deep in the Edinburgh psyche. This railway linked the double institution which became St Margaret's (half of it was later St Hilary's) with one building near Morningside Station and the other in Newington. Both were on what was then the edge of the city. The two schools were built to an identical plan and run by one headmaster (and owner) who commuted between them. To the east of Bruntsfield Links, less far out but definitely South Side, daughters of imposing mansions in the Grange district attended schools just like their homes in appearance. Most have vanished even from memory.

The move of Muriel Spark's school from an earlier Gillespie Crescent house into airy splendour exemplifies a general trend for one building to be replaced by another. Small schools like St Denis and Lansdowne House moved to where the market was in the residential suburbs, likewise St Serf's. St George's sold its Melville Street premises to a boys' school and built again in Murrayfield. Mary Erskine's moved, in the most radical transformation imaginable, from chronic overcrowding to wide open spaces in the west at Ravelston. Quite late in the day George Square was abandoned for Myreside in a co-educational alliance with George Watson's College, one of the Merchant Company boys' schools. Small schools became larger. Mergers took place, and for the weaker sisters that meant closure. Sometimes the name was kept, as with St Denis and Cranley

School. Now this particular gathering up of girls' schools (which also took in St Hilary's) is known by one name, in a final act of merger, as St Margaret's. And since the closure of the Catholic convent school in Whitehouse Loan there is only one St Margaret's.

It might be thought that changes of location would damage a school's traditions, or ethos (the Greeks had a word for it). But one school generation soon follows another, juniors become seniors, and nothing important seems to be lost by moving an entire school from one place to another. Symbolic items are taken along, like the snuff horn of wholesale tobacconist James Gillespie – to be presented annually by the youngest girl in the school and passed round sneezing teachers. A rhyme celebrated the Founder's wealth:

> Wha wad hae thocht it
> That noses had bocht it!

For girls' schools of Edinburgh, a central aspect of what parents have been willing to pay for over the years was single-sex education – the obvious justification for writing two separate books. It is logical to lose interest here in George Watson's girls at the point where they joined the boys in 1974, but co-education has become part of the story. John Watson's School and the Rudolph Steiner School (Alexander McCall Smith's neighbour, convenient for teasing) were always co-educational and all the more unusual for that.

In the year of the George Watson's union, however, Fettes College became the first Scottish boys' school to accept a girl for the two-year run up to A-Level. The following year there were fourteen in the sixth form, and by the centennial year of 1988 girls made up forty-six per cent of this boarding school's roll and were to be found in all classes. A particular version of co-education within the private sector can be seen in an innovative twinning arrangement between Mary Erskine's and two already-merged boys' schools, Daniel Stewart's and Melville College. There is a united primary department and the sixth form is also co-educational, but not the secondary years between. Merchiston Castle School is now the only remaining one in Edinburgh which is restricted to boys. The Edinburgh Academy, hitherto limiting girls to sixth form level, has recently accepted a vote by parents for a fully-mixed school by 2009, as reported in *The Scotsman* under the headline 'Another Bastion Falls…'

But the future may yet be feminist, if it is still permissible to link single-sex girls' schools with that cause. It certainly used to be. St George's began in 1886 as a training college dedicated to the ideal of well-educated female secondary school teachers – at a time when women were unable to study for university degrees. The school was opened two years later to provide classroom experience for adults training to be teachers, and it was almost as a by-product that pupils received a higher-class education equal to that of boys. The title of Nigel Shepley's history is worth quoting in full, *Women of Independent Mind: St George's School, Edinburgh, and the Campaign for Women's Education, 1888–1988.* In an updated 2007 version he addresses the feminist question head on: 'When the first edition was published, discrimination against women and girls in the educational system was still apparent. The defence of all-girls' schools on academic grounds was easy. Men outnumbered women in the higher posts of all the professions, there were still fewer women Members of Parliament than in 1945, and all the research demonstrated beyond doubt that in mixed schools there was discrimination, often unconscious, against girls… Since then, girls nationally, in mixed as well as single sex schools, have outperformed boys in almost all subjects and at all levels. They have also outnumbered men in what were once "male" subjects such as Law and Medicine, and have entered the professions in greater numbers…

'Perhaps this means that the battle is won, and the artificial separation of girls from boys in school is no longer necessary… The Headmistress and governors have had to ask themselves whether there is a future and a purpose for St George's School for Girls. Their answer is unhesitatingly and resoundingly: "Yes!" The latest research still supports single sex education. Although in mixed schools girls do better in examinations than boys, they, and boys too for that matter, do even better in single sex schools. Those who have been educated in girls' schools also tend to go on to earn more and to rise higher in their chosen careers. However, examination results and earning power are not all. The research also concludes that girls' schools inspire greater confidence, independence and ambition in their pupils. When questioned, this is also what parents and students have said and, most compelling of all, it is their belief that the school should retain its current status. St George's will continue to fulfill its mission of the last one hundred and twenty years, to enable girls to acquire the skills and independence of mind to equip them for life.'

As a historical comment on feminism, it may be noted that the two Merchant Company girls' schools were slow to give women a role beyond that of classroom chaperone for girls taught by university men. George Square appointed a female head before Queen Street, but even during the 1920s assumptions persisted in both these girls' schools as to the superior qualities of the male Scots 'dominie'. A positive aspect of this, as progressive people acknowledged at the time, was that girls received teaching in the same subjects as boys and sat the same exams. With the passing years they were even encouraged to look like them in blazers and ties, and share their boyish enthusiasm for sport. Meanwhile small private schools run by their proprietors continued to provide a 'ladylike' education: English and French were emphasised along with art, music and dancing. Mathematics was considered too hard for the girls at these schools – an attitude which was considered backward at the Merchant Company institutions.

Nigel Shepley had a particular point to make in connection with Miss Brodie: 'Muriel Spark omits to tell us where this most renowned of Edinburgh teachers was trained.' Jane Georgina Niven, the most Brodie-like teacher I have come across in the annals, was trained and educated in the Melville Street premises of St George's. Miss Niven took charge of Brunstane School in the eastern suburb of Joppa before transporting it to the South Side as Cranley. There she brought literature vividly to life, Brodie-style. Other Edinburgh headmistresses also trained at St George's.

We are back with Muriel Spark, that icon of single-sex education for girls. Returning to the class photograph of 1930, a caption in *Curriculum Vitae* specified 'James Gillespie's *Girls'* School'. James Gillespie's Boys' School opened nearby at Warrender Park in 1929: previously this had housed mixed primary classes like Muriel's, in exile from the main Gillespie's building where they met in First Infants. Miss Kay's class of the following year coincided with a return to Bruntsfield – the Promised Land – for teacher and pupils, and the boys were left in possession of Warrender Park. Eleven-year-old Muriel Camberg was in at the start of something big, under a teacher who knew it: Miss Kay would scarcely have described her class as the 'crème de la crème' if boys had still been in it.

There is more. Gillespie's had just been authorised by the Scottish Education Department to teach pupils up to Higher Grade, and in 1929 it became a full secondary school. So James Gillespie's High School for Girls was doubly a new creation when Muriel Camberg entered it: as a high school, and for girls. It is possible to forget that *The Prime of Miss Jean Brodie* is more about the years spent after leaving primary education. Two male teachers of music and art are central to the plot. The sexual frisson which carries it along must surely have arisen (in the real world of Gillespie's) from the tension between new education for girls and men in the midst of it. Five male teachers are recalled in Muriel Spark's autobiography, which scarcely mentions what was by that time an anomaly – the male head teacher who guided this changing school for twenty years before retiring in 1936. Muriel Spark never knew the lady who replaced him, and created her own headmistress in Miss Mackay. Of course there were also female role models on the Gillespie's staff apart from Miss Brodie in her prime. Miss Lockhart, presiding powerfully over the science laboratory, comes to mind.

One more thing is interesting about the class photograph. Half the girls including Muriel are in gym tunics, the rest in a variety of skirts and dresses. There is no school uniform, although a third of them wear ties in what appear to be maroon and yellow Gillespie's stripes. This suggests a school in process of establishing itself, which was true, although school uniforms generally were still quite new in the Twenties. Miss Kay's preference for variety over uniformity, it may be surmised, is implied by her comment on drab raincoats: 'Why make a wet day more dreary than it is? We should wear bright coats, and carry blue umbrellas or green.'

Muriel Spark makes a feature of the uniform she wore on first setting out across Bruntsfield Links at the age of five: 'I had a black velours hat with a red and yellow band and a JGS monogrammed band on it. The yellow JGS stood for James Gillespie's School. On my maroon blazer was another badge, a rampant yellow unicorn surmounting the school motto: *Fidelis et Fortis*. My parents had informed themselves that this meant Faithful and Strong. How clever we all were!' Here she misremembered (and admitted it) because the school motto with its accompanying unicorn's head was not introduced until 1927. A House system had just been set up, and the process of ethos-building was gathering strength. The velours hats and straw ones of most Edinburgh girls' schools later gave way to berets, but not at Gillespie's where a distinctive maroon box-hat was adopted. The streets of Scotland's capital city were to provide the stage for a pageant of uniforms in mid-century, and correctly worn headgear topped it off. The next two chapters are about outward appearances: the buildings which girls attended, and what they wore to school.

Chapter 2

Girls' Schools of Edinburgh

This chapter takes girls' schools from their Victorian beginnings to a 'prime' time after the Second World War. It is long, because there were a lot of them. When compulsory education from five to thirteen was introduced in 1872 the great majority of Scotland's girls were educated alongside their brothers, but they left sooner because grammar schools and academies were for '*lads* o' pairts' – talented boys who might come from humble homes. Fees were charged everywhere, but the leading citizens of Edinburgh wanted a higher level of education for their sons and, in time, their daughters. Classical education for boys was available at

CONSIDERATE—VERY !

Master George (alluding to the New Governess, who happened to be within hearing). " Cross, Disagreeable Old Thing, I call her !"
Miss Caroline. " Oh, Georgy ! but we ought to give way to Her ; recollect, dear, She's a very Awkward Age !"

5. *Home education according to* Punch.

the old High School and the new Academy, modern subjects at the Edinburgh Institution in Queen Street. The sons of families in the New Town were well catered for. What of their sisters?

The tradition had been one of 'lock up your daughters', with governesses providing education at home. A School for Ministers' Daughters was opened because of 'their finances not allowing them to employ an accomplished governess.' Charlotte Fenton, founder of Lansdowne House, was a typical lady of culture who had never been to school. She came to the city with four girls to 'make a home for them and educate them with the help of masters and some private classes to which we had been introduced'. This compromise between home and school was not ideal. On every street 'some delicate girl could be seen hurrying from class to class (according as each teacher found their partisans), which were held at their respective houses. These young creatures were generally encumbered with a load of books, and the time lost called for some better plan.' The obvious plan was for teachers to come to pupils. Schools were limited by the accommodation available in private houses, but those known as 'institutions' became relatively large.

The Scottish Institution for the Education of Young Ladies opened in 1833 at 65 Queen Street. It had a resident lady superintendent and ten visiting masters for subjects which extended – remarkably for that day – to 'natural philosophy' or physics. The Scottish Institution was run by 'a native of England' recommended by the Duchess of Buccleuch and Lady Sinclair, 'who have their daughters under the care of Mrs Furlong.' She was the Lady Superintendent. It moved to 15 Great Stuart Street and then 9 Moray Place but closed after nearly forty years when the Merchant Company day schools opened in 1870. At 23 Charlotte Square the Edinburgh Institution for the Education of Young Ladies was opened in 1838 by the same Mrs Furlong, this time as proprietor, but she soon retired to London. One girl, sent there at fifteen, had a considerable journey from home to school as recalled by her sister: 'All the way from George Square to Charlotte Square you kept declaring that you just hated going to a large school, and that it was too bad of me having put father and mother up to sending you, but I knew you would thank me some day.' Mary Erskine's foundation in Queen Street also followed the fashion in naming: for nearly twenty years it was the Edinburgh Institution for Young Ladies. One more school of the same

6. *Edinburgh Ladies' College, Queen Street.*

type, the Edinburgh Ladies' Institution for the Southern Districts, looked away from the New Town though it began at 55 George Street. Later it moved to receive pupils at 37 George Square (a quite different address) before yielding to the lower fees of the Merchant Company girls' school round the corner.

Some schools were short-lived: the North British Academy for the Education of Young Ladies at 121 George Street opened and closed in the 1830s. Similarly the Royal Circus Institution for the Education of Young Ladies provided William Begbie with a living for only ten years. Mr and Mrs Ollendorf opened their Nelson Street home as the Edinburgh Collegiate Institution for the Education of Young Ladies. Alexander Law observed: 'Concentrating, as did most private schools for girls, on languages, music and dancing, this was a popular school; it began about 1850 with 30 pupils, and in three years had 100 on the roll.' Despite moving to Great King Street for a bigger dance floor, the Collegiate Institution closed a few years later. Most institutions had rolls in three figures, but not by much. The majority of pupils were day girls aged from eleven to fifteen. Fees were kept at a level suitable for young ladies, but the parents of some girls paid less for a narrower range of subjects. These pupils sat exams. According to Dr Lindy Moore, public examinations were 'seen by most upper-middle-class parents as appropriate for girls of a lower social class who were intending to become governesses.'

The girls' schools known as institutions invariably ended up being run by men, and two successive headmasters presided over the Merchant Company girls' school which became established in Queen Street. James Pryde was first made responsible for transforming the Merchant Maiden Hospital at Archibald Place in Lauriston, with its seventy-five Foundationers, into a day school for 1,200 'daughters of merchants and well-to-do shopkeepers and members of the professions.' Almost half of those who came to the new school were aged five to twelve. A year after the Lauriston dormitories had been converted into classrooms during the summer of 1870, the building was handed over by Merchant Company decree to George Watson's College. Boys and masters arrived in September, their old boarding hospital having been sold to the Royal Infirmary. Meanwhile James Pryde was starting all over again in Queen Street.

The Edinburgh buildings known as tenements traditionally rose very high, a Scottish architectural phenomenon which may explain why the terraced buildings between 70 and 73 Queen Street had five storeys from street level. Below was a basement. Marjorie Chaplyn, who was both pupil and head teacher, remembered it as 'dusty and dank with, at the end, a forbidden cobwebbed eerie space; I was dumbfounded to learn that when the school moved in from Lauriston that twilit region was the recreation room.' Next door to the former British Hotel (one of the two buildings purchased) the Hopetoun Rooms had been designed for dances and public gatherings: 'The School Hall was famous in Edinburgh as having been the setting for a recital by Chopin on his Scottish tour. [It was] elliptical in shape, with a glass cupola supported by Greek caryatid figures and with a raised area which could be closed off by sliding doors... Architect David McGibbon could do nothing radical to convert the building for school use.'

A two-storey extension to the rear added recreation and luncheon rooms, and plans were drawn up in 1908 to rebuild the central area. They were never carried out, because the Scottish Education Department insisted on a separate primary school and set a limit of 600 on secondary numbers. The primary pupils moved in 1909 to newly-acquired premises at 16 Atholl Crescent, off Shandwick Place. This was convenient for tram cars and trains at the west end of Princes Street. However the dancing mistresses experienced a particular problem travelling between the two sites, and Queen Street's head asked the Merchant Company to approve 'the use of a cab: The total expenditure for 76 hires would be between £2 and £3 per annum. Were this arranged it would be unnecessary for the teachers to change their boots and they would be fresher for their work.'

At Queen Street the youngest children had hitherto relied for exercise on 'a little walk, tiptoeing upstairs from their class-room, along the corridor and down the other stairs, two by two.' Atholl Crescent's veranda and garden to the rear meant unimaginable freedom. Meanwhile in the main school 'congestion in the corridors was relieved, class movements during school intervals greatly simplified and stair climbing much reduced.' A proposed move to what became the Falconhall playing-field in Morningside came to nothing, but in 1912 No. 69 Queen Street became available for eastward expansion. Architect Hippolyte Blanc's plan for an equivalent expansion on the west side fell through, but he deserves to be remembered for the school's distinctive roof garden. The cost was fully £23,000, and heads were shaken when St George's obtained an entire new school shortly after this, along with extensive grounds, for very little more. The Company was financially stretched, and there was to be no more building for half a century.

Early on a Queen Street pupil was nearly hit by falling plaster, but two world wars came and went before the situation was recognised as dangerous. In 1950 the Clerk of Works reported that 'the northern portion of the Old Building has been elaborately shored up and stiffened by cast iron columns and steel beams… In the Staff dining-room during the vacation the painter drew attention to the swinging ceiling; the plasterer immediately investigated this and little or no encouragement was required to bring down approximately two tons of plaster… This ceiling appeared sound, having no cracks or bulges. In view of these disclosures, can any of the ceilings now passed as safe be counted on for one year ahead?'

Six years later thirteen Junior classroom ceilings collapsed during the night. Summoned by phone, headmistress Muriel Jennings 'didn't like the feel of the building.' A flat opposite her home round the corner was promptly purchased, and after three days of frantic activity (pupils kept at home, parents forbidden to make contact) school resumed at 18 Ainslie Place. Worse was to come: 'Scarcely had we recovered from the excitements of the first term when the walls and ceilings of the Junior School began to collapse all at once and a large part of the building had to be evacuated. One third of the school is now sealed off by cardboard partitions behind which workmen are busy tearing down the whole interior of the building. This sudden disintegration surprised no one; indeed it is astonishing that the building lasted as long as it did. While the harassed Higher candidates were furiously trying to acquire some knowledge, the so-called "leisure class" (the VI Form) was tying pieces of coloured string on every chair in sight and then carrying all the furniture in the building up and down several flights of stairs and even along Queen Street. This aroused considerable interest in Edinburgh.'

Faced with all the mess, nine cleaners gave up their jobs. Classes were held in corridors as well as at nearby Simpson House, where pupils had to shift their own chairs and desks every day. Summing up, the redoubtable Miss Jennings wrote: 'No-one can complain that school life is dull.' That

7. Miss Jennings.

summer a survey of the Ravelston estate was carried out. Surrounded by modern villas and young families, it lay to the west of Daniel Stewart's College and St George's School for Girls. Almost ten years were to pass, however, before 'the Great Trek' of 1966 established the Mary Erskine School on its present site – modern, purpose-built and surrounded by greenery. Not everyone approved:

'As sixth-formers with long experience of life at Queen Street we cannot help wondering rather uneasily about the effect of new surroundings on the Mary Erskine girl. The distant sound of a cuckoo (or even a wood-pigeon) can hardly give the same intellectual stimulus as the roar of traffic on Queen Street and the unloading of milk crates in the lane. We fear that easy living at Ravelston may produce poorer physical specimens in years to come. There will no longer be four flights of stairs to scale in double quick time...' But the rising generation saw things differently: 'I have so much space to run about in that when I have run right round the jim I'm quite puffed out. We

8. *The Mary Erskine School at Ravelston.*

have a playground so big that you don't youshally bump into anyone. Yes certainly our new school is better than the old one.'

This concentration on an unsafe building hardly does justice to Queen Street's fine reputation, but it is natural to contrast appearances – as parents did – with those of other girls' schools. St George's was preferred by the upper-middle classes, who paid six guineas a term when Merchant Company fees ranged from 12s. 6d. to £3 a quarter. The first phase of St George's was to do with advancing the cause of women as teachers. Randolph Place, where St George's Training College began with seven students, is linked by a lane to Charlotte Square in the New Town. Two years later in 1888 it moved further into the West End when a 'practising-school' was opened at 3 and 5 Melville Street. St George's was there for twenty-five years, latterly in four buildings characterised by 'a rabbit warren of corridors and stairs'.

Melville Street had been laid out spaciously at the end of the Georgian period and it benefited visually from the soaring spires of St Mary's Cathedral. Old girls cherished their memories: 'The whole thing was so exciting – we had never had a school of that sort in Edinburgh. There were only the rather grim looking institutions known as "George Square" and the "Merchant Maidens", or the small private schools in ordinary houses…

9. St George's at Melville Street.

October 1888 saw flocks of girls leaving the "dining-room table schools" for which Edinburgh was famed and assembling, many without notice, on the doorstep at Melville Street to be examined as to stage of advancement... More and more chairs had to be brought in. Paper and pens also ran short, and a teacher hurried out to buy them in Queensferry Street.'

St George's offered small classes partly because girls of similar age arrived at different levels of attainment. Principal Mary Walker started with three teachers and an intimate atmosphere: 'At first, when the front room of No. 3 held us all, it seemed odd and unnecessary to hear the roll called every morning.' Fifty-six pupils were accepted at the start, and in two years the numbers rose rapidly: 'St George's High School with over 150 girls and an adequate staff of mistresses, with a gym built out behind, was truly something different. The Melville Street buildings were a great advance on anything scholastic then found in Scotland with the golden exception of St Leonard's, St Andrews.' More classrooms were added as Nos. 7 and 9 were acquired, but when the number of pupils rose above 'the optimum 200' St George's felt crowded. By the time a decision was made to start again on a green field site in Murrayfield close to the boarding house at 14 Ravelston Park (a move which took place in the autumn term of 1914) Melville Street had lost its appeal. First, an increase in iron-wheeled traffic over cobbled streets made it noisy, and then the 'acrid, smoky air' of the internal combustion engine gave another reason for closing windows.

The new St George's designed by Balfour Paul was described as 'colonial neo-Georgian', attractive in light-coloured Scottish harling with small-paned windows. An inspector called: 'The building itself looks quite palatial... Its greatest length faces south and west, so as to get the maximum of warmth and sunshine. Its plan suggests the letter E – the classrooms which are most used being in the long bar, with a southern exposure, while the end crossbars form important blocks, and the central one denotes a large and beautiful hall... I was much struck by the care

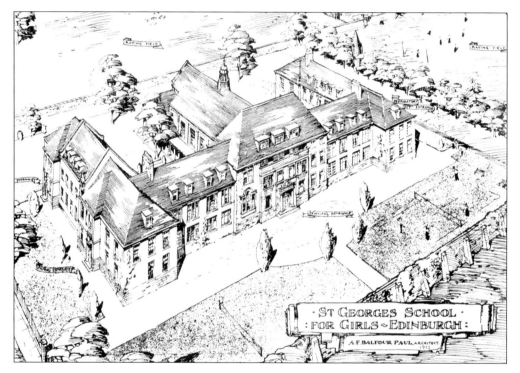

10. *The new St George's.*

which had been given to all the planning, especially in those important and minute details affecting cleanliness, comfort and ventilation... The class-rooms have the artistic touch of decoration which is absent from a boys' school.' Forty years on, the building still gave satisfaction to staff: 'No one would exchange it for the glass and concrete disasters of the 1960s. Its solidity is as comforting and enduring as the founding principles.'

Lansdowne House was another girls' school run by women – though Miss Fenton and her companion were thorough ladies. After two false starts elsewhere in the West End this home-based version of school became established at 21 Lansdowne Crescent, near St Mary's Cathedral, and took the name Lansdowne House. 'Day-boarders' who attended from their homes were still in a minority at the end of the Victorian era, compared with fourteen 'house-girls', and the roll did not reach three figures for half a century. Miss Fenton commented on the standard of health at the first Lansdowne House, thanks to 'the high and healthy position of the estate'. A final move to 36 Coltbridge Terrace in Murrayfield came in 1901, when the old premises were taken over by St Monica's School. The Murrayfield

11. *Lansdowne House.*

mansion had been designed for his own use by the architect responsible for the Episcopalian Gothic of Trinity College, Glenalmond (a boys' boarding school in Perthshire) and was suitably magnificent.

In 1895 Miss Gamgee's School opened at 21 Alva Street between Melville Street and Shandwick Place, following the death of her father at the age of ninety-three. She had grown up in Florence along with three brothers and four sisters, and the original group of day girls and boarders included two nieces. The earliest school photograph shows Miss Gamgee with seven others: the young girl seated on the ground is presumably a niece. Growing numbers resulted in a move to 8 Rothesay Place, and neighbouring No. 10 was also acquired by the school which became known as Rothesay House.

Over the years two other buildings in Rothesay Terrace were added, and No. 1 became the main building with a large School Room which was used for assemblies. Girls entered at age eight, with numbers close to a hundred by the outbreak of the Second World War. Some parents sent their daughters on to English boarding-schools (Sherborne, Tudor Hall, Benenden) or else St Leonard's, so that numbers in the top classes were always small. The roll never passed one hundred and twenty. In the absence of central heating, Rothesay House was cold in winter. 'There were small fires in most classrooms, but a stove in a couple of the larger rooms gave off greater heat. Coal was carried in buckets up many flights of stairs by long-suffering domestic staff.' The PNEU Queen Margaret's in India Street had a similar domestic feel to it, with girls from nursery age to eighteen sharing the owner's kitchen (used for biology) and bathroom.

The school which became St Serf's began at 7 Albany Street on the Broughton edge of the New Town, but Miss Mary Williamson took advantage of the sale of former Lord Provost Sir John Boyd's house to move closer to its heart. In 1892 she led her pupils into the curve of Abercromby Place. No. 11 had four storeys above a two-level basement and looked on to Queen Street Gardens. From the top rear windows there were views across to Fife where St Serf had converted pagans. The 1901 census recorded sixteen rooms in the house and six boarders from counties as far apart as Sutherland and Devon. One girl was born in India. The sister of another pupil helped Miss Williamson in class, and there were two resident governesses – one for music and the other teaching the language of her native France. Miss Williamson's old aunt lived among these young people, and the household was completed by a cook and two maids.

Success (linked to location) turned it into something more than a household. A 1927 advertisement for St Serf's Boarding and Day School had pupils 'prepared for Leaving Certificates by a large staff of Qualified Resident and Visiting Mistresses.' Masters, generally speaking, were no longer visiting girls' schools by this time. The Educational Directory for 1926–27 named Miss Williamson as Principal and Miss Duffes as Headmistress. Transfer of ownership to Miss Duffes followed. She is remembered for wearing a fur coat and headpiece indoors: small coal fires again. A full entry appeared for 1933–34: 'St Serf's School for Girls (Preparatory for Boys). Principal Miss Duffes M.A. (Hons.). Boarding and Day School for

Girls from Kindergarten to University Entrance; Individual Attention from Staff of Specialists; Preparation for University Preliminary, Music and Drawing Examinations. Boys prepared for Edinburgh Academy and other schools.' Boarders were no longer accepted. Following the death of Miss Duffes the school was purchased jointly by two married ladies, possibly widows. The new owners turned the back garden over to netball and – remarkably – a squash court. Demand was high in the Fifties due to the post-war birth rate, and St Serf's flourished along with the other girls' schools.

The school which became St Denis is remarkable for the number of houses which it occupied: six in the thirty-three years from 1855, followed by two more moves in the twentieth century. Miss Simson's School began in Great King Street before shifting along into Royal Circus, then crossing the Dean Bridge to Buckingham Terrace. Jane Simson's Edinburgh period (before she transferred her attention to London's debutantes in season) came to an end at 2 Magdala Crescent off Haymarket Terrace. Miss Simson employed Mlle. le Harivel and Maria M. Gotha as governesses in French and German. Music was taught by a gentleman who went on to become Principal of the Royal Academy of Music, and visiting masters were also responsible for art and elocution. A charming document of the time has survived. Caroline Potter was one of four little girls who shared a bedroom at Magdala Crescent when there were twenty-four older pupils in residence. Seventy-five years later she produced her collection of pupil verses and drawings along with signatures and addresses of staff.

The album of this girl also had the home addresses of her companions. There were Romanes sisters from Lauder and Lawson sisters from Kingskettle in Fife. The brother of Jessie Haig from Dollar became Field-Marshal Haig. The end-of-term journey made by Gloria Coates from Ayr was partly shared with a MacMillan girl who lived at Darvel near Kilmarnock. Sarah Dickson of Thornhill in Nithsdale also came from south-west Scotland: much later, in wartime, St Denis was evacuated to nearby Drumlanrig Castle. The most northerly girls were Lucy Burt, Aberfeldy, and Annie Thomson from Kincarrathie near Perth. Schoolgirl memory is selective, as a later headmistress observed when describing the album: 'Mrs Fergusson's recollections of her activities in her early schooldays are of matters important to a schoolgirl – long, dull walks along the Glasgow Road under the supervision of a governess; visits on Saturdays to Vallance's sweet shop at the West End (now occupied by Rankin's Fruit Market) and, with three whole pennies to spend, the purchase there of rosebuds and toffee drops; Sunday service at West Coates Parish Church situated at the corner of Magdala Crescent, and, for the Seniors, Dr Forrester's Bible Class. And not a word about lessons!'

The proprietor's niece Miss Saunders was one of the five lady teachers. When Miss Simson retired in 1883, the niece transferred the school to its fifth home at 42 Drumsheugh Gardens. She then moved along to No. 14 before leaving for America and marriage. Boarders were restricted to twelve, and Miss Mack's School – new name, new owner – was mainly for day girls. Then in 1908 Miss Bourdass took over: a photograph shows her solemn in spectacles, and there is a word-picture: 'Miss Mack had been a rather tall, commanding sort of woman, Miss Bourdass was tiny, not more than five feet, but we found very soon that the matter of inches did not make any difference.' It was she who first called the school St Denis, having taught English in the Paris suburb of that name, in order to provide 'continuing identity' for a mobile school.

21 Chester Street off Palmerston Place was acquired for St Denis in 1914 with three storeys on a corner site. Maybell Benvie, who was to be the next owner, joined the staff after graduating as a mature student. She looked uncannily like the actress Margaret Rutherford. Miss Benvie spent four years teaching English at Chester Street before going to St Bride's School

St. Denis School, Edinburgh.

12. *St Denis at Chester Street.*

at 5 Ettrick Road. This was in the suburb of Merchiston. Three years later she was invited to take over the ownership of St Denis, and in 1924 Miss Benvie looked to Drumsheugh Gardens for a second site at No. 10. A kindergarten was added so that St Denis now catered for the full age range, although there were still only about seventy girls. When St Bride's closed in 1932 Miss Benvie decided to buy the house, but departure from the West End was not undertaken lightly. A twenty-four-seater bus went round the town in the morning collecting pupils and took them home for lunch. Miss Benvie gathered support from the families, shrewdly turning St Denis into an independent school with shareholders. It now had a

13. *The St Denis bus.*

garden, and she waxed horticultural: 'Two years ago we transplanted, and St Denis of Chester Street and Drumsheugh Gardens is now St Denis of Ettrick Road. For a time we felt perhaps a little bewildered at the sudden change of environment – elevation, space and air. But now we are acclimatised and our roots are searching down into rich soil.'

St Bride's had set out to be a second St George's, with a declared allegiance to 'methods on best High School lines' and a staff of 'university women'. One of these, Catherine Fraser Lee, was briefly in charge before she opened her own school as St Trinnean's. Canaan Park, some of whose pupils transferred to the burgeoning St Denis of Ettrick Road, was a notably academic girls' school like St Bride's. In 1909 a Miss Dick took possession of the Old House at the corner of Canaan Lane. When it became the Astley Ainslie Hospital, 'Canaanites' – staff and pupils – moved on to Blackford Park House in South Oswald Road. On retiring and selling up, Miss Dick 'chose St Denis as the school which most clearly identified with Canaan Park College in ideals,' according to Miss Benvie, 'and particularly because she held the conviction that school should be a happy place.' St Denis certainly became a harder-working place under the influence of these clever newcomers.

The trajectory of Cranley was unusual, starting as Brunstane School in distant Joppa before bumping to land between Merchiston and Polwarth. As a governess at Lippe, Westphalia, the founder Elizabeth Douglas had taught the future Queen of the Netherlands, but it was the strong personality of Jane Georgina Niven (St George's-trained) which brought about considerable change. The plain name – at a time when most girls' schools were being named after saints – implied no want of religious feeling, but came from what was already there at 42 Colinton Road: 'I remember the excitement of the little band of boarders when they caught sight of the name above the gate. We decided to keep that as the name of the school. It had been chosen for the name of their home by a saintly

14. *Cranley School.*

husband and wife.' William Hunter may indeed have been saintly, but he owned a brewery in Fountainbridge.

The roll was seventy-seven in 1920, day girls joining the little band, and it doubled in six years. More space was required: 'The day Miss Niven told us of our new home at Redwood, Spylaw Road, I shall never forget. Our whole class retired to the bathroom to discuss this earth-shaking news. One girl who had started in the K.G. burst into tears and declared, "Our childhood is over! Remember the plasticine models in the Transition and our tree-houses in the woodland?"' Kindergarten and Transition classes were on the ground floor at '42'. Some of the place's intimacy was transferred to 16 Spylaw Road, and on Friday mornings the whole school assembled sitting cross-legged in the largest room. Latterly it was standing-room only, however, with sixth formers in the outer hall. Cranley gained a fine reputation for science – in unpromising circumstances since the laboratories started out as a conservatory and a greenhouse. The first doubled as a sheltered place for drinking milk (third-pint bottles and straws) at morning interval. A water barometer was later erected against the tower of the main building.

Since this is a historical chapter, schools long closed are worth rescuing from oblivion. The Trades Maiden Hospital continued until late in the nineteenth century at Rillbank Terrace, Mary Erskine having also left money for tradesmen's daughters. The site was acquired for the Sick Children's Hospital. The Bell Academy at 15 Lauder Road, owned by Miss Bryden Bell, advertised for 'young ladies' but only took in girls to the age of ten. The Grange Home School which effectively succeeded it was at 123 Grange Loan for half a century. Also a primary school, it peaked at 150 pupils. Craigmount Girls' School in Dick Place had a similar roll for the full age range. Its proprietor Miss Adamson had sold St Elizabeth's School at 1 Rothesay Terrace, which continued under new management as the main building of Rothesay House. She bore away – like trophies – the motto and badge of St Elizabeth's, but Craigmount closed in turn after wartime evacuation. Edinburgh Southern Institution for the Board and Education of Young Ladies opened in 1878 at 11 Strathearn Road in Morningside 'to meet the requirements of the large and growing population of the Southern Suburbs'. Within twelve years, as Strathearn College, it had turned into a school of cookery and domestic economy.

Newington became the most densely populated of these suburbs. The district was served by public transport in the form of horse-drawn trams, with underground cables added for the hills. Electric trams replaced the cable-car system in 1921. Newington Institution for Young Ladies shared 8 Salisbury Place with a boys' academy under the same director. Both moved round the corner to 41 and 43 Newington Road before giving way to enterprises better placed for southward expansion. To the right of the broad downhill thoroughfare which starts as Minto Street, the Institution for the Education of Young Ladies at 5 Duncan Street was followed by the Bellwood Institution at 58 St Alban's Road. Craigmillar Park College at 6 Crawfurd Road developed out of Madame Muriset's 'boarding and day school for girls of all ages'. Back in the New Town, 'all the saints' included St Oran's (named for an abbot of Iona) round the corner from Scotland Street, and there was also a St Anne's at Succoth Place in the West End.

St Hilda's was opened in 1901 beside Liberton Kirk by Miss Rosa Stoltz, a George Square girl who graduated early from Edinburgh University. It left town at the start of the second war and never returned. The founder regarded it as a celebration of place: 'From the age of ten or thereabouts I had lived at the top of a steep hill overlooking Edinburgh. How many hours did I not waste gazing down on this storied city at my feet with its defiant old Castle in the centre richly studded about with domes and spires? As my undergraduate days were drawing to a close, I began to think about the future. Then one night – half awake, half asleep – my path was lit as by a flash of lightning. I would build up a large girls' school – a boarding school complete in itself, now and here – here on this very spot so that future generations of girls might enjoy what I had enjoyed.'

A caricature of St Trinnean's became famous through the cartoonist Ronald Searle. The real school opened in the Grange at 10 Palmerston Road in 1922 but moved after three years. Proprietor Catherine Fraser Lee registered the improvement in accommodation: 'Classes were being held in every nook and cranny... I was most fortunate to be given a lease of St Leonard's, a lovely castellated mansion house with a magnificent outlook over the King's Park and Arthur's Seat in the background... How wonderful it was to have our Playing Field and Tennis Courts in our own ground, and big bright House Rooms, and best of all a room to house our large library where the girls could sit and browse! We had a large well-equipped gymnasium and a garden large enough to allow all four Junior Houses to have their own garden plot.'

Esdaile (otherwise the Ministers' Daughters' College) was described as 'one of Edinburgh's most interesting schools' – the judgement being an architectural one, for the mansion in Kilgraston Road is imposing still. With ministers of the Established Church serving parishes all over Scotland, it was mainly a secondary boarding school. Despite having spacious grounds, Esdaile girls were regularly sent out and about: 'Each walk, with only marginal detours for dire necessity, was referred to by an identity number… The line, or crocodile, of girls frequently stretched several hundred yards, "policed" at intervals by prefects and members of staff at the rear.' There is a *Scottish Field* photograph of the Esdaile column drawn up in front of the school, seniors resplendent in straw hats, dark coats and gloves, with flat black shoes for walking round the Grange.

As daughters of the manse they would have taken more than a passing interest in what went on behind the walls of the Convent in Whitehouse Loan, where St Margaret's girls worked and prayed and sometimes emerged with hockey sticks. Its gate-house hints at the grandeur of Gillespie Graham's chapel from which a great bell rang out the Angelus at noon. The boarding school began soon after the Convent opened in 1834, close to the Episcopal residence in Greenhill Gardens. Later there were two schools: 'The Ursulines of Jesus give a first-class education to young ladies whom they receive as boarders, and also conduct a Day School for young ladies at St Anne's Seminary, Strathearn Road.' This turreted villa known as The Tower is now home to a reduced community of nuns. The school roll rose above three hundred in the Seventies after being small for a record number of years: with the Merchant Maiden Hospital coming into another category, St Margaret's had the distinction of being the oldest Edinburgh girls' school.

Two Catholic schools were also advertised by the Sisters of Mercy at St Catherine's Convent in Lauriston Gardens. Pupils were required to bring sheets and pillow-cases to both, but one was for young ladies and the other for pupil-teachers. A third convent school took over teacher-training when Sacred Heart Sisters from Roehampton in south-west London came to 28 Moray Place. Their students were housed nearby in Ainslie Place. The 1918 Education Act had just brought Scotland's Catholic schools into the state sector and many more teachers were required. After the First World War the Sacred Heart Sisters moved out to Craiglockhart, where shell-shock was treated and war poets met. Formerly a 'hydropathic' hotel, the convent school which was opened for demonstrating lessons to students was unique, among the institutions under discussion, in having a swimming-pool.

The better known St Margaret's began – under a slightly different name – as two identical schools in Morningside and Newington. The enterprise was announced in August 1890: 'THE QUEEN MARGARET COLLEGE FOR YOUNG LADIES, Cluny Drive, Morningside (adjoining Morningside Tennis Courts, and close to the Tramway Terminus). James Buchanan, M.A., Head Master. Session begins 1st October… Parents are invited to call and inspect the building, which is quite new and designed expressly for a Ladies' School.' An equivalent handbill was circulated in Newington to advertise a very similar school at East Suffolk Road. St Margaret's at Cluny Drive served the area west of Blackford Hill where streets were still being laid out on both sides of the city boundary.

The twin schools were the first in Edinburgh to be built for the purpose of educating girls. Buchanan, who had taught at George Square before setting up his own educational business, gave an end of session report: 'The St Margaret's Ladies' Colleges have just closed… They have been very successful, an attendance of no less than 200 pupils having been secured. Alike in every particular, they stand in healthy situations, and are fitted up with every improvement necessary.' Ten classrooms were mainly on the ground floor, with an assembly hall upstairs. Stone staircases at each end deadened sound and satisfied later fire regulations. The south side was restricted to one storey, and had skylights as well as windows (art and drawing a specialty). Buchanan regularly cycled between his two schools, though staff went by train between Newington and Morningside stations. He died of a heart attack just before the start of session 1897–98. Management of the joint enterprise fell to Mrs Buchanan who was then mother to a nine-week-old baby. Nothing daunted, having been a star pupil of her husband's at George Square, she handed the child over to a nursemaid and taught mornings at Newington, afternoons at Morningside.

Two sisters joined her: 'Miss Burnett was our Headmistress, so pleasant, so attractive, so well dressed. Her sister, Miss Violet, was head of Newington, and each School considered that its Miss Burnett excelled the other in looks, dress and manners; these things far out-weighing scholastic attainments!' The Morningside district developed faster than Newington, and for years the Cluny Drive school was more profitable. One effect of opening two girls' schools on the suburban line was that numbers attending the Merchant Company's schools fell at George Square and Queen Street: 'The Company must fight to get its pupils back.' Queen Street also lost pupils when Trinity and Leith Academies, charging lower fees, were opened by the Edinburgh School Board. The north side of Edinburgh included a high proportion of park land, some of which was to be turned into school playing-fields. Lixmount School for Girls at 33 East Trinity Road was the only one of its kind north of Canonmills.

In 1926, to the astonishment of all, Mrs Buchanan sold Cluny Drive. The new owner was Miss C. M. Muirhead, a product of St George's College who had gone to Cambridge for further teacher-training. Her experience of the Hilary Term there must have influenced her choice of name: girls of the new St Hilary's circled a Maypole at the Zoo to publicise the school through English folk-dancing. In 1937 No. 14 Cluny Drive was purchased to obtain extra kitchen space 'for the more practical, less academic pupils', and then No. 16 after the war for additional boarders. Before long St Hilary's had a waiting list.

'Mrs B' also sold her husband's foundation at Newington after thirty-two years as Principal. Grace Matthew, who succeeded, had taught Latin in both schools. She kept the name St Margaret's and negotiated a sticky patch. A small school of sixty-nine day girls and four boarders became

15. *St Margaret's in Newington – or Morningside?*

one of 150 by 1937 – no mean achievement in a period of economic depression. During the second war a reduced day school continued nearby when the main building was requisitioned for military purposes, the head's sister and her husband opening their home at 5 Suffolk Road to forty pupils. A house was also acquired on Mayfield Road for younger girls. When peace was restored a record 200 pupils presented themselves, and there was no room for the evacuees who constituted St Margaret's in Perthshire: like most Edinburgh girls' schools St Margaret's moved to avoid the risk of bombing. There was a separate school of the same name at Auchterarder for many years, and when the lease ended in 1956 staff and pupils finally returned to town – or close to town. The new boarding-house was at Pittendreich House in Lasswade.

George Watson's Ladies' College shared with St Margaret's and St Margaret's Convent the distinction of never leaving its original site – clear exceptions to this chapter's theme of mobility. The first building acquired by the Merchant Company in George Square had been the residence of Henry Dundas, Viscount Melville, who was Prime Minister Pitt's man in North Britain. Melville House became a Ladies' Boarding School and then a boys' school under Alexander Thomson. In 1871 the Merchant Company bought it and kept him on as head. The five hundred girls who first enrolled rose to double by the turn of the century, and the school spread along the north side at a suitably Georgian height of three storeys.

Heating pipes were blamed for headaches, and Mr Thomson became familiar to pupils as the 'man who walks about the school and attends to the ventilation.' Classrooms held fifty pupils: 'I like to think back to the old rooms on the east side with their rows of benches in tiers reaching up to the wall at the back of the room. No single desks and seats then – long benches with long desks in front of them and a good view of everyone.' Tiered classrooms were modern, as also speaking-tubes connecting the head to all corners. Electric bells and lights were introduced following consultation with a Professor of Electrical Engineering. The most striking effect was that of the Central Hall, which was below street level.

When the garden of Melville House was turned into a luncheon room the loss of fresh air was regretted, and pupils were sent out to George Square for seven minutes of every hour (although the residents' garden was closed to them). It was considered fortunate that most walked a

16. *George Square.*

'reasonable distance' to school. For some it was an uphill struggle: 'School life started for me when, at the age of four and adorned in a white hat and coat [no Watson's maroon in these days] I walked with my brothers from the far end of Mayfield Road to school. The building itself was most impressive to a youngster – the overwhelming grandeur as I saw it.' This Woman Watsonian – as George Square old girls were called – gloried in having been part of everything from the start, with 'no Primary or Elementary School to keep the young in isolation'. However Miss Dorothy Nicolson, as headmistress after the Second World War, regarded the primary department at 58 St Alban's Road as her greatest material contribution. A typical example of recycled school accommodation, it had formerly been the Bellwood Institution (mentioned above). Thereafter George Square was dedicated entirely to secondary education. Nooks and crannies were lovingly recorded for the Art Department when closure came in 1974. It would be wrong to assume, however, that girls who attended the schools which moved felt less affection for the buildings which housed them.

Chapter 3

A Variety of Uniforms

School uniforms came to Edinburgh as an 'English thing'. Writing about England's public schools, Jonathon Gathorne-Hardie noted the increasing regimentation of pupils through dress: 'The Godolphin School gives a good chronological picture. In 1889 this was a small old-fashioned private school with about eighteen boarders. There were few rules or restrictions and girls were free to go out with no uniform worn… During the 1890s girls pour in. Houses are introduced, monitors and prefects are started, and some elements of uniform – white hats with black bands, and gym tunics – are worn… By 1904 there are over 200 girls. Eton collars and ties are added… Skirts and regulation coats are added to the uniform. In 1910 the final articles of clothing unspecified – blouses and shoes – are regulated.' Scotland followed on.

But London's Blue Coat School reminds us that uniforms go back to the sixteenth century in charitable institutions, and Edinburgh's Merchant Maiden Hospital had a uniform of sorts: in 1733 (to control how often items were supplied) the Merchant Company instituted a 'Rule for the Cloathing of the Girls in time coming', although it allowed the Sunday gown to be 'dyed blue or green or any other colour that the treasurer and auditors shall direct'. The committee only insisted that gowns of cotton drugget should have 'a colour different from that now wore by the Girls of the Trades Maiden Hospital'. One Merchant Maiden Governess objected to 'the impropriety of girls going to church in different coloured Hats and Bonnets, that part of their dress being furnished by their friends'. Sunday black prevailed.

An illustration of approved Merchant Maiden winter and summer dress for 1841 suggests uniform, but later studio photographs display a variety of attire. The last Governess is shown with six of her girls. All are in sumptuous silks of the mid-Victorian era, three buttons from neck to hem for the darker gowns and single buttons for light ones. Neckwear and material also vary: they are more like fashion plates than schoolgirls, which points to an explanation. Dress-making was given particular attention

Merchant Maiden summer and winter dress, 1841

17. Uniforms for Hospital girls?

at the Hospital, where it was assumed that most pupils would become governesses or milliners. But even Scottish hospital schools laid no great stress on pupils being dressed the same.

English influence can be seen at St Leonard's School in the university town of St Andrews. It formed the link between Cheltenham Ladies' College and Edinburgh, customs emanating from the south being passed on from St Andrews to St George's as the city representative of High School ideals. When St Leonard's opened in 1877 no thought was given to uniformity of appearance, but ten years later there was a change: 'Miss Dove, casting her eye over her house, felt she could no longer brook the patchy appearance offered by the endless varieties of attire. Hats at any rate might be dealt with, and a school hat was then and there determined on. It was easy to carry out the intention, for the long reign of the sailor hat as fashionable headgear had begun… A wave of the wand, so to speak, and school blossomed into neat straw hats, trimmed with the house colours recently adopted.' A woollen tam-o'-shanter 'fell into disuse with the quickly growing habit of discarding the wear of any kind of hat in the playground.'

On the other side of the Forth a similar fashion appeared among the pupils of Brunstane School in Joppa. There, straw boaters or 'biffs' were held in place by elastic under the chin, and 'a black and red band carrying the letters B. S. told the world who we were.' They were the young ladies of Miss Douglas's Classes in Montebello, close to Portobello, where the name of Brunstane Road was borrowed. An old girl giving the Cranley Founder's Day address recalled these 'straw bashers'. One of her friends 'had an unusual shape of head and her hat always seemed to be perched precariously on the very top. On one occasion her hat blew off and was run over by an old cable tram car.' Avenues led down to the Promenade, where winds were bracing. Here, more than anywhere, Edwardian schoolgirls dressed for the weather:

'There was no central heating or electric light – just coal fire and incandescent gas. The fires were replenished at the mid-morning break by Jeannie the school maid. We wore combinations, wool in winter and cotton in summer: blue knickers with a white fleecy underlining replaced in summer by white cotton knickers. We wore long black stockings kept up with black elastic garters, and ankle length boots changing into slippers for school wear. I can remember the thrill when long black lacing boots came into fashion! We wore one or two petticoats under our dress. I can still remember wearing a blue serge dress which scratched!' One old girl linked being sent to the headmistress with 'that sure manifestation of

18. *No uniforms at Queen Street.*

schoolgirl nerves, a hitching-up of long black stockings, before knocking timidly on the study door.'

Outer garb can be seen in photographs advertising the new Mary Erskine school at Queen Street. Senior girls gathered with the headmaster have only a high, demure neckline in common. In one of Queen Street's south-facing classrooms a class group shows the photographer's use of natural light and – once again – a range of display from the drapers' shops of Edinburgh. For a dancing class in the hall, however, small girls all wore

19. *Senior pupils and staff.*

calf-length tunics, light aprons and black stockings. This Mabel Lucy Atwell look became normal day wear for junior classes. A change from stockings to socks is seen at Atholl Crescent in country dance. Seniors were more dignified in light blouse and long dark skirt. Several of these Edwardian young women wore ties, but not the same ties. Shortly before the war some Queen Street girls were ready for a change: 'We tried to start a uniform with a navy skirt, a white blouse and a blue and white striped tie in my senior year, but it was not taken up.'

'Gym slips' provide familiar shorthand for girls' school uniform, and it would be easy to forget that they started in the gymnasium. A Victorian gymnastic class posed at Queen Street demonstrates a range of not very strenuous exercises, some pupils confining themselves to deep breathing with hands on hips. All wear 'pumps' more suggestive of the minuet than physical execise. Woollen dresses are calf-length and individual in design: 'For Gym if you were posh you wore bloomers, otherwise an ordinary frock.' Edinburgh dress codes for the gymnasium started with St George's (following St Leonard's) although some scope was left for a mother's imagination – at least as far as younger girls were concerned:

'Girls in the six lower forms – i.e., up to and including the Upper Third Remove – have Gymnastics in the morning as part of their regular curriculum. Girls who wear smocked or yoked frocks not reaching below the knee only require knickerbockers to match their frocks... If the ordinary dress is not suitable, a gymnastic costume must be worn during the lesson, and this necessitates waste of time in changing. A pair of tennis shoes is required in all cases, and must be kept at School.' A group demonstrates 'free exercises': free of apparatus, that is, for their movements are in unison. Shoes vary but black is the only colour for stockings. Dark wool dresses are gathered at the waist in a variety of styles. However...

'In forms above the Upper Third Remove, the Gymnastic lesson is given in the afternoon, and the subject is therefore optional. Girls in these forms who take Gymnastics *must all wear the costume.*' The costume was new, St Leonard's having borrowed it from the convent schools of Belgium: 'The colour is dark navy, and the suit consists of knickerbockers and tunic, with a *very* loose belt of the same colour and material. (A fine make of serge is recommended.) The knickerbockers are made like those of boys, closed and buttoned at either side, with a pocket, and gathered with elastic (without a band) just above the knee. The tunic is loose, either smocked, gathered, or hanging from a yoke, it reaches *just* below the knee, and is fastened in front. The sleeves are wide and perfectly straight (like ordinary nightdress sleeves, with a gusset), and gathered into a frill with elastic at the wrist. The belt should be attached to the tunic at the back, and kept loose. No corset must be worn with this costume.' Senior girls balancing on the bar are shown in boyish

20. *Gym tunics at St George's.*

knickerbockers but their tunics have evolved, losing the sleeves. This outfit became popular in the grassy 'playground' where team games took place, but was too outlandish for schoolgirls on the street. No uniform was worn to and from school.

Miss Walker the founding head of St George's had reservations about competitive sport, but her successor Elizabeth Stevenson believed in it strongly. She went so far as to insist on spectators wearing the school hat, hatband and badge, giving her reasons in a 1911 letter to parents: 'Some element of uniformity is essential to satisfy the eye when a large number of girls are grouped together. Further, a distinctive mark is helpful to mistresses in charge of the girls in public places. Finally, the sense of *esprit de corps* and responsibility is fostered by even the outward signs of membership of a corporate body.' Ravelston boarders were the most regular spectators at sports events. The following year (1912) Miss Stevenson produced an outfit list for them:

'2 dark blue serge Coats and Skirts (no white or coloured trimming) – one for Sunday and one for every-day wear. 1 warm Dress for every evening wear (not white). 1 simple white Dress, for School Parties, Concerts, etc. 2 plain dark blue woollen Blouses (no stripes or spots), to be worn with white collars... 1 white silk Blouse, for Sunday (optional). [For Summer wear, two or three plain blue cotton or linen blouses (not pale) with white collars.]' The complex rules on underwear ran to 40 items (flannelette garments forbidden) and ended with '2 pairs washing corsets (if worn).' It is not clear whether this final item registered the start of a change away from stiff decorum or merely distinguished older girls from younger ones. Wartime shortages loosened things up, and a later boarder's memories were simple: 'I was very happy with my uniform. It was a blue gym tunic; a navy blouse in winter, in summer we had cotton ones; black shoes and stockings.'

Some of these requirements also applied to day girls. Boots and shoes had to be black, with rubber-soled ones for the gym. For games on grass 'the heels must not exceed 1 inch in height in the highest part.' Evening shoes at Ravelston were different from indoor ones, the latter having 'low, broad, leather heels (one pair for use in day school). Snow boots and slippers completed the list of footwear. A Queen Street girl confirmed its importance: 'You wore boots to school and changed them for slippers;

everyone needed at least three pairs of shoes. They were carried along with books in school bags; these were never worn on the back, that was for boys. Queen Street girls either slung them over one shoulder or carried them.'

The Great War helped women towards greater freedom, as is well known, but the clothing of schoolgirls became increasingly standardised after it. There was a before-and-after contrast in the school which left Joppa for Colinton Road. Cranley pupils all wore 'pleated navy gym tunics with three-inch belts loose on the hips, black woollen stockings and strap shoes... Out of doors we had cosy navy reefer coats, knitted "jelly bag" caps and galoshes at play-time.' One area of freedom remained: 'There was a craze for growing our hair, so we wore it in shaving brushes with large bows, which some grew into hawser-like waist-length pigtails. The seniors had Marcel waves, kept rigid by many kirbie grips.' Merchant Maiden pigtails are seen in a Class 7 Junior photo. At this time

21. *Sisters, primary and secondary.*

prep school girls all wore white smocks before progressing to gym slips: a photograph of two sisters – my mother and aunt outside their home in Hart Street – serves to make the distinction.

At the risk of fast-forwarding into confusion, this is a good point to bring in an Esdaile Old Girl writing about ministers' daughters of the Swinging Sixties:

> *When I was young* – the old familiar phrase –
> It wasn't nylon stockings in those days.
> 'When I was just a schoolgirl,' I would say,
> 'We had to wear black stockings every day.'

'But that's non-U,' my daughters answered back.
'You surely wouldn't want us to wear black.
The fashion's different now you must agree.
Our friends would call us squares and laugh with glee.'

One year has passed: still Mother is the square,
She hasn't got a clue what girls should wear.
'We don't wear silly nylons,' they both cry.
'We must have long black stockings or we'll die.'

'They look so smashing. They're the latest thing.
Just everyone is wearing them this spring!
We must be in the fashion – just like you.
You always wore them back in '32.'

When *Scottish Field* captured Esdaile starting the neighbourhood walk, light-coloured nylons were worn by senior girls. St Margaret's chroniclers are helpful: 'The 1920s had seen some emancipation from black or brown stockings and shoes, but light stockings were mainly lisle thread, silk being an expensive luxury. In the 1930s, rayon, usually pinkish, became available, but the glamorous sheen stopped at the knee; the rest was cotton.' At Mary Erskine prize-giving ceremonies, however, 'white dresses were worn with silk stockings and dancing pumps.' At the Convent schools girls changed to white stockings, together with white veils and gloves, on feast days.

Normal wear for St Margaret's Convent girls featured navy blue blazers with purple and white piping. Perhaps the Ursuline Order's French origins explains the adoption of berets – before the Second World War and well ahead of most schools. Sacred Heart pupils wore bottle green tunics and blazers in the Fifties and a tussore silk dress for summer: its light brown has to be imagined in a black and white photograph of some two hundred pupils lined up in front of the Craiglockhart building. Then the headmistress devised a new uniform when she was on the point of leaving to take charge of the Order's boarding-school at Kilgraston near Perth: 'Another reminder of Mother Ranaghan is the neat felt grey hat that now perches on our heads instead of the ubiquitous beret of longstanding, together with the little green skirt worn by the seniors. These, along with the smart uniform shoes, a new green coat in 1968 with a pac-a-mac to wear over it, were all chosen by her before she slipped away quietly in the summer holidays. Alas! That "mini-skirts" came into fashion at the same time and Mother MacMahon had to tell us so often to unroll the waist bands of our new skirts until they hung at the correct school length!'

The old school tie is another shorthand phrase – about networking after schooldays by men. Here the new school tie adopted by girls' schools was part of the trend to uniformity. A 1916 Queen Street photograph shows the start. Head teacher Mary Clarke, who came from Roedean by way of St Leonard's, had just created the school's first prefects. However even at this formal level some of those setting an example to others are tie-less. What was to become familiar as the Mary Erskine tie – in broad stripes of red and navy blue – is worn by several, but the stripes go in different directions: early days for school outfitters. Ties come in different shapes and sizes (one resembles a scarf) and are worn loose below an open neck. The look is feminine. For girls of the high uniform period, however, ties were to be knotted tight with the top button closed – even when representing the school in a hockey or tennis match. St Margaret's pupils wore ties in the gym.

One school's uniform contrasted with the cartoon version: 'The St Trinnean's girls didn't deserve those hideous gym slips and wrinkly black

22. *The new school tie.*

stockings; they were in fact rather elegant in powder-blue gym slips and beige stockings, the envy of all other Edinburgh schools including mine.' Miss Fraser Lee provided the background: 'Ah yes, for our uniform was taken from nature, the blue sea and golden sand and the brown seaweed of lovely Iona, where I had spent many happy summers, gave me the colours – the coat a Harris crotal tweed and the saxe-blue tunic and tussore silk blouse…' No less intense about it all, the founder of St Hilda's opted for black with a tie striped in white and gold: 'White for the pure and good; black for the darkness and evil in the world; while the golden bar which is both gay and bold represents the hope in the heart of man which can never know defeat.'

St Denis already had an upmarket dress code at Chester Street: 'The wearing of uniform was strictly observed – navy gym tunics with a girdle in the school colours, and in winter a navy blouse with white stripes and a white piqué collar and tie.' White collar and green blouse were to become distinctly St Denis. 'When the pupils were working at their desks, green sleeves were worn to protect the blouse or jersey which was also navy with green and white bands on cuffs and pocket.' When St Denis moved to Merchiston and took over the premises of St Bride's, the girls in residence were absorbed, but could be identified by the blue and white stripes they continued to wear. Girls who transferred from Canaan Park kept their white blouses for a year or so rather than change to what had become settled as St Denis green – a variety of uniforms indeed. Still greater variety came later to the classes of Lansdowne House, when most Edinburgh schools moved out of the city: 'At the beginning of the war there was only one other girls' school left in Edinburgh, and very soon after we reopened girls whose parents had not wished them to evacuate joined our numbers. At one time it was possible to count six uniforms.'

Lansdowne House was the first school to wear what became a staple item: 'In 1923 the School adopted a Blazer in which the School colours were represented. It was itself navy blue, bound with light blue braid and embroidered on the pocket with a monogram of L.H. in gold. At that time there was no further uniform except the School tie.' St George's resisted blazers, but light tweed costumes with buttoned jackets were introduced in 1938. The green, navy and red stripes which made the Cranley blazer so distinctive came from the dress tartan of the Royal Scots Regiment. It featured in a post-war comment on clothes rationing: 'Some boarders began to display rows of suits and shoes to the envious discontent of their dorm-mates. This worried the parents. With a uniform every mother, however far away, can be assured that her child is as well dressed as any. It was not long before our school outfitters contrived to reissue the striped Cranley blazer. It was made of gabardine, not flannel, and amazingly durable.'

Blazers came to Queen Street in due season: 'Summer saw blazers and panamas with sprigged Tobralco dresses, pink, blue or green... The uniform list was staggering and must have represented a very large outlay for a family with no older sisters or cousins to hand things on. The school pupil of the '30s dressed from the skin out in a vest, a liberty bodice, navy bloomers (worn for gym), black stockings held up with suspenders or garters, a gym slip (but seniors wore skirts), white blouse with tie and square-necked blouses for gym and games. Over all this went a navy Melton coat or a gabardine (both were obligatory) worn with a velours hat or a navy woollen cap for cold weather which could pull down to cover the ears. Brown leather gloves were always worn and black laced shoes... The high spot of the end of the summer holidays was a visit to one of the city's school outfitters: Jenner's had the arms of all its customer schools round the school department walls.'

Headgear for schoolgirls flourished in the middle years of last century, although one fashion never caught on: the St Margaret's school cap 'knitted in dark green, with yellow and white piping down the seams – like the modern Wolf Cub's cap, peak and all'. *Fortiter Vivamus*, the centenary book of St Margaret's, features a flat straw boater at the head of early chapters and a rounded affair thereafter. 'Miss Gertrude Kirk in 1930', all of ten years old when captured by the lens, displays the new version. Her straw hat goes with the blazer (buttoned on the girl's side) and summer dress in a different shade of green, along with short white socks and sandals – also a chiffon scarf over the shoulder which must have reflected her mother's sense of style. That year J. & R. Allan's Maids' Department (part of this prominent department store, and

23. *St Margaret's pupil in 1930.*

24. *Uniforms established.*

nothing to do with domestic servants) advertised maroon blazers in the *George Square Chronicle*, demonstrating that a version of what became the distinctive Gillespie's box-hat was also tried at George Watson's Ladies' College.

During the Thirties navy felt hats were standard for girls' schools. At St George's, where boarders were first put in regulation dress from head to foot, there developed a resistance to rules about what should be worn on the touch-line: 'Hats caused endless vexation. Miss Aitken retreated, insisting only that girls should wear hats going through the town.' Thereafter the schools outfitter Aitken & Niven advertised hats for boarders and berets for the rest. Wartime evacuation was marked by a wonderful photo of St Denis girls milling about in Waverley Station, some in felt winter hats, others in summer hats of straw, still others with berets. These modern-seeming items (which were soon to gain added cachet from servicemen) were introduced to Edinburgh streets before the First World War by French 'Onion Johnnies'. At school level they were destined to drive out French velours. A George Square senior looked back:

'Occasionally one may perceive a small blushing junior running out of school "à toutes jambes" as the French would say. This unusual haste is caused, I think, by the susceptibility of such a hat to draw critical attention to the owner as, in our school at any rate, velours seems to be on the way out. The article of clothing commonly known as a hat was intended originally to keep the head dry. It now appears, from an exclusive and careful study of our school berets, that this idea is quite primitive. Although initially they were similar in appearance, being maroon, eight-gored constructions, by the time they have been worn day after day for several years each one has obtained a distinct character of its own. In the juniors, girls are taught to pull their berets tightly over their ears and forehead so that there is not the slightest chance of their coming off. Older girls with pony-tails have the greatest difficulty, and so mostly the beret looks like an oversize sagging pancake perched on the back of some spirited horse. However by the time a girl has reached the dizzy heights of the sixth form she has also acquired a certain mode of putting on her beret which only requires a few seconds, a couple of kirby grips and some ingenious movements of her hands.'

Velours was in short supply when coupons were required under rationing, but there was in any case a pleasant informality about the beret. Women wore head-scarves to work in wartime, and hats never recovered. In 1952 the Merchant Company ignored them when expressing concern that 'a Corporation school had recently adopted a uniform similar to that worn by the Mary Erskine school with the same tie and scarf.' The example of fee-paying schools encouraged others into uniform. James Ritchie's 1964 book *The Singing Street* shows girls (bare-headed) in the blazers of Norton Park School on the border of Edinburgh and Leith. When the Lord Provost took the Queen Mother to Gillespie's, box-hats were worn by primary pupils. These were nowhere to be seen on the variously styled heads of their seniors.

School headgear was increasingly reserved for the very young. The knitted 'jelly-bag' associated early with Cranley appeared late as a

pixie-hat on the heads of St Margaret's girls starting school, while the 1990 cover of *Fortiter Vivamus* was given over to straw-hatted five-year-olds. Mothers dressed up their daughters in headgear which would be discarded long before secondary school. But there was an exception. During the Seventies at Lansdowne House berets gave way to 'jaunty deerstalkers', taken over from Rothesay House when that school's pupils were enrolled, and 'cool' Baker Boy hats for summer. Hats had 'to be worn at all times outside or risk a disorder mark.'

25. *St Margaret's girls in woolly hats.*

By this time in a number of schools prefects were becoming distinguished from lesser mortals by the distinctive ties which they wore, along with brooches and other more traditional badges of office. Sporting prowess also led to an elaboration of the uniform and sometimes the two were combined on one head, as at George Square: 'The prefects' berets are adorned by white stripes as well, running up the seams of the beret rather like the tentacles of an octopus. However the crowning glory is a tassel. This can be attached to the centre of the beret when the owner has played six matches in a hockey team. The first eleven has a long white tassel, the lower extremity of which is liable to become extremely dirty. The second eleven has, at the moment, a somewhat undernourished maroon-and-white one whose appearance is rather overshadowed by the plump and healthy-looking maroon tassel of the thirds... The berets of the sixth are decorated to the limit of their capacity with badges, dates, tassels and stripes.' In general the further a girl rose in age, achievement and dignity during the Fifties the more elaborate her uniform was liable to become, as with officers in the armed forces.

At Queen Street the powerful influence of Miss Jennings moved school-wear in a different direction, however. Light cotton dresses were already established there as kind of summer relief from uniform – 'dresses, pink, blue or green'. Miss Jennings went further: 'The Head took great pleasure in seeing her well turned-out girls at state occasions; always an elegant dresser, she liked to see the whole school on parade in summer dresses "like a lot of sweet peas", while the Duke of Edinburgh's praise of the prefect's summer dresses which she had designed, worn in 1955 when they lunched at the Merchants' Hall, was a source of great pride.'

In India Street a much smaller number of girls shared an outfit with fifty similar schools in England: 'The uniform consisted of a blue blouse with the PNEU tie of blue, white and brown stripes, a grey striped dress in the summer, grey cardigan and grey blazer with PNEU badge or grey tweed coat in winter with a PNEU blue, white and brown scarf. In the summer we wore a panama hat and in winter a grey tweed hat, both with a blue, white and brown ribbon round it and the school badge. Senior girls were allowed to replace the hat with a grey beret. We were proud of our uniform and thought it the best in Edinburgh, but perhaps we were biased.'

School outfitters did well although times were hard – perhaps because times were hard. An advertisement by Peter Allan's of South Bridge emphasised 'Sound, Durable School Clothes' tailored for 'these days of strict economy'. In a 1953 issue of *The Servitor* Aitken & Niven requested 'the pleasure of the company of The Young Ladies of St Serf's School and their parents to view their collection of School Wear.' The shop at 46 Queensferry Street was billed as 'outfitters to all the leading Edinburgh schools'. St Serf's navy blazers were of flannel; only the coats came in gabardine. Poplin square-necked blouses encouraged the idea of a standard games kit. They were worn with navy 'shorts' or split skirts. The day blouse had a collar, and cashmere ties of differing lengths were available for junior and senior pupils. St Serf's school jerseys were optional, but there was no evading the blazer badge at three and thruppence or the beret one at 1/9. Uniform school scarves came late and were never compulsory.

One Rothesay House old girl, formerly Susan Bell-Scott, started her recall of what she wore with a parental response to small coal fires: 'A comfortable uniform of warm Viyella shirt; gym tunic; navy, red and white striped tie; tweed coat in speckled navy; navy woollen hat with tiny RH badge sewn on… In summer we wore plaid grey cotton dresses designed, I am convinced, by our headmistress who had worked in Australia as they so strongly resembled school dresses still worn in their TV soaps – but considerably longer. In summer we wore blazers and "bowlers", the latter being navy felt hats with school ribbon band. "Bashers" were also permitted, which were straw hats not the least suited to Edinburgh's climate. Once or at most twice a year we wore dresses of flimsy silk fabric patterned with white spots on a pale blue ground. Known as "spotties", they drove our mothers wild as they tried to squeeze their daughters into them for a prizegiving or dancing display at the Walpole Hall.'

British 'youth' rejected much of what uniforms stood for in the Sixties, and Gillespie's girls were not the only ones to go bareheaded. George Square pupils pocketed their berets when meeting Heriot's boys in the Meadows. Of course headgear was being abandoned by adults too, despite the unavailing slogan 'If You Want to Get Ahead, Get a Hat'. Girls rolled up their skirts for the roundabout return from school to home by way of Princes Street, and short skirts were accepted by school authorities in the course of time. Girls also expressed the spirit of rebellion by wearing their ties as loosely as possible. Towards the end of the high uniform era there was a more tolerant approach to dress on the part of authority. A 1955

St Margaret's primary class featuring 'Mr Buchanan's original desks' shows considerable variety: skirts, dresses, gym slips, cardigans, blazers – some girls wearing ties and others without – but all in the defining St Margaret's colour. Thirty years later '700 little green Martians' were piped aboard a special train to York.

By then kilts in tartan of the pupil's choice – still more unity in diversity – had come in. The girls at co-educational George Watson's and George Heriot's nowadays wear standard kilts designed for the uniform. Only in the pipe band are these traditional items of male attire worn by boys. A tartan was devised for St George's, that most 'English' of Edinburgh schools, and modelled splendidly in a costume by Dr Judith McClure, the head. St George's minikilts have since made an appearance. Mary Erskine produced a tercentenary tartan for 1994: just below knee-length, kilt pins optional.

There is one more thing to be said about 'female' attire and the schoolgirls of this spacious campus. Some of the most striking tercentenary illustrations show Mary Erskine girls in Army khaki and RAF blue uniforms as members of the Stewart's Melville Combined Cadet Force. Mary Erskine remains a girls' school, though twinned at the top and merged below, and girls are still required to wear the navy and red uniform until they leave. Indeed, since the scarlet blazer of Melville College has been retained for sporting and other 'colours', sixth year Mary Erskine girls can now be seen – in a further degree of distinction – wearing this item of clothing.

St George's has opted for a different approach. Gone are the prefects' ties and badges; colours blazers are nowhere to be seen. Instead, by way of preparation for the modern world, senior girls wear 'smart street clothes' of their choice. There is still a dress code which bans jeans as normal school wear, but trouser-suits give an impression of power-dressing for the careers that beckon. On the evidence of clothing, this school has returned – at sixth form level – to its origins as a young ladies' college.

Chapter 4

Ethos and Authority

Many things contribute to a school's ethos. Work and games are discussed separately, but general aspects of 'school spirit' exist beyond the classroom and sports field. It is a Speech Day commonplace to say that the institution being celebrated 'gives the girls something that no other school does.' Rarely do listeners learn what it is. The ethos of a school may be hard to describe, though the dictionary has 'the characteristic spirit or attitudes of a community'. That seems to be specific to one school, but should it be? At the start of last century the magazine of St George's High School (as the Melville Street institution was then called) carried an article celebrating the 'subtle bond which unites us all as High School girls and makes us so wonderfully alike, come we from London or Edinburgh, Oxford or Liverpool, Brighton or Sheffield.'

A common ethos may perhaps be discovered in the girls' schools of Edinburgh – at least by contrast with boys' ones. When one master moved to Queen Street at the end of the Great War, after teaching Watson's boys, he was struck by the difference: 'The first thing that impressed me on entering the girls' school was the perfect orderliness and charming quietness of the whole assembly of considerably over twelve hundred girls. It was the manners of the drawing room at Queen Street.' Obviously the warning given by friends of the first headmaster had been mistaken: 'You surely don't know what girls are… Man, they'll worry you to death before the year is out.' Credit is due to the Matron at Edinburgh Ladies' College who from the early days 'wore a black bonnet and rang the bell between classes.' The Lady Superintendent also dressed in black and inspired respect. To a considerable extent it was these female presences which set the tone.

26. *Queen Street Matron.*

Authority starts at the top – almost literally at George Square, where Charlotte Ainslie presided from on high: 'I looked up at that hallowed spot on the gallery every morning, and there she was. To me she was a goddess, and she looked and spoke just like one. Her dignity, her lovely white hair, and her graceful dress left one in no doubt that she was the Head… Dr Ainslie was always called the Head – not Headmistress – but perhaps that was because she followed a Headmaster. To me she was quite un-approachable… Woe betide any girl who was sent to the Tiled Hall for a spell if the Head happened to find her there. A cold, terrifying reprimand would destroy her. I should know, having had the experience. She was a strict disciplinarian, and rightly so.' Another Woman Watsonian confirmed that Miss Ainslie (the doctorate came later) was 'majestic and forbidding. Most girls were scared of her.' Dorothy Nicolson, who herself took charge at George Square in the Forties, 'laughed to remember when, not being shy, she cheerfully greeted Miss Ainslie in town on a Saturday morning. On the Monday she was summoned to the presence and told that this must never happen again.'

27. Dr Charlotte Ainslie of George Square.

Headmistresses presiding majestically over assemblies belong to a world of school songs and prize-giving ceremonies. School mottos also played their symbolic part, and badges were designed with care. School rules provide a rough guide to the intangible heart of the matter. There were sanctions against breaking them, but never the corporal punishment which was such a feature of boys' schools – nor were girls spared the strap in normal co-educational schools throughout Scotland. Only in fee-paying girls' schools did ethos come first. Elsewhere the heading would have to be 'Authority and Ethos'.

The authority of girls' school teachers came to be supported by prefects whose introduction strengthened school spirit at the top. Down all the age groups, however, the pupils contributed something. Mary Tweedie, a head whose Queen Street schooldays began in the 1880s, was aware of it: 'I have seen no fundamental change in the pulsing life that calls down to my room from the Roof Garden or bubbles in happy laughter from the class-rooms… The young Victorian played the same human pranks.' There is more to ethos than authority.

In Melville Street a sense of mission – for the higher education of women no less – was positively inspiring: 'At last the encumbrances of prejudice and the Scottish educational tradition could be challenged effectively. St George had rescued the Scottish maiden.' There have been three versions of the St George's badge, the latest lacking a dragon. School badge and motto become traditional over time, but linking St George with *Trouthe and Honour, Freedom and Curteisye* was inspirational from the start. Girls sat 'on the stair while the committee conferred, waiting breathless to hear the decision. Finally the door opened and the members emerged, and I shall never forget the thrill of the announcement and the immediate recognition that the choice of Chaucer's description of his knight was the inevitably right one.' The founder of St Hilda's came up with a curious motto which had a similar feeling of medieval chivalry, *Gentle Herte Kytheth Gentillesse*. 'Kythe' comes from an old word meaning the opposite of uncouth.

On the other side of Coltbridge Terrace from St George's, Lansdowne House pupils were calmly exhorted to live by the principles of *Gentleness and Justice*. Excitement was reserved for house badges: 'Wallace a dark blue sword on a gold background, Bruce a green spider on a gold background, and Douglas a red heart on a similar background… It was often amusing to see the pride with which a child coming up into the School from the Preparatory Department (who do not share in the Houses) wore her badge with a corresponding sense of importance.' End of session prizes at Lansdowne House were bound in the school colours of blue and white: 'For the occasion the girls in each form wore one carnation of a chosen colour. On the prize-table stood a bowl of carnations of all colours. Form I and Preparatory wore white sweet peas.'

Cranley had crossed torches. When former pupils wanted a title for their magazine in the Twenties, 'What could be better than *The Torch* – symbol of learning and held high by the figure above the Old College [of Edinburgh University] where at the time most of us were studying?'

An editor mused: 'A torch has, for us, many symbolic attributes, suggesting as it does youthful achievement, the search for learning, a communication between generation and generation, between friend and friend the world over. A burning torch has a unique enchantment with its flame creating weird shadows and its whiff of redolent wax. We caught its magic recently when we saw the students' Torchlight Procession flowing down the Mound and along Princes Street like a river of fire.' The magazine for Cranley pupils bore the curious name *FEHOMI* from the school motto *Forsan et haec olim memenisse iuvabit*, 'Perchance these things will one day be remembered with joy'. Shortened to 'Forward Remembering', the motto was meant to be positive. Virgil's own meaning in *The Aeneid*, however, gave the happiest days of your life an ironic twist with 'even these things'.

Badges must be simple for a hat band, but something more elaborate may be devised for a book-plate. On taking over at St Denis the drama-loving Miss Maybell Benvie asked her art teacher Miss E. A. Molyneaux for what turned out to be a very elaborate display. The St Denis prize book-plate began with a ship representing the barque of life viewed through a door: 'The beautiful Norman doorway with the School motto across the lintel stands open for those who cross its threshold to set out on the voyage of life and for those who wish to return to their School. The Franco-Scottish tradition of St Denis is symbolised by the *fleur-de-lys* and thistles on the door-posts. The doorway is surmounted by the lamp of learning and the monogram "St D". Overall is a silhouette of the Abbaye de St Denis, and, in front St Denis himself, clad in armour, ready for battle, but with sword reversed, indicative of peace.' St Denis (patron saint of France) may have been invoked for away matches:

> St George he was for England,
> St Denys was for France,
> Singing 'Honi soit, qui mal y pense'.

However girls of the Lycée St Denis (later twinned with the Edinburgh school) were convinced that the figure on the book-plate was Bayard, the '*chevalier sans peur et sans reproche*' whose statue stood in front of their Abbey. His reputation is echoed in the St Denis motto *Loyauté sans Reproche*, but the chivalrous Bayard was never depicted – as in Miss Molyneaux's display – with the halo of sanctity. Which French saint wore armour? Two years after commissioning the book-plate Miss Benvie acquired 10 Drumsheugh Gardens for a boarding-house, calling it St Joan. France's second patron was celebrated soon after the move to Ettrick Road in a production of Shaw's play about the Maid of Orleans. St Denys, a bishop, was beheaded on Montmartre. Confusion is worse confounded by the fact that the French boarding-school was opened for the daughters of Napoleon's dead and wounded, '*les filles de mes braves*'. Marching behind the *tricouleur*, never the Bourbon *fleur-de-lys*, they were inclined to favour the guillotining of bishops.

The St Denis French motto was unusual for an Edinburgh school. Equally so was the Gaelic *Solas agus Sonas* (Light and Joy) of St Trinnean's. Catherine Fraser Lee came from Nairn, whose patron saint is Ninian or Trinnean. St Ninian brought Christianity to Scotland at *Candida Casa* on the Solway Firth, and White House was named after it in a language which even the youngest girls could understand. The St Trinnean's badge was a Celtic Cross. The school's remaining eight 'houses' (junior and senior) were all associated linguistically with Scotland's Celtic past, though Gaelic was not on the syllabus. The most aptly chosen name for a house, given Miss Fraser Lee's enthusiasm for fresh air, was Fuaranringy, evoking a well in the 'dear little cold place'.

The head's claim never to have met a naughty child was confirmed by her version of the prefect system: 'In Comaraigh, the sanctuary, abode the virtual rulers of the school – Group Five, from which the highest class in each house elected for itself two prefects every year. Here they studied, debated, considered, meted out such punishment as a notably clement system devised.' An ex-pupil recalls the head's domination: 'Miss C. Fraser Lee had very blue eyes and a tremendous "presence". She was also a perfect disciplinarian. If a class heard her voice in the distance – and it was a distinctive one – the girls all sat up with very good deportment and you could hear a pin drop as she approached. Not that I remember the classes being anything but well-behaved.'

Latin was generally the language for badges. The pride which Muriel Spark's parents took in finding out the meaning of *Fidelis et Fortis* has been noted. The St Margaret's motto for surviving the Thirties' slump in support for fee-paying was *Fortiter Vivamus*, or 'Let us Live Bravely'. It was given musical expression:

St Margaret, Queen of Scotland, we take for name and guide,
Beneath her noble title we work and play with pride,
And *Fortiter Vivamus* is the watchword on our crest,
That Living Bravely we may give each other of our best.
Fortiter Vivamus, Fortiter Vivamus!

Grace Matthew who introduced it in 1929 (when she took over from Mrs Buchanan in Newington) was a Latin teacher. When she left Cluny Drive for East Suffolk Road the language left with her. Miss Muirhead (of St Hilary's Maypole-dancing) settled for *Quietness and Confidence our Strength* as the Morningside school's motto. It comes as a surprise to discover that Hilary was male – a heresy-fighting Bishop of Poitiers. The school's episcopal purple may have owed something to him, but the cedar tree of the badge had no obvious connection. When St Hilary's was briefly re-absorbed into St Margaret's in 1983 a parent with heraldic skills produced a combined badge. (The original lozenge-shaped one had emerged from a competition organised by Miss Matthews.) In the new badge the St Margaret's cross with four 'martlets' (heraldic martins lacking claws) was on top, and the motto continued as the Latin one of the dominant partner. The St Serf's badge displayed a simple 'SS' intertwined in yellow on a navy blue background. There were

28. *St Margaret's badge plus St Hilary's.*

at least two Celtic monks named Serf or Servanus (in different centuries) which may explain why the school in Abercromby Place never ventured to adopt a motto in any language.

The Ministers' Daughters' College founded by the Rev. David Esdaile came to be known as 'MDC'. This matched *Mores Dirigat Caritas* (Let love direct your ways) which kept the school's origins in mind when the name changed to Esdaile. The badge was a plain St Andrew's Cross, distinct from the national Saltire in being dark upon white. Navy blue predominated in the uniform. The St Margaret's Convent badge was enclosed in a pointed oval aureole such as icon-writers reserve for divine and saintly figures. Queen Margaret was shown – in light blue and gold – holding a cross in one hand and a sceptre in the other. The motto was *Scio*

29. *Gentle and strong.*

Cui Servio (I know Whom I serve). Latin Mass made the language familiar to pupils. PNEU founder Charlotte Mason's motto 'I am, I can, I ought, I will' encircled an aspirational (early feminist?) skylark.

George Watson's Ladies' College shared a badge with the boys, which may explain why it became a legitimate target for humour: 'On every hat or beret there is a school badge, a remarkable piece of structure crowned by a heart which is often misinterpreted by the ignorant as a carrot, and the words *Ex corde caritas* which, for the benefit of those who have not had the doubtful privilege of studying Latin, means "Love from the heart".' A merchant ship in full sail dominates the formal Mary Erskine's coat of arms, registered after the war 'as a cadet of the Merchant Company whose arms were displayed on a lozenge, heraldically correct for females, while the traditional motto *Mitis et Fortis* was now officially adopted.' By then the Merchant Maidens had been 'Gentle and Strong' for some time. On a fund-raising wartime postcard of December 1914 *Mitis* appears under a gentle lady – the Red Cross is also on display – with *Fortis* near a kilted soldier. The motto predated the arrival of Mary Clarke but it was she who, about the time the guns fell silent, introduced morning assembly, uniforms, prefects, a school song, and a house system named after Scottish nobles:

Play the game nor heed the scar,
Hark! The slogan of the clans,
Erskine, Hopetoun, Marischal, Mar,
Mitis et Fortis!

Queen Street's hall was highly suitable for assemblies and never more so than on Founders' Day – another new tradition. In the summer term of 1922, having perceived 'a need to stimulate common loyalties and enthusiasms', Miss Clarke commissioned a play and *Mary Erskine* was performed on the day. Merchant Maiden Hospital years were recalled and old associations pushed to the limit with the broom of the Erskine Earls of Mar: 'The deep yellow of the emblematic broom and the brilliant hoods of academic dress gave colour to the scene. The banner stood in its appointed place. Several distinguished former pupils were present and the Master of the Merchant Company and the convenor attended in their robes of office'. The banner was embroidered by pupils of the Art Department. Lydia Skinner (who has put on record her disappointment at the loss of hall and caryatids) described the event with obvious relish:

'The first Friday in June was for generations of girls a red-letter day, starting from their arrival at school an hour later than usual, hair brushed and braided, uniform immaculate...

30. *Queen Street banner.*

The tradition grew that the classrooms should be decorated with flowers for Founders' Day, so Edinburgh gardens were scoured for the essential yellow sprays and for anything else that an early Scots summer could provide. Drooping lupins and magenta ponticums were combined with Solomon's Seal and crammed into vases and jam-jars on any available flat surface. Then it was down to the Hall and the joy of studying the outfits of the distinguished visitors before the Founders' Day hymn brought everyone to their feet.' It ended:

> Before us and beside us
> Still holden in Thy hand
> A cloud of unseen witnesses
> Our elder comrades stand.
> One family unbroken
> We join with one acclaim
> One heart, one voice uplifting
> To glorify Thy name.

Cranley's regular Friday assembly took up the same idea of former pupils present in spirit: 'O Lord of Love, who art not far from any of Thy children, watch with Thy care those who are far away from us.' Queen Street was unusual in having a school hymn as well as a song. St George's tried out several versions of their school song ('never considered really satisfactory') and rejected all the efforts which came from a Jubilee competition of 1938. In the opening years of the twenty-first century those involved were still debating whether they needed a school song. Rothesay House solved the problem by adopting the hymn 'Be Thou My Vision' – 'sung often' – and ended the annual Walpole Hall prize-giving with 'Land of Hope and Glory'.

The non-competitive ethos of St George's rejected the public awarding of prizes, but elsewhere it became general. School halls are designed to hold pupils and staff, so that when Edinburgh parents were invited to the annual prize-giving it was generally held elsewhere. The St Denis Speech Day began in windy garden party conditions at Ettrick Road before the ceremony was taken to the Music Hall in George Street. The largest girls' schools favoured the grandeur of the Usher Hall. Muriel Spark, a regular prize-winner at Gillespie's, recalled (with pardonable exaggeration) that a choir 'of at least seven hundred girls in white dresses and black stockings rendered many a rousing number, to the apparent delight of our parents and their friends. We ended with Blake's "Jerusalem" accompanied on the organ by Herbert Wiseman, Edinburgh's organist No. 1.'

A Queen Street photograph shows the same crowded platform with some three hundred girls rising row upon row to the booming pipes behind. In addition to the school hymn and song there was 'synchronised marching into the organ gallery to Miss Badger's school march on the organ, the solemn moment when the Banner was carried onto the stage by

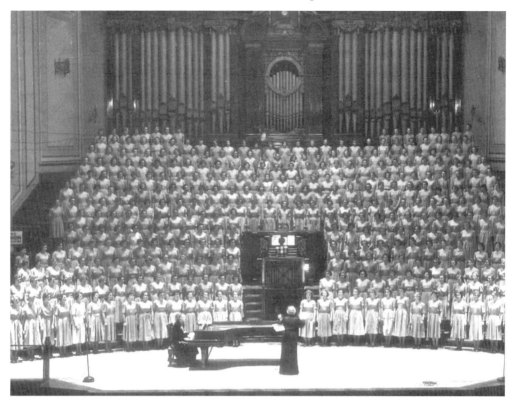

31. *Usher Hall prize-giving.*

the Senior Prefect, its supporting cords held by the Games Captain and the Dux.' More like a Girl Guide church parade than the Fascist affairs which were choreographed for Il Duce, it ended in smiles: 'The Dux's great moment came at the culmination of the prize-giving; she generally had quite a pile of prizes and it was not considered suitable for her to carry them off herself, so she made her curtsey and walked off empty-handed, followed by the Janitor carrying her trophies for her. Both James and his successor Henry wore tail-coats, and Henry had a distinct swagger on stage which caused great joy.'

The Queen Street Senior Prefect was head girl in other schools. A St Margaret's sequence began in 1927, and photos of St Denis head girls survive from nine years before that – although there were no prefects. Cranley never had a head girl, on principle, but prefects were appointed in due course. One of Miss Ainslie's first acts on coming to

George Square in 1902 had been to appoint prefects, well ahead of any other Edinburgh girls' school. Wearing maroon and white rosettes, they were responsible for keeping records of 'misdemeanours', some passed on from class teachers, which were conveyed to parents in the form of conduct reports. A Woman Watsonian remembered even these things with joy: 'There was quite a lot of movement in the classrooms, for these were the days of Good and Bad Rings; those who answered or did not answer moved up and down the class. There was an order book, too, in each class and in it was entered the name of anyone who had forgotten a book or broken a rule. If no further Order Entry was incurred for a month, the order mark was stamped out and the culprit could start afresh.' The prefect system spread from George Square to other Edinburgh girls' schools at a time when the parliamentary franchise was being extended to women, and then to women under thirty.

Another ethos-building innovation began at George Square: 'I remember when the school was first divided into Houses, the excitement of hearing their names, the first sight of the badges with their designs, the joy of wearing the badge firmly stitched on one's tunic and the satisfaction of belonging to a House. But the joy didn't stop there. Now one worked and played for one's House, and games and sports at the playing field took on a new meaning.' The size of this school provided an obvious reason for creating smaller units, but Lansdowne House also had house competitions when the roll was still in double figures: 'The Captains kept records of places gained by their respective members in the three-weekly Form Lists – over 80 per cent scored so many marks for the House, under 40 per cent lost so many. Conduct, neatness and punctuality marks lost scored against the house. Very soon other competitions arose: Drama, Reading and Sports' cups were awarded. Each year each House gave a one-act play, entirely produced by the House and judged by an outside authority; passages for reading aloud in prose and poetry were set… There were also inter-House Hockey, Tennis, Netball and Badminton matches.' One distinctive feature of a school catering for the top end of the social scale was the Deportment Cup. It was awarded by an old girl on the Founder's principle of making an entrance to a room: 'My dear, don't try to come through the keyhole.'

Ruth Freer became headmistress of St George's after Redland High School for Girls in Bristol, and her version of the house system was highly serious: 'From 1922 disorder marks meant a loss of house points and a Conduct House Trophy was awarded. The school sat in houses at dinner every day and there was "keen rivalry as to which house could get up with least noise or shunting of forms"… By the time Miss Freer left in 1927 houses were described as "the dominant factor in the life of the School"; their purpose, according to the history mistress, was that "greater unity in the School community may be achieved by bringing the elder and the younger girls into touch with each other".' Prefect authority grew, with badges to make it visible. They patrolled the corridors, allocated girls to houses, and invited staff to tea. A Prefects' Court summoned two girls for 'disgraceful behaviour in the tram car coming to school' and their house badges were confiscated for a week. 'The extension of the franchise for the selection of prefects and the establishment of a Girls' Committee with prefect and form representatives to discuss school matters and suggest policies put the finishing touches to Miss Freer's system of responsible self-government.' That solemn phrase was borrowed from changes in the British Empire.

Weekly House Meetings were held at St Margaret's Convent, and there was a monthly Mark Reading for the school as a whole under the headings of study, order and punctuality. Competition became very keen as numbers rose in the Sixties and Seventies: 'Inter-house matches were fiercely contested – hockey, netball, badminton, sports day – and in the summer term there was an art competition leading up to the last day of school. The whole morning was devoted to Inter-house. The Hall was divided in four with each house in its own area. Everyone was there. There was a table with all the cups won to date, each with the ribbon of the winning house, but the Inter-house Cup was still there to be won. Points for each house to date were on the blackboard and the maths teacher was ready, chalk in hand, to keep the score with running totals. The programme could include a balloon debate, or a music competition on a common theme. The excitement was always at fever pitch right to the end. It was a high note to end the year on and everyone went off exhausted.'

When the Girls' High School movement was making its first advance through England, rules achieved an exaggerated importance. Those introduced at North London Collegiate by Miss Buss were so numerous as to be 'in small print and double columns, like the blue by-laws on the trams.' By way of contrast Mary Walker told her first group of St George's girls there would only be one rule, 'Be good'. Even then one girl got it wrong: 'Be careful of the paint.' In fact St George's rules were also numbered and in print, but they mainly came down to girls being silent at appropriate times. Ethos also works by stealth: as a St George's boarder put it, 'We didn't seem to have any rules. We just behaved!'

The influence of teachers is important in any school worth paying for, and more so if they are secure enough to accept being made the object of collective fun. This St Denis fragment owes an obvious debt to Gilbert and Sullivan:

> When a teacher's not engaged in stern correction
> Or in giving order-marks to all the form,
> Her activities are in the right direction,
> The heart that beats beneath her gown is warm.
> Our yearning to suppress the truth or twist it,
> Or indulgence in the rougher kinds of fun,
> Is really just because we can't resist it:
> A schoolgirl's life is not a happy one.
>
> When the Latin mistress isn't teaching Latin,
> When the Science mistress isn't giving lines,
> They love to deck themselves in silk or satin
> And study all the latest dress designs.
> When the matron isn't giving an injection
> She loves to crack a joke or make a pun.
> Ah, this indeed must be our sad reflection:
> A schoolgirl's life is not a happy one.

'The heart that beats beneath the gown' recalls that it was not only head teachers who swished the corridors in black. But at Lansdowne House Miss Wynne, who taught English and 'enough Latin to be able to translate quotations that you meet in books', wore a red gown. She was remembered for saying: 'Give me a girl with reverence and a sense of humour, and all is well.' Academic gowns represent scholarly values, but the younger pupils could scarcely be expected to know that: 'Miss Matthew wears a cloak and we kneel at prayers.' The St Margaret's head seems to have been an Episcopalian. After her time, Craigmillar Park Presbyterian Church was taken over and used for school assemblies: 'From the soaring vault incident to a church has been fashioned, by some architectural wizardry, this splendid Hall.'

Public prayer helped to create the ethos of these schools although religion also found expression in good works. The Zenana Bible and Medical Mission operated in India, and by St Denis pupils it was 'affectionately known as the "Banana" Mission'. During much of the twentieth century, church attendance was general among the families which patronised fee-paying schools, with a variety of Sunday morning destinations: 'The official religion of James Gillespie's School was Presbyterian of the Church of Scotland; much later this rule was expanded to include Episcopalian doctrines. But in my day Tolerance was decidedly the prevailing religion, always with a puritanical slant.' Thus Muriel Spark, who grew up Jewish and became Catholic. She added: 'To enquire into the differences between the professed religions around us might have been construed as intolerant.' The grandparents of Miss Niven, head of Cranley, had been Baptist missionaries in India. She belonged to Dublin Street Baptist Church where the father of actor Tom Fleming preached, but accompanied her boarders to Sunday morning service at North Morningside. It stands at an Edinburgh crossroads known, for its four churches, as 'Holy Corner'.

Behind convent walls schoolgirls experienced the full theatre of religion. At Craiglockhart the Feast of the Immaculate Conception was celebrated on 8 December: 'We wore a white veil, white pleated skirt, white shirt and carried a white flower, preferably a lily although I always had a chrysanthemum due to cost. The flower was offered at the altar after a long procession in the dark with just torches on, singing hymns mostly in Latin. It was very atmospheric. The older girls carried candles, which made life interesting when Sandra L'Estrange's veil caught fire and singed her hair.' St Margaret's put more emphasis on Corpus Christi in the summer term: 'We processed to the right side of the Chapel where an altar was set up. It seems to me the weather was always warm and we enjoyed ourselves. The altar was beautifully dressed with candles and the family of one of the girls gave flowers, usually roses.' And from another witness: 'We made mosaics on the ground with flower petals pressed into sand. The Sisters worked with us to create designs such as chalices or monstrances.' Laburnum trees provided the next best thing to gold.

Irene Young, author of the autobiographical *Enigma Variations* (World War II code-breaking) was a convent girl before she joined the ministers' daughters at Esdaile: 'When I was sixteen the school appointed a new headmistress, Mrs Dorothy Calembert, who had considerable influence on my later adolescent years. She was the unlikely daughter of a Church of Scotland missionary to Rajputana, and was charming, brilliant and unconventional. She had married a Belgian Catholic (an official of the Belgian air ministry, subsequently killed in the R101 airship disaster) and had refused to raise her only daughter in the Faith, which in those less liberal days showed considerable courage.'

Esdaile girls entering by the school's front door were faced with the image of St Columba, dove descending, and there was more stained glass on the stairs. For convent girls May was the month of Mary; across Strathearn Road at Esdaile it was the month of the General Assembly. On Moderator's Day the Church of Scotland's representative for the year attended a concert party. Throughout the year Sunday mornings saw a procession to Grange Parish Church where several girls sang in the choir, and sixth year pupils also went to Youth Fellowship there. Esdaile's last headmistress returned to Scotland from the Girls' High School in Kikuyu – a living witness to the national church's missionary work in Africa. A sense of links with many lands was strengthened by talks, some illustrated by 'colour transparencies', after evening prayers. On one occasion the head of Lansdowne House visited Esdaile to tell staff and pupils about her summer vacation in the Holy Land.

Lansdowne exemplified the English public school ideal of chapel at the centre of school life. Made out of the original drawing room, the chapel was enlarged for the 1929 Jubilee and consecrated by the Bishop of Edinburgh. Boarders used it daily for morning and evening prayers, and religious instruction classes were held there. Sunday morning service was at the Cathedral in Palmerston Place and alternate Sunday evenings at the Episcopalian Church of the Good Shepherd in Murrayfield. The other Sunday evening was given over to a service organised by senior girls, for which 'friends among the clergy were very kind in sending sermons'. On one occasion a visitor asked to attend, but it 'was not a Home Service Sunday. The Headmistress asked the head-girl if they could arrange it on such short notice, and she went to consult her fellows. She returned in a few minutes and said, "Would you mind if we didn't have the Service this evening? We think we should feel that we were just having it as a kind of show."' The Principal of the Theological College at Coates Hall (now St Mary's Music School) was one of several Episcopalian clergymen who involved themselves in the life of the school.

However it would be wrong to present Lansdowne as a Church of England school in Scotland. For one thing the Founder 'would have thought it indescribably mean to use her influence in favour of her own church principles'. Boarders from Presbyterian homes attended Murrayfield Parish

32. Lansdowne House at Sunday worship.

Church on Sunday mornings. The school's chapel was quite bare in appearance, with High Church art left to Phoebe Traquair, an artist parent who decorated the walls of the Cathedral Song School: her murals are still admired in the former Catholic Apostolic Church (quite different from the Roman Catholic Church) at the foot of Broughton Street. The atmosphere of a very small school in Victorian times is caught by evenings at Lansdowne Crescent: 'We were all in the drawing-room after dinner, Miss Fenton and Miss Emerson in their armchairs each side of the fire, and we in the recess part, doing needlework, etc., while Miss Emerson read aloud to us. Dora Hole, the artist's daughter, was allowed in reading time to draw illustrations of what was being read – also another artist's daughter, Hilda Traquair.'

Queen Street has been characterised, from the school song, as a 'family unbroken'. The intention is to celebrate continuity down the years, but there is irony in the phrase since other schools distanced themselves from such large institutions by emphasising 'family atmosphere'. At St Hilary's

Miss Muirhead had a policy (ahead of its time, but well suited to residential Morningside) of involving parents, and she subscribed to the magazine *Home and School.* As the title implies the progressive PNEU ethos extended beyond the schools, and Charlotte Mason's *The Parents' Review: A Monthy Magazine of Home-Training and Culture* expressed the fact. St Hilary's prefects were introduced for the sake of involving older girls with younger ones, as in a family. At St Hilary's it was said that small classes made it possible to give 'the individual help and encouragement that can make so much difference in cultivating a right attitude to study and ensuring progress. This is especially valuable for those who would feel quite lost in the less intimate atmosphere of a large school.' They said the same at other small schools which closed.

When the owners of St Serf's announced their intention to sell up in 1965, the move to Wester Coates Gardens introduced something quite new. Newspapers went beyond the facts in calling it a parent-run school, but St Serf's was certainly different. A father recalled the early days when the self-help spirit of the playgroup movement was harnessed to education: 'When we moved here the parents themselves had to come in and scrub the floors and shovel the rubble out of the building to get it ready for the pupils. We took a film at the time and this is often shown just to remind everyone of how it began.'

The question posed at the start was whether 'ethos' was specific to one school or something more general. The answer is clear. Even when two schools were built to a common architectural plan and linked by a railway which made it possible for the same staff to teach in both, differences emerged. Alice Keys (who presided over East Suffolk Road while Grace Matthew was with the boarders in Perthshire) knew St Margaret's under both its aspects: 'The twin schools were by no means identical, though Mrs Buchanan's plans for them were. The Newington branch had, I think, the happier atmosphere, while the Morningside one, under Miss Wilkie, was more meticulously organised and more strictly disciplined.' Convent schools can be used to make the same point, with the Sacred Heart ethos noticeably stricter than that of the Ursulines at St Margaret's. When a young teacher reared in one went to work in the other she automatically drew in to the wall with a curtsey to let one of the Order pass by, only to discover that this was not expected at Whitehouse Loan. Large schools and small schools are always liable to be different, of course, but that is by no means the end of the story.

33. Dressed up Merchant Maidens.

34. Lansdowne House at Lansdowne Crescent.

35. *Rothesay House – 'earliest school photograph'.*

36. *Publicity for a new venture.*

THE

QUEEN MARGARET COLLEGE

FOR YOUNG LADIES,

CLUNY DRIVE, MORNINGSIDE.

(Adjoining Morningside Tennis Courts, and close to the Tramway Terminus.)

JAMES BUCHANAN, M.A., Head Master.

Session begins 1st October.

PUPILS ENROLLED AT THE COLLEGE DAILY DURING
SEPTEMBER, FROM 10 TO 12.

Thorough Education from the most Elementary
(Kindergarten) to the most Advanced Stages.

FEES MODERATE AND INCLUSIVE.   NO EXTRAS.

BOYS UNDER EIGHT MAY ATTEND.

N.B.—Parents are invited to call and inspect the
building, which is quite new, and designed expressly for
a Ladies' School.

The arrangements for heating and ventilating are of
the best description, and there is excellent playground
accommodation.

Prospectus will be sent on receipt of Post Card
addressed to

MR BUCHANAN,

SHERWOOD,

SOUTH LAUDER ROAD.

37. *James Buchanan of St Margaret's and family.*

38. *No uniforms at Queen Street.*

39. *Informal dress in the gymnasium.*

40. *Queen Street hockey eleven.*

41. *The Hall at George Square.*

42. Upstairs to class.

43. Miss Rosa Stoltz, founder of St Hilda's.

44. St Hilda's in Liberton.

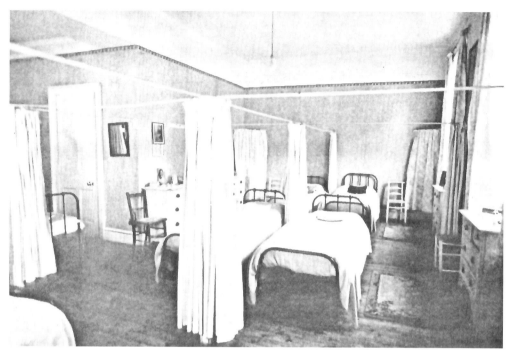

45. *Dormitory, St Hilda's.*

46. *St Trinnean's at St Leonard's.*

47. *Queen Street extension.*

48. *St George's School for Girls.*

49. *George Square girls in the Thirties.*

50. *The Balcony, George Square.*

Chapter 5

Schoolgirls at Work

In Victorian times the distinction between home, where you relaxed, and school, where you worked, was not always clear. The name of Lansdowne House makes the point, and one of its first pupils was conscious of bridging two eras: 'We had always studied at home with governesses who, I am sure, were good teachers, but I think about five of them left as finding me quite hopelessly impossible, and I confidently believed I was incapable of anything but war. Somehow when I went to live with Miss Fenton and Miss Emerson I gained confidence and keenness, and a totally different outlook on life.' But whatever may be said in favour of a small school's 'family atmosphere', the point of formal education is that it provides opportunities which are not available at home. Schools may be more or less happy places, but even the most benign exist to provide an environment for schoolgirls at work.

The Girls' High School movement represented a conscious break from home education. Classes were quite large, and if the teaching was sometimes as dull as that of boys' schools, so much the better: equality was the aim. Miss Buss of North London Collegiate had obtained medical evidence that maths was not harmful to girls after all, and she was a pioneer. By the time St George's Training College opened in Edinburgh, however, 'women of independent mind' had become more flexible in their search for good teaching. Mary Walker, who returned to Edinburgh from the Maria Grey College in London to

51. *Miss Mary Walker of St George's.*

take charge of the enterprise, had absorbed modern ideas and saw learning as an active process for the individual pupil. Poor mathematicians were accepted at St George's. The school's ethos sought to combine high academic standards with an absence of strain. Competition between pupil and pupil was discouraged, work was discussed rather than graded, and there were no form places.

The Victorians believed that girls were more liable to illness (truly the weaker sex) and early entries in the St George's register show girls being reclaimed by their mothers as 'too delicate for school', or 'father considered her overworked'. There was a lot of illness about, and eight girls died during the first five years – out of more than 700 who passed through, most of them quite briefly. In a corner of the schoolroom at Lansdowne House there was 'a sloped reclining board, especially for girls with weak backs. I was one, and spent many half hours there with my history or other book.' In the small schools of the New Town and the West End a morning's schoolwork was considered enough for young ladies who might nevertheless go home to labour at piano practice or embroidery.

Miss Gamgee has been mentioned as the founder of Rothesay House, a late example of the small private school. She came from a remarkable family. The father, Joseph Gamgee, had run a very successful veterinary practice in Florence and her brother John set up a rival institution, more science-based, to Edinburgh's Dick Vet. College. Opened in Drummond Street in 1857, it flourished for eight years as the Edinburgh New Veterinary College until he left for London. Miss Gamgee's two other brothers had distinguished medical careers, and Joseph Samson Gamgee (after whom a widely-used dressing was named) is said to have been the first surgeon to wash his hands before as well as after operations.

But the family's connection with school was through marriage. In *The Clacken and the Slate* Magnus Magnusson honoured Classics teacher D'Arcy Wentworth Thompson with a chapter, otherwise reserved for rectors of the Edinburgh Academy. Thomson was married to one of the Gamgee girls, and in *Day-Dreams of a Schoolmaster* he gave his reason for giving up the leather belt or tawse, which his wife found in his pocket 'then thrust it back hurriedly, as though it had been a something venomous. And over a very gentle face passed a look of surprise not unmingled with reproof.' She died giving birth to the future Sir D'Arcy Wentworth Thompson, Professor of Natural Philosophy at St Andrews for sixty-four years. The widowed Classics teacher left for University College Galway, and his son was enrolled at the Academy as part of the

Gamgee household. Magnusson described Thomson's teaching methods as a hundred years ahead of their time. Rothesay House is nevertheless remembered by Susan Bell-Scott as 'definitely old-fashioned, with emphasis on homework (always with something to learn by heart) and termly exams from age eight. We wrote with dip pens and watery blue-black ink for the first two years.'

The Merchant Company schools challenged genteel tradition in presenting themselves as colleges. The more demanding timetable at Queen Street and George Square went from 9 a.m. to 3 p.m., with a short interval in the middle of the day and periods of one hour. At the start of the twentieth century this was changed by shortening the periods and granting an hour's break at 1.30 p.m. The afternoon, which now ended at four, was given over to special classes and preparation. The founder of St Margaret's sought a similar compromise with regard to afternoon work: 'The curriculum is large, but the school and not the home is transformed into the place of study, the afternoon being devoted to the preparation of next day's lessons.' In practice the timetabling challenge of having teachers in Morningside and Newington, morning and afternoon, limited this to the younger pupils of the Lower School. At St George's, afternoon school was still optional in the Twenties.

The work ethic of Esdaile was strong, starting with a conscious rejection of drawing-room accomplishments: 'Esdaile was founded with the declared purpose of providing clergy daughters with the education then available only to the sons of the manse. Thus the School declared its academic status at the outset. Some girls went on to higher education around the turn of last century and by the 1930s bright girls were expected to aspire to university. Learning was respected and the slur "swot" was not a peer comment! Seating positions were determined by the previous term's examination results and friendships were often formed according to such proximity. Games were a strong feature, but practices were not allowed to encroach on lesson time. These took place after lunch, but then there was a return to school work until 5.15 p.m. Gymnastics were similarly removed from the working day and scheduled at 8 a.m.'

English was generally well taught in girls' schools. At Queen Street the head of department for almost three decades was Logie Robertson, who had made his name as a poet in Edinburgh literary circles: 'We felt, young as we were, that his literature was life and our daily contact with the pioneer of the Scottish renaissance was an influence that struck deep.' When the Scottish Leaving Certificate was introduced in 1888 the best results were achieved in English. Lansdowne did not participate in the new examination system, preferring University Prelims. The Dean of Arts

52. *James Logie Robertson.*

at St Andrews was content: 'Lansdowne House turns out the kind of girl we want at the University.' One Lansdowne girl found English at Edinburgh University easy because 'we've done most of it already.' All senior pupils entered for the prize poem and prize essay, English Literature being 'almost the dominant subject'. The Leaving Certificate exam system treated history and geography as part of English, but the head of Brunstane School (later Cranley) went further in the 'unifaction of studies'. An inspector reported: 'Neither Geography nor History nor Literature is treated by Miss Niven and her colleagues in isolation. The geographical character of the country is considered as largely determining the history of the people and both together as combining to determine the literature and consequently to explain and illustrate it.'

St Denis may be taken to represent a foreign languages emphasis which was quite general, with girls speaking French or German at meals for a week at a time. The tradition of 'French Table' was maintained long after German became a casualty of the Kaiser's War. Pupils were expected 'to conform to high standards of good manners, to make suitable conversation at table.' The foreigners who taught them how to pass the salt, however, were liable to suffer from schoolgirl mischief: 'I remember going up Arthur's Seat one Saturday afternoon with a few girls. Both Mademoiselle and Fräulein were in charge. We got to the top and, as we were tired of going down the way we had come up, we decided to try another. I think it would be the south-west side, as it was rather steep and rocky and to us looked a real adventure. I fear neither Mademoiselle nor Fräulein could do anything about it, so we set off and, to a chorus of "Mon Dieu" and "Mein Gott", which continued all the way down amid gales of laughter from us, we reached the bottom in safety.'

The last headmistress of St Margaret's in Morningside was renowned for the pages of French phrases which she gave the girls to learn. Languages were also taken seriously at Queen Street under Auguste Evrard and Charles le Harivel who succeeded him. Mary Tweedie, a Queen Street pupil who went on to become headmistress, began the custom of annual trips to France: 'Many friends, amongst whom was Miss Tweedie and a little dog wearing the school colours in our honour, saw us off at Waverley.' When Charlotte Ainslie was put in charge of George Square and encouraged to 'take women of culture and of character from wherever you can find them,' she looked for those who had studied abroad. They were expected to teach by the 'direct method', encouraging pupils' oral confidence, and Clara Fairgrieve banished fear from the language classroom at George Square: 'It was transformed into a delightful party, at which dolls often played an important part.'

Art continued to be more important in girls' schools than elsewhere in Scotland, but nothing as messy as paint was allowed. At both St Margaret's buildings arrangements were made to ensure good light, and a feature was

53. *Art class, Queen Street.*

made of 'the art and drawing classes under the supervision of Mr David J. Vallance. When the children enter the school they are immediately taught drawing, and are brought up by easy stages to the more advanced studies.' Drawing was listed among the wide range of subjects advertised by the Merchant Company, with art consisting of Freehand and Chalk Drawing for many years. St George's girls won prizes from the Royal Drawing Society of Great Britain and Ireland for 'shaded drawings from the cast', and also for botanical diagrams. At Brunstane Road a link was made between 'drawing and nature studies – e.g. various types of seed vessels being used for art work.' Water colour painting gradually made its way into schools. A St Denis old girl who returned to teach art, E. A. Molyneaux, was elected to the Royal Society of Painters in Water Colours – 'a rare distinction for a woman'.

In the early twentieth century every respectable Edinburgh household had a piano, and at the Merchant Company schools lessons were provided 'at no extra fee'. George Square acquired thirty-three new upright pianos after Miss Ainslie's appointment: 'Suddenly the classroom door opens and a music mistress looks in. She need not say a word for even by then the girl who has forgotten to take up her music or has not arrived for her lesson is making her way along the bench, sweeping rulers and jotters to the floor in her effort to reach the door. Those were the days of music

54. *Piano-playing at Queen Street.*

lessons for all and the music department was a busy place, away high up at the top of the school – so many little rooms, from each of which came the sound of music in the making.' Little music rooms were an advance on Queen Street, where eight girls played in unison during their twice-weekly lessons. There were nineteen full-time instructors at Queen Street and a host of part-time music teachers. No fewer than 758 girls were involved at the point when compulsory piano lessons were abandoned in 1924, setting free resources which led to an outburst of choral singing.

Mathematics and science came first to the largest schools. It was a maths inspector who said: 'The institution of the Merchant Company's Schools for Girls has to a great extent created the Secondary education of girls.' Queen Street's second head Robert Robertson was an internal appointment from the maths department: 'Its work was of a very high standard and its watchwords accuracy, lucidity and concentrated endeavour dominated the tone of the whole school… There was no specialisation that could eliminate Mathematics and the pupils bred on it seemed to do well in any and every form of knowledge.' Older pupils, however, were allowed to drop algebra and geometry.

Early results in the Leaving Certificate confirmed that Victorian girls' schools had neglected maths. Sarah Siddons Mair admitted that women 'to whom discussions on "the Good, the Beautiful and the True" were as fascinating as any novel, shuddered at the idea of wrestling with vulgar fractions.' Mathematics gained ground steadily, with trigonometry added in some schools, but as late as 1912 an inspector felt bound to defend St George's: 'In the curriculum of this school it is not to be expected that very lengthy and elaborate courses of Mathematics and Physical Science would be given. These are not – as it seems to me – the most essential features in the education of girls, and time saved on these subjects is devoted to other important branches of learning.'

Science was even slower to find a place in girls' schools, being limited at first to lectures on nature study by visiting speakers. The two Ladies' Colleges agreed on a common course of action, and in 1895 physiology and zoology classes were introduced for seniors and botany for juniors. Eight years later an extension to the building in George Square made possible the addition of two laboratories, one for chemistry and one for physics. A single science master was sufficient for the early level of demand, although the subject's importance was growing at national level thanks to German advances in technology. Grants were made available to secondary schools, including those opened by county councils, and the effect of this spread north after 1907 when the extension of the Scottish Intermediate Certificate to 'higher class' secondary schools made practical science compulsory. It could still be ignored by high-fliers heading for university, however, and by private schools in general.

St George's eventually followed the Merchant Company lead, but there were difficulties. Melville Street lacked space for a laboratory, and the shortage of science teachers applied even more to a school which employed only women. The school's ruling body had resisted exp-erimental science in a series of letters to the Scotch Education Department in London. Having accepted the Department's inspectors, however, those responsible for the school had to respond: 'The Committee would deprec-ate any change involving the curtailment of the time now devoted to the study of English language and literature … and they see considerable difficulty in the way of limiting the pupils to the study of only one language other than English.' Eventually the school gave way and a science teacher was found. Meanwhile Miss Niven had stolen a march on her former St George's colleagues. The Brunstane conservatory was turned into a half-scale version of the best laboratories in Edinburgh. It served senior girls with medical careers in mind. There, as the 1914 inspection noted, science was taught by 'a visiting mistress with full qualifications'.

So far the story is one of a widening curriculum, resisted in the areas of maths and science but leading to what anyone would recognise as progress in girls' education. During these years before the First World War, however, there was controversy over the subject known as Domestic Science. In the old Merchant Maiden Hospital a firm distinction had been made between the value of needlecraft on the one hand (all girls making their own clothes) and domestic skills – which were not taught. Contact with cooks and laundry maids was discouraged. Following this tradition, only sewing was included in the original curriculum at Queen Street, although the first prospectus at George Square ended the list of subjects (after Drill, Callisthenics, Dancing) with Needlework and Cookery.

In the mid-Nineties both Merchant Company schools introduced Scientific Cutting-Out and Dressmaking. Practical Cooking began as a

55. *George Square teaching kitchen.*

lecture course, but after the purchase of Nos. 6 and 7 George Square a laundry and cookery room became available. The rooms were formally opened in 1911 by the Marchioness of Tullibardine, a former pupil. She recalled that in the early days it had been necessary to give girls the same education as boys so as to prove that they could benefit from it, but that had been achieved: 'I think that sometimes we are a little apt to overlook this fact; that the aim of an education such as you are receiving here is to turn out women.' The head thanked her for helping 'by her very presence here to refute a somewhat widespread fallacy… that intellectual tastes in women are incompatible with interest and aptitude in domestic matters.'

An even grander advocate in support of better 'artisan cookery and cleaning' was Queen Victoria's daughter Princess Louise. She was patron of the Edinburgh School of Cooking and Domestic Economy which became known as Atholl Crescent. It was the poor physical condition of men coming before Boer War recruiting officers which led to the spread of cookery and laundry classes in state schools. Girls' schools for the upper and middle classes stood aloof, until the demand for domestic science teachers led to some overlapping between the sectors. Girls from George Watson's Ladies' College took early advantage of the bursaries which were now on offer. Queen Street was slower to move in this direction, but after Robert Robertson gave way to Mary Clarke in 1914

56. *Support for Domestic Science.*

the new head made a point of being photographed with the domestic science class: eleven girls in white, their teacher wearing the cook's cap of Atholl Crescent with pride.

The Excellent Women is a history of this institution which became Queen Margaret College at Clermiston. In it Tom Begg discusses feminist objections to the domestic direction which girls' education took in the early twentieth century, concluding that it was justified. The Education Act of 1908 required the feeding of 'necessitous' children and encouraged the development of domestic science in schools. Alexander Darroch, as Professor of Education at Edinburgh University, supported the policy and stated that a fundamental aim of girls' education was to reduce infant mortality through 'a race of healthy, intelligent and morally earnest wives, housekeepers and mothers.' Darroch was involved with St George's as a women's training college, but saw the school as different from others. He did not wish to limit any of its girls to 'a narrow domesticity'.

Headmistress Elizabeth Stevenson agreed. She refused to introduce a subject which would widen the difference between schools for girls and boys, and was unimpressed by inspectors who pointed out that the standard of sewing at St George's was below that of the worst elementary schools. Miss Stevenson denied that housecraft belonged to education: it was only a matter of training. According to the school's historian, 'It would have been a costly and wasteful effort to have introduced domestic science to girls who would neither be servants nor, for the most part, house-keepers.' St George's girls did not go to Atholl Crescent.

Queen Street girls were also academically inclined, for the most part, but the school catered for many talents. Miss Tweedie (who succeeded Miss Clarke) continued to encourage domestic science, and time could always be found for dressmaking: 'Some hundreds of summer frocks, dressing gowns, overalls, pyjamas and other garments made by the pupils were displayed and some presented in a march past.' The economic depression of the Thirties led to changes as parents weighed costs and outcomes. Between 1924 and 1937 the number of women students in Scottish universities fell by a quarter. At Queen Street fewer pupils went to university, 'except for Honours degrees; these number twelve as against twenty entering the College of Domestic Science.' Home-friendly St Hilary's had to wait until the war was over for progress on the domestic front. The purchase of 16 Cluny Drive fulfilled a long-held dream of the head – ex-St George's Training College – with 'a really large, roomy and convenient kitchen for the Domestic Science Department, with gas and electric cookers, washing machine, and spin drier.'

Commercial Education was another 'non-academic' subject which took some time to find a place in the girls' schools of Edinburgh. When the 1892 *Chambers' Encyclopaedia* described the Remington typewriter which had recently come on to the American market, it was explained that 'a rapid operator uses both hands and generally uses his [*sic*] fingers like a piano-player's.' This recalls the telegraph operators (male) who tapped out news from coast to coast. Female stenographers had not yet made the typewriter their own. In that same year a Merchant Company deputation which included the heads of girls' and boys' schools visited Blair Lodge, a boys' boarding school at Polmont. What impressed them was the 'Commercial Room where each boy had a japanned tin box for his books, had his money deposited in the School bank and his banking done for him by the Commercial pupils.' William Budge was released from teaching English at George Square to investigate Commercial Education in Europe, and in 1893 a Commercial course was introduced to both Merchant Company girls' schools. It included Shorthand, as required for the new Civil Service exam: Queen Street pupils came top and second top in successive years, and Typewriting was soon added. At the turn of the century young women were beginning to apply for office jobs which had formerly been the preserve of male clerks. By the Sixties no fewer than seven Cranley old girls were secretaries of Edinburgh University departments.

It became possible to continue a Commercial course to the top of at least one academically-inclined school, but according to the *George Square Chronicle* other seniors regarded these 'moderns' with a touch of resentment. The sixth year common room was taken over by those with least studying to do. 'Reading matter varies considerably – cartoons on Wednesday and fortunes on Thursday… The Modern section consists, as the name implies, of "Bright Young Things". These are also split into two sections: those who doggedly peg away at secretarial subjects with the view to keeping themselves (until they get married) and those who aspire to the mysteries of domestic subjects with the avowed intention of getting married.' The lack of servants in middle class homes had turned domestic science into a new 'accomplishment'. But matrimony appealed to all, and the George Square satirist would also have had it in mind while aiming for her Honours degree.

That is a feminist issue, but there were gender-free concerns about more and less intellectually able pupils. In the largest schools around the turn of the twentieth century secondary teachers of English were the only ones who worked with the full range of pupils enrolled – and many were refused admission to the Merchant Company schools. Setting was applied in other subjects. Arithmetic (which included mathematics) was tackled at four levels or 'divisions', as also Latin, French and German: by this system even the most challenging subjects could be taught to all. Latin was more challenging than most subjects, with Leaving Certificate success well below the near-universal pass rates achieved in French and German.

The school day was divided up by timetables of increasing complexity: Queen Street's first one had been the product of a few hour's work by the Lady Superintendent. At George Square period changes were announced by the janitor: 'As a performer on the resonant gong he might be relied on with the punctuality of the one o'clock gun.' This Canton gong was remembered by many: 'Upstairs I go and reach the tiled hall, a busy place with much coming and going. There stands the great gong… So many girls longed to sound that gong for it had a wonderful deep note heard all over the school.' At Chester Street St Denis pupils were allowed to try their hand: 'As there was a certain skill required to produce the volume of noise necessary to penetrate to the classrooms on the upper floors, the art of starting gently and working up to a crescendo was passed on from one Gong Monitress to another.' The installation of electricity ended this way of dividing up the days of schoolgirls at work, though not everywhere. St Margaret's Convent pupils still walked the corridors in the 1980s with a hand bell to warn teachers that a move to their next class was imminent.

At Queen Street the relationship between home and school was formalised by a report card which had to be 'kept clean, regularly signed and returned'. Class marks were forwarded to parents with their daughter's percentage mark in each subject compared to the class average. Class places were not recorded, although girls sat on their benches in order. There were two sets of examinations each year, and again marks were shown in relation to the rest of the class. Music, like conduct, was initialled from V.G. (Very Good) downward. Times absent and late were recorded, and overall progress (with additional space for Remarks), was indicated on a scale from Highly Satisfactory to Unsatisfactory.

57. *Reporting to parents.*

Different degrees of aptitude for school work have always challenged the ingenuity of heads and teachers. At Queen Street Muriel Jennings stated her intention to provide 'a varied course for pupils of all abilities … I feel we should try to be less rigid in our syllabuses and give the A classes more and varied mental food and the C classes a completely different approach. We should start from the known, the practical, the every-day angle and not expect too much in the way of written work.' By the time Lydia Skinner joined the staff as a history teacher, classes were known by the form teacher's initials rather than A to C. The top classes were nevertheless taught by senior members of staff, and the school's future chronicler found herself boosting the confidence of less favoured pupils. The rapport Mrs Skinner achieved was acknowledged in a back-handed compliment: 'When we have lessons with Miss X she's so clever that we don't understand what she's saying, but you're like us, you're not clever and we can understand you quite well.'

The large schools which were so popular with Edinburgh parents had entrance tests from the start, with hundreds turned away. Between the wars psychology became influential. Tests were administered which produced an 'Intelligence Quotient' to encourage the idea of wide-ranging 'mental age' among children of the same chronological age. At St George's 'a greater social than intellectual homogeneity' led to the division of classes in French and maths. St Bride's went further, advertising 'two sides in Upper School'. Differentiation came to St Denis after the move to Ettrick Road, when the first Higher Leaving Certificate to be awarded went to a newly arrived Canaanite. Cranley never used an entrance test ('indeed we were sometimes the last hope for the rejected') or divided pupils into sets. There 'Improvers' who had struggled to pass 'O' Level Arithmetic were equally applauded at session's end along with 'First Class Averagers' who had won university scholarships.

Teacher training colleges fostered an interest in 'modern methods', and St George's continued to train women secondary teachers until the outbreak of the Second World War. The college magazine was full of new ideas, some of which were tried out in practice. Miss 'Pea' Green the Latin teacher was renowned for ignoring grammar and making the learning of vocabulary optional: 'The theory was you just absorbed it. To this day I am vague about prepositions and conjunctions! Nearly everyone had extra coaching in Latin to get university qualifications.' The geography mistress favoured audio-visual aids: 'Miss Crawford wanted a film projector. The Council [formerly the School Committee] refused to pay the full cost (as it had refused to pay for a gramophone a few years earlier for the Music Department) apparently considering it a frivolous expense, detracting from the serious business of education. Miss Crawford borrowed some projectors on free trial and won her point. Her classes also saw pictures through an epidiascope.' It projected images onto a screen. Further aids to learning followed, including radio, gramophone and film.

There was plenty of publicity for 'progressive' education. Identified by newspaper editors as the 'Do As You Please' school, Summerhill in Suffolk was the prime example. Its founder A. S. Neill rejected Scottish education in general and the harsh methods of his father the Forfar dominie in particular. Instead, Neill's boarding pupils – male and female – experienced a 'free' school where attendance at classes was optional. The closest that any Edinburgh girls' school came to Summerhill was St Trinnean's. Catherine Fraser Lee wrote articles for the *St George's College Magazine*, lectured on education and enrolled the daughters of liberal parents. She introduced the Dalton Plan to Edinburgh. This was a development of the individualised learning which had been pioneered by Maria Montessori. Its chief features were an hour of free study at the start of the day and homework given out for a month ahead. Pupils had to take responsibility for their work in the manner of university students.

In 1966, along with half a dozen other pupils in the top class, Diane Maxwell left Queen Margaret's after GCE O Levels. Scottish Highers could readily be acquired elsewhere (Napier College of Further Education) with PNEU thinking skills encouraged by methods taught to the Charlotte Mason students at Ambleside: 'If you understand it, you will remember it.' A distinctive feature of the approach was Narration. Explaining to others work covered independently encouraged concentration and banished day-dreams. On offer was 'a liberal education for all'. The approach rejected textbooks in favour of Living Books – by authors able to make contact with young minds, regularly changed to keep things fresh. Progressive education was on the horizon in 1899 when a Blogg (Miss Frances) presented these possibilities to parents of the New Town.

The Belles of St Trinian's presented a very different version of 'the school where they do what they like', but Miss Fraser Lee was nothing like Alistair Sim's irascible Miss Umbrage: 'The average of examination passes was good, not because of cramming, of late nights or extra tutors, but because all was calm, all was orderly.' A former pupil paid tribute to the head's own teaching skill: 'After a period of being absent through illness, when I returned to school I had missed learning about fractions and how to deal with them. Miss Lee was present in the classroom to see how we were getting on (or possibly observing the new young teacher) and noticed that I did not understand fractions. She spent a short time teaching me individually and I completely understood at the end of ten minutes. They have never been a problem to me since… She was very modern in her approach to sex education: I was at school between 1924 and 1936. Miss Lee took the class of ten-year-olds. We had a very good book called *Yourself and Your Body* written by a well known doctor whose name I have forgotten. We had to tell our parents before she started the talks which lasted eight weeks, and we had to write an essay on fathers and mothers.'

After the Second War 'secondary education for all' came in through state schools intended to supply – at no cost to parents – the same facilities as private ones. Could the elite institutions continue to offer something better for 'schoolgirls at work'? In state schools large classes followed the post-war high birth rate ('the bulge') so that the girls' fee-paying institutions were able to maintain an edge through more individual attention. St Serf's competed so well that it grew too big for Abercromby Place.

The group requirement of the Scottish Leaving Certificate (failure in a single subject meant no award) was relaxed in 1951 so that it became possible to resit subjects failed and add extra ones. Even at overcrowded Queen Street space was found for those who stayed on, and soon there were seventy in the sixth form. Some took English A Levels, with Oxbridge applications encouraged by Miss Jennings. All schools became increasingly dominated by exams. Ordinary Grades were introduced to fourth year and then gave way to Standard Grades; the Certificate of Sixth Year Studies was replaced by Advanced Highers. The grading of results provided feedback and a basis for comparison: 'Year after year some of the mathematics candidates from little Cranley topped the lists in company with boys or girls from the biggest, most competitive, schools in the country.'

Kathleen Dyne's father withdrew her from a local school at the end of primary and then found it difficult to find a secondary place. Her enrolment at St Margaret's Convent was more or less a matter of chance. Later dux of the school (and later still a convert to Catholicism) she looked back with gratitude: 'Because St Margaret's was a small school it was able to make provision for individual needs. As well as learning the organ, I had expressed an interest in doing German. When I went into Senior 4 Mother Cuthbert arrived in retirement from the house in Berwick. She was then in her eighties but wanted one German pupil to keep up her interest, so I was duly told to report to the Chapel parlour at 9 a.m. on Monday. She was an immensely civilised lady, extremely well read and with a great interest in everything. I was lucky to have three years' one-to-one tuition, gaining Higher German and taking it as a university subject. I also had the chance to learn some Spanish… One or two girls needed Chemistry and Physics as well as Biology so they went out to one of the colleges. Because classes were small many girls got help and support and the chance to do more subjects at Higher level, and better grades, than they might have had at a bigger school. And a few who might have been put to "special needs" had the chance of a normal education.'

The former reluctance of girls' schools to embrace the physical sciences was turned round completely after the war. The new National Health Service widened the range of occupations requiring scientific knowledge – more doctors and nurses, of course, but also new opportunities in pharmacology, dietetics, radiography, physiotherapy and so on. Many girls came to share the satisfactions recalled by Muriel Spark: 'I loved the science room, with its benches and sinks, its Bunsen burners, its burettes, pipettes, test tubes and tripod stands… I see again the apparatus – bell jar, phosphorus, crucible lid, the trough, the water. I smell again the peculiar and dynamic smell of Gillespie's science room.' During a ten-year expansion to 1986

58. *Lab work at George Square.*

St Margaret's opened six laboratories – 'a far cry from Biology in the Pavilion'. When newspaper concern was expressed about young people's reluctance to study science, St George's in its centenary year could claim to be going 'in the opposite direction to the national trend: more pupils are now taking the sciences than taking the arts, and next year Physics is the most popular A level subject'.

Shortly before this, Sara Delamont carried out an 'ethnological' study of an Edinburgh girls' school which she concealed under the name of St Luke's. The school was St George's. Academic standards were high, she reported, with an entrance test ensuring an IQ well above average. Delamont distinguished between two broad categories of day girls: 'debs and dollies' and 'swots and weeds' – the phrases being used by each group of the other. Debs and dollies were fashion conscious, detested the uniform, and wore make-up whenever the eye of authority was off them. They drank, smoked and had boy friends, but they were also ambitious, accepted school values in general, and enjoyed sport. Debs and dollies regarded classroom learning as necessary for achievement. They were consumers of knowledge, keen on exam success for the sake of the job market. Swots and weeds were different. They saw 'the creation of school knowledge as a shared activity, in which they had a role to play, and not as a fixed body of material which they merely had to learn passively.' From professional backgrounds, their mothers usually had careers. Scholarly by inclination, swots and weeds had very little interest in sport. Sara Delamont ended with a reassuring judgement for staff and parents: both types of schoolgirl were committed to learning, in classrooms that were 'quiet, orderly and academic places'.

Chapter 6

Schoolgirls at Play

Girls are more playful than boys. They have always played more traditional games, particularly those which draw on imagination or take the form of drama. Singing games have a long pedigree, and in the Victorian era they were decorous – reflecting the formality of adult relationships. One of the commonest Scottish ones began:

> Here we go the jingo-ring,
> The jingo-ring, the jingo ring,
> Here we go the jingo-ring,
> About the merry-ma-tanzie.

'Merry-ma-tanzie' comes from a time when skirts were long and girls circled and curtseyed as they sang. By mid-twentieth century there were livelier expressions of childishness, with 'Chinese' skipping over joined-up elastic bands and fast handclapping games. And the remarkable thing is that more of these self-organised games are found in the all-age, single-sex playground of girls' fee-paying schools than anywhere else. Read all about it in my *Out to Play: The Middle Years of Childhood*.

Physical education is not meant to be playful, even today. It was first introduced to schools as a form of classroom exercise for pupils who spent most of their days sitting still. The first physical exercise in big halls was military drill, and the Edinburgh School Board introduced it to encourage 'habits of sharp obedience, smartness and cleanliness'. Aimed first at boys who were later to advance obediently against machine-gun fire, it was adapted for girls. Sergeant Donnelly taught drill at both Merchant Company ladies' colleges before being dismissed for turning up in a 'condition unfitting him for his duties'. Queen Street janitor James Auchinachie, a veteran of Khartoum, helped with another kind of exercise:

'James provided spare red and blue elastic chest expanders for girls who had forgotten to bring their own to dancing lessons which took place in the Hall.' Emmeline Fleming, a George Square girl of that Edwardian era who later wrote about her South Side childhood, clarified their purpose:

'We each had our own peg to hang our slipper bag on. This gave me a curious thrill. It was the first time I had something entirely mine. The bag contained pumps for the dancing class and gym shoes. It also contained a strange expanding belt thing covered in blue and red cloth, like some sort of snake. Its use was not explained until the first dancing class when we were shown how to exercise our arms by means of stretching and relaxing the belt. After a few minutes of this unusual but exciting game the teacher clapped her hands and we had to stop and fix the belt round our waists in a fetching clinch. Some of us had signally failed to do this correctly and Miss Graham, a rather terrifying and extremely agile lady, leapt to the scene and said, "Come along now, dear, what is your name – Maisie. Well Maisie, you must try to do it yourself like this." I and the trembling Maisie eventually did so and we clever ones clasped and unclasped the metal prongs with a sense of superior achievement.'

Long after this the girls of St Hilda's were photographed – for publicity purposes – outdoors in high and windy Liberton doing drill in gym tunics. Rothesay House girls had outdoor gymnastics, weather permitting, in Drumsheugh Gardens. At Queen Street Swedish exercises replaced drill when Miss Lund and Miss Henriksen joined the staff. Margit Lund was well named: the University of Lund was where P. H. Ling opened the Royal Central Institute of Gymnastics to revive 'the ancient vigour of the sagas'. Most of the exercises in Ling's system were for the upper body and required no equipment, proving ideal for schools when there were neither playing fields nor gymnasiums. Ling's system was first exported to Sheffield High School and spread rapidly through girls' schools of the same type. The Osterburg college in London trained five hundred students before the Great War.

The Ling system became a feature of teacher-training at St George's, and variations developed over time. Shortly after the move of St George's from Melville Street, music and movement were added through the eurhythmics system of Emile Jacques-Dalcroze. It also found expression at St Trinnean's: 'I recall a considerable feeling of embarrassment when I first started Eurhythmics, dancing about in a floating garment pretending to be a gentle breeze or a puff of smoke; and at a Parents' Day in early youth my class did a demonstration in the rose garden. After giving impersonations of giants,

59. *'Free exercise,' St George's.*

fairies, birds and flowers, sunset was presumed to fall and we all had to fall asleep in artistic postures. I unfortunately overbalanced, sat down on a rose tree, and swiftly gave a vivid dramatisation of someone punctured in a very vulnerable place, to the great amusement of the audience.'

When St Margaret's opened on two sites posture-improving exercises were taught in identical upstairs halls, but P.E. never stands still: 'In the days of Indian Clubs and the quietish movements of Callisthenics, Mr Buchanan cannot have envisaged the difficulties of teaching in a ground-floor room while overhead a vaulting class was in progress.' Wall bars were added, and by the middle of the twentieth century gyms invariably had badminton court lines on the floor. A St Margaret's photo shows only the teacher in a gym tunic, pupils having merely removed their skirts to take exercise. Gymnasiums continued to improve, but change did not suit everyone: 'All the modern equipment and facilities at Ravelston hold no fascination for some of us. I am referring to those new contraptions and apparatus in the gyms – ideal for games-mad enthusiasts but to inferior gymnasts like myself sheer torture. How often have I longed for those dark shadowy corners in the little gyms at Queen Street where we were so crammed that there was no room to indulge in the fantastic head-stands and spectacular leaps that we do here.'

Girls' sport came to Edinburgh from England by way of St Andrews: 'Many, no doubt, were the critical eyes which from the back windows watched our little playground, and the heads which wagged in disapproval of girls playing "boys' games". Games can be overdone. But those who with me remember the dreary "crocodile" walk, that apology for healthy exercise, and the hours spent on the reclining board which was supposed to keep children's backs straight, only they can realise the change and the health and happiness which games have brought to girls – and more – what lessons in self-control, good temper, love of fair play, and service not for praise or gain, but in some cause beyond self, are learned in the playground.' This was a grass-covered games field. At Cheltenham Ladies' College Miss Beale had been reluctant to allow tennis. When the pioneer of women's education first witnessed the roughness of hockey, she ordered several balls to brought on to the field – presumably so that girls would be less at risk through physical contact. However at St Leonard's, where ex-Cheltenham teacher Louisa Lumsden took charge, it was said that the games mistress could overrule the Head.

Tennis was the first game to be played by pupils of George Watson's Ladies' College when access was granted to the boys' courts at Lauriston. There had been nothing like that when the Merchant Maiden Hospital were in residence, for the game had yet to be invented. During the closing years of the nineteenth century nets were lowered to their present height and the dimensions of courts were standardised. Lawn tennis was not always played on grass. At Chester Street there was a 'paved tennis area' which also served as the playground where hop-scotch came round in season. A St Denis photo captioned 'Tennis styles of 1920s' shows dark back court set off by white dresses and stockings. No doubt the 'squash court' in the basement of Abercromby Place was a variant, although St Serf's also rented a lawn at Scotland Street. A photo presents this school's tennis eight at the cusp of fashion change, their white skirts both at and below knee level with stockings yielding to socks.

Tennis court lawns expanded into wider grassy areas where girls could run about. In 1889 the Merchant Company purchased the Falconhall grounds in Morningside. Previously Falcon Hall had housed a boys' boarding school which prepared pupils for Indian Civil Service exams and the Royal Military College at Sandhurst. An idea of the dimensions may be gained from the fact that an unsuccessful bidder had planned to create a race-course. The grounds were already suitable for boys' physical training, obviously, but the new owners introduced a new set of activities. The earliest sporting event recorded in the *George Square Chronicle* was a Teachers' Potato Race. (In another school magazine it was a St Margaret's girl who greeted the introduction of novelty races with the words, 'At last here was something I might win.') The wide open spaces at Falconhall

60. *Falconhall playing field.*

were mainly given over to hockey, but a version of golf – much-reduced – was played on ground later occupied by the Dominion Cinema.

Girls travelled by tram to the stop before Morningside Station: 'I can see the little wooden door in the high wall that surrounded Falconhall, only a few yards from the busy main road, and the lovely green of the grass as one entered, the games that were played and the excitement of Sports Day. I can see Falconhall on Saturday afternoons in summer with games of tennis being played and groups of staff and girls having tea under the lovely old trees that shed their shade over the grass.' Access was easier for George Square pupils than for Queen Street ones on the other side of town. Perhaps that explains early tennis victories by GWLC over ELC – that, or the fact (from medical records) that 'the George Square girl averages at various stages from 5–12 lb. above the anthropometric standard.' Miss Ainslie further noted 'the curious fact that girls at GWLC are taller and heavier than those at the Ladies' College'.

In the last year of the nineteenth century St George's acquired a games field. Prior to this there had been no mention of games in the prospectus, for Miss Walker was committed to the gentler values of gymnastics. As the announcement made clear, however, 'a strong desire for such a field has for some time been expressed by parents and pupils.' The six-acre site, entered off Queensferry Road, was behind what became the new St George's building after Melville Street. The games field was also convenient for Craigleith Station, eight minutes by suburban line from the 'Caley' (or Caledonian) Station at the west end of Princes Street. The alternative, as parents were told, was a fifteen-minute bicycle ride by way of the Dean Bridge. They were assured that there would be 'proper supervision of girls while in the Field'. Furthermore (as the *Chronicle* put it) 'a palisade round part of the field and a care-taker of the sterner sex will also tend to secure us in our gambols.' Ground was levelled for hockey, cricket and tennis, and changing-rooms provided in a games pavilion. A photograph shows the bicycle (symbol of young women's liberation) propped beside it. More greenery was acquired when the school itself moved out of town. Miss Blott ran the boarding house and,

61. *St George's pavilion.*

'against all the rules, walked across the playing fields and then censured pupils for the same fault.'

All the girls' schools obtained access to games fields in time, but often not their own. St Margaret's paid £10 a year for two pitches at Craigmillar Park in the shadow of Blackford Hill. The premises were shared with rugby teams, and 'many were the stipulations about the exact half of the Pavilion, the leaving of everything absolutely tidy after Saturday morning's matches, and above all the careful replacing of divots in the goal area lest some rugby player might sustain injury during his afternoon game.' While the two halves of St Margaret's were still part of one system there was an annual sports day at Carlton Cricket Club: 'Loud were the arguments on the rules of the slow cycling race, which Newington always seemed to win; but the climax of the affair was the tug-of-war, when staff and girls shouted themselves hoarse, and the respective staffs were with difficulty restrained from taking a pull.'

St Margaret's Convent had ample space for a hockey pitch in the grounds as well as tennis courts and a 'top field' for rounders. When the grass was uncut it was possible to hide and briefly ignore the bell for classes. A Pirie Watson (one of three sisters) reported recently from New Zealand: 'We had an hour of sport every day after lunch. According to the seasons we played netball, hockey, cricket, tennis and badminton. Netball or hockey matches were also held on Saturday mornings. I was a member of the Hockey team in 1938–9 starting at the early age of twelve. I always imagined that it was because I was not afraid to tackle my big sister Diana, who could slog the ball from one end of the field to the other!'

Gillespie's played on municipal turf at Meggetland. Esdaile made use of a park at South Oswald Road as well as the school's extensive tennis area. St Serf's rented ground at Warriston near Canonmills. The spacious garden of Lansdowne House lent itself to rounders. This was very much a girls' game, and it 'never declined in Cranley popularity' at Spylaw Road. Cranley abandoned lacrosse after the war but hockey and tennis became strong when agreements were made with the University and with Craig-lockhart Tennis Club for winter and summer sports. St Denis began as playing-field tenants of the Dean College of Nursing before moving to Atholl Crescent's fine hockey pitches at Succoth Avenue. When that ground was sold to a developer, St Denis hockey players had their matches closer to school – but on muddier ground – at Craighouse in Morningside. There were tennis courts and space for other forms of St Denis recreation at Ettrick Road. Lansdowne House girls (who had one hard tennis court and two grass ones) also used Succoth Avenue for hockey, lacrosse and cricket. This followed an early period of paying rent to the Murrayfield Polo Club, until the Scottish Rugby Union moved in.

That move made the international pitch at Inverleith available and it was acquired by the Merchant Company, primarily for the rugby players of Daniel Stewart's College, together with a much larger area behind the stand. Part of that was set aside for other purposes, girls only, as reported by the *Merchant Maiden*: 'In the late afternoon of 4th June, 1923, a gay procession of girls wearing Queen Street colours might have been seen making its way down Ferry Road; by five o'clock a considerable number had assembled. Did ever tennis courts look over so glorious a stretch of country? Who would not barter the beeches of Falconhall for the prospect of the Pentlands and mist-clothed Edinburgh? The ceremony was simple and dignified. Miss Clarke expressed as excellently as mere words could our abundant thanks to the Merchant Company. With what rapt eyes did

62. *Playing field, Inverleith.*

we watch her serve the first ball on our very own courts!' This left George Square in sole possession of Falconhall, until new playing-fields were bought for the school at Liberton and the old one was sold.

Sport was not compulsory at Inverleith, and indeed Queen Street parents paid additional fees for the games field – an annual five shillings, plus a one-shilling supplement in winter and two and six for summer games. Tennis was the most popular activity with over three hundred signing up. Two hundred and ten girls joined the Hockey Club soon after the field was acquired but only fifty chose cricket: a wide-angle photograph shows fielders in gym tunics. Netball was introduced as another option. It took six years before Junior girls were admitted to Inverleith, but then they were also granted the privilege of being bussed to games and back: 'Their elders either took the Goldenacre tram or walked by Church Lane and Comely Bank – pleasant going down but killing coming up again.'

Hockey is the game most frequently associated with schoolgirls, not least through St Trinian's, but lacrosse was preferred at the real St Trinnean's. St George's provided opposition in the Easter term. In the early days St George's generally lost their matches against other schools: 'The hockey players at first showed a great tendency to forget their places and collect at some particular spot to fight over the ball in one seething mass, but latterly there was a slight improvement in this particular.' The school was staffed for excellence in gymnastics, so that hockey was hardly coached. Results improved when Miss Stevenson took over as head in 1911 and turned the Gymnastic Mistress into a Games and Gymnastic Mistress. The whole atmosphere quickly changed: 'We were all very keen on games – hockey, cricket, lacrosse and tennis. I have a vivid memory of a "Sevens" hockey tournament in 1924, which we won. We practised endlessly, staying on after 4 o'clock.' Results improved against other schools, even after afternoon games time was reduced because of exam pressure.

Small-scale hockey was popular, Falconhall photos suggesting teams of eight. However the earliest team photograph in the Queen Street archives, dated 1906, shows eleven girls. Their box-pleated gym tunics come down to mid-calf above black stockings and boots. White blouses are buttoned at wrist and neck, and each girl wears a tie – although this had not yet been adopted as day wear. No doubt ties were meant to distinguish one team from another in inter-school matches, giving way to the coloured diagonal bands which became standard in the Twenties. This early group of hockey enthusiasts, whose outfits are set off by their teacher's floral hat, would never have been seen wearing gym tunics in class. Early St George's hockey teams took the field in their day wear of ankle-length skirts, which must have contributed to their lack of success. Having set other schools the example of ties for vigorous exercise, Queen Street then led the way into square-necked blouses. Navy gym tunics, worn with sturdy black stockings, rose to knee level in the Twenties. St Serf's did not take up hockey until the Fifties, when the 1st XI were still wearing ties to the field although split skirts had replaced gym tunics. As late as 1957–58 the top team at St Denis wore ties for hockey, their only concession to sport a rolling up of sleeves on leaving the classroom.

Hockey boots began as normal day wear, but by the time Muriel Camberg (Spark) moved on to the secondary department at Gillespie's they had acquired studs. Muriel's father surprised her with a second-hand pair: 'I was overjoyed, especially as those boots had a rather kicked-about and experienced look; they were not at all novices in the field.' Never to rise above five feet in height, the future novelist was regarded by the school's hockey captain as a 'mere spectator on the field of play'. Typically her chief memory was of watching teachers, especially Miss Anderson the games mistress: 'When the staff annually played the school's first hockey eleven, how vigorous they all were. How they pounded down the field, waving their sticks, especially Coolie [the art master] and large, lusty, red-

63. *George Square hockey.*

haired Mr Tate... The staff players sometimes slipped and fell on the muddy field, to the heartless applause and ironic encouragement of the onlookers assembled round the edge. Andie led the staff team, sometimes to glory. ("Go it, Nippy!" "Well saved, Andie!").'

At that time Queen Street were unbeatable and won the Edinburgh Schools' Challenge Shield three years running. George Square's hockey-playing seniors were held in high regard by the rest of the school: 'Firstly, there is the Sports Notice-Board. Athletically-minded maidens haunt its precincts in the hope of seeing their name in its hallowed lists. Starry-eyed juniors taste the delights of the forbidden in marking their "crush's" name with a surreptitious fingernail. Lofty first-year hockey experts discuss knowledgeably, and with a strictly limited vocabulary, the team selection… One morning, however, a new notice appears requesting all girls desirous of playing hockey on Saturday morning at the break of dawn to sign below. Hidden eyes watch the Captain as she pins up the momentous missive and at once a wild rush ensues among the first and second years, each and everyone of whom longs for the glory of being the first to sign.' The 'crush' admired by younger girls was conspicuous leaving the building due to the white tassel on her maroon beret. Full colours and half colours were restricted to members of the 1st XI, but tassel-wearing for regular team members began in the Thirds.

Hockey fixture lists grew longer as more Edinburgh girls' schools took up the game. In session 1948–49 St Hilary's, only recently big enough to compete, won all their matches. Four years later St Serf's fielded the school's first hockey team. Linked with its 'rather discouraging results', perhaps, a photograph in *The Servitor* showed the novice First Eleven gathered modestly behind the school in normal school uniform. A year later, in square-necked blouses, divided skirts and ankle socks, the team presented an altogether more athletic appearance at the front door in Abercromby Place. Helped by well-drained grass at Succoth Avenue and excellent coaching, St Denis bullied off to great effect, regularly beating teams from larger schools. There was also a Second Eleven: even quite small schools like Cranley began putting out two teams. Lansdowne House made a point of playing matches above schoolgirl level against Atholl Crescent, Moray House, the Art College, and Edinburgh Western Ladies.

By the last quarter of the twentieth century Lansdowne no longer needed hockey pitches, nor did other schools which had ceased to exist. However daughters and grand-daughters of previous generations were to be found playing for George Heriot's School at Goldenacre, a ground renowned for rugby and cricket. George Watson's Ladies had already joined their brothers in the other large-scale co-educational venture, with girls' hockey played on Myreside's holy ground. One of the first co-eds – who campaigned successfully for admission to the boys' primary school football team and ended up as captain – progressed to hockey: 'I spent many afternoons and weekends at Myreside with knees turning blue in the cold! I vividly remember the taste of that half-time orange quarter held in numb hands, and the time spent in the changing-room after each match running warm water and feeling the biting pain in them as circulation gradually returned. I also remember the clicking of our boot studs as we crossed Myreside Road; they've now installed a footbridge so that teams no longer have to make that perilous crossing.' For some time after the move from George Square to Colinton Road *The Watsonian* carried team photos of the First Eleven at half the size of the First Fifteen, rugby players like Gavin Hastings having been traditionally celebrated as the heroes of this school's sporting life; a similar imbalance applied to the summer sports of girls' tennis and boys' cricket.

Since then Watson's girls have acquired a cricket team of their own (dark leggings preferred to white shorts) and photographs as big as any. Cricket was only played in a few of these Edinburgh schools under discussion, with girls bowling underhand – as in rounders. Lansdowne House, though short of opposition, moved beyond that level through the coaching of the Rev. John Watt, 'himself an ardent cricketer'. At one stage the school fielded twin sisters who were feared by other teams as overhand bowlers from alternate ends of the pitch: 'How well I remember Miss Hale giving us tea at the Zoo when we once succeeded in beating St George's at cricket!' Eventually the sport was given up, even there, as 'not a Scottish game'. When England's most characteristic sporting activity began at St George's, cricket matches were often called off – not only for rain but also because of what the headmistress considered excessive heat.

Tennis, first of the modern sports to appeal to women, remained popular with girls from first to last, though only a few schools played on grass. Hard courts were built for all the schools in time, and became netball courts during the darker months of winter. Some members of the undefeated St Hilary's hockey team were in the Tennis Six which enjoyed an equal measure of success. The boarders of Esdaile, from manses all over Scotland, had ample opportunity for practice on courts in their own grounds. Seventeen George Square girls entered for the 1964 East of Scotland and Junior Championships, with Queen Street represented in similar numbers. Cranley often had girls in the finals at Craiglockhart Tennis Club, their weekly visits to the home of Scottish tennis providing an incentive for the girls in striped blazers.

Swimming was another summer activity. Drumsheugh Baths, convenient for St Denis at Chester Street, continued to be patronised after the move to Ettrick Road. Other schools bussed their pupils there for weekly sessions, with Warrender Baths providing another option. Among the facilities taken over at Craiglockhart, when the Sacred Heart Sisters moved in, was the indoor pool of the former hydropathic hotel, and the Mary Erskine School had a new swimming pool built at Ravelston. Learning to swim became a serious matter for girls as young as eight, but it was the fun of water play which encouraged them to persevere. RNLI life-saving badges were gained by seniors, who included artificial respiration – and even the kiss of life – in their rescue skills. Every school had a swimming gala. The crowning event of the Lansdowne House gala was traditionally the race between boarders and day girls, but this straightforward rivalry came to be seen as unhealthy and gave way to a three-way competition between houses.

The house systems adopted by most schools often extended the spirit of competition into non-athletic areas, but the highest levels of excitement were generated by team games and cheering spectators. Schools had house shields for hockey and netball, and in summer for tennis and swimming, but the high point was Sports Day. The Mary Erskine School Sports at Ravelston became a social occasion of sufficient importance to be reported in the local press. Track and field events developed a precision of their own in terms of marked lines and accurate measurement, as sport turned into athletics. The George Square Senior and Upper School Sports at Liberton were taken as seriously as athletics matches with rival schools. And beyond that level, individual winners were coached for stop-watch events like the 80 metres hurdles at the East District Championships.

Nowadays there are fewer girls' schools, so fewer gripping contests against old rivals. Hockey remains the most popular sport. It is still possible to play against George Watson's girls – an echo of the past – and there are new girls' hockey teams at Heriot's, Loretto and Fettes. There is also private school opposition to be found in Perthshire and the west of Scotland, but for Mary Erskine hockey players, coached to success as Scottish Champions in 2002 by a former Scotland captain, the high point of the season was still 'thrashing St George's in the semi-final of the East District Knockout Cup!' Magazine photos show the huge pads and boots of today's goalkeepers (face-guarding helmet removed for recognition purposes) and the general adoption of what seem to be rugby stockings. Girls' teams now wear the halved or quartered shirts associated with men's hockey. However a more obvious change in the modern age is the lack of prominence granted to First Elevens in school magazines. Once upon a

64. *Mary Erskine hockey.*

time the only photographs found in such publications were of prefects, hockey elevens and tennis sixes.

Tennis today is covered quite briefly in the *St George's Chronicle* with only a single fixture reported: 'A "friendly" match for seniors was arranged with Heriot's for anyone who wished to play. Five couples from each school took part and thoroughly enjoyed the event. Less importantly St George's scored a narrow victory… Participation and enjoyment are the main aims. The emphasis in school tennis is to encourage as many people as possible to play.' Tennis colours and half colours are nevertheless awarded, as for all sports. The trend towards social tennis was noted early in the co-educational school magazine of Watson's College, although scores achieved by the First Six in winning all ten matches against other schools were recorded with care: *The Watsonian* is a journal of record. Against expectation, the girls' tennis team photos of today at Watson's show a range of tops based on Wimbledon fashions. The 2002 *Merchant Maiden* gave no tennis results but followed tradition in publishing photos of the First and Second Six. Younger year group photos – the numbers vary but all wear white – show Mary Erskine's social side under the inclusive heading 'Anyone for Tennis?'

Surprisingly, one might think, mixed doubles are missing from team events at those schools where tennis is played by boys as well as girls, although they do feature in the traditionally social sport of badminton – St George's teaming up with Merchiston to be part of it. Shooting is another sport where girls are admitted on equal terms through the Combined Cadet Corps. Curling has gone co-ed at George Watson's College, and also fencing: girls of today score points with épée and foil in teams of both sexes. The Forth and Clyde Canal's proximity to Myreside has made rowing a natural sport for Watson's boys down the years, and girls took it up after the merger. They have since taken over the Boat Club, for boys no longer row. By contrast Heriot's boys and girls both compete in single-sex crews on the river – and not only the Scottish river, such are the standards achieved all over Britain by their coxless pairs, fours and eights.

Lacrosse has long featured in a minority of the Edinburgh girls' schools, and St Margaret's joined them as the roll of the school rose steadily in the Seventies. St George's girls have played lacrosse from the earliest period of the move from gymnastics into sport, and it has every appearance of being the school's dominant game today. Two tours have been made to the USA's eastern seaboard, where lacrosse (including men's lacrosse) is billed as the fastest growing sport. At home, on grass and astro-turf, young girls of Year 6 and the Remove are introduced to the game. The St George's First Twelve were very strong in the season when thirteen of the senior squad were selected for the East District. *Chronicle* photos abound of lacrosse-playing debs and dollies.

Choice of sport from a widening range is a feature of today's large girls' schools. Volleyball and basketball have ousted netball. Squash and skiing are valued as social sports, liable to be carried into adult life. Queen Street girls of the inter-war period took up golf in the same spirit, but it has only recently been granted a club notice-board at Mary Erskine – as noted by 'the first games captain to begin and end the year on crutches'. Athletics now includes cross-country running as well the jumps and javelins of track and field. From there it is only a step to orienteering. When does sport become outdoor activity? The simplest answer has to be when it fails to be mentioned in the Games Captain's Report.

Chapter 7

Out of School, Out of Edinburgh

The actress Hannah Gordon, who was a mere Second Eleven hockey player in her last year at St Denis, described a weekend expedition to Melrose Youth Hostel. Her contribution to the school magazine presented a corrective, cheerful view of the notoriously gloomy Scottish Sabbath. Her group of boarders was in the charge of a teacher and their goal was the country home of Miss Ramsay, who was in her last term as headmistress of St Denis: 'Supper over, we set off to have a look at the monument erected on the site where the Roman camp of "Trimontium" stood, and resolved to remember it as a red herring for Monday morning's Latin lesson. When we arrived back at the hostel we were still game for some dancing, in which other hostellers joined, and we rounded off a most successful evening with the Epilogue, conducted by Miss Garvie.

'Sunday morning saw us up early and the "breakfast squad" frying mounds of aromatic sausages and eggs. Then a three and a half mile walk to the tiny and very lovely old church at Bowden, where the minister who had been informed, or perhaps I should say warned, of our visit welcomed us warmly. Miss Ramsay had kindly invited us to her delightful cottage for soup after the service, and there we gleefully consumed vast quantities from a pot that never seemed to get any emptier. Miss Ramsay then suggested another route for our return, and accompanied us part of the way. Two of the other hostellers – cyclists – who had come to church rejoined the party and this was their undoing, as the "road" provided fences to be climbed, burns to be crossed and slopes to be scrambled up. However it was exciting, and photographs will show people balanced precariously mid-stream on slippery rocks, and others wading across with bicycles held aloft in one hand and shoes in the other. We reached the hostel in time to collect our rucksacks. Then we were pelting down the road towards the bus stop in a torrential downpour which soaked us in a few minutes, but we were all too happy to care.'

'Reading the *Merchant Maiden* for the '80s often gives the impression that the girls were rarely in School, such was the range of their expeditions and trips.' Lydia Skinner's observation also rings true for the present day. During the first two years of secondary school Mary Erskine pupils undergo a Projects' Week in summer while the older ones have study leave to prepare for exams. It gives them experience of scuba diving (in the Stewart's Melville pool, so hardly out of school); artificial rock-climbing in Leith; country park activities near Linlithgow; and hill-walking in Perthshire. The country park offers real rock-climbing, plus an exercise called Pioneering: 'The first challenge was to build a stretcher that would hold a member of the group without breaking. It sounds easy but we were only allowed to use ten pieces of wood and twenty pieces of rope... We then had to carry the stretcher to the next challenge, to build a bridge across a burn without going to the other side... The last was to build a free-standing swing for the whole group to stand or sit on for ten seconds.' Rival groups of boys add to the challenge; early doubts are mostly overcome: 'However tiring (extremely) it was, Projects' Week was one of the most exciting times of my life. I can hardly wait for next year's new challenges!'

Water is the common element in three of Mary Erskine's S2 (second year secondary) exercises, with a former naval base at South Queensferry providing opportunities for dinghy sailing and kayaking in the Firth of Forth: 'If I continued to paddle it would be less likely to capsize. Swoop. Up into the air. Crash. Down into the waves.' White-water rafting on the Tay is less alarming, with an adult instructor to guarantee safe passage through the rapids. Abseiling down cliffs provides natural progression from climbing up them in the previous year. A day on the beach at North Berwick is not much of a hardship for those who opt to stay out of the chilly brine, in contrast to mountain-biking at a Fife country park which is agreed to be the most physically challenging activity: 'At the end of the week I was extremely tired, covered in bruises and never wanted to see another coach for at least a year. But in spite of all these things I had a good time and I'm looking forward to Carbisdale next year.'

65. *Kayaking in the Highlands.*

Carbisdale Castle is a late-Victorian mansion in Sutherland which for many years has been the grandest of Scotland's youth hostels. Third year pupils from Mary Erskine and Stewart's Melville fill the dormitories over a ten-day period which is broken by a visit to Inchnadamph on Loch Assynt. The setting is truly Highland, and two Munros are climbed on the first day. Orienteering is the only specific advance on Projects' Week but day after day spent outdoors – rain, shine or midges, traversing mountain and marsh – builds up stamina and confidence. The Bothy Walk is described in tones of heroic resignation: 'This small stone-built cottage stood alone amongst the rolling hills. It had its own huge outdoor toilet. What else could we possibly want after a wet day roaming over endless hills? In the evening we cooked our delicious meal of packet pasta and noodles, cleaned our dishes in the burn and played games. After an uncomfortable sleep on a cold wooden floor surrounded by snoring boys, and a hearty traditional breakfast of Scots porridge, we were ready to walk back. We reached the minibus after a couple of hours, tired, cold and in desperate need of a shower.'

The effect of example is hard to pin down, but it does appear that George Watson's led the way. George Square girls followed the College boys outdoors to Glenmore Lodge at Loch Morlich. Then in 1968 they began basing their own programme on what was organised from Colinton Road. Balquhidder Youth Hostel and Loch Earn were used by fifth year volunteers until a Merchant Company Outdoor Centre opened at Ardtrostan on the loch side. Projects brought third year pupils out of Edinburgh for a fortnight in May, and shortly before the end of the George Square era they became compulsory. Groups went to a range of hostels and outdoor centres including Ardrostan (since destroyed by fire) and the effect was dramatic: 'Our classroom for the whole two weeks was the stunning beauty of the Cairngorms. No cathedral could lead us to anything more uplifting.'

All the activities so far described are conducted under the immediate eye of

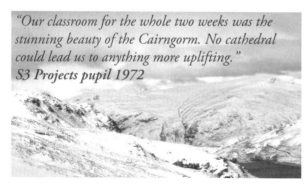

"Our classroom for the whole two weeks was the stunning beauty of the Cairngorm. No cathedral could lead us to anything more uplifting."
S3 Projects pupil 1972

66. *Beyond the George Square classroom.*

responsible adults (and in safety gear) but the Duke of Edinburgh's Award scheme leads third year girls towards independence by stages. This is for volunteers – a couple of dozen Bronze aspirants when St Margaret's took up the scheme in the Eighties – who go to youth hostels in groups and walk such trails as the Loch Lomond leg of the West Highland Way. Reporting on historical features like castles and crannogs (lake-dwellings) elevates these journeys above the level of physical effort. The Silver Award involves sleeping under canvas and travelling longer distances – by bike. The wide-ranging nature of the scheme is described by a St Margaret's girl: 'After climbing every mountain, fording every stream and enduring untold hardships, eight of us Golden Oldies finally made it to Holyrood Palace on 3rd July to receive our awards. This year we've explored from Arran to the Caledonian Canal to Normandy, and served the community in a variety of ways such as helping at Crosswinds and grooming retired horses at Balerno. Keeping body and soul together, we participated in judo, yoga and swimming. Perhaps the most enjoyable part was doing our residential projects in Wales, Norfolk and Dunkeld, just a few of the places where we sweated blood and tears. Meeting the Duke of Edinburgh was the climax of four years' hard work and endurance.'

The contrast of being ladylike in summer dresses – and hats until quite recently – for the royal garden party adds an element of enjoyment for these toughened up young women. There is nothing like that for an equivalent group who enlist in the Combined Cadet Force. St George's pupils followed the lead of Mary Erskine to combine with boys – in their case with those of the Merchiston Castle School. Numbers having increased, however, an all-girl unit has recently been created out of

Merchiston/St George's CCF. All the outdoor activities already described are on offer to girls in khaki, leading up to summer camp and night ops in combat gear. The firing ranges at Culty-braggan add a specifically military element, giving point to winter naming of parts and weapons training:

67. Girls of the Combined Cadet Force.

St George's girls have

competed well as members of the Merchiston shooting team. The highlight of CCF life for some of the Mary Erskine girls is admission to the RAF Section of the Stewart's Melville CCF, with scope for flying, gliding and parachute-jumping.

After all that out-of-school excitement the popularity of ski trips abroad (as far as Maine, USA, in the case of St Margaret's) seems hardly worth mentioning. However this sport which has long been favoured by stylish young women provides a link with foreign travel generally. Examples of that can be found as far back as 1908, when a Queen Street group travelled to Germany. They visited the picturesque medieval town of Hildesheim in Hanover for the sake of a connection which went back further still. Five dux-medallists of the Edinburgh Ladies' College were among those who had continued their education there. One young 'old girl' was responsible for laying out the Hildesheim tennis court, and a half holiday was declared so that the game could be demonstrated by the girl from Edinburgh. However she was unable to persuade the frauleins (or their guardians) to risk playing hockey. One of the Queen Street girls who studied in Germany was Mary Tweedie, but by the time she took over as headmistress in 1924 annual trips by senior pupils were invariably to French destinations. Journeys of up to twenty-six hours were undertaken by rail, with slatted wooden seats on the other side of the Channel.

Thanks to a Danish Consul in Leith whose daughters were at St Trinnean's, a party of fifty parents, pupils and staff crossed the North Sea to Jutland in 1935. Everything in Denmark impressed the visitors, from tethered cows in unfenced pasture to the Tivoli Gardens – and never a hill in sight: 'There is no doubt that this entirely novel experience made a profound impression on all, but particularly on the girls who saw a new way of life for the first time among a robust, healthy and happy people.' George Square girls were no less impressed by healthy Hitler Youth. Meanwhile the Ursuline Sisters, uncloistered in summer, took St Margaret's Convent boarders to their spiritual homeland: 'We stayed in a Paris hotel for a week, then a convent in Anger where we put hankies soaked in eau de cologne around our faces before going to the loo. Finally we had a fortnight in a convent close to a beach near Bordeaux.'

Arduous train journeys were still the order of the day when educational travel became general in the Fifties. School exchanges took place between the two very different institutions called St Denis, and George Square pupils experienced the life of a similar girls' *lycée* in Paris: 'The school is colossal. Multiply Watson's Boys by two and you will have a rough idea of the size. The corridors are all tiled and very slippery. Between periods they are filled by screaming French girls, all in blue overalls, who behave as if they were on a skating rink.' Channel ferries were a feature of the journey: 'Our misfortune was at Dieppe, when one suitcase fell into the sea. It was quickly retrieved, but the other passengers were regaled with the sight of the owner's clothes being dried. The French customs officer did not examine cases but pinched the cheek of one of our number.' School journeys to Switzerland were undertaken by St Denis, which was also 'the first Independent School in Scotland to send a party of girls on one of the British India School Cruises on the "Devonia"'. PNEU girls also cruised, including Diana Maxwell: 'At sixteen I was one of twelve Queen Margaret's pupils who flew from Gatwick to join the "Devonia" at Venice. I don't think there was one of us who had been abroad before. We toured the Acropolis, Pompeii and the Temple of Ephesus, all places we had read about in Ancient History.' Aeroplanes were soon to transform the nature of foreign travel, but the photo of a Mary Erskine party hot, tired and unhappy on the Spanish Steps in Rome acts as a reminder that trips abroad were never meant to be easy.

68. *To Rome in summer.*

Nowadays school exchanges are arranged on a regular basis, sometimes to France (Dax is a regular Mary Erskine destination) but more often for girls who have been learning German for a couple of years – to Nuremberg (St Margaret's), Giessen (Mary Erskine), Bad Godesberg (St George's). Access to Rhine cruises and the Phantasialand theme park near Bonn help to decide the location. The mode of travel varies; sometimes it is a long coach journey. Over recent years Giessen has alternated 'work experience' – days spent in kindergartens or lawyers' offices – with a Young Reporters scheme. This impels nervous teenagers into German shops bearing tape-recorders, with 'I have no money, do you have free cakes?' as a standard greeting. Hospitality given by local families is returned in Edinburgh.

Germantown Friends School in Pennsylvania has been linked with St George's for more than three decades, and teachers as well as pupils are exchanged for periods of up to a month. Art and Religious Education are two areas where fruitful comparisons have been made by staff: there is no R.E. course in the Quaker school, but a weekly Meet for Worship session, with silences, allows issues to be worked through calmly. For their part St George's girls come to terms with first-naming teachers, absence of school uniform, and the laid back style of co-ed students in a downtown melting-pot. Exchanges with places more like the girls' schools of Edinburgh have also been set up in Canada.

European visits are not always aimed at developing confidence in a foreign language. History gives teachers another kind of reason to take groups abroad, and not only history teachers when it comes to the First World War battlefields of Ypres and the Somme. In English classes the poetry of Rupert Brooke and Wilfred Owen prepares susceptible teen-agers for empathy. There are connections to be made in foreign fields: 'We all collected six names of soldiers who died in the fighting. They were chosen at random, or because they were part-icularly young, or famous, or heroic.

69. *Battlefield education.*

Later in school more information was gleaned from the Commonwealth War Graves website.' Fifteen-year-old Valentine Strudwick, the youngest casualty who patriotically lied about his age, is a common choice. So far, so educational, but the neatly-trimmed sites bear little relation to the actual conditions of that war: there is something incongruous about smiling girls in smooth grassy trenches. St Margaret's visited the Normandy beaches of another world war while the Queen was there. St George's and Mary Erskine have ventured into Eastern Europe as far as Warsaw and Moscow since the Berlin Wall came down.

At the risk of turning this into a travelogue, even more remote destinations may be mentioned. Geography (the subject) lay behind a 2004 expedition to Iceland by second year pupils of Mary Erskine and Stewart's Melville, or MES-SMC: lava fields, steaming 'fumeroles' in the ground and volcanoes rising above it. The first day featured swimming in 'a pale blue pool of effluent from the Svartsengi power plant' – a bizarrely Simpsons-style exercise which is nevertheless said to be curative because of the silica mud. That summer a group of senior pupils organised a World Challenge Expedition to Malawi, where they repaired the tourist rest-house beside a waterfall in Livingstonia. They also handed out much-needed equipment – brought from Edinburgh – to the local primary school. During their thirty-two day stay the girls struggled up the slopes of the country's highest peak but admitted defeat at about the level of Ben Nevis. An equivalent world challenge took St George's girls to Uganda, where they became bricklayers in the building of new classrooms.

Thanks to cheap air flights, schoolgirls now go to the ends of the earth, but usually in small numbers. From the earliest primary classes, and up through the years, teachers have long been taking all their pupils out of class to places as far as Hadrian's Wall. For sheer headmistressly chutzpah, however, there has never been anything to match what was carried through by one Edinburgh girls' school: 'Mrs Hiddleston's reign at St Margaret's ended with the most ambitious of all school trips. Two special trains took most of the girls and staff, together with some parents, governors and domestic staff, on a day visit to York on Wednesday June 27, 1984. "It was incredible," as a comment in the *Chronicle* puts it, "seeing 700 little green Martians being piped on board their British Rail Spaceships at Waverley – an experience never to be forgotten.' York bore up under the green invasion. This was 'its biggest ever school party, and a thoroughly enjoyable day was spent by everyone. All toured the Minster, for many the highlight of the visit; all went for a sail on the river,

70. The longest day for St Margaret's School.

and groups visited York's many museums – the journey through the reconstruction of Viking Jorvik being the lot of the privileged Sixth Form.'

For old girls of a certain generation, however, the truly memorable experience was being removed from Edinburgh in time of war. Influenced by the Spanish Civil War and Guernica, British politicians, press and public were greatly concerned about bombing raids. It was calculated that in the first twenty-four hours of war the German air force would be able to drop 3,500 tons of bombs on London. The Ministry of Health expected 600,000 civilian dead and twice as many wounded in six months. A plan was drawn up, well before the outbreak of war, to evacuate city children to the country. By the time Germany invaded Poland and Britain declared war on 3 September 1939, destinations were identified for all. Edinburgh girls' schools were unusual, most leaving town as communities. Some were away quite briefly, others for the duration of the war and even beyond it. The two largest went out of school but not, as it happened, out of Edinburgh.

When the Merchant Company schools were breaking up for summer that July it was decided that trenches would be dug in Queen Street Gardens and George Square. Parents were to be consulted on the possibility of evacuating the girls' schools, with Queen Street seen as a particular fire hazard. Meanwhile part-time education would be provided on a shift system at Daniel Stewart's College. As with George Square (sent part-time to George Watson's College) city centre schools were considered to be at greater risk. The autumn term began with Queen Street abandoned and the girls getting used to a system of morning or afternoon school at Queensferry Road. Some George Square girls went there too because of transport difficulties. During March of the following year meetings were held to discuss a proposal for evacuation to St Leonard's at St Andrews. Parents were not in favour, and Galashiels was also rejected. But part-time education was no great success, and after repeated requests the Senior School were allowed to return to Queen Street on 11 November 1940: 'The girls and Staff settled thankfully back into familiar surroundings; they were still cramped, owing to shelters in the basement and a First Aid Post in the Exam Hall, but they were home.'

The parallel story of George Square emerges from the reconstructions of Sheila Henderson, who became Head Girl ten years later. They start in the weeks before war broke out: 'Early that summer Melville House had been taken over by the Red Cross as a depot, and during the holidays pupils' mothers were asked to help roll bandages and pack sphagnum moss for dressing. As children we knew little or nothing of the fears and problems besetting our parents and the decisions that had to be taken about our schooling. It was years later that I learned of the crash courses taken by the George Square staff in first aid and fire-fighting during these phoney war months, and the anxieties of how and where to keep our education functioning. Before the end of the previous session there had been serious talk of the school being evacuated to Elgin. Over the holidays some of my friends disappeared as their parents made alternative family arrangements.

'In mid-September I found myself in Crieff, Perthshire, living with Aunt Jess and Uncle Jim in the lodge beside the Boys' School gate and going happily enough to Morrison's Academy, a co-educational independent day school. I knew these relatives so well and had spent so many happy holidays with them that it was a comfortable place to be, even without my parents, and I think I looked on this period as an unusually prolonged holiday with a dash of school thrown in. And yet it was a disjointed time too, for I was at an age when a weekly letter written laboriously to my parents was the limit of my correspondence skills, and there was no contact with any former classmates. Instead there were two or three new friends who lived nearby and who came to play in the extensive school grounds. My mother, too, came up by bus occasionally to visit.

'For some reason my class of boys and girls was not taught in the school itself, but in the nearby North Church Hall. Like George Square, there were dark corners in the passages and cloakroom areas. My teacher was a slim, quietly spoken lady with fascinating dark hair which she wore coiled in two "earphones". There were two lessons that I never seemed to master: one was Mental Arithmetic, at which I was desperately slow, and the other was Handwriting. The writing taught at Morrison's was longhand, and how I struggled with the slopes and loops after George Square's vertical loop-free style!

'That first wartime term must have been a nightmare for Merchant Company governors and staff. Our school was moved lock, stock and barrel to the boys' premises at Colinton Road. A half-day timetable was adopted. The "flitting" from George Square took time to plan and execute and for the first week or two a stop-gap scheme was put in place by which small groups of girls were taught in someone's home for a few hours daily by a member of staff living in the locality. There was a home-taught Liberton contingent which ended up going to Lasswade School.

'After a few months the drift back home began, and in the early spring of 1940 I was suddenly transplanted back to Edinburgh to discover that my school was no longer where I thought it was. Here was another new experience. For the first time I was in a modern, custom-built school at Colinton Road… In time the Red Cross vacated 5 George Square. The first stage of a staggered return took place in September 1941 when sufficient outside and basement air raid shelters had been built to take all the Senior classes plus 4 and 5 Junior. At the start of the next session my year followed… In July 1943 the last two Junior classes "came home" and we were all once again under one roof, with the exception of the Prep classes which went to new premises at St Alban's Road.'

With a roll of almost 290 St George's was the largest of the other city girls' schools, and the arrangements were correspondingly elaborate. As early as 30 January 1939 a meeting of parents agreed to their daughters being evacuated in the event of war to the Borders, an 'approved area' in terms of the regulations. Three large houses had already been secured for the teaching and accommodation of senior classes around the village of Bonchester Bridge near Hawick, and possibilities for younger children were being explored. Finance was crucial, and help was sought from Edinburgh City Council. Fees would continue as usual, apart from some 'extras', with a charge of 35/- a week for board, lodging and laundry. Priority was to be given to boarders, and parents were urged to return their request for a place within six weeks. A 67-item emergency outfit list was already drawn up for each girl to carry in one suitcase ('if room, hot water bottle') with gas mask over the shoulder. Enamel plates gave a sense of going to camp, and girls were asked to bring a 'bicycle if possible'.

In the event bikes were of greatest use to teachers hurrying between classes in fulfilment of the carefully devised timetable. Teachers also bought

Hallrule House, Bonchester Bridge. NB

71. St George's in the Borders.

food for the scattered community and did the pupils' washing, along with most of the other domestic chores – a future head was remembered for scrubbing the stone steps in front of Hallrule House. Girls who had grown up with at least one servant at home were also kept busy: 'Every morning at 7.30 we were wakened by the clang of a brass hand-bell. Each of us had our own special jobs to do in the morning – one week it was setting breakfast, the next washing up, then cleaning dormitories and so on. The "setters" were the most unlucky, as they were wakened before the wretched bell rang!' Old girls recalled sharpened appetites in the country air as rationing tightened, but hard-pressed staff took it all in their stride as part of the war effort – some confided that it was 'great fun!'

After the aerial Battle of Britain the threat of invasion receded, and numbers fell to 91 fee-paying pupils: 'The school was on its last legs. They realized in '42 that if they didn't bring it back to Edinburgh there wouldn't be a school in '43.' Three houses were secured in Garscube Terrace, and the new St George's session opened 'at the very gate of its real home'. Soldiers were everywhere in the school premises and grounds, with the gymnasium used for sleeping quarters. Across the road fifteen officers and their batmen lived better at Lansdowne House. Miss Aitken the St George's headmistress managed to negotiate access to gym and lab. Pupils returned, some from Lansdowne which had stayed open as a day school – after entrusting boarders to Oxenfoord Castle School in East Lothian. St George's was saved, but getting back to normal took time:

'Even the goalpost nets, lost in transit from Wolfelee, could not be replaced until 1947.'

For a while St Serf's and Lansdowne House were the only girls' schools in their normal Edinburgh premises. All-boarding St Hilda's was at the opposite end of the spectrum, since it had already experienced a move to Alva House near Alloa during the Great War. Under the joint ownership of Miss Cooper and Miss Hill, the 1939 move to Ballikinrain Castle near Balfron in Stirlingshire was managed effortlessly. Recently redecorated as a hotel, and with central heating, it had hot and cold water in every bedroom. There was 'accommodation for 100 resident pupils under one roof. A large central hall is used for cinema shows and is the main sitting room for the girls.' This was not a hardship posting. When an opportunity to buy the property arose the co-principals took it, although the intention had always been to return to Liberton: 'When the war ended it was seen that the main building of St Hilda's needed entire reconstruction. It was impossible to get building permits for this and the final decision was made to sell the houses, to construct extra tennis courts at Ballikinrain, and to carry out the conversion of rooms there as extra class rooms.' Pressure of events caused this Edinburgh girls' school to leave the city for good, although it flourished in the country for many years to come.

Part of St Margaret's also continued as boarding-school out of town after peace was restored. Some day school pupils stayed in the vicinity of buildings requisitioned in Newington, and the site was never fully yielded up to the military. Meanwhile Miss Matthew took her share of pupils from Strathtay to Dunkeld and finally to Auchterarder. After a very primitive seven months at Strathtay, a decent house was obtained further down river at Dunkeld. Five years were spent there: 'All the principal subjects – English, Latin, French, German, Mathematics, Science – are in the charge of Honours Graduates… The curriculum includes music, art, gymnastics, games and dancing taught by fully qualified mistresses… The staff is also well equipped on the domestic side, and the children's physical welfare is carefully supervised by experienced matrons… The fee of £40 per term is inclusive of tuition, board, dancing, games and laundry. The only "extra" subject is pianoforte…' Dunkeld House had to be given up before the school's Edinburgh premises (which included some boarding accommodation) were relinquished by the military, and the final

Perthshire move to Auchterarder lasted until 1956. Pittendreich House at Lasswade then became home to girls who were bussed to East Suffolk Road for classes.

St Denis also experienced a false start at Swinton House near Coldstream, where conditions were cramped and there was a water shortage. The train then took them from Waverley Station to Lauder in Dumfriesshire, where Drumlanrig Castle had been made available. There was no mid-term break, and once a week Miss Molyneaux, Miss Booth and Miss Turner-Robertson came down to teach Art, Dancing and Elocution: 'Lessons were given out-of-doors whenever possible, sometimes on the magnolia terrace... The girls trained hard for the inter-house hockey matches by running round the Castle oval several times before breakfast.' Esdaile went first to Ancrum House near Jedburgh, then Ayton Castle at Eyemouth. The Earl of Lauderdale made Thirlestane Castle near Galashiels available to eighty St Hilary's pupils and their teachers. There, in an atmosphere created by old paintings and 'a profusion of elaborately carved chimney-pieces', a rota of pupils helped to maintain fires and as well as doing other domestic duties. Forty-seven Rothesay House boarders spent all five of the war years at Paxton House outside Berwick-upon-Tweed while the A.T.S. occupied No. 1 Rothesay Terrace.

St Trinnean's went to Gala House, a Scots Baronial mansion which resembled the school they knew so well. In the memory which follows it is hard to avoid comparison with train journeys to horrifying destinations in war-torn Europe: 'After the evacuation notice was given and we found ourselves at Duddingston Station there was a space of waiting, somewhat dazed, wondering if this extraordinary thing could really be true. Here we were, each one of us a piece of human luggage, labelled and carrying a gas-mask like all the other parties of children, mothers and babies who thronged the platform and all approaches to the station. Two train-loads of such freight were sent off before it was our turn to be packed up, locked in, and despatched by the busy and kindly officials.' On arrival the metaphor changed from luggage to insects: 'Yes, I felt not unlike an ant with its comical white bundle of egg as I lumped my bedding to its appointed place. And each time, during the first week, when a vanload arrived at the front door or private cars yielded up their unwonted but by no means unwanted cargoes, the whole hive of workers streamed forth, and under the potent, magic spell of co-operation, disposed of beds, desks, chairs, pots and pans, crockery, jam, mops, ink, books, more desks, still more beds, books, books, books – whew!' In

September 1946 the closure of St Trinnean's (Miss Fraser Lee choosing to retire) was marked by a church service and then a garden party at Gala House.

The distant Highlands also provided accommodation for Edinburgh girls' schools. St Margaret's Convent was given the use of Lunga House on the mainland looking across to Jura, and when conditions were right the tidal whirlpool known as the Corryvreckan could be heard – that or (by nuns gathered for night prayers) bombs falling on Clydebank. Two Pickford vans reached the house without difficulty, but a coach bringing girls from the station at Oban could not negotiate the rear gateway. They had to carry their cases a very long way on a very hot day: 'Only Mother di Pazzi, Miss Campbell, Miss Tansley and Mother Mary Bernardine were able to arrive in some style in Miss Campbell's car.' When a father drove his daughters to Lunga they saw men gathered with pitchforks.

72. *St Margaret's Convent at Lunga.*

They turned out be the Home Guard responding to an invasion alert.

Cranley went north, as a young teacher recollects: 'Armed with galoshes, gum-boots and two really warm dresses, I took the train to Grantown-on-Spey. How can I describe the warm friendly atmosphere among pupils and staff as I rushed from scrubbing the baths at Highfield to my much-loved Juniors in Ardlarig, two houses down Station Road, overall flying? Here in the sunny empty drawing room we constructed nature tables and cupboards with bright cretonne curtains, not as yet on clothing coupons. We found many uses for apple boxes and enticed the rare crested tit to our bird table... I still have a child's drawing of "Tree-creeper on Miss McLaren's thumb". Most of our work was done out of doors at small tables in fine weather, unhampered by the dread of Inspectors. What fungus forays the 11-year-olds and I had in the pine woods in autumn and bicycle runs with ponding nets to dragonfly marshes in summer. What hectic speed the teenagers achieved on bicycles headed by the games staff to all the surrounding lochs, while I panted in the rear with the younger ones.'

Like all evacuated Edinburgh schoolgirls, Cranley's Catriona Watson wrote Sunday letters home. They give the impression of a lively fourteen-year-old in affectionate and practical contact with her family. 'I don't think I'll need any more soap for ages yet. My huge cake is still going strong.' A sheet torn in the laundry becomes a focus of concern and family rugs go missing. Thanks are regularly returned for the weekly food parcel (sometimes with sweets) and there are discussions about knitting and ration coupons. Skating gives great joy in Highland winters, but the weather can also be trying: 'This morning we had to go to church in driving snow. All last night it snowed and this morning there was an awful wind. We spent one half of our church-time in thawing and the other in getting warm before going out again into the howling blast.' Holidays at home in Edinburgh were keenly anticipated.

No doubt there was occasional homesickness, but old girls of one school after another recalled their time out of Edinburgh as 'The Happiest Days' – title of a *St Margaret's Chronicle* article. 'The Great Perthshire Adventure' strengthens that impression in the centenary history *Fortiter Vivamus*, and St Margaret's may be allowed to speak for other evacuated schools at the last: 'Brownies, Guides and Rangers – we had them all, and none of us will forget the camps, cheese dreams and half-burned sausages. We took badges by the sleeveful, as many weekends were given to testing. We had so much more free time than one ever had as a day girl… We were treated with great care during those war years at school, and none of us could feel we had been "evacuated" in the true sense of the word. We ate well, we slept well, we all grew (and how!) normally; we had remarkably carefree school life – thanks to the staff who always filled in when there were disappointments, for instance not getting home at mid-term at the last minute because of some National Emergency… But the tears were also of sadness when, in the Sixth Year, it was time to move on. Much as we loved throwing our Panama hats over the Forth Bridge on our train journey home, it was sad to say goodbye.'

Chapter 8

Music and Drama – and Dancing

'Schoolgirls at Work' and 'Schoolgirls at Play' may make good chapter-headings but they do not cover all the activities of a school year. 'Extra-curricular activities' (a grim label for happy times) in the girls' schools have included literary and debating societies, photography and wildlife clubs, Scripture Union and the Edinburgh Schools' Citizenship Association – the last of these bringing girls into contact with pupils of other schools, including boys. Regarding those activities with the highest profile, however, the capital must be acknowledged as a city of culture. This chapter-heading pays homage to the Edinburgh Festival of Music and Drama.

Girls' schools have traditionally provided music and drama in good measure, these activities mainly finding their expression outside the classroom. Music lessons are one thing, school choirs are another; and school plays developed from the work of elocution teachers. Acting and musical performances have developed over the years, so that the variety of what goes on today in the girls' schools may be compared with Edinburgh's Festival Fringe. Stilt-walkers and jugglers enliven the city streets in August; modern schoolgirls too will try anything. And they have always loved to perform.

Drama demands a setting, and when Lansdowne House moved to the sloping garden at Coltbridge Terrace in 1901 they were able to imitate the theatre of the Greeks: 'The lower lawn with its background of trees made an excellent stage, and several plays were thus acted out of doors. The first was Shakespeare's *As You Like It*… We were usually very fortunate with the weather, but on the second occasion of Tennyson's *Princess* the rain came down in torrents on the morning of the day, and there was nothing for it but to arrange things in the drawing-room, which was thus called upon to accommodate twenty-seven actors and some ninety guests. The orchestra, consisting in their kindness of the music masters, occupied the conservatory, which, sad to relate, did not prove entirely waterproof!'

St Margaret's End Concert which brought the school year to an close in Edwardian times required adjustments to the gymnasium-*cum*-hall: 'Unromantic objects like drill forms were moved out, 150 or so chairs were arranged, extra pianos brought in, sometimes even a grand piano and – crowning romance – a potted palm or two hired for the occasion.' In the school's centennial history an illustration of the programme is captioned 'The Marathon of the End Concert'. An early start was made at 6.45 p.m. in order to get through fully three dozen offerings. There was music in plenty, alternating junior and senior choirs, with piano solos, duets and trios. Kindergarten action games provided drama from the youngest children, who also demonstrated dumb-bell drill. The Second Half began with the playlet *Tom-Tit-Tot*: curious entertainments of that era included *Bo-Peep and Boy Blue, The Spanish Gypsies* and *A Garden of Japan*.

Even before they had a stage George Watson's young ladies put on tableaux from Scripture, and (with Hellfire the common theme?) Dante's *Inferno*: teacher-arranged tableaux, akin to a still life, led on to pageants – still silent, but mobile – during the inter-war period. There was a League of Nations Pageant and another for the delayed Coronation of 1937. The third centenary of Shakespeare's death had been celebrated in 1916 by extracts from his plays introduced, 'with lucidity', by the senior English master at George Square; the quatercentenary of Shakespeare's birth in 1964 prompted trips to Stratford-on-Avon from several Edinburgh schools. School history alternated with the Bard when it came to the marking of dates, and the first George Watson's Ladies' College House drama competition in 1921 took the form of a comparison of sporting eras: 'A game of clock golf was in progress, although a conversation about weddings and Bismarck's occupation of Paris engrossed the actors' attention more than the ball. The next scene shifted to Falconhall where girls were playing hockey, and then we were all asked to imagine girls fifty years from now playing rugby! The team did not look unattractive!' The Ministers' Daughters' College did something similar with three one-act plays fifty years apart, the middle one evoking the excitement of girls whose fathers had come to town for Assembly Week.

A new stage at Queen Street was first used for the performance of *Mary Erskine*, celebrating half a century since the end of Merchant Maiden Hospital days. Written by English teacher and school historian Mary Sommerville, its leading parts were played by former pupils. The large cast included thirty-six acting roles for pupils, and younger children were also on stage for the prologue and epilogue. Typical of the genre, it again consisted of scenes down the ages. When the 250th anniversary of the Merchant Company in 1931 was marked by all four schools together, a masque was put on in the Usher Hall which included an adaptation of the

Mary Erskine play. By the time a second full production was mounted in school four years later there were proper stage curtains; also footlights which had already served to brighten *The Glen is Mine* and *Quality Street.*

Full-length productions became common in the Thirties. As a boarding-school St Hilda's was well placed for rehearsal and preparation, and the Dramatis Personae for *Monsieur Beaucaire* by Booth Tarkington ran to fifty-seven pupils including dancers. A recent old girl, having just finished her RADA course by playing Bianca in the *Taming of the Shrew,* was touring with the Bristol Rep. St Denis reached unaccustomed heights with Shaw's *Saint Joan,* thanks to their elocution teacher. It was the first time any amateur group (never mind a school) had attempted the play in Scotland: 'No one can deny that this venture is unparalleled, and the fact that in spite of all difficulties the play was such a success is due in great measure to the splendid team work done by the girls. Some were outstanding, but all were enthusiasts, which is the chief thing. As everyone knows, Miss Turner Robertson's productions are always on a high level, and this time her task was unusual as "Saint Joan" is such a difficult play for schoolgirls.' Ann Turner Robertson also produced plays for St Hilda's, starting with *Quality Street* in the Lauriston Hall and moving to the Little Theatre with a biennial series which included *Berkeley Square* and *Pride and Prejudice.* Rothesay House also put on plays in the small Pleasance setting, old girls recalling 'the excitement of getting there by bus, and grease-paint'. Other ambitious productions of the time included Barrie's *The Admirable Crichton* at George Square and Purcell's opera *Dido and Aeneas* at St George's.

Long before there was an Edinburgh Festival the city acted as a magnet for high quality music and drama, which partly explains why girls were sent to school there. All St Denis pupils experienced a rich diet of cultural activities but going out to orchestral concerts in the evening was for boarders. Miss Benvie the headmistress also took senior House girls to see Sir Henry Lytton in *The Mikado* and to productions of the Shakespeare Society, of which she was an enthusiastic member. The experience of St George's boarders is recorded in a pupil diary of 1937: 'February 15th – We were taken to Barbirolli's last Edinburgh concert as he is going away to America… He said he was sorry to be going away, but hoped to come back again and conduct in the Usher Hall. March 5th – "1066 and All That" in Lyceum thoroughly enjoyed by all. May 22nd – The whole

73. *St Hilda's pageant c.1935.*

boarding house acted two plays called "Fat King Melon" and "Scenes from Pickwick Papers". October 16th – Miss Blott arranged to take some of the boarders to T. S. Elliot's "Murder in the Cathedral". The meaning was rather deep and Miss Blott kindly explained it to us afterwards.'

In the following year a Nativity play at Lansdowne House offered by the head teacher, Miss Ellen Hale, was acted on a new stage in the new gymnasium. The play was performed over three days, and silver collections were given to St Saviour's Child Garden in the Canongate. The Episcopalian Church's *Scottish Guardian* wrote an appreciative account which ended: 'Previously the audience had been asked not to applaud but perhaps this was almost an unnecessary request, for in that atmosphere of sincerity and devotion those present seemed instinctively to understand that they were not merely onlookers, but had also the privilege of sharing in an act of service to the glory of God.' Forty years on, and a further advance was made in the new Ellen Hale Hall: 'It was very exciting to have our own stage, with good curtains, proper lighting and adequate green-rooms. A spacious wardrobe has been installed under the stage, which will

74. Queen Street's first orchestra.

save many expeditions up and down the stairs of the tower, where for many years dresses and "props" have had to be stored.'

Music, which also developed from modest beginnings, was sometimes mixed with drama. The second issue of the *George Square Chronicle* reported such an occasion, as rendered by the school's historian Liz Smith: 'A "red-letter night" took place in the Lawnmarket's Orwell Halls on the evening of 3 February 1911 when the girls of George Square combined with the Guards Brigade (musically only we presume) to provide what became an annual concert for both parents and members of the public. As well as the girls providing a varied programme of both song and dance, the Guards Brigade during the interval apparently provided a demonstration of how to get someone into an ambulance.' Shades of the Edinburgh Military Tattoo which lay in the future. By this time W. B. Ross had begun his thirty-year reign as the school's music master. Ross achieved a great reputation through organ recitals in the Usher Hall and St Mary's Cathedral, and Oxford University awarded him the degree of Doctor of Music. As well as composing music for Dr Ainslie's school hymn, Dr Ross was instrumental in ending 'the ghastly ordeal of the Annual Recital in the Assembly Rooms, George Street, when eight pianos were placed in a row on the platform and three "pianists" sat at each hammering out an operatic overture.'

It has already been stated that the end of compulsory piano lessons at Queen Street freed staff energies for choral work, but the change was gradual. In the Thirties three hundred Edinburgh Ladies' College girls were still taking piano lessons and more than half of them were taught in pairs. The senior choir had come into its own by then, however, and an inspector (with curious choice of words) praised their 'virility, a feature of the highest classes in their choral work'. The newly formed school orchestra – which was made up entirely of string players – included five members of staff. George Square had an orchestra too, but its reputation as a centre of musical excellence came rather from seminars on topics like the romanticism of French composers and the centenary of Beethoven's death. Near the end of the decade an invitation was extended by Dr Ross to a choir from the Berlin College of Music, but air raid sirens were soon to drown out all music with melancholy warnings.

At St Margaret's in East Suffolk Road, the ending of hostilities was celebrated with a Victory Pageant. Since it had been impossible to mark the school's first fifty years in wartime, even greater effort was put into the Diamond Jubilee in 1950. Scenes from *The Saxon Saint* by Edinburgh playwright Robert Kemp were presented out of doors. There were production difficulties: 'Scottish costume was less well documented then than now; there was very little suitable in the wardrobe and materials were almost impossible to obtain without clothing coupons. Parents were naturally

75. *Drama at East Suffolk Road.*

reluctant to sacrifice these; even an almost derelict shirt could hardly be wrung from any father whose daughter was in Malcolm's army, but in the end all were equipped. The shirts were died saffron, the tunics made from couponless floor cloths; spearheads and "jewellery" made from cardboard and paint. Providentially the government were selling off, at a very low price, redundant and variously coloured parachutes which had been used for dropping supplies to beleaguered areas of war, and these provided the voluminous robes required by the Saint and her ladies.'

Pupils from St Margaret's Convent had the custom of visiting St Margaret's Chapel at Edinburgh Castle on her feast day of 16 November, often a cold and windy one. In an associated school production one of the girls had a 'non-speaking part as a guard who carried a spear'. This was *The Pearl Precious* by J. M. Burke, a play in three acts about St Margaret of Scotland which was put on in December 1949. But every year there was drama, with Mass in the morning and a Supper Dance (attended by former pupils) at the end of a day out of class – holy day and feast combined. In the same session as the Jubilee garden party at East Suffolk Road, the Convent celebrated a Marian Year with its own pageant *Causa Nostra Laetitia* (Cause of Our Joy) which ended with angelic girls in white paying homage to the Blessed Virgin Mary. Gregorian Plainchant was taught to volunteer pupils until the Ursuline Sisters stopped using it in Chapel because of wartime evacuation. The teacher who wrote out the pieces for each singer also played the organ, which in these days required hand pumping.

At Esdaile, schoolgirl Irene Young harboured ambitions to become a Shakespearian actress and won prizes out of school. She became 'the school's principal diseuse, and was called upon to perform at entertainments such as those put on for the annual visit of the Lord High Commissioner.' This is taken from her autobiographical *Enigma Variations*, where the grandeur associated with this quasi-State occasion is conveyed. The author provided further information by letter: 'Emphasis was placed on good speech and an itinerant teacher gave elocution lessons to individuals as an extra. She also taught Drama and prepared those with talent for entry in the annual Shakespeare festival in the Music Hall. Encouraged by the school's attitude to drama, each dormitory put on an entertainment on certain Saturday evenings which day girls were permitted to attend! The teachers produced a play once a year in which they deliberately and endearingly made fools of themselves, to the delight of their pupils. Music was strongly featured…'

After the return from evacuation to Grantown-on-Spey, Cranley music was given a higher profile by Kathleen Kelly. She succeeded Miss Niven (and Miss Milne who enjoyed almost equal status through long association) as joint principal. Miss Porteous, the other half, described her contribution to Cranley life: 'Miss Kelly was a good example of an "enabler". The Music staff she chose were selected not only for knowledge and high technique, though never lacking in these. They found and encouraged gifts and interest in individual pupils, classes and small choirs, and in time Cranley girls were carrying off the highest awards in the Music (Competition) Festival, playing in the Usher Hall, singing in St Giles. Quite early in our time a Music inspector was so impressed by our madrigal singing that he arranged for a group of our songsters to accompany him to a conference in England to show what skill schoolgirls could display in those lovely complicated musical forms.' Small schools could do great things, and it was on the initiative of St Hilary's that five years of Usher Hall concerts, in combination with other schools, began in 1950.

St Margaret's began to lay more emphasis on drama at East Suffolk Road, replacing the End Concert with two performances in each session. The second was always a play: Wilde, *The Importance of Being Earnest* (1951); Bennett, *Milestones* (1952); Shaw, *Arms and the Man* (1955); Bridie, *Tobias and the Angel* (1957). The head teacher Alice Keys was a gifted producer 'with a keen sense of the dramatist's purpose, integrity in its interpretation, and a remarkable talent for eliciting from the most unlikely actress, in an unfamiliar situation, a stunning performance. Outsiders could never fathom how, from a chair in the middle of the hall floor, she could inspire a douce schoolgirl to flirt; to think herself into the emotions of an earlier age; to adapt her athletic movements to those of, for instance, Tobias's old blind father; or to be funny without breaking into giggles.'

The Little Theatre continued to serve the needs of smaller schools, and Hannah Gordon made her acting debut there in a St Denis production of *H.M.S. Pinafore*. Music flourished quite generally in the Seventies, and St Margaret's choirs competed in the Llangollen International Eisteddfod: 'An expedition to the little Welsh town, so welcoming and colourful with its performers from many parts of the world, became an annual event, and

76. *St Margaret's victorious.*

singing in the flower-decked giant marquee a long-remembered thrill. Many were the successes in the face of stiff competition.' 1984 (the year of the day trip to York) was one of special success at Llangollen. On the instrumental side, a wind band came into being alongside orchestras at junior and senior levels.

Meanwhile Mary Erskine was mounting productions of Shakespeare, Molière, and Sheridan, and the orchestra grew to forty-nine players. Royal visits to Edinburgh led to the senior and junior choirs combining with those of George Square, and the 1970 centenary concert for the four Merchant Company schools brought male and female voices together in *Veni Creator Spiritus*, commissioned from William Mathias for the occasion. Lydia Skinner's testimony comes from the orchestra stalls: 'During the 1980s the schools consolidated their reputation for joint productions in music and drama. The juniors were included in Edinburgh Fesival performances of *Noye's Fludde* and *The Tower of Babel* and a series of musical and dramatic events developed their reputation as young singers, players and actors. The Seniors' productions drew on the skills of the Art, Music and Home Economics Departments in increasingly lavish and professional productions, whether in drama with *Le Bourgeois Gentilhomme* and *The Business of Good Government* or in musicals such as *The Boy Friend* and *Guys and Dolls*.'

It was not only girls' schools under shared Merchant Company patronage which came to see advantage in having boys play male characters on stage. St Margaret's made a safe start, teaming up with Loretto at Primary Seven level for *Alice* and 'finding the opposite sex was not so strange.' Available records do not show a repeat of this venture with older pupils, but in the centenary year St Margaret's Singers, 'now a mixed voice choir made up of former pupils, parents and friends', carried all before them at

the Edinburgh (Competitive) Music Festival. The Mary Erskine School – MES, now merged at sixth year level as Erskine Stewart's Melville, ESM – is well placed for mixed drama. Nor is this limited to those who study together and put on *Singin' in the Rain*. Younger pupils of separated sexes – after their primary education together – have met again for *Bugsy Malone*. Bridges can also be crossed between single-sex schools. St George's girls have shared the stage with Merchiston boys (*Romeo and Juliet, Blood Wedding*) but it was along with more familiar counterparts that they performed – inevitably – *The Boy Friend*: 'Everyone sang and danced

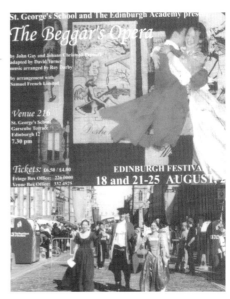

77. *Drama at the Festival.*

(yes, even the boys from the Academy!).' *The Beggar's Opera* was taken by the same pairing of schools to the Millennium Festival Fringe, where 'particularly strong performances came from the girls.'

Sadness touches Cranley's only venture into mixed performance, as recorded in the final issue of *FEHOMI* following the school's sudden closure in 1979. The last head teacher (who made it clear in that issue that she saw no future for 'small independent girls' schools') turned the event into a statement on behalf of co-education: 'The highlight of the session was – without the slightest shadow of doubt – the four performances of *H.M.S. Pinafore* at George Heriot's School in June. Cranley girls had been invited to join Heriot's boys in the production. The request was regarded as a great honour and the event as a great thrill. Twenty-seven girls participated, rehearsing weekly throughout the session. The Gala Performance will remain a fond memory in the minds of performers and listeners alike: it was an unforgettable success.' Elsewhere praise was bestowed on Cranley's performers: 'I could be biased, but I felt they outshone the boys who seemed less at ease on stage, at least on the night I was there.' In yet another corner of the Cranley magazine there appeared a short piece from Primary Two: 'I went to Heriot's today. I had a test. I saw lots of boys.' Soon there were lots of girls at Heriot's, for this was the year when co-education began there.

Acting on stage is only one part of drama. The *Merchant Maiden* magazine gave credit to the sound crew behind a combined production (Mary Erskine and Stewart's Melville) of *Kiss Me Kate* in 2003. The Stage Crew Girls were also invited to explain their part in making things run smoothly ('manoeuvring scenery, sorting props and most importantly opening and closing the curtains on cue') but to anyone from even a slightly older generation the most striking phenomenon was that of a six-girl lighting crew. Anything technical used to be reserved to males of the species. Not any more: 'We put up the follow spots, control desk and scaffolding tower; we move heavy lanterns around and hang them from bars; we discuss the coloured filters to use, cut them out and install them in the lanterns; we operate smoke machines, mirror balls and set off the pyrotechnic explosive devices.' There is expensive technology behind the modern thespian, but also professional expertise in the form of Drama teachers – who preside over studios as well as stages. It would be wrong

78. *Mary Erskine lighting crew.*

to imply that all this is exclusive to fee-paying schools, but they are certainly well to the fore.

Music has also come a long way since the days of mass piano-playing, although mass playing of stringed instruments in the early secondary years is the route to school orchestras – that or a wind band. By the senior years musicians may find themselves playing anything from classical music to jazz. Brass consorts and ceilidh bands also form part of the mix. Instrumental music and choral singing (which includes madrigal groups) are increasingly taken out of school. St Mary's Cathedral is a familiar venue during the Christmas season; Edinburgh University's Playfair Library provides a natural setting for chamber music. Less predictably, since coming to Edinburgh Harvey Nichols (the upmarket department store) has made space for school orchestras and jazz bands. And after the excitement of the Leavers' Concert, instruments large and small are sometimes transported overseas. In the summer of 2004 the ESM Concert Band entertained locals and holidaymakers in southern Spain with selections which included marches by Sousa. They ended, 'as always, with "Highland Cathedral" on the bagpipes.' Meanwhile the musicians of St George's Chamber Orchestra were touring in northern Italy:

'Our first concert was high up in the hills in the almost Alpine village of Fai Della Paganella: we had a huge welcome from the local audience who hummed and clapped along with great gusto!... And so to our final and most memorable concert, this time in the beautiful lakeside resort of Bardolino in the gorgeous Baroque church of San Nicolo e Severo. A final concert is often emotionally charged, and this one was no exception! The mixture of a week of sun, exploring wonderful places, and sharing music in exciting venues had lifted everyone on to another level, and the orchestra gave of their best. It was thrilling to see the four hundred strong audience giving us a standing ovation at the end of the concert, and then to walk down the café-lined street to the lakeside afterwards with people clapping us on our way!'

Dancing deserves to be mentioned as an extension of music and drama. It was important from the first in schools for young ladies, of course, with quasi-debutantes regularly conducted to the ball by carriage. Polkas and quadrilles were taught and practised. Pressure of work at the large academic schools led to dancing being focused on quite young children, however, either under the Queen Street caryatids or below ground level at George Square. As they progressed, white gloves became *de rigueur* as well as pumps. The footwear problems of dancing-teachers making their way between Queen Street and Atholl Crescent have been noted.

In time the gloves came off for Mary Erskine girls who escorted each other round to the rhythm of waltz, foxtrot and quickstep. Ankle socks, on view in one photo, seem more apt for Scottish country dancing – which

79. *Ballroom dancing at Queen Street.*

was also taught. (MES has since progressed to highly competitive Highland dancing and joint events with the Stewart's Melville pipe band.) A girl who saw out the George Square era remembers 'dancing to "Windmills of Your Mind" in my gym tunic with the teacher we called Leapy Lee. I guess she was Miss Lee. We had coloured cotton tunics with what seemed like huge pants in the same colour – yellow for Falconhall House, of course.'

Victorian young ladies who danced with male partners had chaperones in attendance, and the encounters were never in school. This continued to be an absolute rule until well into the second half of last century. At

George Square there was an annual event known as the Cookie-Shine ('jocular' term for tea-party, according to the Chambers Dictionary) which stimulated dress-making in the weeks before Christmas. It was a supper dance for fifth and sixth year girls, formal enough to have a dance card so that the small number of male teachers could be shared. Female teachers were also popular, as a surviving card shows, in what was mainly a programme of country dancing. It was revived after the war as 'the pride and joy of the Upper School, and it was not until 1955 that the Senior Prefect of the time, Margaret Sommerville, was despatched by her peers to approach the Headmistress Miss Nicolson and ask if partners might be permitted. To the huge surprise of everyone (and by all accounts the horror of some staff!) Miss Nicolson agreed, although not without first enforcing some strict rules. The girl's parents had to write to the Headmistress informing her of the name of both the boy and his school; if the boy was at University he must be in the first year of undergraduate study and he could not be a medical student.'

The compiler of this book generally keeps a low profile but cannot resist saying that he was there, all unaware of the historic nature of the occasion. As Liz Smith points out in *George Watson's College*, 'finding partners was no easy matter for many girls as few had boy friends... Mothers had to work quickly to find the male offspring of some long-lost cousin.' That describes my case exactly, the artificiality of the relationship exaggerated by me being younger and smaller than the George Square athlete in question. The dimly lit subterranean awe of being introduced to Miss Nicolson lingers in memory still. Moving on to St Margaret's, by amazing coincidence – for I was no more confident with girls than the average Edinburgh college boy of that time – an occasional doubles partner from the local tennis club issued an invitation in the following Easter term. The Highers were over, and 'on March 29th the Sixth Forms held their dance in the School Hall, which was beautifully decorated; a three-piece band provided the music and refreshments were available in the form of a running buffet. The dance was a great success and will, we hope, be repeated next year.' St Margaret's did not in fact turn it into a regular event, but George Square Cookie-Shiners met in summer with seniors of the other Merchant Company schools (George Watson's College the venue on at least one occasion) for the Quad Dance.

Over the years which followed most girls' schools found occasion to allow partners from carefully chosen boys' schools. Even in the Fifties a Saturday night Reel Club had linked St George's with the Edinburgh

Academy through Scottish country dancing. A recent Lower School Cake and Candy at St George's produced photos of kilted juveniles doing the Gay Gordon with girls of the Remove and Year 6Q. Meanwhile young ladies who had worn tartan since their first day at Mary Erskine were unfazed by male Highland dress: 'On 13th December 2004 the class of 2004 celebrated their Christmas Ball in style. Preparations for some began months before, with frantic attempts at finding a partner and endless searches for the perfect dress. Others seemed to enjoy the last minute anxiety of getting ready the week before. Come Saturday night, though, everyone without exception looked amazing. Most of the guys went for kilts and it can be noted that there was many a true Scotsman within the year group! On the Friday night before the ball a huge team of volunteers stayed behind to transform the hall into a winter wonderland… The evening itself started with photos and many exclamations of "No, you look gorgeous!" We then had a buffet meal accompanied by some good chat and exactly one glass of wine each. The ceilidh band then kicked off and many hours of enthusiastic dancing followed.'

80. *The Esdaile neighbourhood walk.*

81. *Gillespie's box-hats – and bare heads.*

82. *Queen Street in fashion.*

83. *The Hall at St George's.*

84. *Church into school at St Margaret's, East Suffolk Road.*

85. *St Denis, Ettrick Road.*

86. *George Square juniors.*

87. *Ties in the gym at St Margaret's.*

88. *Convent doors open.*

89. *St Margaret's Convent.*

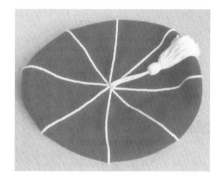

90. *George Square berets.*

91. *Straw hats for the smallest.*

92. *Modern gymnastics, Mary Erskine.*

93. *Making a splash in the pool at Ravelston.*

94. *Mary Erskine kilt and blazer.*

95. *Learning Mandarin Chinese.*

Chapter 9

Girls' School Stories

In their well-known survey of girls' fiction, *You're a Brick, Angela!*, Mary Cadogan and Patricia Craig identify the period between the two world wars as the golden age of school stories. At a time when *esprit de corps* was being encouraged by head teachers and staff in all sorts of ways, from uniforms to field sports and prefects, school stories were often mildly subversive, presenting school life from a mischievous girl's point of view. What effect did reading about fictional schools in books and magazines have upon pupils who attended the girls' schools of Edinburgh?

A survey of the field, starting with Angela Brazil (pronounced 'Brazzle') who more or less invented the girls' school story in 1906 with *The Fortunes of Philippa*, gives the impression of a predominantly English phenomenon. It was gathering momentum before the Great War. Cadogan and Craig acknowledge Angela Brazil's popularity while pointing to limitations which had the effect of making the subject comical to outsiders: 'Schoolgirls had been well primed for the blossoming of the school story by the early books of Angela Brazil whose energetic form captains and prefects are silly, exuberant and intense in a way which is highly caricaturable… The schoolgirl as a joke owes its inception in part to Angela Brazil – an unfortunate result of her efforts to free the girls' story from the conventions which had governed it… Instead of boring her readers with a long-winded narrative view of events, she adopted as far as possible their vocabulary and their viewpoint, to achieve a zest and immediacy which the Edwardian schoolgirl must have relished.'

After the war men came to play a significant part in the world of female junior fiction. Amalgamated Press turned to Charles Hamilton, the creator of Billy Bunter, for stories about Bunter's sister Bessie when they launched the *School Friend* under a male

96. *Billy Bunter's sister.*

editor, R. T. Eves. Changing his pen name from Frank to Hilda Richards, Hamilton started a new series set in Cliff House School for Girls. Unfortunately the stories were not a success, and a different writer – also male – took over the pen name and reworked the character of Bessie Bunter. A recurrent theme in the *School Friend* saw scholarship girls from poor homes winning acceptance in schools for the rich, which helps to explain the wide appeal of such papers.

One young man who developed the humorous potential of head-mistresses and schoolgirls was Arthur Marshall, then a boarding-school master at Oundle. He began what became a regular Christmas feature reviewing girls' school stories in a 1935 issue of the *New Statesman*. One of the books was Dorita Fairlie Bruce's *Nancy in the Sixth*: 'Life in schools for girls is clearly an exciting business. They go the pace. Lights are put out in the cubicles and one would think that the girls, exhausted by the strain of ragging Miss Bellamy, would be ready for refreshing sleep. But all that the merry madcaps seem to want is the ginger-pop hidden under Bertha's bolster and a moonlight climb over the roofs. And doubtless the readers of these stories would not have it otherwise.'

Another of Dorita Fairlie Bruce's books was the object of gentle ridicule in the following year: 'The girls are all fearfully keen on a ripping games mistress called Miss Stewart, and can one wonder? "It isn't her beauty and her auburn colouring, but she's got that – that sort of glamour." She abandons lacrosse momentarily in order to go for walks with a plucky little junior called Faith Kersey, who has "eyes like drowned violets" and is an "undeveloped genius at throwing in".' Marshall's humour was somewhat in the style of Wodehouse. He felt that the books chosen for review were well enough written to stand a little mockery, and was hardly ironic at all in suggesting that the readers 'would not have it otherwise'. These books were for schoolgirls, not adult bystanders. Ten to fifteen was the age range, with the Fourth Form often chosen to represent the heart of school life. Although Arthur Marshall headed one of his columns 'Memsahibs in the Making' (many boarders had connections with the Raj), he seemed unconcerned about social implications, in contrast to George Orwell with his well-known critique of 'right-wing' boys' weeklies. Marshall has inevitably come in for feminist critique.

Angela Brazil has been described as 'easy to grow out of', and older girls were liable to take a detached view of school fiction. A George Square senior parodied the *Schoolgirls' Own* around the time that Marshall's career was taking off: 'Enter the Coterie with a noisy rush. Gaily flinging down their books, they group themselves gracefully on the window sill, regarding Betty Berneaud their famous form captain.' Ten years later, shortly after the Second War, another meted out similar treatment to the *School Friend*, and asked: 'Is it not strange that we should have made so little attempt to model ourselves on those heroines?' The question of how Edinburgh schoolgirls responded to them is addressed by Linda Murison, now a librarian and collector of the school story genre, but then a pupil at Lansdowne House:

'I read my first school story when I was about seven or eight; at the recovery stage of being ill in bed, I had run out of books of my own and in desperation took down an unappetising jacketless dark blue book from my sister's shelf. It was Enid Blyton's *Summer Term at St Clare's*, and I can still call back the wonder I felt, discovering the sheer entertainment lurking between those boring covers. I had no idea that fifty years later the genre would still be amusing me. However, I don't remember as a child ever discussing school stories with school friends, although one girl had Elinor Brent-Dyer's *Heather Leaves School* and Angela Brazil's *Nesta's New School* on her shelves at home.

'The appeal of school stories wasn't that they bore an exact resemblance to real life as I knew it. I read them because they presented a familiar life tidied up and made manageable. The different fictional schools reflected facets of the school I knew which had just enough in common with St Clare's or the Chalet School to make me feel that I was attending a vaguely unsatisfactory version. (I was too young to realise that this was life versus art.) As for the ethos of these establishments, I had swallowed enough of it whole to feel that I was definitely unsatisfactory as an inmate. It was comforting to think that had I gone to the Chalet School, either Joey or Mary-Lou would have sorted me out by the end of the first term. In size Lansdowne House was very like St Clare's, and Miss Bennett shared many of the qualities of the fictional headmistress. When Claudine pushed a spoilt fashion-plate of a mother into the St Clare's swimming pool, and clothes had to be borrowed from the dignified head, Miss Theobald, I knew exactly how incongruous they would be.'

In the period between the wars the girls' school story was developed by Dorita Fairlie Bruce (of the Dimsie series), Elsie Oxenham (Abbey Girls) and Elinor Brent-Dyer (the Chalet School), although Angela Brazil continued to produce a book a year until her death, aged 78, at the end of the Second World War. Not all the school stories had English settings, however; some had a distinctly Scottish flavour. Dorita Fairlie Bruce – the author whose gentle ribbing by Arthur Marshall has been noted – was the daughter of a Scottish engineer. She was born in Spain (hence the Spanish nickname for Dorothy) but grew up in the Stirlingshire village of Blanefield and the town of Blairgowrie.

When Dorita was ten the family moved to London, where her father built a reservoir at Staines, and she spent enjoyable schooldays at Clarence House, Roehampton. Dorita had stories and poetry published (in *Girls' Realm* and elsewhere) for fifteen years before her first book *The Senior Prefect* appeared in 1920. It was republished as *Dimsie Goes to School* – Daphne Isabel Maitland was the lead character – in a series of adventures on the Kent coast. There the Anti-Soppist League directed its efforts against excessive schoolgirl femininity. Arthur Marshall was also hostile to 'beauty culture' and said so: 'Girls, shy away your bath-cubes and freesia soap. A moonlit night and a rope ladder were all your mothers needed to make them happy.'

Dorita remained Scottish to the core, holidaying every year with her mother's parents in Ayrshire. It was there that she set a fictional boarding-school on an island very like Great Cumbrae for a series about Nancy Caird. It culminated with *Nancy Returns to St Bride's* (1938). Nancy had failed to live up to the 'good' reputation of her mother and aunt as pupils at the school by organising one escapade after another. She was expelled, and this led to other, less successful books about a day school called Maudsley. The author's fullest account of boarding-school life (Springdale, with Rae Merchiston as the main protagonist) was set on the Ayrshire coast at Largs. The town and its surrounding countryside recently attracted a visit by the Dorita Fairlie Bruce Society.

Sweden's Eva Margaret Löfgren attributes this author's lasting appeal partly to an avoidance of slang, which quickly dates. She further observes that Dorita Fairlie Bruce was 'more concentrated on the intrinsic themes offered by the boarding-school as a small society of girls than those by many other writers. Her plots are skilfully built around the relations between schoolgirls of the same or different ages: friendship, rivalry, conflicts. Teachers and lessons play a comparatively smaller part. "Outside" adventures and mysteries are normally well incorporated in the central plot, often inspired by her great interest in history, local legends and archaeology.' Friends often fall out over a misunderstanding, only to be reconciled in the last chapter. Sport is always prominent, with a somewhat unlikely emphasis on girls' cricket beside the rainy Firth of Clyde.

The death of her father allowed Dorita Fairlie Bruce to leave London for Skelmorlie on the Ayrshire coast, where she spent her remaining years. All her Scottish books are more or less interconnected, unlike those of Angela Brazil who used a fresh set of characters every time. Even Dimsie – who is prominent nowadays due to reprints – had her family home in Argyll. Competent judges rate Fairlie Bruce's St Bride's and Springdale series above the rest of her work. On the question of Scottish connections, it is of some interest to find that three of Elinor Brent-Dyer's late Chalet School books were

97. *Cricket by the Firth of Clyde.*

dedicated to the Schwarz daughters of an editor at Chambers (her publisher) who had been educated at George Square. The three girls were also pupils of George Watson's Ladies' College.

Edinburgh was home to Ethel Talbot, whose *The School on the Moor* (her first book) appeared soon after the Armistice. She and Edith Mary de Foubert shared a cottage at Pitlochry at a time when patriotic Girl Guides (and Guide leaders like themselves) were gathering natural disinfectant to dress the wounds of Jocks and Tommies: 'Picking sphagnum moss is ripping; quite apart from the jolly feeling that you're really doing something to help things along, there's always the chance of being bogged.' Although most of her forty-six books between then and the outbreak of another war had school settings, Ethel Talbot also wrote about Brownies, Guides and Rangers, including Sea Rangers. At first the Girl Guides – as military as their sex was permitted to become in that war – copied the khaki of their Boy Scout brothers: 'At St Bride's School the first school company in the city showed resource in 1917 when their company was inspected by the County Commissioner. Uniforms were difficult to buy so the unfortunate boarders had to make their own, and on the fateful day their stitches were not in time and safety pins had to take the strain of seams!' – this from a history of Guiding in Scotland.

Ethel Talbot's next book *Peggy's Last Term* (1920) shows Sylvia Armstrong as a tenderfoot Guide who 'doesn't know a Union Jack from a Stars and Stripes, you bet, and I don't suppose she knows a granny from a reef knot.' Members of the patrol coach her in Guide Law, the Salute, woodcraft and the national flag. Sylvia carves a Union Jack on her school desk to aid memory. She also keeps a long piece of string under her pillow in the dormitory for practising reef knots, sheet bends, clove hitches and bow lines. Her enthusiasm for winning the Patrol Cup leads to an uprooting of plants in the gardens of rival patrols. '"I did it for you," she tells Peggy (her Patrol Leader heroine) whose answer is stern: '"Don't you know when a thing is playing the game and when it isn't? Don't you know how to be sporting, and – clean, and – straight?"'

Conformity to an honour system is stressed again and again by Ethel Talbot, although in *Patricia, Prefect* (1925) she reveals sympathy for the outsider and for the crushes which girls often felt for their seniors. But Linda Murison observes of real-life seniors: 'There was no sign of prefects agonising over our morals at Lansdowne House, let alone courting double pneumonia and death to bring us back to the fold. Ethel Talbot's prefect, Patricia, slips happily from life knowing that young Veronica has been brought round to the spirit of St Chad's, but our prefects seemed far more concerned to give us pneumonia at "chucking out time", when we were forced out into the cold at break.'

Ethel's life was as strange as any fiction. After a London childhood, she had a first story accepted at the age of fifteen in 1895. Her relationship with Herman George Scheffauer, an American of German extraction, developed through the capital's literary circles: there was no question of writing for schoolgirls then. Scheffauer, who was four years older, arrived from San Francisco with a fine reputation as a poet ('The Ruined Temple' was inspired by that city's earthquake) and gained another as a translator between English and German on behalf of authors such as Thomas Mann and Frank Harris. (Ethel also translated in both directions when her production of school stories was slowing down in the Thirties.) Around the time of her marriage to Scheffauer in 1912 she had poems in *Harper's Weekly*, *The Smart Set* and the *Poetry Magazine*, and in that same year Cassell brought out *London Windows* by Ethel Talbot.

War changed everything. Scheffauer was among those who hoped for a negotiated peace after two years of stalemate. He opposed the United States entering the war, and an American source tells us that he was 'run out of England'. American citizenship saved him from worse. Scheffauer translated a German newspaper, according to Rupert Hughes, and contrived to have it 'distributed to soldiers by various devices. I proposed to the Department of Justice that he be found guilty of high treason… This was done, and served as a precedent for Ezra Pound and the others. Scheffauer died in Germany a few years after the war. He wrote excellent poetry.' He also continued to play an important role in cultural exchange, explaining the Bauhaus movement to readers of English in *The New Vision in German Arts* (New York, 1924). Three years later he died after falling out of a window.

Photographs held at Berkeley's Bancroft Library (and made available on the internet) tell their own story. The first, dated 1908, is inscribed 'The Sons of Baldur. For Ethel Talbot from her friend Herman Scheffauer'. It draws on Germanic myth as exhibited at the Bohemian Grove. A spear fashioned from mistletoe which killed Baldur, son of Odin, leans against a wooden throne carved with animal heads. Herman sits on it, incongruous in modern dress. In another photo he is rowing 'with Ethel Talbot' on what is probably the Thames. She wears a broad flowered hat of the Edwardian era. Her poem 'Give Love Today' dates from this time. A third photograph shows Ethel Talbot Scheffauer with her husband in a horse-drawn sleigh, possibly on honeymoon at Augsburg where his parents were born. Finally there is one featuring a German funfair and the mock-up of a coal mine entrance. From it emerge 'Uncle Herman and Aunt Ethel' and their daughter Fiona astride a four-wheeled trolley. Above are the words '*Glück auf*', the miners' good luck greeting. The fashions in the photo are interwar. The pretty girl with the Scottish name is about six years of age.

Among the more prolific writers of schoolgirl fiction Ethel Talbot has the closest connection with Edinburgh's schools. In 1916, when her friend Edith Mary de Foubert was Sixth Form Mistress at St George's, Ethel joined her at 5 Roseburn Cliff beside St George's. Both of them left the city for Perthshire soon after (Edith is said to have kept chickens) but five years later Ethel was listed in the Edinburgh Post Office Directory as an 'authoress'. The two women were living together a year before Herman met his sudden end. It would appear that Fiona was born after her father had been 'run out of England' (he brought out *The Work and Wealth of Austro-Hungary* in Berlin in 1916) and that in her early years Ethel and Edith looked after her. No doubt the presence of a child and a schoolmistress in the household helped to turn Ethel in the direction of girls' fiction.

One can only guess how the sphagnum-collecting patriot felt about the departed Herman. He was not free to return to Britain after the war and Ethel stayed only a short time with him in Germany. She wrote no books for two years after *Peggy's Last Term*. Then, showing a commendable intention to pay her way while living once more with Edith de Foubert, she wrote eight school stories in two years. Shortly before her husband's death in 1927 Ethel Talbot Scheffauer went with Fiona to live at Shooters Hill in London, and remained there until her death in the last year of the Second World War. Her involvement in translating Paula Shaefer's *The Catholic Regeneration of the Church of England* (1935) suggests religious affiliation and possibly a fashionable conversion. Ethel Talbot wrote until the paper ran out: *Terry's Only Term* (1939) was her last school story.

Housemates and friends, Ethel Talbot and Edith de Foubert each dedicated a book to the other. It is the teacher Edith Mary de Foubert who provides the only example of school stories written by someone with direct experience of Edinburgh girls' schools. She appears to have come from an Anglo-Irish family and the surname suggests a Huguenot connection. One of her books, *For the Sake of Shirley* (1935), starts with an impoverished gentry family in County Kerry seeking education for the youngest sister in England. It may well have been inspired by events in her own life. The name de Foubert is found in County Cork. Adelaide D. E. de Foubert who qualified as a teacher from Cork School of Art in 1897 may have been Edith's sister. Mrs Barbara de Foubert (her sister-in-law?) was confirmed in the Church of Ireland at St Michael's, Blackrock, in 1925. An astonishing seventy-eight years later, she was still singing in the choir. The evidence is circumstantial and the Scottish capital some distance from that corner of Ireland. At any rate Edith de Foubert became a teacher at St George's after a course at the Training College in Edinburgh.

The beginnings of St George's School in Melville Street have already been described, but there is more to be said about the college. It began in 1886 as St George's Hall Classes in Randolph Place, a cul-de-sac at the east end of Melville Street, before moving into the school premises. After preparing women (mainly by correspondence) for the St Andrews University Lady Literate in Arts examinations, and then for entry to full university courses in the Nineties, St George's Training College worked towards the Cambridge Certificate. Intended for women teachers in secondary and higher grade schools, the college was admitting a majority of graduates by the turn of the century. Five years into it, Education Department funds were directed towards training centres in Edinburgh (at Moray House) and other Scottish cities. Independent St George's found that the level of fees made it difficult to compete. Numbers fell from an average twenty-five to seven, but a solution was found when school and college amalgamated.

A 1909 photograph showing Edith with eight other young women is held at St George's, where she was to teach English and History. Edith herself was not directly involved with the school's boarders but lived at 37 Palmerston Place round the corner from Melville Street. Midway through the war she gave up her post when Ethel Talbot and her child came to Roseburn Cliff. Close to the new St George's in Murrayfield, this consisted of houses designed by the visionary urban architect Patrick Geddes. By the time Edith de Foubert began to write for money she was describing herself as a lecturer.

Edith's collecting of sphagnum moss for the wounded of the Western Front reminds one of Muriel Spark and *The Prime of Miss Jean Brodie*: "'I was engaged to a young man at the beginning of the War but he fell on Flanders' Field,' said Miss Brodie. "… He fell the week before the Armistice was declared. He fell like an autumn leaf, although he was only twenty-two years of age… After that there was a general election and people were saying "Hang the Kaiser!" Hugh was one of the Flowers of

98. *Edith de Foubert fourth from left.*

the Forest, lying in his grave."' Miss de Foubert belonged to the same generation of women whose brothers and fiancés were cut down in No Man's Land, young officers leading their men over the top. Single ladies taught, as a result, and sometimes wrote.

E. M. de Foubert's first book came out in 1924 and proved to be her most successful: *Every Girl's Book of Hobbies* was reissued twice in four years. It ran to 393 pages with fifteen photo plates and countless drawings. The board cover shows a girl hand-painting a Rockwood pottery vase from the Arts and Crafts movement. The hobbies range from embroidery to birds' eggs, and include toy-making, book-binding, gardening, etching, lacework, butterflies, enamel metal work and much more. *The Great Big Glorious Book for Girls* compiled in our own time by Rosemary Davidson and Sarah Vine is very much in the same tradition. Edith and Ethel's home at Roseburn Cliff must have borne much evidence of craftwork. No doubt teenage girls were encouraged to try their hands after morning school at a time when devotion to sport had hardly started.

The book has a chapter on Girl Guides and Brownies. The St George's Company, started in 1921, was seen by one head as equivalent to the Officer Training Corps in 'upholding traditions of loyalty and offering training which can make service effective.' Fifteen years later her successor informed parents that 'we have decided to give up the Brownie Pack at St George's after this term. I feel that in a school like St George's the children get the training which the Brownie Pack is supposed to give them more naturally in their normal school life.' Edith de Foubert and Ethel Talbot both contributed to Collins' *Cubs' and Brownies' Annual*. The range of their outlets is worth emphasising. The two women also appeared together in a volume of Cassell's *British Girls' Annual*, in which Ethel's story 'The Feud' had been published in 1916. It was followed by fifteen contributions in seven years to magazines which included the *Boy's Own Paper* and *Chums*. Edith started later and wrote less, but she was the lead contributor to a mid-Thirties *Hulton's Girls' Stories: The Best Annual Ever*. She also wrote for the *Girl's Own Paper* which boasted an international (mainly colonial) readership.

The first of eleven full-length school stories by E. M. de Foubert (as she always appears) was *That Term at the Towers* (1927). Others followed in each of three succeeding years up to *The Fourth Form Mystery* (1930). It was still in print seven years later, on the evidence of a prize bookplate. The plot concerns the relationship between 'milk-and-waterish' day-boarder Sonia Tregarth, who is chauffeur-driven to Sarum School from a house in the woods, and the super-confident girls of the Middle Fourth. Sonia's mother is an invalid under the care of Cousin Charlotte, whose lorgnette-glaring disapproval of 'thoughtless' modern girls is made very clear. Urged by the visiting doctor to cheer her mother up by bringing friends home from school, Sonia has an added incentive to join the 'brotherhood' – a tomboyish group which is anything but cliquish. As Babs the leader puts it, 'Sarum School never lets new people lie about wondering what comes next. It always shows them the ropes.'

She is talking about new girls Zara and Zuleika Ionides, Greek Cypriots who are – for comic and symbolic effect – shown to be scared of a cricket ball. The illness of Sonia's mother is linked to some dark event in Cyprus. The mystery unfolds through outside events involving foreigners, while the inside story shows Sonia winning approval for her 'pluck'. Younger and older Ionides sisters join the cast. We are introduced to Gitra, whose thwarted desire to be an English schoolgirl is expressed by the Sarum uniform which she wears, though confined to home, and the Sarum textbooks she reads alone; also by slang: '"Topping – top-hole – sporting," she ticked them off on her fingers. "I must go and put all your new words down in my notebook."' The story ends in the drama of a Saturday evening play put on by the Middle Fourth and the discovery that Gitra is Sonia's sister, not lost in Cyprus as had previously been thought. The unravelling is as complex as all good mysteries require, and the book ends with 'dormie' lights out: 'Neither Sonia nor Gitra would be lonely again; and the mother would be well and happy… Good old Sonia! She had proved herself now.'

At St George's, where there is a set of de Foubert books, the best of them is considered to be *The Fighting Fourth* (1934). Strong group loyalty has been formed during 'rags' led by Pat Desmond, whose 'black-lashed eyes of Irish blue' (her home is a castle in Kerry) stand for madcap daring. But in the opening crisis Pat's eyes go 'dark with sudden resentment'. Her best friend Anne is the sensible one, and their relationship falls apart when the head announces that the badly-behaved Fourth Form is to be broken up at the end of term. The Manor School has semi-official form flags in each room, but the Fourth have gone further with their own class magazine: 'Into the several volumes of *Ragged Robin* had gone plain unvarnished accounts of all their rags (there was an allusion to these lawless occasions in the title) for years past, also records of matches, attempts of budding authorship, cartoons, snapshots, jokes, poetry even!'

Pat ceremonially and publicly tears up all the back numbers. Later Anne picks up the pieces – both literally and figuratively. She declines to join an illicit visit to Shelbourne Magna's cinema, where the 'Coming Attraction' has

SHE WAS HOLDING ZINNY IN HER ARMS

THE FIGHTING FOURTH

By

E. M. de FOUBERT

Illustrated by

REGINALD MILLS

OXFORD UNIVERSITY PRESS
LONDON : HUMPHREY MILFORD

99. *Highly rated at St George's.*

Russians fleeing by sledge. Also at 'the flicks' are slum children from the school's Holiday House and one of them, a girl called Zinny, faints at the high point of drama. Near the end of the book it emerges that she comes from a White Russian family which fled from the Bolsheviks. Again the outside story has foreigners, while the deeper theme is of form loyalty being turned to school-approved ends. The Fourth is now fighting for the head's approval while taking turns to supply Zinny with necessities in a ruined tower out of bounds. It is this good-heartedness, in which Pat and Anne are reconciled – rather than the unexciting project of 'no blacklisting, hard-swotting, general order and punc.' – which wins the headmistress to change her mind.

It is remarkable how much Edith de Foubert builds into a story while virtually ignoring 'the H.M.' and the teachers. Outside adults do appear, however, not all of them villains. Prefects hardly feature at all. The book deals with leadership at fifteen years of age, contrasting Clare, the Head of Form who becomes an in-house villain, with Pat whose qualities are indescribable even to a reconciled friend: 'Damp and draggled, tear-stained and cold, and sneezing – yet completely happy and light-hearted, and at peace with all the world, Anne tramped back to school. Not one of all those thorny questions which had caused all the trouble, with reference to "rags" and "good times" versus keeping the laws and "having proper pride", had been so much as mentioned between them. And yet everything was all right, somehow. Anne was dead sure it was. It mightn't be with an ordinary girl, but Pat wasn't ordinary: you couldn't measure her at all by ordinary ways.' And it is while recovering from their woodland exposure in the 'San' that the two girls glue *Ragged Robin* together again.

Edith de Foubert cannot be called a post-war author, although her last book *Penny in Search of a School* was reissued in 1949. In *You're a Brick, Angela!* Cadogan and Craig argue that the Fifties were 'in many ways the most retrogressive decade of the century' in terms of the themes presented to girl readers in books and in weeklies like *School Friend*. Linda Murison's schooldays failed to match those portrayed by the classic authors still in circulation: 'According to the books, Irish girls were wild and Scottish girls were canny; our Edinburgh school should have been crammed with the likes of Enid Blyton's Jean, the shrewd form captain. Where were they all? We were just ordinary. We never planned jokes on a grand scale, and the only gang I remember enrolled its members in the bicycle shed with a painful ceremony involving holly leaves, and held general knowledge tests – a far cry from the happy lunacy of Nancy Breary's gangs.'

100. *Changing illustration, from* Penny in Search of a School.

Nancy Breary is the best example of a post-war author, and indeed several of her books came out during paper shortages. She wrote at least twenty-five girls' school stories between *Give a Form a Bad Name* (1943) and *The Fourth Was Fun for Philippa* (1961) which, according to Arthur Marshall, 'begins delightfully with the whole of the check-ginghamed Lower Fourth plunging, screaming, into a pond from a collapsed pseudo-Japanese bridge.' The schools vary – Greyladies, Creighton Towers, the Croft School – but they all reflect the author's experience as a boarder at Kingsdown School in Dorking. Blackie the publisher could not persuade Miss Breary to set even one late story in a comprehensive, popular as she had always been with 'the boarding-school purists'. Today's adult readers associated with FOLLY (Fans of Light Literature for the Young) regard her as 'the P. G. Wodehouse of school stories … one of the funniest.'

School stories lost prominence in the Sixties at the same time as juvenile magazines were exchanging their closely printed columns for picture strips. They survived a while longer in comic strip form. *Bunty* readers were reminded each week that 'The Four Marys were pupils in the Third Form at St Elmo's School for Girls. They shared a study and were great friends.' The setting was timelessly D. C. Thomson – teachers wore gowns and mortarboards, and loyalty to the school was the common factor in stories about hockey, burglars and the Pharaoh's Curse. There was very little concern with social class in the St Elmo's stories. This was not the case in other magazines, where snobbery was regularly put before girls as the great social evil. A typical storyline from *Mandy* was that of 'I Hate Her', a tale of tennis rivalry between two girls from sharply contrasted worlds: 'Gwen, who attended a private school, considered Sue to be rough and bad-mannered, while Sue, who is a pupil at the local school, thought Gwen was stuck up and snobby.'

To many it seemed that the gently conservative bias of the old school stories had been replaced by an egalitarianism which made inverted snobbery into a neurosis. But if anyone – publishers, for example – thought that stories set in a school environment had lost their appeal for children, they were in for a rude awakening. Of course Hogwarts is not a run-of-the-mill boarding school, but the success of J. K. Rowling's series of Harry Potter books does suggest that schools – of one kind or another – will continue to provide a fictional environment for children's adventures for the foreseeable future. Let Linda Murison have the last word:

'Looking back, school stories were comforting but unreal. Even those with Scottish settings failed to reflect my Edinburgh experience because of the gap between boarding and day schools – and also because we had entered the Sixties. Sadly my schoolmates and I failed to live up to our paper counterparts. The school story we passed round was a piece of pre-Jilly Cooper nonsense called *The Passion Flower Hotel*, and no boarding school in fiction would have kept us. I never discovered Antonia Forest's distinguished Kingscote series as a child, but from *Autumn Term* (1948) to *The Attic Term* (1976) her portrayal of school life – with its edgy alliances and uncertainties – rings true to my memories. My Edinburgh schooldays were a cross between Kingscote and *The Prime of Miss Jean Brodie*; and as preparation for life, none the worse for that.'

Chapter 10

Chronicles – for Old Girls?

'*Ragged Robin* was purely private and personal to *their* form, a very, very precious possession (not at all to be confused with *Manor School Chronicle*, an official and dignified publication for the whole school which was dealt with by a real printer and appeared half yearly) dating far back to days in Junior school. It was a motley production, half straggly writing, half laborious hand-printing, varied by an occasional crazy attempt at typescript, when Pat had been able to wheedle Miss Darrell, the school Secretary, into giving her the loan of her typewriter.' That extract from *The Fighting Fourth* by Edith de Foubert makes a contrast between amateur efforts and official publications. The focus in this chapter will be on magazines which were, by and large, 'official and dignified' – at least until the end of last century. (Advances in technology and the advent of colour have since turned them into something quite different.)

Girls' schools did not always have magazines, and in fact St George's was unusual in bringing out its *Chronicle* within six years of the start. It was a relaxed, social affair: an article on how to ride a bicycle set the tone. The idea of a 'chronicle' which recorded events was widely adopted in the titles of school magazine, but the Edinburgh Ladies' College in Queen Street went its own way with the *Merchant Maiden,* started in 1906 'partly to maintain links between Former Pupils and between them and the School.' The *George Square Chronicle* followed two years later, with headmistress Charlotte Ainslie setting the agenda: 'History speaks to us not only in the textbooks of the classrooms, but in the sober and dignified houses which we see from our windows, and which will be famous to all time because they have sheltered such honoured heads. Imagination might perhaps conjure up an old world figure, resolute and alert, listening with interest to history lessons dealing with naval victories and silently approving the growth of pious and patriotic sentiment among the present occupants of his home.' The reference is to Admiral Duncan, victor of Camperdown in 1797, who came home from sea to live in Melville House.

School magazines can be directed mainly to pupils or else to former ones. The first Canaan Park College magazine came out in April 1909, when all the Old Girls were young and very few were married. The editor struck a note of nostalgia: 'After all, if we were permitted only a bare list of events we should still be glad of this little record. Such a list kindles for us again pleasures that were bright at the time. It sends a light through our memories, illumining the corners where sleep the pleasant records of old delights; it makes us grateful for the past.' There were two issues a year. The November 1910 number has also survived to confirm that although school news came first, reviving memory, it was followed by a much longer section on former pupil concerns. Contributions on a range of topics came in from old girls without difficulty: 'Some Castles on the Loire' ran to two issues.

Former pupils came first more often than not. The Brunstane Club produced two booklets for the ladies who had gone to school from addresses in Joppa and Portobello. In each of them only one page out of sixteen touched on current school affairs. The booklets were headed *Forward – Remembering.* Shortly after the move to 'Cranley' in Colinton Road, *The Torch* (which was also for adults) started to appear annually, and it was not until 1966 that a magazine for both pupils and former pupils was produced in school under the title *FEHOMI.* (As readers may remember, this came from the initial letters of Virgil's Latin: *Forsan et haec olim memenisse iuvabit.*) The first issue was mainly for former pupils – to the extent of the first two-thirds of a fifty-page magazine. However when the final *FEHOMI* appeared in 1980 it was truly the 'Cranley School Magazine' of the cover, without any news of Old Girls. A newsletter was promised them.

The Saint Hildan started within a year of admitting the school's first pupils, Miss Stoltz explaining its purpose as 'to make general what has been of interest to anyone amongst us, and also to put on permanent record the doings of the school, to further the *esprit de corps* of the small community which was our

Forward – Remembering

Brunstane Club.

1913.

101. *Old Girls pre-Cranley.*

world so that some part of it is likely to remain with us when school walls no longer bound our horizon, and to carry to our homes and elsewhere the enthusiasm, generosity and unselfishness which are its characteristics.' Vol. VII, No. 14 appeared as double number 1929–31 with editorial apologies for a seven-term gap. School news, the 'permanent record', came first in the form of remarkably comprehensive lists (examination successes, prefects, new girls, leavers, games results) but hardly a word of comment. Four times as many pages followed (to page 51) in which only an account of 'Monsieur Beaucaire' as acted by pupils, along with the occasional poem, had anything to do with the school.

102. *Hand-crafted cover.*

Chronicles of school affairs became commoner in the Thirties, the *George Square Chronicle* acting as a journal of record more thoroughly than most with three solid issues a year. Two members of staff (male) produced it, although pupil 'representatives' were elected early and soon rose to twenty-five in number. Their task was to bring in material from all levels of the school. There was a golden period of prose and verse when 'the editors were snowed under with so many contributions of a high standard that they could not print them all.' William Mackay Budge, English and History master from 1895 until 1931, was

103. *A journal of record.*

responsible for anthologising magazine items as *A Book of George Square Verse*. It was published two years after his death. A poem by Catherine Brown, one of his last pupils, ends:

> Silver and gold together form the chain
> That twines about my heart its fettering bands,
> Gold of the gorse, and silver of the loch,
> Gold sunsets, and the silver Morar sands.

Most schools were putting out a magazine by then. The authors of the St Margaret's centenary book *Fortiter Vivamus* imply the existence of earlier occasional magazines to do with the Newington school when recording that now (after the war) they 'came out regularly and increased in size'. The issue of the St Denis magazine which celebrated the move from Chester Street derived a certain charm from pupil material which included drawings, but it was very much an in-house production with typescript turned out on the office duplicator. By way of contrast the *Lansdowne House Chronicle* boasted a gold band on a dark blue cover. When it was revived after World War II without any band – austerity being the watchword – London Old Girls' Guild complained. Retired headmistress Ellen Hale came up with £3 a year to restore it.

With the example of *St George's Chronicle* behind her, Miss Fraser Lee produced a high quality magazine from the start of her St Trinnean's venture. She made a point of celebrating the St Ninian's Centenary pilgrimage to Whithorn on 16 September 1932 in Vol. 1, Part X of *Lochran Cuimhne* (The Light of Memory). An article told of taking the school banner to Galloway uncompleted so that 'the few remaining stitches might be put in on the sacred soil and 'neath the shadow of the Chapel'. This item covered pages 487–9, indicating a substantial output over the years. The print is professional, and there is a full-page photo of the beach where St Ninian landed – also one of a procession being led through Whithorn by the Moderator of the Church of Scotland. Father to a St Trinnean's girl, he (or his wife) had obviously decided against the Ministers' Daughters' College. The equivalent magazine for Esdaile was well written and full of interest, but the stern black type-setting is that of a printer accustomed to Kirk Committees.

Most school magazines ceased to appear after the German occupation of Norway blocked off an important source of paper, but at George Square there was a determination to carry on regardless. The summer 1941 *Chronicle* was 'the sixth to appear since Hitler let slip his dogs of war'. It had come out each term as usual, with only a slight increase in charges to purchasers and advertisers. However Vol. XXXIII of July 1943 was labelled WAR-TIME ISSUE and carried an apology: 'Because of the Paper Control Regulations, we have not been able to publish more than one number of the *Chronicle*. We had regretfully to abandon our advertisements.' Two years later the Chairman of the Magazine Committee wrote a farewell article on resigning after nineteen years. He recalled 'many pleasant meetings at the beginning of each year when we discussed plans, finance, letterpress and illustrations,' and ended by hoping that 'the scope of the *Chronicle*, once we are freed from war-time restrictions, will be enlarged to cover new activities and new features.' But July 1946 still had cramped pages, mainly records of school activities to the exclusion of literary material, and members of staff leaving with 'scant acknowledgement'.

Although the routine of an issue each term was not revived, things returned to something like normal with two issues a year in December and July. March was the month of the Scottish Leaving Certificate, and a previously unknown level of exam pressure partly explains the demise of the April *Chronicle*. To compensate, the summer issue extended to sixty-eight pages. The two members of staff now editing it were male and female, and teachers retained control for a further two decades. When the handover to pupils finally took place, times had changed: 'In recent years the editors continually complain about the lack of response to their appeals for articles from the school. When the magazine representatives have succeeded, as they invariably do, in extorting poetry, prose, illustrations and club reports from the seemingly reluctant school, the editorial committee leaps into a frenzy of activity as the printers' deadline approaches... The onus of compiling a magazine from this conglomerate material now falls on the two editors, who set about the laborious task of counting the number of words and lines of each contribution.'

St Margaret's Chronicle returned as an occasional publication, much as it had been before the outbreak of hostilities, but the stimulus of the Coronation issue in 1953 led to annual productions. Four years later the first combined magazine for pupils and former pupils appeared, and from then on a Report of Former Pupils' Club rounded off each issue – usually quite briefly, except on those occasions when an updated list of names and addresses was included. The editor, a senior pupil, was supported by four girls and three teachers. Her editorial on the school motto 'Fortiter Vivamus' is good enough to quote: 'This is an excellent motto with which to face the perils of the world which awaits us when we leave the confines of school for the last time... As we who have survived sail all too rapidly down the last stretches of the river of education it is obvious that only supreme courage could have enabled us to brave the terrible early stages of our river. Who but the brave could have survived the ordeal of gluing scarlet tulips to purple foliage in the early terms?' And so on, through the seven ages of schoolgirl-hood. 1956–57 was also the session when the Perthshire contingent returned, an event which created a cramped staffroom and classrooms. At that time school magazines usually had the same three photos as their only form of illustration: Prefects, Hockey Eleven, Tennis Six. On this occasion Pittendreich House at Lasswade was also shown as the new home to sixty boarders.

By 1964 *St Margaret's Chronicle* – still annual – had expanded from 48 to 60 pages, all of them now as glossy as the inevitable team photos. These now included lacrosse. There were also photographs of two artistic objects along with three drawings of pupils by other pupils – all provided by the Art Department. Many poems added white space. All sorts of 'reports' appeared – visit to Stratford, Literary and Debating Society, the Dramatic Society. Reports from the four houses – a feature of the magazine which was undergoing a makeover – ranged from verse to a television-style interview format. Having won practically everything Melville House was modest in straightforward prose. Amidst a range of 'creative writing' by pupils of all ages, nothing quite matched the factual report of a third year visit to the slaughter-house:

'From outside the buildings looked clean and tidy. There was no evidence of death. Then a shot rang out, an animal emitted a tortured scream and silence, like a smothering blanket, followed. As we drew nearer a stench of blood began to penetrate our noses. I looked through some open doors and there was a room with carcasses, dripping blood, hanging from the ceiling. The blood oozed to the floor, making it look like a small scarlet lake. Men in long wellingtons and blood-spattered aprons strode in the slippery sea hanging up warm, pink bodies... In a large indoor space off the pens a white calf was being tied up. Strong arms threw it to the floor, a pistol was pointed at its head, and while it bawled and kicked to regain its freedom the trigger was pulled. Immediately the body shuddered and lay still. Death marched slowly past the body; there was an eerie silence. Then the men dragged away the body and a skinny Tamworth boar took its place.'

A surviving *Lansdowne House Chronicle* of December 1969 has its five shilling price on a cover lacking the gold band. The editor, who was probably not old enough to drink alcohol in public, included her own 'Ode to Alka Seltzer' (apologies to Keats) which ended with 'expel this hangover dim' – suggesting a lack of teacher supervision in the editorial sphere. There is a measurable rise in art work from the magazines of previous decades (one lino-cut, five drawings) and a non-team photo – a chimpanzee which, according to the Director of the Zoo, had been adopted by 'the young ladies of Lansdowne House School'. Thirty pages are reserved for pupils, leaving nine for the Old Girls' Guild. The youngest children come first with entries to amuse: 'I wer a cot and a skaf bekos it is wet.' Lower IV provides a puppy piece, before two Upper VI girls write at greater length. There is a crossword. A sponsored pony ride near Grantown-on-Spey ('Tosca and I were both in need of a good feed after our tiring but most enjoyable day.') contrasts with mule-back adventure at the Grand Canyon: 'We almost died of fatigue and thirst after riding down.'

By the Sixties school magazines were mainly aimed at schoolgirls, but Craiglockhart Convent was the exception with *Annals of the Associations of the Sacred Heart, Ireland and Scotland* making its first appearance in 1966. Aimed at the 'alumnae' of four Irish Sacred Heart schools and three Scottish ones (including Aberdeen and Kilgraston outside Perth) it ran to 121 pages and was paid for out of the £1 annual subscriptions of some 1,500 members. Members of the Craiglockhart Association, linked more to the training college than 'the day school', belonged to an international organisation which included the neighbouring Province of England and Wales, but their own School News never amounted to more than a page or two. Occasional wedding photos were included, never team ones. There was a Craiglockhart College magazine, *The Buckle*, but not a school one. By contrast the annual magazine put out by St Margaret's Convent devoted most of its generous space (about a hundred pages) to pupils, with Ursuline items at the start and Old Girl news tucked in at the end. It was unusual among school magazines for the number of advertisements carried and the almost complete absence of photos – only the Convent itself, which appeared regularly above the editorial. But the quality of reporting was good and creative writing better – largely thanks to 'Inter-House' competition, it may be supposed.

St Margaret's in Newington may serve to illustrate changes in school magazines around the end of the black-and-white era. One shows a yearning to move out of it: by 1975 the central Junior section was on green paper, and it changed colour from year to year thereafter. Art increasingly prevailed over sport, which this year was limited to a single illustration – a photo of the Third Year Lacrosse XII as winners of the Scottish Schools' Junior Tournament. A second rare celebration of tradition showed the elegant headmistress in the midst of her twenty-six prefects. The only traditional thing about the abstract cover of squares and triangles, however, was the colour green. By 1984 (when Mrs Hiddleston left to take up a headship in South Africa) it had changed to blue, although the imagery was that of a St Margaret's blazer pocket with badge and pens. Inside, visual ambition struggled with the limits of affordable print technology: illustrations of interesting subjects usually turned out dull. But every effort was made to produce a 1991 *Chronicle* worthy of the centennial celebrations of the previous year. The cover made a virtue of black on white with a fine figurative collage. The Photography Club's darkroom and studio facilities were used to good effect. Action photos of high-jumping and hurdling, set against a hockey cartoon, provided reminders of where magazine illustration had come from.

104. *Collage in black and white.*

Modern school magazines are amazing: lively, glossy, multi-coloured. Who are they for? The *Merchant Maiden* editor addressed pupils directly: 'I hope that the following pages will rekindle fond memories of the past year and inspire you to keep making the most of all the wonderful opportunities that the school and its staff offer you; you never know, we might see you in the next issue as well.' Elsewhere the headmaster made reference to seventy clubs and societies. Sport has made a comeback: there are thirteen small team photos for hockey alone (available to buy at full size, no doubt) and the number of pupils who do appear in the magazine is past counting. For one year (2002) the opening page shows head-shots of ten girls – the only black-and-white in evidence: 'We aspiring journalists of the *Merchant Maiden* are happy to bring back to you memories of the frantically busy year which we have left behind us. It has been a long and perilous journey for the girls of the editorial team, as we tracked down articles and scavenged for reports. However it has all been done and we are proud to present to you an action-packed magazine.'

This seems to answer a second question: who are the magazines by? Seven of the girls here were in fifth year, at the top of the all-girl secondary department, the rest a year younger. No such group features in the next issue, nor do sixth year pupils take part. Recent magazines have carried a high proportion of pupil writing (in all colours of print and paper) which probably represents the intervention of teachers. Nine members of staff are heavily involved in *Merchant Maiden*, an art teacher showing his pupils' work while doubling as one of the five named sources of phot-ography. Advertisements add to the impression that this is more than a pupil affair. School outfitters offer Gents' and Ladies' Wear (Barbour being featured) as well as blazers and sports gear. More remarkable, in this context, are the adverts for expensive housing and cars, architects and law firms. Diamonds are displayed with a '10% discount on production of this advert at either store'. Clearly parents are being congratulated on being able to afford school fees as well as everything else.

The *Chronicle* No. 183 put out by St George's in 2002 carried no advert-isements, Aitken & Niven having long ceased to draw attention to 'Ancient Red' cardigans from 36/9 and 'The Tweed Coat' from £8-14-6. But the magazine itself – under one aspect at least – is a marketing exercise. The St George's Futures project which has taken the school into the new millennium requires it. Student art is used to marvellous effect on the covers – and throughout – in collaboration with an outside media company. Even bad news has a fashionable connection with stand-up comedians and the Festival Fringe: 'The Editorial Team apologise for the late publishing date of the 2002 *Chronicle*. Our designers were located in an office above the Gilded Balloon and they were making good progress until the Cowgate fire destroyed everything.' Computer back-up saved the day. Editor Nigel

Shepley (who wrote *Women of Independent Mind*) maintains a balancing sense of tradition, with material from the archives – photographs in sepia, and sometimes black-and-white.

No doubt St George's girls of all ages respond to articles about themselves – as well as parents and potential parents. But soon after fire put the annual magazine at risk two new organs, more frequent and more focused, came into being: *Termly Times* for the Juniors and *Independent Women* for the Upper School. Sixth form students have future careers in mind: 'The production teams practise their skills in journalism, art and design, desk top publishing, and planning and strategy meetings. There is a breakfast

105. *Is that a dragon below St George?*

meeting every week in the Junior School which is well attended, whilst the sixth formers tend to organise themselves with just a little help from staff.' Perhaps this represents the start of a trend to termly production, as represented by the staff-produced *Horizon* at St Margaret's, and by *News Update* in which the Principal of Erskine Stewart's Melville Schools reports to 'parents, guardians and friends'.

Old girls were meanwhile reduced to communicating through newsletters, until St George's came up with something new – *The OGA*, launched in January 2004. Produced by the same company at a quieter time of year, its glossy fifty-seven pages (and growing) are stiffer than those of *The Chronicle's* eighty. There is also more solid reading but no shortage of cheerful illustration. Ten-yearly reunions, as in The Class of '54, make use of the newly constructed St George's Centre. Archival material is again presented by the irrepressible Mr Shepley who, as teachers' representative on the Old Girls' Association, contributes a Letter from the Staffroom. There are a few school-focused items: one on the Early Stages unit clearly has young mothers in mind. The teenage 'Riff Raff' entertained at a Fizz 'n' Jazz

106. *The OGA.*

function where the oppor-
tunity was taken to photograph
five O.G. mothers with five
daughters in the band. The
height of the Upper School
Library is used to good effect
('fine view of the Castle') for
September's Festival Fireworks. The school has become
a focus of Tatleresque social
events, and *The OGA* promotes
them. But there is also the
usual news of Old Girls and
former staff (long service leads
to honorary membership) as well as marriages and births. The magazine
ends with obituaries, presented as Appreciations, of those whose association
with St George's has finally come to an end.

It is time to move by way of *The OGA* to Old Girls' associations in general.
How do they work? By what means are mature women with busy lives
persuaded to maintain a connection with their schooldays? It is unlikely
that changing the label has ever had a significant effect, but there are
variations. Mary Erskine opted for Former Pupils' Guild fourteen years after
the founding of the day school; St Margaret's waited until 1927 before
appointing its first Former Pupils' Club President. Craiglockhart's alumnae
are unique in Scotland, like the almost equally international Women
Watsonians – who started as the George Square Former Pupils' Club.
Catherine Fraser Lee of St Trinnean's typically came up with something
different: Old Friends. However the O.G. idea was obvious enough to be
used widely, in particular by Canaan College, St Hilda's, St Margaret's
Convent, Cranley, Lansdowne House and Esdaile, where it was the Old
Girls' Union. A youthful Esdaile school leaver confronted paradox in verse:

> What a shock to my sensitive nerves
> Was given one day of last year,
> When the news of the title 'Old Girl'
> First came to my wondering ear.

Old girl! Is old age then approaching?
Will my hair soon be silvery white?
Will my muscles grow stiffer and stiffer?
The thought makes me tremble with fright.

The seventeen-year-old poet had just been informed in the *Esdaile Chronicle* that 'an O.G. Blazer, trimmed with cord and badge, costing about 6 gns., may be obtained from Messrs. Aitken & Niven, 79 George Street ... on presentation of an order form from Miss H. M. Ewan or Miss Jean Russell [headmistress and O.G.U. secretary]. Girls, when they leave school, may obtain four and a half yards of cord from the same firm, to convert a school blazer into an O.G. blazer.' The effect of such generous piping on what had previously been plain black must have been striking. St Hilda's offered a choice of black or white blazers, with piping in reverse, and Old Girls' Ties post-free from the Club Secretary. Badges had to be designed, Watsonian women finally reaching a decision on theirs in 1931. The wearing of blazers by those who wished to associate themselves with schooldays in this way began in the Twenties and lingered into the Sixties.

107. *F.P. blazers on young old girls.*

The fashion varied from school to school, with a boarding institution for the daughters of ministers calling up special affection: 'That the girls enjoy their life at Esdaile is proved by the strength of the Old Girls' Union, which Old Girls like to think has no rival in its loyalty to its School. Founded as an official body in 1900, with 48 enrolled members, it now has a steady membership of over 700.' That is an impressive figure for one of Edinburgh's smallest schools. It certainly compares favourably with 1,366 Women Watsonians – a minority of those who had attended in the twentieth century by the time George Square was abandoned. Much of Esdaile's success in keeping former pupils in touch was due to someone who had taught rather than learned there: 'An item in the O.G.U's history which must surely be unique is that its first Honorary Secretary, Mrs Hill Stewart (who, as Miss Milligan, had been a member of staff before her marriage) remained in office for fifty years, winning the friendship of generations of Old Girls.' Fund-raising – familiar to ministers' daughters – resulted in almost annual contributions to improve the facilities at Esdaile: a shared sense of purpose fostered loyalty. And the scattered nature of Scotland's parishes seems to have actually helped through the creation of five local centres, 'each with an active life of its own'.

The Women Watsonians' Club illustrates the range of possibilities opened up by large numbers, especially since many former pupils were living in the Edinburgh area. Reunions in the atmospheric building were easy to arrange. Early in the Thirties William Mackay Budge, the compiler of *George Square Verse*, made an appearance in order to invite contributions. The occasion was not a literary one: 'Generally speaking, things were much as usual this year. There was dancing in the Central Hall and the Gymnasium where the bands were bright and vigorous… Certain intimations of general interest were made from the Gallery by Mrs Tullo, and Mr Budge made a strong appeal for more support for the "Chronicle" by former pupils… We returned home with aching toes, and throats decidedly hoarse.' It was Folk Dancing then; after the war Scottish Country Dancing was taught at weekly sessions after choir practice. The Annual Dinner, partnered as a white-tie affair, also began at this time. It developed into a social event of toasts and speeches, with place settings reserved for the press.

Women Watsonian branches appeared outside Edinburgh: Glasgow, London, even Vancouver – whence came an early cablegram. Aberdeen followed in the Fifties, and there was a Perth pairing – out of a chance meeting between two George Square old girls – which led to something larger. Attempts to set up branches in northern England failed, but London meetings always attracted good numbers. The London branch organised a visit to Hampton Court and another to Crosby Hall in Chelsea, where Dame Rebecca West was guest speaker. As Cicely Fairfield, she had been a pupil early in the century. The writer and social critic humorously described her several visits to Buckingham Palace – starting with the kitchens as a cub reporter – and also her return to George Square after forty years. On another occasion London branch members were welcomed to Westminster by Dame Florence Horsbrugh, the Unionist Party's only female M.P. over a period of twenty years and Minister of Education in a Conservative government. (From 1912 to 1965 the Unionist Party, formed by a merger between Conservatives and Liberal Unionists, was Scotland's equivalent to England's Conservatives.) Dame Florence started school as a day boarder at Lansdowne Crescent from her family home round the corner in Grosvenor Street.

In London there was some coming together with the former pupils of other Merchant Company schools, and in Edinburgh there was the 'Mercator' Dramatic Club which put on a Dodie Smith play at the YMCA Theatre in 1950: 'Since its post-war revival the Club has staged only one other full-length play; thus considerable courage was required to produce "Autumn Crocus", which is fraught with difficulties.' Golfing women joined with male Watsonians once a year in a mixed pairs competition with Stewart's men and Queen Street women, but otherwise ELC v GWLC was a straight contest, keenly fought, as in other sports during schooldays and after.

Inter-club hockey matches (never tennis, for which there were neighbourhood clubs) provided the most stirring occasions for blazer-wearing. Three George Square F.P. elevens played before the war, with members gaining East District and international honours. However a post-war heyday was followed by decline, and a further shocking example of convergence. Both Merchant Company F.P. hockey clubs found it increasingly difficult to field second elevens and in 1972 (to the disapproval of many) a combined Merchant Ladies' Hockey Club was formed. It has since been unformed. Sport is central to the success of male F.P. clubs, and Alexander McCall Smith has made a running joke out of George Watson's College and rugby. Women are simply Watsonians now, a second merger having been edgily arranged for former pupils, but they could hardly be teased in these latter days for being too sporty.

Keeping in touch with classmates, for these women, goes well beyond sport. Childhood friendships may be continued in adult life without organisation, or renewed through Friends Reunited (by computer) but leadership and a club can certainly help. When St Hildans formed theirs in 1930 Miss Cooper (owner and co-principal along with Miss Hill) was not a happy editor: 'Why won't the Old Girls send up contributions? Alas, they do not even send in notices of births or marriages, but leave us to cull these from the pages of the *Scotsman*… It is often the same with Old Girls' news. By angling round we bring some fish to our net, but a great big interesting fish escapes us.' Alice Stewart, first O.G. president, English teacher and poet, aspired to have membership 'co-extensive with the whole body of old St Hildans', although she conceded a difficulty for those living abroad. By the Fifties, the *St Hildan News Chronicle* gave an impression of what had been achieved.

A remarkable 370 women featured under Old Girls' News in the 1952–3 issue. Miss Cooper had retired with Miss Hill to Liberton but they paid weekly visits to Ballikinrain as directors. The following year Miss Cooper passed on responsibility for school news to the headmistress but kept a firm grip on the many pages devoted to former pupils. At the suggestion of the Founder Mrs Waugh (*née* Stoltz) the magazine began to come out after Christmas: 'News would be more up-to-date, and it would also be easier for St Hildans to notify changes of address or to give any news to be included when they send their cards.' Substantial items appeared in From the Editor's Postbag, whereas the alphabetically-arranged (by maiden name) news section tended to be limited to a line about someone's latest activity or address: a Lebanese former pupil was in Beirut 'according to Xmas card post mark.' The school having scarcely passed the half-century mark, only a couple of deaths per year were reported but upwards of thirty births. Whether 'culled' from newspapers or not, the number of marriages more or less matched the score or so of annual leavers. Merchant Company F.P. clubs could not hope to provide anything like this level of personal interest among so many.

Finally in search of what 'works', post-war minutes of the Lansdowne House Old Girls' Guild may be consulted. Some credit should perhaps go to kindly tradition. The original Guild, founded in the reign of Edward VII, had an Autumn Soirée attended by monitresses, with twelve-year-olds and upwards admitted 'after the lecture to supper, and dancing in the schoolroom. But those still younger appeared in their dressing-gowns on the front stairs during supper and were fed by the Old Girls.' At a meeting in the school library on Saturday 24th November 1951 Miss Hale, retired head and chronicler, 'gave a vivid sketch of the Guild and its many activities in the past.'

But times had changed. Minutes in various hands show the committee trying in vain to persuade members to attend the Annual General Meeting: a sherry party before the first one only attracted twenty. The School's 75th Anniversary in summer 1954 provided a boost, but only sixteen turned up at the December AGM. There it was decided that 'if subscriptions lapsed for three years the members would be warned that they could no longer be considered members of the Guild.' The all-important register of names and addresses took a further two years to complete. The *Chronicle* published these in an O.G. section, first fully then briefly to register changes of address. One problem which emerged from these lists was the high proportion of old girls living at a distance: eighty apologies were received in the year when Miss Hale hosted a tea party for twenty-four in London University's Women's Club.

More day girls attended Lansdowne House in the Fifties. By the end of the following decade at least half of the 250-plus Guild members lived in Edinburgh, most having left school in the Sixties. Meanwhile committee members had learned the value of entertainment, and the chance to socialise: 'The evening started with an excellent and most amusing talk by old girl Miss Winifred Shand on her work with Highland Home Industries, based at Lochboisdale in South Uist. Not only did she keep us in fits of laughter but she contrived to bring the atmosphere of the Western Isles into the Music Room. Her coloured slides were quite lovely.' Buffet suppers rang the changes from Danish open sandwiches to wine and cheese, with committee members vying – co-operatively – to provide desserts. 'A terrific buzz of conversation during the coffee' was regularly minuted – evidence that Friends Reunited beats Approval of Minutes every time. It is a general phenomenon (at George Square described as 'the usual contest of tongues') which goes far to explain why old girls still gather after old buildings have been closed to them.

Chapter 11

Bringing Back to Mind

Memories are the making of a book like this: set them alongside facts and a story emerges. Some people can hardly remember anything about childhood, never mind school – they 'put it behind them' – while others have what seems like total recall. If the latter take pleasure in writing then memories may be shaped, and a few go as far as putting them into print. Word-processors come to the aid of even quite elderly women nowadays. The one who 'reconstructed' the wartime experience of George Square – inquiry plus memory – was glad to have been nudged into organising her notes from a time, years ago, when she helped to organise a reunion. Another old girl, dux of a different school, sent seven thousand words beautifully hand-written in a notebook. A telephone inquiry confirmed that this was not a fair copy ('no time to do it twice') nor was it a careful construction. It reads very well, despite apologies: 'I'm afraid the request landed at a difficult time of year – I didn't think I'd find so much to write.'

Once the process of bringing back to mind is begun, memories increase – perhaps by interview, or listening to a guest speaker on the subject of schooldays (one group imaginatively hosted a 'Crème de la Crème Tea'). It may work better in association with others, but reading about schools in general regenerates thoughts of one school in the solitary page-turner. Memories tend to be positive, which probably explains the adage that schooldays are 'the happiest days of your life'. Unhappy days surface less often. Commanding headmistresses always remain. Favourite teachers are often credited with a positive influence, usually put down to 'personality'. They are rarely praised for lessons taught, exercises marked, or the actual work of teaching. At the other extreme, few people think to mention these daily sessions in the playground where, it has been argued (by me among others) children learn to be social beings through their play.

Former pupils have had interesting things to say about most of the topics arranged here in chapters, but memories cannot always be pigeon-holed for the sake of a theme. Some are too particular to mean much to anyone who was not at that school then. You had to be there. But curious, wonderful stories about school life remain to be told. If there were no other justification for the unclassifiable collection which follows, it would be that so far nothing has been said about school dinners. Food takes first place here with a variation on the dormitory feast of schoolgirl fiction. It comes from St Hildans looking back to their boarding-school days in the Edwardian period – under the influence of Angela Brazil. The school's cubicled dormitories were photographed for the prospectus, but the place chosen on this occasion was a music room on the top floor. On lights duty, Mademoiselle had reported to higher authority:

'A quick firm step approached the door. Rat-tat-tat! We were chilled to the core. This must be the H.M. herself. We all looked at each other in despair, then quietly scuttled around trying to cover up the goodies which had so delighted us a few minutes before. Rat-a-tat again – "Open your door at once!" Someone reluctantly turned the key. What a funny bunch we must have seemed. She looked round coldly and said, "Do you not know that night is not the time for eating but for sleeping? Get a tray and take all this fine collection down to the kitchen. It is all confiscate." Then Gussie Graves Law stood up (how pretty she looked with her blue eyes matching her dressing gown and her fair loose hair falling to the shoulder – how could anyone resist her?). She seized a plateful of éclairs, and holding it out said, "Please eat those at once, Miss Stoltz, they won't keep." The H.M. pulled out her handkerchief and seemed to ram it against her mouth… The last we heard as we filed out was, "Don't trail your eiderdowns on the stairs that way." This was our first full-scale midnight feast, but let no one think it was our last.'

Quite often those with the least recall of school are young women a few years away from it. To an extent (but with a sad nod towards senile dementia) the opposite applies. An A.G.M. of the Lansdowne House Old Girls' Guild took place on 24 September 1977: 'Among the apologies was a card from the oldest member, Mrs Daisy Pearson (*née* Paul, 1886–89) aged 104, who informed us that the African violets sent on her 100th birthday were still alive.' When young Daisy Paul moved with her parents into a newly built house in Strathearn Place, as she recalled, horses were the only traffic hazard. At the time the card was posted she was living in another family home at Balerno with two daughters and a son, still active in pursuit of her knitting and writing. Three years later an old girl told the Guild Secretary that her nine-year-old was in the same class as Mrs Pearson's great-grandson, 'and he came home full of information about the 107th birthday of this grand old lady.' She finally expired in the following year.

Old women remember. Dorothy Robertson went to Craiglockhart at the age of ten, shortly after the Sacred Heart Sisters moved there from Manor Place. In the following session there were still only about twenty girls in the Junior School and five in her class, including younger sister Mary. She spent seven years as a boarder, returning to her St Andrews home at half-term holidays, and left school in 1927. Seventy years later, interviewed on tape, she spoke very well: 'Mary and I both had slight Fife accents when we first went, and we weren't allowed in the school plays until we got rid of them. No dialects were permitted, so we had elocution lessons which cost extra. Sometimes at weekends we went by tram to the King's Theatre escorted by an adult. I remember seeing "Macbeth" there. The tickets were paid for by our parents, and we always had a box to keep us separate from the "plebs"! Mary and I got half a crown pocket money each when we went back to school at the start of term. You could get a lot for that then. I usually spent mine quickly but Mary always had some left at the end of term.

'Reverend Mother Walsh the headmistress was awe-inspiring; she put the fear of God into you. We had "notes" every week, of course. You went up as your name was called out. I remember when one of the three wee boy boarders pulled a chair away from a Nun and she landed on the floor. He got a "bad note". If you got one of these it was flung on the table and you had to pick it up… Grandmother always used to say that of all her grandchildren Mary and I were the ones who knew how to behave and conduct ourselves. That came from School – and also from home. Mother was English. I mean you would never have gone into a room and sat down before your parents, and you always held the door open for them. We stood up in class automatically if anyone came in and waited to be told to sit down again.

'I think the discipline, although quite strict, did more good than harm. You wouldn't speak in the corridors or when you were in playground "lines", or talk in bed at night – we shared three to a room. A Nun walked up and down outside in case you did. But we did do some things which were not expected of Convent girls! Once there was a crowd of us going home for the holidays by train. We were at Waverley Station and had saved up enough pocket money for a packet of cigarettes. We got a compartment to ourselves, and pretended we had whooping cough to stop any one else from coming in to it. The trains had no corridors then. We lit up, but whenever the train came to a stop and one of us was getting off out went the cigarettes. Mother used to say to us, "I wish you wouldn't get into a

compartment with people who smoke." It was years before she found out.'
Dorothy Robertson still lives in St Andrews, her mind as clear as ever.

A wide photo taken on the Craiglockhart lawn in the Fifties shows two
hundred pupils, of whom twenty-three are small boys sitting cross-legged in
front. According to a former pupil who was there in the Sixties (at a time
when the roll had grown considerably) 'Nuns had difficulty disciplining the
boys, and I remember one being regularly locked in a dark cupboard, with
kicking and screaming going on.' Mrs Pat Marin, for many years President of
the Associated Alumnae of the Sacred Heart, Scotland, describes a more
positive approach: 'During the Christmas season the younger children had a
crib with steps going up to the figures of the Holy Family. Each of us was
given a small woollen lamb with our name tied round its neck. We all started
on the bottom step, and the idea was that if you were good and thoughtful
towards others your lamb would progress. Some lambs almost galloped up,
while others went more sedately. I remember very well that one boy had

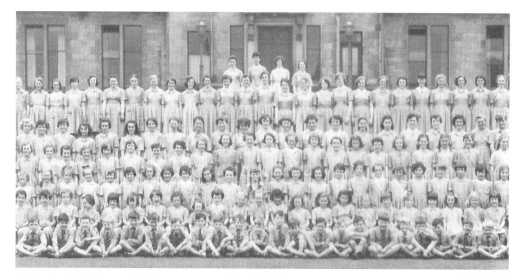

108. *Craiglockhart: little boys among girls of all sizes.*

a black lamb which always seemed to take two steps up and one back, but
by Christmas all lambs reached the crib. The owner of the black lamb
always declared he was "set up". I know this, because I married the black
sheep of Craiglockhart!'

A word is due in defence of little boys surrounded by girls of all sizes
– most of the smaller schools took in boys to about the age of eight. Sandy
Macfarlane began at St Brendan's, otherwise Eskbank Girls' School near
Dalkeith: 'On Sports Day it was a beautiful morning and I won everything

from egg-and-spoon to sack race – not forgetting the sprint and the obstacle race. Particularly pleasing were victories over my closest rival, a dark-haired girl whose name I've forgotten. Then the Games Mistress announced that the morning's events were only a rehearsal. In the afternoon I lost every race. There was another girl in my class who was given permission to leave school early one day a week in order to go shopping with her mother in Edinburgh. This seemed worth trying and it worked for several weeks, until the Headmistress phoned to ask my mother if she had enjoyed her shopping. Red face and tears for me! Miss Smith was a tough cookie. On going up to the Edinburgh Academy Prep School the first person I met was the Headmistress, also Miss Smith and an exact facsimile of her St B's counterpart. I believed for many years that all headmistresses were called Miss Smith – an essential requirement for the job.' Tam Dalyell's education began at St George's before he went to Eton (by way of the same Academy Prep School). Maybe the experience prepared him for standing up to Margaret Thatcher.

Thinking back to schooldays, most people start by recollecting the end of them – as an athlete or scholar or prefect, perhaps. It is more impressive when someone who was not only a prefect but Head Girl remembers the earliest years quite clearly, as with Sheila Henderson (now Mrs Dinwoodie). Having the brains to be almost a dux (*proxime accessit*) must help recall: 'Along with my best friend Joyce, who also lived in Macdowell Road, I began school life in September 1937 a month before my fifth birthday. In these early days George Square itself was merely a vague background, its cobbled streets surrounding a railinged garden where paths disappeared into hidden depths and no children played. The north side was dominated by our school in Melville House. To small newcomers it seemed an immense building, swallowing up thousands of uniformed girls of all shapes and sizes who then vanished from our ken until the following morning…

'The Elementary cloakrooms lay to the left along a short, gloomy basement corridor. Our special toilets were nearby. You had to "go" before lessons and at break times: after the first few weeks, only in a dire emergency were you allowed out of class. Sound training for later life! When the bell rang we formed a line and were led upstairs by our teacher. The Elementary Department consisted of two bright, spacious rooms overlooking the Square and a double-sized room divided by a partition at the back. In each room there was a big teacher's desk and rows of individual small desks. One wall was taken up by the windows; on another was a roller blackboard and on the remaining two walls, above the line of a three-foot varnished wood surround, was dotted a kaleidoscope of colourful pictures and charts. Apart from our weekly visit to the gym, and

our daily foray downstairs to the stone-floored Central Court for milk and biscuits, the classroom was virtually our school world and we were blissfully unaware what went on beyond its boundaries. Our school day was over by lunchtime… The final ritual was lining up to shake hands with the Elementary head teacher. Having said clearly and politely, "Good afternoon, Miss Bowman," we walked in orderly fashion to the basement door and spilled outside.'

109. *Sheila Henderson's box hat.*

Class photographs, and one of the soon to be redundant maroon box hats, add to the feeling of 'being there'. Mrs Dinwoodie's account of George Square is substantial enough to make a booklet of its own and really ought to appear as one, especially after the recent publication of *George Watson's College: An Illustrated History*, where George Square is sandwiched between sections about the boys' school and co-educational George Watson's. Here we can only take a few steps along a very special path: 'My first teacher was Miss Wilson, or "Baby Miss Wilson" as we affectionately called her from lofty Junior and Senior class heights. She was a small, bustling yet calm lady with a sweet, gentle expression and endless patience. I remember her teaching us to write…'

'When I was about ten, I was sent to a boarding school in Edinburgh; whilst there, one particular incident stands out in my mind.' Hannah Gordon was trained to remember lines for her roles on the stage, but this strong memory came from earlier times. The setting was St Denis in Ettrick Road. 'Down in the basement under a large house where our dormitories were situated there was a big heavy door which was always locked. None of the girls had ever seen it open and there were plenty of stories about what was hidden behind it: perhaps a secret room, perhaps something dark hidden away that no-one was allowed to know about except the most senior teachers. Maybe it was only opened late at night, or during the holidays when there were no pupils around to see.

'Anyway, it was a big mystery and one day, in a great show of bravado, I said I wasn't afraid to open it. Nobody believed that I would, but having got that far I couldn't back out – I would never have lived it down. So screwing up my courage I secretly got hold of the key, a large spooky iron thing. It looked very old and just the thing to keep a monster in check, or perhaps a great heap of treasure that the headmistress had somehow discovered, maybe even the remains of some pupils that had tried to run away. Well, now was the time to find out whatever the cost.

'Some of the girls stayed upstairs, but one or two of my particular friends came down with me although they stayed well away from the door, peeping round the corner of the passageway and all ready to run. I managed to get the key into the rather rusty lock. It didn't want to turn at first, it obviously hadn't been opened for a very long time. At last, using two hands, I was able to turn the old key. It moved with a clunk, and then nothing happened. There was a hiss of encouragement from the little party at the other end of the corridor… "Go on Hanny, open it!" I turned the knob of the door using two hands again, then – WHOOSH … RUMBLE … RUMBLE, CLATTER, CLONK, Clonk, Clonk. Clatter, clatter, clonk, clonk, and so on. The corridor was filled with choking black dust… I staggered back against the wall coughing and spluttering. The party at the end of the corridor had fled, leaving me up to my knees in … coal.'

Having taught in several of the girls' schools, Mrs Sylvia Ritchie has proved a marvellous contact-maker. Her own earliest memories pay tribute to a small Morningside school, St Ann's in Hope Terrace. Sylvia Wood-Hawks started there during the war (no uniform for small civilians) making the short journey from home in St Alban's Road on a tricycle. At first there was the postman for company; later, having mastered the balancing challenge, Sylvia went alone on her fairy cycle: 'Miss Perceval was the owner and headmistress, and Miss Riddell taught primary one. The main feature of 11 Hope Terrace was a large beautiful rocking horse which stood in the bay window. I was very happy there and must have received a good grounding because I was well ahead when I went to Cranley in primary four. I chose it over St Hilary's because someone was playing "Rustle of Spring" on the piano.' Sylvia Wood-Hawks became a stalwart of Cranley sport. St Ann's moved to Strathearn Road, rocking-horse and all.

'Rustle of Spring' recalled in tranquillity may be contrasted with Cranley's musical co-principal, as described by another old girl in *The Torch*: 'I have vivid recollections of Miss Kelly at morning prayers in the hall here. She would come over from 42 Colinton Road and usually she played the hymns. She had a "thing" about slow-dragging hymn-singing and she literally rushed us through all the hymns at top speed. This was ideal in most cases but occasionally there was a hymn which was what I might call a "good-going" one in any case, and at Miss Kelly's pace it was a bit of a race. We always managed to reach the end of the hymn at the same time as Miss Kelly but we were all breathless and panting... After prayers Miss Kelly would play a brisk rousing march and we would all file out of the hall smartly – no slouching out with shuffling footsteps when Miss Kelly was at the piano. I'm sure this livened us up for the rest of the day.'

Memory comes in many forms, witness another item from *The Torch*: 'As I write, the power of reminiscence is so strong that, though I have a bowl of fragrant lily-of-of-the-valley on my desk, for the life of me all I can smell is that curious black soap we had to use in School, and the paint-stained rags and sewing-wool's smell of the "Art" room, and the tadpole-filled jars of the "Garden" room! I wonder if anyone else shares my inability to hear of the Prime Minister going to Chequers without conjuring up

110. *Miss Niven of Cranley.*

the image of an afternoon class in the "Chequers" room, pondering the immensities of history with Miss Porteous, or grappling (vainly, perchance?) with the intricacies of Pythagoras under Miss Macdonald?' Cranley's founder Jane Georgina Niven was never allowed to be forgotten, thanks to an oil-painting in the hall. After her death a special issue of the magazine was full of stories:

'She wore pince-nez and always a long golden chain or beads with her watch chained to her dress,' according to Kirstie Watson, one of the first pupils in the Cranley building. She recalled 'how one of our class, acting a headmistress in a form play, parodied Miss Niven's well-known gesture of rumpling her hair with the palm of her hand, then playing with the long gold chain, borrowed for the occasion.' Several stories about the head made reference to the 'chuckle that we all knew and enjoyed'. Impressed by pupil cycle trips round Grantown-on-Spey, Miss Niven 'decided she would try to ride a bicycle again. We all thought she was brave trying at all, but when disaster came and she burst out laughing we thought she was marvellous.' A form of joint leadership had been shared from Brunstane days with Henrietta Milne: 'Miss Niven had the vision and dreamed the dreams, but it was largely due to Miss Milne that these dreams became reality… She never sought the limelight for herself. She was content to organise and work on quietly… Miss Milne showed amazing patience as Miss Niven grew older.'

Another respected lady was commemorated in 2006 by Sir Roger Young, former headmaster of George Watson's College: 'I first met Margaret Bennett in 1959–60, shortly after arriving in Edinburgh. We went to St Columba's Episcopal Church by the Castle and I happened to sit next to her at coffee afterwards. In conversation, I asked what she did and, putting her hand in front of her mouth, she whispered: "I am a headmistress. What do you do?" I also put my hand in front of my mouth and whispered back: "I am a headmaster."' Perhaps Miss Bennett's mock secrecy was a form of response to the caricatures of Arthur Marshall and Ronald Searle. Sir Roger praised Margaret Bennett for what he learned from her as head of a very different school, Lansdowne House.

Not long before her death Miss Bennett returned to Edinburgh for a remarkable

Lansdowne House Old Girls Guild Newsletter 2006

Welcome to the Newsletter for 2006.
Since the last newsletter we have to report the sad news of the death of our Patron Miss Bennett earlier this year. Appreciations and memories of Miss Bennett's life and work follow in this publication, as do appreciations of Miss Scroggie and Mrs Mitchell both of whom died in 2005.

MARGARET E. BENNETT, HEADMISTRESS OF LANSDOWNE HOUSE SCHOOL
I first met Margaret Bennett in 1959/1960, shortly after arriving in Edinburgh. We went to St Columba's by the Castle and I happened to sit next to her at coffee afterwards. In conversation I asked what she did and, putting her hand in front of her mouth, she whispered: "I am a Headmistress. What do you do?"

111. *Bringing back…*

occasion celebrating 125 years since the founding of this school which had closed – or merged with St George's – three decades before. In advance of a social occasion which brought many former pupils back together she wrote: 'When I first heard of the great Anniversary celebrations I thought, "How odd, when the School is no longer in existence!" But then it occurred to me that it is very much in existence in the lives of the many old girls, not, I mean, in this or any other get-together but in the way you live your individual lives, carrying on the ideals and ethos of the School.' That applies equally to others who go 'forward remembering' whose schools are no longer in existence, but a special edition of the *Lansdowne House Chronicle* claims attention. Its editor went through all the school's classes as Beverley Reid. Now Bev Wright, she rang the changes on different types of memory:

'I remember the sound of the school bell and Miss Bennett's voice in church, bell-like in its clarity; the Gong which rang at lunch time and the trouble Christine got into for putting some absurd sticker in the middle of it. I remember the taste of school dinners and the chore of dinner duty: of setting and clearing and of ordering "smalls" or "seconds" depending on your appetite. I remember smuggling poly bags into the dining room when liver was "on" so that Gilly B's portion could be smuggled out without detection! Also Chucking Out Time when prefects would patrol to ensure that all girls went out to play. I remember playing in the "Den", losing many tennis balls over the Practice Board and leaping over piles of leaves in the Catwalk like joyful horses during autumn term. And I remember anticipating the first day of each new session by setting my alarm clock early enough to ensure a good seat next to my best friend in each new classroom.

'There was the touch of old books when they were handed out for the year – and how I would immediately look inside the cover, curious to see who the previous owner had been. I recall the smell of Sports Day when we were allowed to buy crisps and fizzy drinks and how we were encouraged to take part even if, like me, "your vocation lay elsewhere." (I still have my little red ribbon for the potato race!) I remember the sight of fellow sixth formers on the brink of exciting new adventures, their time at Lansdowne over, tearfully saying goodbye and promising to keep in touch … and keeping that promise. Of course we still have our beloved Elephant which used to stand at the bottom of the very grand carpeted stairway upon which no girl was allowed to set foot. I remember being dared to run up and down it whilst Miss Bennett was in her office – a feat I accomplished, in spite of being sure she would catch me so loud was my thumping heart!

'What a singular headmistress she was! To me as a little girl she was a bit like the Queen but without the hat: always neatly turned out in a smart suit, polished shoes with heels at a sensible height from the ground, a string of pearls round her neck and not a hair out of place. Like the Queen she had a majestic way of carrying herself and never seemed to be in a hurry or get flustered or even angry … although she could look very stern if you had been sent to her for any misdemeanour. This sternness also combined with a look of disappointment which somehow managed to reach the depths of your soul and made you feel completely penitent. As one got older and taller she became more and more approachable and I often marvelled how she could remember everyone's name. That wasn't all she remembered and I can recall on several occasions when I had achieved something outside school I would receive a congratulatory note or comment from her about it. She was always proud of her girls and especially when they did well.'

Patricia Gow set off 'Down Memory Lane' (her title) offering a promise of criticism: 'Our 125th Reunion certainly prompted many memories – some good, some not so good. I arrived at Lansdowne in 1954 aged seven having come from Glenrothes Primary School in Fife – which was not known for its genteel behaviour! It was an enormous upheaval coming to Edinburgh, which lived up to its name "Auld Reekie" by being very dirty and smelly. I was in Miss Douglas's Preparatory Department. Some of my earliest memories are of watching the "big girls" (not the modern connotation!) go to church. They all looked very elegant and tall. From then on I wanted a beret with a tassel and eventually I did get into the first eleven.

'My first classroom was to the left in the room which became the Biology classroom and Form One was in the room up the stairs on the north side. I remember Miss Mann coming to help me with my letter shapes, and that peculiar smell of rubber and chalk. The culture of Edinburgh, the way its "society" was organised, was also a shock because I soon found out that if your parents did not meet certain people doors did not open easily. Life seemed to revolve around what your father did and what school you attended!! I seemed to attract disorder marks like a magnet. At one point in Miss Scroggie's class I congratulated myself that I had managed to evade them, only to end up with eleven by the end of term. I never felt good owning up to the Douglas House "big girls", and I did try to get stars, honest!' Art provided this rebel with an outlet – apart from hockey – and nothing truly negative emerged.

112. *Margaret Morgan at home in Hart Street.*

This section is different in being supported by a pupil's photographs. Margaret Morgan was born on 19 October 1907 at 4 Hart Street in the Broughton district of Edinburgh, and this continued to be her home during Queen Street days. She started school in September 1912, when the daily journey to and from the Atholl Crescent Preparatory Department was by tram from Broughton Street by way of Princes Street to the West End. Two years later Margaret began taking her younger sister Dorothy to school. Sometimes they walked the whole way home to save the fare. In April 1921, aged thirteen, Margaret Morgan was given a camera and started taking 'snaps' of home and school. Sports events at the Falconhall ground featured among them, with photos of classmates and admired older girls including prefects. Names were carefully noted on the back of all prints. Margaret completed her primary education in session 1919–20. The first term report for Class 5A that year showed Good for French, History and Botany, with other subjects Fair or Fairly Good. The teacher wrote: 'Margaret must learn to be less talkative.'

As a secondary pupil she descended to 2D. She must have been popular, for in due course Margaret Morgan was 'elected Head of Clan Erskine' according to her younger son Martin Roberts – for it is his mother and mine being brought back to mind. It is good to think that a girl of lively personality could be chosen ahead of others with more aptitude for work or games. Keenness personified, Margaret earned certificates of merit for sewing, gymnastics and singing. In July 1923, aged fifteen, she was photographed with other girls on the Roof Garden; Mr McCallum's 4B maths class is badly lit by comparison. She ended the following session with five passes at Lower Grade in the Scottish Leaving Certificate,

113. *The Roof Garden.*

114. *Maths class.*

having played for the Second Hockey Eleven. Margaret took up golf after it had been introduced to the school and was still playing at Prestonfield in her late seventies. After school she did a secretarial course at Whitley's Business College in Castle Street, reaching 100 words per minute in Pitman Shorthand. She acquired an F.P. blazer and wore it at Gstaad while skating. As a member of the Merchant Maiden Dramatic Club Margaret Morgan played the part of a pupil in *Children in Uniform,* adapted from *Gestern und Heute* ('Yesterday and Today'). In pre-war Germany, more than elsewhere, tomorrow was supposed to belong to children in uniform.

115. *Skating at Gstaad.*

Even elderly teachers could be playful: 'We had fun at Queen Margaret's PNEU School too. Putting on plays like *Toad of Toad Hall* at Adam House in Chambers Street and the unforgettable Elizabethan Fair, where we performed Morris Dancing and sang songs from Shakespeare's *Midsummer Night's Dream* (which I still remember). Miss Moffat walked there in Elizabethan dress. We were afraid that people would think she was mad, but she held her head up high and said they would know she was going to a function. In summer we went to places like Traquair House in the Borders, and I can still see Miss Moffat taking off her stockings to cross a stream.'

The chapter began with remembered schoolgirl mischief and ends with more of the same: 'The PNEU teachers at India Street were very trusting. I travelled from Fife every day with another girl in my class. We were often late and always blamed the trains – on one occasion we said there was a cow on the line and they believed us ... Miss Smith the head and Miss Moffat were strict about unforms and every so often would carry out a beret or hat inspection. Miss Moffat would stand outside the locker room while each student passed, one by one, with the appropriate headgear on. Little did she know that half the school went out with the same beret on, as it was passed through the locker room window. As the last of us caught the beret flying through the window, Miss Moffat arrived in time to witness this crime. She was horrified: "You deceitful girl!" she cried.'

For much of the four years or so this book has been in the making there was a frustrating lack of information about the convent schools of Edinburgh. Then, months from the end, a dam burst through the intervention of retired history teacher Sheila King. Stories about St Margaret's Convent began arriving by telephone and e-mail and post (including packages with magazines and photos) on a regular and sometimes daily basis. Old classmates drew in others, sister spoke to sister – and sometimes to Ursuline Sister. A book could be written about St Margaret's in Whitehouse Loan. The Convent was never one of Edinburgh's better-known schools, despite being 150 years old when it closed: perhaps the Catholics of Scotland's capital city kept too much to themselves. But several of the best contributions came from Protestants – who never felt uncomfortable there. Responding to this rush of interest in school memories further encouraged the process, and the day when e-mails went off to two sisters in Canada and New Zealand was one for the world wide web.

Three daughters of an Edinburgh surgeon called Pirie Watson were at St Margaret's, the oldest of them (Diana Temple) leaving school in 1938. The memories of this lady, in Toronto for half a century, tend to the outrageous: 'In 1927 Mother Catherine was our headmistress, followed by Mother Pius, whom we called Pie. The first two years were Kindergarten and Form One. I remember standing in the corner with a dunce's cap on, also being hit over the knuckles with a wooden bar which was painted half blue, half pink. Our Form Two teacher was Mother Winifred – we called her Winnipeg. We had a fireplace in the classroom which was always lit in the winter time and Winnipeg used to dry her undies there during class. Stink bombs in the waste basket and sneezing powder were the vogue that year... Form Six was mostly taught by Pie, although we also had Miss Green for maths. No science. Pie taught Latin. We had to say amo, amas, amat, etc., time and time again while she would go off to sleep. I knitted a sweater with five colours of wool during these sleepy occasions. Once I put the ice from the small bird bath on her chair. She sat through class without feeling anything because she had so much clothing on...

'There were always about ten or eleven boarders during my time. They lived in a house called St Crescentia's across the road from the Convent, and we day girls felt sorry for them. The nuns kept pigs between the refectory and the outside wall. The pig door to the main street was out of bounds but we used to nip out and hope not to get caught. In my second last year the school was divided into three houses. Joan, Yvonne and I decided we needed a shield for the winning house, so we went down to Thornton's on Princes Street and ordered a suitable one. Then we went up to Archbishop MacDonald's house in Greenhill Gardens (he was a relative on my mother's side) and asked if he would like to pay for it. He agreed. All hell broke loose when Pie heard, but we got the shield. All in all, I had a good education and lots of fun.'

To round up this chapter the oldest of these correspondents gives way to the youngest, Anita Gallo who left St Margaret's in 1984: 'St Crescentia was fed to the lions for her faith at the age of twelve. Her remains are in the Chapel. Each year on her feast day the front panel of the box was removed to display her bones. I think she was meant to inspire us but these bones scared the living daylights out of me! There is a crypt under the Chapel – out of bounds, so of course a very interesting place to go. It was hard to get to because that part of the building was used only by nuns, but there are ventilation gratings on each side of the steps, and you could climb down to the crypt. A girl in my year discovered that if you put your head back up you created the effect of a human head with no body on the steps. The crypt has passageways leading away from the centre with lead-lined coffins on shelves (at least I seriously hope they are lead-lined!) and the rumour was that if you went to the end – no lights, cobwebs – there were collapsed coffins with human bones. I have no idea if this is true …'

We pass swiftly over stories of sex education with Sister, and the bottle of Blue Nun which exploded from contact with the Sixth Form Common Room's heating system. As a playwright and poet, Anita Gallo will no doubt find a use for them. Of course not all her memories – or those of the many others – are at the level of horror in the crypt or 'lots of fun'. She gave a thoughtful reply to the question of happy schooldays in hindsight: 'You're right, I did like the school. I came to it from a primary school I didn't enjoy and found the family atmosphere of the Convent very reassuring. I was racking my brain for negatives but all I could think of came from a former classmate at an informal reunion last year. She thought the school cosseted us and did not prepare us for life outside. She found the transition to university really hard. I can see how that might have happened, but my parents owned a B&B and I worked there every summer so had no problems moving on from the "safety" of the Convent.'

Chapter 12

Fin de Siècle

This chapter is about what happened to the once quite numerous girls' schools of Edinburgh, of which there are now only two. Perhaps the title is rather contrived for the sake of a French book-end to match *Crème de la Crème.* Is it accurate as to *siècle,* meaning century? There were Victorian beginnings and up-to-date endings, but yes – the story is mainly a twentieth-century one. True, the phrase is normally applied to the last decade of a century, whereas the decline and fall of several well known schools took place over a longer period. Perhaps the chapter title is inaccurate in another way, *Fin de Siècle* suggesting a weariness which hardly applies to two large schools which flourish in the new century: Mary Erskine and St George's. French book-ends, at any rate, appeal to the author.

Schools began closing much earlier, and Lydia Skinner identified the Twenties as particularly challenging: 'The post-war years brought problems for many of Scotland's independent schools. Rising costs and falling incomes hit parents and school managers alike, and some old foundations found it impossible to survive on their original endowments. Of the thirty-four independent schools recognised under the 1882 Educational Endowments Act, only thirteen were left by the 1920s. Some, like Merchiston and Glasgow Academy, had survived by setting up trusts and becoming private companies, but many went under, most passing into the hands of the Local Education Authority.' Girls' schools like the Bell Academy and the Bellwood Institution closed in the Twenties; St Bride's and Canaan Park followed in the Thirties.

Between the wars low birth rate added to the problem of finding pupils, but thanks to the post-war 'bulge' (two million extra schoolchildren between 1947 and 1961) all the girls' schools found themselves turning applicants away. The roll of James Gillespie's School for Girls rose above 1,300 with only a one in four chance of admission at age five. The head of one of Edinburgh's non-fee-paying schools, Forbes Macgregor, expressed himself feelingly: 'Very many infant entrants who had been rejected by one

116. *Gallery classroom, South Morningside School.*

or more fee-paying schools, Merchant Company or Corporation, were brought to me... The innocent cause of the family upset was a normal intelligent child upon whose wondering head the inverted pyramid of family prestige pressed quite unfairly. I can cite numerous cases where these "failed" infants proceeded after the primary course at South Morningside School to the secondary division of the fee-paying school which had initially failed them, and obtained dux or other high academic distinction.'

As Macgregor knew only too well, the fee-paying option was attractive compared with classes over forty in an old building and primitive outdoor toilets. These were, in his experience, 'the sole cause of many parents withdrawing their children'. Double desks with iron legs and slots for slates in sloping gallery classrooms reinforced the impression that no improvements had been made since Victorian times. Then there was the dreaded Qualifying exam, England's Eleven-plus, which could only be avoided by getting your child into a fee-paying primary department: 'The alternatives to success presented a nightmare to the socially conscious parents and pupils of South Edinburgh. I do not speak in metaphors. The district doctors told me that for years the endemic neurosis had led to a general prescription of phenol-barbiturates to alleviate bed-wetting and night fears.' Qualification was for senior secondary school (England's grammar school) and failure to pass meant three years in a Junior Secondary before entering the world of work at fifteen.

The story of St Serf's illustrates parental demand. Mrs Mackinnon and Mrs Pringle bought the school in 1950, 'since when the School's scope and activities have greatly increased.' The roll soon passed three hundred, but there was limited scope for development on the Abercromby Place site.

The school's best years came in the Fifties, when pupils went on to do well at college and university. Music was taught by the only male member of staff. He 'could not control girls' but helped to produce at least one teacher who could – Angela Hardman of St George's. Pupil addresses in the suburbs of Blackhall and Newington reflect the widespread demand for places at schools like St Serf's.

The crisis which broke in March 1965 came from having 309 pupils in an old building. Having completed his inspection of private schools, the head of the local Fire Brigade insisted that costly fire doors were required in every corridor to isolate the stair well. Twenty-six members of staff were as shocked as pupils and parents when closure of St Serf's was announced for the end of session. When fund-raising was proposed the two heads refused to take part. By April they were speaking through a lawyer: 'Any statement to the effect that St Serf's will resume at the premises in Abercromby Place next September is without authority from the principals. No negotiations have taken place for the sale of these premises. They are still in the open market to any interested party.'

Parents responded with a campaign run by fathers, one of whom had professional fund-raising experience. 'Keep St Serf's Alive' meetings were held in Leith Town Hall, and a covenant scheme was introduced. The chairman had it 'on good authority that the teachers are behind us.' Removal from Abercromby Place became inevitable, and the Charlotte Square halls of St George's West Church were considered: 'We do not intend to go out to the suburbs. We shall do our best to acquire a central site.' 5 Wester Coates Gardens was purchased in the West End, with planning permission

117. *St Serf's at Wester Coates Gardens.*

obtained in time for the new session. The DIY efforts of parents have been described in Chapter 4.

When the school reopened in September the roll had dropped to 180 and the committee were 'struggling as far as funds are concerned'. Numbers fell to 140 in 1972, when the decision was taken to admit sixty boys. More came later to St Serf's School – 'for Girls' having been dropped.

Headmaster David Wate spoke to the press in December 1981: 'There are certain things that we cannot give that are standard in a comprehensive school – the technical subjects, woodwork, metalwork and domestic science. But I think that we have a role to play…We have many applications to take older children who are not happy in comprehensive schools.' Some came from outside Edinburgh by train to Haymarket. A further comment helps to explain the survival of small schools in difficult times: 'We are fortunate in Edinburgh, where there are a lot of women teachers who have married and left the profession. We are able to be flexible and offer part-time hours to suit them, and this allows us to have a high standard in recruiting staff.'

The St Serf's head was soon wishing he had kept quiet. On 10 June 1982 the Edinburgh Evening News ran an article under PRIVATE SCHOOL TEACHERS EXPLOITED, SAY UNION: 'Teachers at a private school in Edinburgh are being "grossly exploited" with salaries of just £2,600 a year – a third of the proper level, a union official said today. Now St Serf's School – who charge the lowest fees in the city – are being pressed by the Educational Institute of Scotland to pay a fair wage to their staff. The case was taken to the EIS by four primary teachers and today Mr Fred Forrester said the union had been "deeply shocked" by what the teachers had told them.' According to this spokesman, 'In theory the teachers are all part-timers but in fact they do not work many fewer hours than a full-time teacher… We have put forward a very reasonable suggestion to the school that the salaries should be increased gradually over five years to bring the teachers to the proper level.' The school refused to back down and one teacher was dismissed. When she threatened to take her case to an industrial tribunal, however, the school settled out of court. Since then St Serf's has moved out of Edinburgh.

When the Labour Government set forth its 'comprehensivisation' policy in 1965, James Gillespie's School for Girls was one of seven Edinburgh Corporation fee-paying schools. Two others were significant, the Royal High School (for boys, fee-paying to age twelve) and Trinity Academy which was co-educational at primary and secondary levels. With fees of £15 a year, it selected pupils from Leith and beyond. The remainder were primary schools. In light of the Government's intention to end selection for state secondary education, it was impossible to ignore the fact that the secondary department of Gillespie's selected one applicant in five – two extra classes of thirty-five pupils broadening the roll at this stage. Parents were only too willing to pay the £40 annual fee and buy all necessary uniform.

In *A School of One's Choice*, John Highet drew on coffee morning lore: 'It's no holds barred… The girls are always talking about it round the coffee table. "Has she not passed her test yet?" is one of the commonest questions you hear. Tremendous tension. As for … [mentioning a girls' school] they really lose their heads and go high-hatted when their daughters get in there… These coffee ladies! They can be absolute bitches – the acme, the epitome of bitchiness. A little girl said to me, with her mother present, "I'm going to …, which Mummy says is a better school than Gillespie's." Her mother knew my daughter was at Gillespie's and her face went scarlet.' Highet felt bound to comment: 'These (all of them) are the lady's own words: she felt very deeply about the matter. The unnamed school is not better than Gillespie's.'

Fee-paying local authority schools were on the wane, and by the end of the Sixties there were only about twenty in Scotland, mostly for under-twelves. It was increasingly difficult to make a case for them. When there were free senior secondary places for those who passed the 'Quali' they could be ignored, but not now. Edinburgh's officials and those of Glasgow (where there were also seven such schools) began talks with government – but were still talking at the decade's end. Edinburgh Corporation had just spent ratepayers' money on a new secondary department for their only girls' school, with larger laboratories and so on. Highet compared it with the Royal High School and Trinity Academy:

'Of the three, pressure on places has been most severe at Gillespie's… There is a limited choice in Edinburgh for those favouring one-sex fee-paying schooling for their daughters, yet not so keen on paying the expensive fees at girls' private schools… Many who send to an expensive school have tried for a not-so-expensive one first. And this demand falls more heavily on Gillespie's.' Headmistress Mary Steel – more forthcoming than most – revealed that even in these harsh times consideration was given to '"family connection" – a daughter of an F.P., a girl who has a brother at the Royal High or James Gillespie's Boys' … [provided she] satisfied the school's requirements, at least to the extent of being borderline.'

Edinburgh Corporation finally agreed to stop charging fees, despite protests from parents and talk of Gillespie's going independent. At the start of session 1973–74 boys were admitted along with girls to the renamed James Gillespie's High School. They came into S1 (first year secondary) without having passed any test, for it was now an area comprehensive school. That year's highly-selected S2 girls progressed up the school, and the last of the original Gillespie's girls left in summer 1978. It has remained a successful school in terms of exam passes and other aspects, with an emphasis on multiculturalism. A statement explains this in English, Gaelic, French, German, Spanish, Urdu, Punjabi and Cantonese. Two hundred pupils are admitted to eight S1 classes. Up to sixty places regularly go to applicants from outside the area.

George Watson's Ladies' College, the grant-aided school which shared the colour maroon with Gillespie's, was already under pressure when the political climate changed. The University of Edinburgh was expanding into George Square, and the school premises were already 'earmarked'. In 1964 Merchant Company officials raised the possibility of a new girls' school next to the Watsonian playing-fields at Myreside. Headmistress Hilda Fleming pressed instead for a co-educational merger on the George Watson's College site. Three years later the Merchant Company announced that this would happen 'in the foreseeable future'. National policy had brought about cuts in the forty per cent government grant towards annual running costs. One very large school (1,050 primary pupils and

118. *Co-educational George Watson's College.*

1,400 in Senior School as it turned out) was better adapted for the challenge. Scottish Education Department approval was given, and the merger became official on 1 October 1974. A joint assembly was held that day, senior girls joining in a new school song, *Ex Corde Caritas*. Miss Fleming had already presented her pupils and staff with the George Square song on a souvenir card. 'The Amalgamation' has since advanced by stages.

Edward Heath's short-lived Conservative Government restored grant aid, but ways were sought of co-ordinating Merchant Company schools with those of the Local Authority. Mary Erskine was vulnerable because an increase in Scottish teachers' pay meant that higher numbers were required for the new structure of promoted posts. Headmistress Jean Thow (her title changed to Principal) announced that the roll had risen to six hundred as a result of comprehensive education: 'Dissatisfaction with the City's policy of non-selection has this year brought many applications which we have been unable to consider. The first year in the Senior School for the autumn of 1973 is already over-subscribed.' The second election of 1974 returned a Labour majority, and the phasing out of grant aid was announced. Fee rises of up to twenty-five per cent were foreseen at a time when one Mary Erskine parent in six was already receiving financial assistance from the Merchant Company.

The Company was responsible for three schools: co-educational George Watson's, the already merged Daniel Stewart's and Melville College, and Mary Erskine. Faced with a choice for its schools between full independence, integration with local authority schools and a combination of the two, the Company announced in June 1975 that Watson's and Stewart's Melville were to be have 'endowed independence' while Mary Erskine would be integrated. Lothian Region (by now the local authority) saw potential for expansion at Ravelston. Parents had been removing their daughters from Mary Erskine because of high fees, but now others besieged the office seeking admission to what would effectively be a free Merchant Company school. Confusion reigned: 'During the summer term there has been continuous manoeuvring of parents with children in Senior II at Ravelston to transfer their daughters to join brothers at Watson's, and of parents at Colinton Road to allow their daughters to quit the larger school for Ravelston.'

Pupils and staff went home for the holidays uncertain whether they would be back for session 1976–77. Lothian Region had agreed to accept primary pupils of Mary Erskine into secondary 'as far as possible'. The school name would be unchanged during their six years in attendance, with the uniform 'retained on a voluntary basis'. Then in December 1976 government rejected the proposal on the grounds that there were now too many schools in north-west Edinburgh, the Royal High School having moved out to Barnton and become co-educational:

'The Secretary of State appreciates that the freezing of grant to the Grant-Aided Schools has already caused a sizeable number of pupils to leave these schools and he accepts that this process is liable to continue. Places have been found for all those who have so far transferred to the public sector and the Secretary of State is not satisfied that accommodation difficulties are likely to become so acute as to justify, at a time of severe financial stringency, the very large expenditure of public money that would be required to purchase the Mary Erskine School.' The decision was heavily criticised by Lothian's Education Committee as well as by the Merchant Company. It was said that 'The Mary Erskine School would have provided roughly one thousand desperately needed secondary places'. In January 1976 Lothian Region made a final attempt to purchase the school through a twenty-five year annuity but this was also refused. A way forward would have to be found for Mary Erskine as an independent school.

Rothesay House was the first of the small schools to close. The connection with Sir D'Arcy Wentworth Thompson has been noted, and it was the professor's daughter Ruth, writing above the initials R. D'A. T., who provided an explanation at the last: 'The announcement, at New Year 1957, of the closing of Rothesay House at the end of the present session came as a great shock to all Old Girls, and to many of them – outside scholastic circles – as an inexplicable happening. To others more conversant with the enormous problems of running schools in these days it was not difficult to understand. Rothesay House has always been one of the smallest of the Edinburgh Private Schools and its resources must have been taxed to the limit from its inception as a Company. Almost at once there was a big expense incurred over a bad outbreak of dry rot in No. 1… Expansion into No. 4 was faced and met in 1953, but by now the steep rise in daily expenses, domestic help, and the upkeep of property that even private people found difficult, was making itself felt, and also unfortunately the number of pupils, though steady during these years, did not rise accordingly.'

Miss D'Arcy Thompson went on to discuss 'the problem of the boarders' Waiting List', but her main point concerned the staff: 'The crucial moment came two years ago when teachers' salaries were raised by Government decree; our fees were raised shortly afterwards but the spiral continued a second and a third time, and still continues, for another such rise is to take place… It is not necessary to state here that throughout this difficult and anxious time the Staff, always so loyal and devoted, have given their services with love and no thought for themselves, only for the School, for we were unable to do all we wanted for them or even to give what was their due.' Years later a similar point was made by a Cranley head: 'Before 1957, when we entered the SED Superannuation Scheme, teachers joining us were entering a backwater financially and career-wise.'

The two Convent schools (St Catherine's having closed earlier) may be treated together. Shortly before the Craiglockhart school came to an end, John Highet drew attention to its almost unique status (along with Jordanhill in Glasgow) as a Fee-paying Demonstration School. 'Dem' schools had closed in other training colleges, as teaching practice in normal schools came to be preferred. The school only charged about £45 a year and was not regarded in the same light as the mainly boarding Aberdeen and Kilgraston schools. Towards the end the Craiglockhart roll reached 250 pupils with about a hundred of these in the Senior School. Ample notice was given of the intention to close, but meanwhile there was the Golden Jubilee of the Sisters' arrival at Manor Place to celebrate, and then the news that Archbishop Gordon Grey had been granted a cardinal's hat:

'This has been a year of many happenings, both sad and joyful. During the Easter term came the sad news of the closing of the day school in 1970. Our hearts are still too full to say more about that… We were a much smaller school when we reassembled in September after the summer holidays, for many parents whose children were at the beginning of their secondary education felt it right to find another school for them as soon as possible. The top and the bottom of the school, however, were as large as ever, and there was a splendid spirit abroad.' Very late in the day the internationally standard First Class was renamed Fifth Year, and the 'experiment' was tried of a school council elected by senior pupils. The final gathering resembled a requiem: 'Craiglockhart Day School closed its doors for the last time on 30 June 1970, after forty-six years of existence. It was a sad day for all of us. We kept our spirits up until the Mass at eleven o'clock, but then it was only the Juniors that managed to keep the singing going.'

St Margaret's Convent provided a refuge, and the school roll there topped 350 in the Seventies. Post-war setbacks had already been overcome, first when the gardener's room at the top of the Tower collapsed into the laboratory and started a fire. For a year it was 'science lessons theory only.' Then in 1957, fortunately during the Easter holidays, the roof of the boarding-school and four attic bedrooms were similarly destroyed. An outside fire escape was added. Two years later dry rot was found in the

119. *Fire escape, St Margaret's Convent.*

Convent. Teaching areas were not affected, but the *Edinburgh Evening News* observed that the necessary work would 'place a very heavy financial strain on this self-supporting house.' Parents rallied round and presented Reverend Mother with £1,000. However a shortage of vocations to the religious life led to an increased reliance on lay teachers, and salary costs were behind the decision (highly unpopular with parents) to close in the summer of 1986. The oldest girls' school in Edinburgh survived a century and a half, but only just.

As schools began to close, landmark years were sometimes celebrated with no sense of the shortness of time ahead. In the case of the Convent school's neighbour in the Grange, *Esdaile 1863–1963* celebrated the building of new classrooms – as well as the passage of a hundred years – without any suggestion that they might soon be empty. Reference was made to 'the courage to consider such an undertaking at post-war costs', but the difficulties were not all financial. With standards rising in local high schools there was less incentive for a minister to send his daughters to Edinburgh. A new Day Girls' Cloakroom was opened in the centenary session for the sake of thirty local pupils who had previously been marginal: one recalled being reprimanded as 'an unimportant little day girl'. The lack of a primary department meant that day girls were hard to find, and it was the school's inability to rise beyond 110 boarders in the Sixties which made the closure of Esdaile inevitable. The PNEU school in India Street came to a quiet conclusion with the retiral of two ladies well past retirement age.

Meanwhile Lansdowne House had become a substantial day school with less of its former limiting connection to the Episcopal Church of Scotland. But it was still a question of expand or go under, and younger children were targeted. In 1972 Miss Bennett reported that 'the decision had been made, backed by a vote of confidence from the parents, to go ahead and raise funds for the building of a new junior school and nursery department.' The nursery had already opened in the Good Shepherd church hall. A year later doubts began to surface: 'In the main school plans have had to be cut back because of rising costs... However the Sixth Form Common Room, the new office and Sick Room were all completed by the start of the new term. The Science Department has an animal breeding room where the old wash-hand basins used to be. The Nursery Class now has eleven members working in the Church Hall and the Kindergarten is up to twenty with a waiting-list.'

Despite these hopeful signs Lansdowne House closed in July 1976. The President of the Old Girls' Guild addressed the A.G.M. in September: 'She mentioned the various council meetings and the demand by the parents for an amalgamation with St George's. Since the start of the autumn term St George's had been using the Lansdowne building as their middle school... While on holiday in the summer, Mrs Potter had visited Miss Ysabel and Miss Evelyn Hale, Miss Hale's nieces in Oxford, as she wished to tell them personally about the school's closure. They sent their best wishes to the Guild and gave four badges engraved with "Gentleness and Justice" which were worn by the head girls and the monitors during the early years of the school.' One of those present suggested that Miss MacDonald, Lansdowne's transitional 'co-head' at St George's, should report on the joint school's first year – this for the sake of helping Mrs Clanchy, the new head of St George's: 'She is Judy Smith's husband's cousin. She started this past year and has done very well.' As with mergers elsewhere there were some hurt feelings at the time, but today's Lansdowne reunions are equally well attended in the modern St George's Centre and the old building.

The last *FEHOMI*, produced after the final 1978–79 session, set out the views of three Cranley heads. Helen Porteous's account of the years 1944–64 later appeared in a history of the school with a fuller explanation of the school's financial problems: 'We had survived as the last personally-owned school in Edinburgh... Like our predecessor Miss Niven we had year by year spent the school income with no building up of profits or a reserve fund. But now with the passing of the years, and with bigger numbers, floors and furniture were wearing out. For years willing hands (including mine) had covered quilts and made curtains and bed covers... The gardens required renovation. More help was required in the office... Miss Kelly and I and the accountant sadly put aside the architect's plans for classrooms and cloakrooms in the back garden... The school was still not much below its maximum 320 mark, but these were mostly seniors, not being replaced by juniors – all schools had places now, for the birth-rate was falling.'

Isabella Turnbull reported on her thirteen years which began in 1964 with her as one of three Directors and Principals. A former science

120. *Cranley farewell.*

teacher at Cranley (in 'the garden laboratory') she had given up the headship of a girls' high school in Derbyshire in an attempt to turn things round. It was a period of change for schools on both sides of the Border, and Miss Turnbull was well placed to introduce Nuffield maths and a language laboratory. She was generous in praise of colleagues: 'Teaching is a matter of good teachers, even more than the systems or methods, and for that reason expensive facilities and much of educational gadgetry are of little value compared with caring and conscientious teachers.'

But Jean Hunter, whose fate it was to preside over the last two years of the school's life, criticised some members of her staff: 'The final edition is no place to indulge in recriminations or to attempt to analyse the reasons for our demise. It is, perhaps, the place to state that many of those in our ranks who quarrelled so bitterly during the Easter Vacation and the Summer Term of 1979 had this in common, that they wished the best, as they saw it, for Cranley, those who advocated the merger with St Denis no less than those who opposed it.

'The days of the small independent school for girls are passing. Cranley has gone the way of Lansdowne and Esdaile, and no doubt in time others will follow us. Recognition of the irreversible trend towards co-education, of the falling birth rate and of the growing difficulties facing schools which have neither state aid nor endowments to rely on, was a major factor in our governors' decision to merge with St Denis, a neighbouring girls' school with a declining roll, in the belief that an amicable amalgamation was better than extinction, and that Cranley and St Denis could offer each other mutual support. Sadly, pride, intransigence and that odd kind of obtuseness that deludes itself that it is being particularly sharp, have so bedevilled the amalgamation that only two-full-time teachers and about fifty girls have transferred to St Denis and Cranley.'

St Denis had built up a stronger position over the years. After the war businessmen were co-opted and income was set aside for development. In 1950 the school roll was 170, 'either just too large or considerably too small to be an economic unit.' It stood at 380 in 1964, extra houses for boarders having been purchased: 'The position which Miss Ramsay has built up is such that to come to St Denis is a privilege for any girl, and it has been possible for her to select those whom she wished to come.' Ten years later, when St Denis was said to be 'still a small school', the roll reached 450. The Science conservatory had been replaced by separate labs, and there was a new kindergarten on the old tennis court. A nursery class came later. There were no more hutted Garden Classrooms – 'those venerable buildings which for so long had presented great problems to successive Head-mistresses and Staff, as they were below modern standards, difficult to heat and sometimes festooned with intrusive greenery from the plants outside… Still, many of us felt a pang…'

Jennifer Cochrane (former head girl and hockey international) became the school's first deputy head before succeeding to the top post as Mrs Munro. In 1988 a plan was presented for new building. A two-storey block of thirteen teaching units, including four laboratories, was to be paid for by selling the Teviot Lawn: 'While nostalgia for school past may hold rosy memories for many, the distribution of the buildings makes for inefficient and what must sometimes be inconvenient communication (particularly in bad weather) through the many labyrinthine pathways.' More pupils were needed than appeared. St Denis and

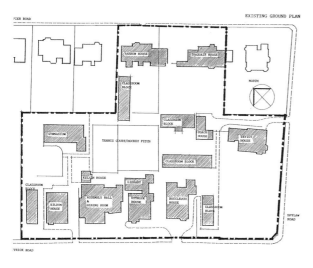

121. *Developing St Denis.*

Cranley Day and Boarding School for Girls aged 3 to 18 years could not compete with the stronger expansion at East Suffolk Road, and the final merger with St Margaret's took place in 1998.

The success of St Margaret's was attributed to the fact that in 1960 Miss Matthew transferred the school 'on very generous terms' to a Board of Governors. Nine years later Craigmillar Park Church was turned into an assembly hall and classrooms, then Matthew House was built on the old tennis courts (despite 'a certain agreeable chaos') as the roll rose from 350 to five hundred by 1973. The school's popularity continuing, the Oratava Hotel was turned into a senior school. All claims for the superiority of small schools abandoned, St Margaret's reached 850 in 1984, adding Dunard (the former Grange Home School) and the Arranmore Hotel in Craigmillar Park for young children including pre-schoolers. These changes were financed by the sale of St Hilary's at Cluny Drive. When Miss Muirhead retired in 1983 the twin buildings in Newington and Morningside were briefly reunited, and for one session Cluny Drive took St Margaret's senior classes. The railway was no more but a school bus linked the sites. Then the Morningside buildings were sold as a home for the elderly: no doubt some old ladies have enjoyed a second child-hood there. St Hilary's House in Newington (the name re-tained) is now billed as a Home from Home, with day and even overnight care on offer for chil-dren as young as three months.

122. *East Suffolk Road and beyond.*

After the Merchant Company's bid to sell Mary Erskine to the local authority failed, the school was reinvented as a part of Erskine Stewart's Melville. For a while there were two Principals at Ravelston, at least when Robin Morgan came over and Jean Thow (successor to Muriel Jennings) stayed in her office. Miss Thow resigned three years before Mr Morgan. Humour, old-fashioned and sexist, helped him through: 'Twinning policy has been seen at Carbisdale, in the Combined Cadet Force and at joint concerts. The first Corps camp is to be held on my mother-in-law's estate in Wester Ross and two of the girls will be with me at Bisley, disarming the opposition by their charm and putting them off their aim.' In 1988 a million-pound appeal was launched to provide technology courses for both sexes. A year later Patrick Tobin succeeded as Principal of the twinned schools; in retirement he was to write an eloquent defence of the ESM compromise with co-education. As long as five years of single-sex secondary education survive, however, Mary Erskine remains one of the girls' schools of Edinburgh.

Nigel Shepley is upbeat in his updated account of St George's: 'The physical features of the school emphasise the continuities. Despite much recent building work, any girl who had entered the main building in 1914, would still be able to recognise her school today. However, it is the attitude to its buildings, rather than the physical features themselves, which links past and present. The enduring idea is that the buildings must be made to provide the best educational facilities possible. Melville Street in 1888 was far bigger and better equipped than any of the old proprietary "dining room table" schools…

'Another almost unchanging feature is the background of the students. The school register and census returns show that the pupils of the 1890s came from professional middle class and prosperous business families. An analysis of the school roll in 2000 showed little change… There are strong links also between the curriculum and teaching methods of the founders and their modern successors. At the core there is still the same academic curriculum, which was so novel for girls in 1888, including Mathematics, languages, classics and sciences. There are no barriers to girls taking subjects like Physics, which have usually been studied mainly by boys. There remains too the early hunger to experiment and to try new courses, to remain at the forefront and to respond to demand. St George's recently became the first school in Scotland to have Mandarin as a main language.'

There is a future as well as a past for St George's, as also no doubt for Mary Erskine. Alas St Margaret's is no more, closed in summer 2010 after the idea of a buy-out by parents and friends came to nothing. 'The days of the small independent school for girls' may well be over, but the two large ones remaining have a degree of financial security which was never there before. A fresh attack, more or less political, on the 'charitable status' enjoyed by them in terms of tax relief appears to have been warded off. All shades of opinion now favour choice in education. Although the relative cost to parents is greater than ever, the number of girls (and boys) attending independent schools is increasing slightly at a time when the rolls of state schools are in decline. Of course many of these girls attend former boys' schools of Edinburgh, now co-educational. It will be interesting to see the effect of the decision – following a vote by parents – to accept girls at all stages to the Edinburgh Academy. Parental demand will decide.

Charitable status depends on value to the wider community on the basis of access to facilities (athletic in particular) and the availability of places to girls whose parents cannot afford the fees. Beyond that, the case for Edinburgh's girls' schools rests partly on example and a reputation for excellence. Educational policy-makers may learn from paying more attention to them – specifically about girls and learning – while student-teachers continue to benefit from what is now an unusual variation of classroom practice. So far, so positive, but what is to be said at the last of those schools which have closed? Regarded as a whole they have been, at the very least, interesting. Muriel Spark described Christina Kay's classroom as 'pure theatre', and throughout the book there has been a sense of drama, of events which linger in the mind. Arthur Marshall poked fun at girls' schools, and the 'ethos' chapter (only) sometimes comes close to that: confusion over mottos and badges; school hymn, song, march *and* banner. But the teacher who called up the atmosphere of competition on the last day of the session went on to contrast it with the way in which most schools approach the summer holidays. Inter-House was 'a high note to end the year on'; as such it provides a high note to end the book on.

Index